Lecture Notes in Computer Science　　9822

Commenced Publication in 1973
Founding and Former Series Editors:
Gerhard Goos, Juris Hartmanis, and Jan van Leeuwen

Editorial Board

More information about this series at http://www.springer.com/series/7409

Norbert Fuhr · Paulo Quaresma
Teresa Gonçalves · Birger Larsen
Krisztian Balog · Craig Macdonald
Linda Cappellato · Nicola Ferro (Eds.)

Experimental IR Meets Multilinguality, Multimodality, and Interaction

7th International Conference
of the CLEF Association, CLEF 2016
Évora, Portugal, September 5–8, 2016
Proceedings

 Springer

Editors

Norbert Fuhr
Universität Duisburg-Essen
Duisburg
Germany

Paulo Quaresma
University of Évora
Évora
Portugal

Teresa Gonçalves
University of Évora
Évora
Portugal

Birger Larsen
University of Aalborg
Copenhagen
Denmark

Krisztian Balog
University of Stavanger
Stavanger
Norway

Craig Macdonald
University of Glasgow
Glasgow
UK

Linda Cappellato
University of Padua
Padua
Italy

Nicola Ferro
University of Padua
Padua
Italy

ISSN 0302-9743   ISSN 1611-3349   (electronic)
Lecture Notes in Computer Science
ISBN 978-3-319-44563-2   ISBN 978-3-319-44564-9   (eBook)
DOI 10.1007/978-3-319-44564-9

Library of Congress Control Number: 2016947485

LNCS Sublibrary: SL3 – Information Systems and Applications, incl. Internet/Web, and HCI

Printed on acid-free paper

This Springer imprint is published by Springer Nature
The registered company is Springer International Publishing AG Switzerland

Preface

Since 2000, the Conference and Labs of the Evaluation Forum (CLEF) has played a leading role in stimulating research and innovation in the domain of multimodal and multilingual information access. Initially founded as the *Cross-Language Evaluation Forum* and running in conjunction with the *European Conference on Digital Libraries* (ECDL/TPDL), CLEF became a standalone event in 2010 combining a peer-reviewed conference with a multitrack evaluation forum.

CLEF 2016[1] was hosted by the Computer Science Department of the School of Sciences and Technology of the University of Évora, Portugal, during September 5–8, 2016.

The CLEF Conference addresses all aspects of information access in any modality and language.

The conference has a clear focus on experimental IR as done at evaluation forums (CLEF Labs, TREC, NTCIR, FIRE, MediaEval, RomIP, TAC, etc.) with special attention to the challenges of multimodality, multilinguality, and interactive search ranging from unstructured, to semistructured, and structured data. We invited submissions on significant new insights demonstrated on the resulting IR test collections, on analysis of IR test collections, and evaluation measures, as well as on concrete proposals to push the boundaries of the Cranfield/TREC/CLEF paradigm.

The conference format consisted of keynotes, contributed papers, lab sessions, and poster sessions, including reports from other benchmarking initiatives from around the world.

The following scholars were invited to give a keynote talk at CLEF 2016: Djoerd Hiemstra (University of Twente, The Netherlands), Andreas Rauber (Technical University of Vienna, Austria), and Isabel Trancoso (INESC-TEC, Portugal).

CLEF 2016 received a total of 36 submissions. Each submission was reviewed by three Program Committee (PC) members, and the two program chairs oversaw the reviewing and follow-up discussions.

CLEF 2016 continued a novel track introduced at CLEF 2015, i.e., inviting CLEF 2015 lab organizers to nominate a "best of the labs" paper that was reviewed as a full paper submission to the CLEF 2016 conference according to the same review criteria and the same PC. This resulted in five full papers accepted, corresponding to four out of the eight CLEF 2015 labs.

We received 23 regular full paper submissions, of which 10 (43 %) were accepted for regular oral presentation and five (22 %, making a total of 65 %) for short oral presentation and poster presentation. We received seven short paper submissions, and accepted three (43 %).

---

[1] http://clef2016.clef-initiative.eu/

The conference teamed up with a series of workshops presenting the results of lab-based comparative evaluation. CLEF 2016 was the seventh year of the CLEF Conference and the 17th year of the CLEF initiative as a forum for IR evaluation.

In addition to these talks, the eight benchmarking labs reported results of their year-long activities in overview talks and lab sessions[2].

The seven labs and one workshops running as part of CLEF 2016 were as follows:

CLEFeHealth[3] provides scenarios that aim to ease patients and nurses understanding and accessing of eHealth information. The goals of the lab are to develop processing methods and resources in a multilingual setting to enrich difficult-to-understand eHealth texts, and provide valuable documentation. The tasks are: handover information extraction; multilingual information extraction; and, patient-centered information retrieval.

ImageCLEF[4] organizes three main tasks with a global objective of benchmarking automatic annotation, indexing, and retrieval of images. The tasks tackle different aspects of the annotation and retrieval problem and are aimed at supporting and promoting cutting-edge research addressing the key challenges in the field. A wide range of source images and objectives are considered, such as general multi-domain images for object or concept detection, as well as domain-specific tasks such as labelling and separation of compound figures from biomedical literature and scanned pages from historical documents.

LifeCLEF[5] proposes three data-oriented challenges related to this vision, in the continuity of the two previous editions of the lab, but with several consistent novelties intended to push the boundaries of the state of the art in several research directions at the frontier of information retrieval, machine learning, and knowledge engineering including: an audio record-based bird identification task (BirdCLEF); an image-based plant identification task (PlantCLEF); and a fish video surveillance task (FishCLEF).

Living Labs for IR (LL4IR)[6] inprovides a benchmarking platform for researchers to evaluate their ranking systems in a live setting with real users in their natural task environments. The lab acts as a proxy between commercial organizations (live environments) and lab participants (experimental systems), facilitates data exchange, and makes comparison between the participating systems. The task focuses on on-line product search.

News Recommendation Evaluation Lab (NEWSREEL)[7] provides two tasks designed to address the challenge of real-time news recommendation. Participants can: (a) develop news recommendation algorithms and (b) have them tested by millions of users over the period of a few weeks in a living lab. The tasks are: benchmark news

---

[2] The full details for each lab are contained in a separate publication, the Working Notes, which are available online at http://ceur-ws.org/Vol-1609/.

[3] https://sites.google.com/site/clefehealth2016/

[4] http://www.imageclef.org/2016

[5] http://www.imageclef.org/node/197

[6] http://living-labs.net/clef-ll4ir-2016/

[7] http://www.clef-newsreel.org/

recommendations in a living lab; benchmarking news recommendations in a simulated environment.

Uncovering Plagiarism, Authorship, and Social Software Misuse (PAN)[8] provides evaluation of uncovering plagiarism, authorship, and social software misuse. PAN offered three tasks at CLEF 2016 with new evaluation resources consisting of large-scale corpora, performance measures, and Web services that allow for meaningful evaluations. The main goal is to provide for sustainable and reproducible evaluations, to get a clear view of the capabilities of state-of-the-art-algorithms. The tasks are: author identification; author profiling; and, author obfuscation.

Social Book Search (SBS)[9] provides evaluation of real-world information needs that are generally complex, yet almost all research focuses instead on either relatively simple search based on queries or recommendation based on profiles. The goal of the Social Book Search Lab is to investigate techniques to support users in complex book search tasks that involve more than just a query and results list. The tasks are: a user-oriented interactive task investigating systems that support users in each of multiple stages of a complex search tasks; a system-oriented task for systems to suggest books based on rich search requests combining several topical and contextual relevance signals, as well as user profiles and real-world relevance judgements; and an NLP/text mining track focusing on detecting and linking book titles in online book discussion forums, as well as detecting book search research in forum posts for automatic book recommendation.

Cultural Microblog Contextualization (CMC) Workshop[10] aims at developing processing methods for social media mining. The focus is on festivals that are organized or that have a large presence on social media. For its first edition, this workshop gives access to a massive collection of microblogs and urls and allows researchers in IR and NLP to experiment a broad variety of multilingual microblog search techniques (WikiPedia entity search, automatic summarization, and more).

A rich social program was organized in conjunction with the conference. A guided visit to the university's historic building was provided and the university's choir performed at the welcome reception; on the last night "Cante Alentejano" (a UNESCO Intangible Cultural Heritage) was staged for the participants. As the conference took place in Évora city center, participants were also able to visit this historic UNESCO city while going to the venue.

The success of CLEF 2016 would not have been possible without the huge effort of several people and organizations, including the CLEF Association[11] and the University of Évora, the Program Committee, the Lab Organizing Committee, the local

---

[8]   http://pan.webis.de/

[9]   http://social-book-search.humanities.uva.nl/

[10]   https://mc2.talne.eu/~cmc/spip/

[11]   http://www.clef-initiative.eu/association

Organizing Committee in Évora, the reviewers, and the many students and volunteers who contributed along the way. We thank you all!

July 2016

Norbert Fuhr
Paulo Quaresma
Teresa Gonçalves
Birger Larsen
Krisztian Balog
Craig Macdonald
Linda Cappellato
Nicola Ferro

Organization

CLEF 2016, Conference and Labs of the Evaluation Forum – Experimental IR meets Multilinguality, Multimodality, and Interaction, was organized by the Computer Science Department of the School of Sciences and Technology of the University of Évora.

General Chairs

Norbert Fuhr   University of Duisburg-Essen, Germany
Paulo Quaresma   University of Évora, Portugal

Program Chairs

Teresa Gonçalves   University of Évora, Portugal
Birger Larsen   University of Aalborg, Denmark

Lab Chairs

Krisztian Balog   University of Stavanger, Norway
Craig Macdonald   University of Glasgow, UK

Local Organizations

Irene Rodrigues   University of Évora, Portugal
José Saias   University of Évora, Portugal
Luís Rato   University of Évora, Portugal

Contents

CLEF 2016 Labs Overviews

Cross Language Information Retrieval and Evaluation

Show Me How to Tie a Tie:
Evaluation of Cross-Lingual Video Retrieval

Pavel Braslavski[1]([✉]), Suzan Verberne[2], and Ruslan Talipov[1]

[1] Ural Federal University, Yekaterinburg, Russia
pbras@yandex.ru, roosh90@mail.ru
[2] Radboud University, Nijmegen, The Netherlands
s.verberne@cs.ru.nl

Abstract. In this study we investigate the potential of cross-lingual video retrieval for *how-to* questions. *How-to* questions are the most frequent among *wh*-questions and constitute almost 1 % of the entire query stream. At the same time, *how-to* videos are popular on video sharing services. We analyzed a dataset of 500M+ Russian *how-to* questions. First, we carried out manual labelling of 1,000 queries that shows that about two thirds of all *how-to* question queries are potentially suitable for answers in the form of video in a language other than the language of the query. Then, we evaluated video retrieval quality for original and machine translated queries on a crowdsourcing platform. The evaluation reveals that machine translated questions yield video search quality comparable to the quality for original questions. Cross-lingual video search for *how-to* queries can improve recall and diversity of search results, as well as compensate the shortage of original content in emerging markets.

Keywords: How-to questions · Video retrieval · Question answering · Cross-lingual information retrieval · Machine translation · Query translation · Evaluation

1   Introduction

Several studies reported an increase in the share of question-like queries in search engine logs in recent years [11,19]. This phenomenon can be explained by different trends: users' desire for a more natural interface, users' laziness or low search proficiency, a large amount of Web content in the form of questions and answers that can be found through search engines, as well as proliferation of voice search. *How-to* questions are the most frequent question type in community question answering (CQA) [17] and Web search [11,19].[1] The substantial share of question queries and prevalence of *how-to* questions mark a significant evolution in user behavior in the last decade. For example, in the late 1990s, queries in question form comprised less than 1 % of the entire search engine query stream and the

---

[1] https://www.google.com/trends/2014/story/top-questions.html.

© Springer International Publishing Switzerland 2016
N. Fuhr et al. (Eds.): CLEF 2016, LNCS 9822, pp. 3–15, 2016.
DOI: 10.1007/978-3-319-44564-9_1

most common question type was *where can i find. . . for general information on a topic* [16].

Another modern trend is the proliferation of multimedia content on the Web, video in particular. Pew Research Center found in 2013 that 72 % of adult Internet users use video sharing services and that *how-to* videos are among the top interests, watched by 56 % of online adults.[2] Video is a natural medium for answering many *how-to* questions [3,18]. One aspect that distinguishes video from text is that videos can often be understood with visual information only. This means that even if the textual information accompanying the video is in a language that is not well-understood by the user who asked the question, they might still consider their question answered by the video. As a result, retrieving videos in a different language than the user's query language can potentially give a higher recall for the user's question. In the countries with emerging Web and growing Internet access, content creation in the users' first language lags behind the demand, and cross-language video retrieval can enrich the supply. Further, most *how-to* questions are longer and more coherent than the average search query, which makes them more suitable for machine translation (MT).

In this study, we investigate the potential of cross-lingual video retrieval for *how-to* questions. The main goals of the study are to

1. get a better understanding of *how-to* question queries, their properties, structure, and topics; as well as their potential for video results in a language other than the language of the original query;
2. evaluate Russian→English machine translation quality for *how-to* questions;
3. evaluate the complete pipeline for cross-lingual *how-to* video retrieval.

We used a large log of Russian *how-to* questions worth 500M+ queries submitted throughout a year, which constitutes almost 1 % of the entire query stream. We performed a thorough automatic analysis of the data and manually labeled a considerable subset of queries. We retrieved videos through the YouTube API both for original Russian queries and their machine translations. After that we performed search results evaluation on a crowdsourcing platform.

The contributions of this paper compared to previous work are two-fold: First, we show an in-depth analysis of Russian *how-to* queries in order to estimate the proportion of queries for which cross-lingual video retrieval would be valuable. Second, we evaluate the pipeline for cross-lingual video retrieval step by step on a sample of queries from a leading Russian search engine, using crowd judgments for assessing video relevance.

2   Related Work

Cross-language question answering (QA) was investigated before in the context of the well-known IR evaluation campaigns CLEF [5] and NTCIR [9]. The

---

[2] http://www.pewinternet.org/2013/10/10/online-video-2013/.

study [13] explores a translingual QA scenario, where search results are translated into the language of the query. The authors discuss implementation strategies and specific MT errors that are critical to solving the problem.

A rich set of features for ranking answers from CQA archives in response to *how-to* questions is investigated in [17]. Weber et al. [20] first extract queries with *how-to* intent from a search log, then answer them with "tips" from CQA.

Research in multimedia QA started over a decade ago with mono-lingual video retrieval. The early work focuses on factoid questions and uses a speech interface, transcribing the queries and the videos using automatic speech recognition [2,22]. The first work addressing cross-language video QA aims at answering questions in English using a corpus of videos in Chinese [21]. The authors use OCR to extract text from videos, and MT to translate the video text to English. Their QA module takes a classic approach, applying question analysis, passage retrieval and answer selection.

In the late 2000s, it was found that non-factoid questions are more frequent than factoid questions on the web, and that *how-to* questions constitute a large proportion of *wh*-questions [17]. Thus, the scope of research in multimedia QA was broadened from factoid questions to non-factoids such as *how-to* questions. It was argued that video retrieval is especially relevant for *how-to* questions [3]. The approach taken by Chua et al. [3] consists of two steps: (1) finding similar questions on Yahoo! Answers with which the terminology from the original question is expanded, and retrieving videos from YouTube for those expanded queries; and (2) re-ranking the retrieved videos based on their relevance to the original question. The authors evaluate their system on 24 *how-to* queries from Yahoo!Answers that have corresponding video answers in YouTube. In two follow-up papers [7,8], Li et al. improve the analysis of *how-to* questions in order to extract better key phrases from the question. They also improve video re-ranking using visual features, user comments and video redundancy.

In their overview paper [6], Hong et al. identify three directions for research in multimedia QA: (1) the creation of large corpora for evaluation, especially for definition and *how-to* QA; (2) the development of better techniques for concept detection and multimedia event detection; and (3) extension of the existing approaches to general domains. The latter of these three goals is addressed by [10].

In the current paper, we address the problem of answering *how-to*-questions with videos. We use Russian queries as a source, and retrieve videos for both the original query and its English translation. Our main contribution compared to previous work is that we show the large potential of *cross-lingual* video retrieval for answering *how-to* questions.

3   Data

Our study uses a subset of question-like Russian queries submitted to a major Russian search engine. The initial dataset comprises of all queries for the year 2012 containing question words and their variants. Under the agreement with the search engine, we only have access to the queries containing question words for research purposes; we have no access to the other queries issued by the same users or to the search results. The nearly 2 billion initially acquired questions form about 3–4 % of the actual query log.

The initial data underwent a multi-step cleaning to keep only queries that represent actual question-asking information needs. First, spam and bot users were removed from the log based on total number of submitted queries, unnatural query 'bursts', very long queries, and long sequences of almost identical questions. Second, only queries with a question word in the first position were retained. Further, we filtered out queries matching Wikipedia titles, crossword puzzles formulations and questions from TV game shows. Finally, we filtered out those question queries that contain only one word after we removed stopwords and question words. The cleaning removed more than half of the originally sampled questions; the remaining dataset contains about 915 million question queries from about 145 million users. This represents up to 2 % of the entire query stream. A detailed description of log cleaning can be found in [19].

For the current study we extracted all queries starting with *как (how)* from the cleaned log, which resulted in $573,129,599$ total queries ($237,846,014$ unique queries). *How-to* questions comprise about 63 % of all question queries and up to 1 % of the entire search engine query stream.

Table 1. Top-10 most frequent queries.

Query	Count
How to download music from vkontakte[a]	1,048,845
How to kiss in a right way	880,326
How to remove page in odnoklassniki[a]	717,639
How to make a slime toy	691,358
How to do it in a right way	545,554
How to download video from youtube	542,397
How to make a magic wand	396,700
How to earn money	345,653
How to quit smoking	297,358
How to build a website	286,657

[a]Popular Russian social network sites.

Table 1 cites the top-10 *how-to* questions along with their log frequencies (here and in subsequent tables the Russian queries and distinct terms have been translated for the reader's convenience). Table 2 summarizes the most frequent last words of the questions (suffixes) that are a good indicator of query intent. The list supports our hypotheses that many *how-to* questions seek for easy-to-perform instructions (*at home* in different formulations and *DIY*) and visual

Table 2. Most frequent words in the last position of the question.

Suffix	Count	%
At home	9,342,893	1.63
Video	8,409,924	1.47
[*windows*] 7	3,421,005	0.60
Minecraft	3,415,061	0.60
vkontakte	3,321,133	0.58
DIY	2,794,189	0.49
Photo	2,715,022	0.47
Free	2,441,100	0.43
Odniklassniki	2,409,490	0.42
At home	2,148,758	0.37

Table 3. Most frequent Latin character words in Russian question queries.

Query term	Count	%
Windows	5,699,513	0.99
Minecraft	5,418,118	0.95
iphone	2,229,155	0.39
Wifi	1,758,564	0.31
Samsung	1,486,654	0.26
XP	1,346,204	0.23
CS (counter strike)	1,304,039	0.23
Nokia	1,236,462	0.22
ipad	1,165,871	0.20
Youtube	1,158,642	0.20

information (*video, photo*). *How-to* questions reflect also the ubiquity and popularity of social networks (*vkontakte, odnoklassniki*). 14.2 % of the queries contain Latin characters. The presence of the Latin characters can be seen as an indirect signal that it might be useful to translate the query because the topic is potentially non-local. Table 3 lists the top-10 words in Latin script. The table shows that the most frequent words in Latin script are foreign words related to computer software, games and mobile devices. Presence of *youtube* in the list again supports our assumption that many *how-to* questions seek for visual content.

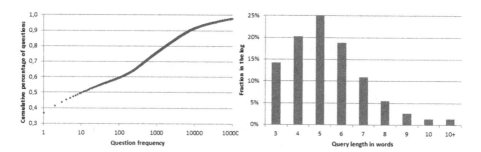

Fig. 1. Question frequency distribution.

Fig. 2. Question length distribution.

Figure 1 shows cumulative query frequency distribution. Unique queries comprise 36.9 % of the whole query mass; only 55 queries have frequencies larger than 10^5. Figure 2 shows length distribution of *how-to* questions (note that two-word questions were removed on the previous log cleaning stage). Question queries are longer than average web queries: the most frequently occurring query length in our data sample is five words, constituting one fourth of all *how-to* questions.

4   Results

In this section, we will first present the results of the in-depth manual analysis of a small query sample (Sect. 4.1), then evaluate the automatic translation of Russian queries (Sect. 4.2) and finally present the results of video retrieval evaluation (Sect. 4.3).

4.1   Manual Analysis of 1,000 Queries

To get a better understanding of *how-to* queries and the potential of answer them with videos in a different language, we randomly sampled 1,000 unique queries with frequencies 100 and higher from the dataset and analyzed them manually. This sample corresponds to 564, 866 queries submitted by users. Despite the fact that special attention was paid to cleaning the initial data from non-interrogative queries that look like questions (see previous section), two queries of this sort – a song title and a TV series title – were found in the sample.

The thousand queries were labeled by two authors in regard to three facets: (1) whether or not video would be a good answer medium for this question; (2) whether or not results in English (regardless – text or video) would be useful; (3) what the question's topical category is. The questions were first labeled by two authors independently; then the labels were discussed and discrepancies were reconciled. In cases where the authors could not interpret the information need behind the question, the question was labeled as *hard to answer*. Some opposed decisions (*yes/no* for facets 1 and 2) resulted in averaging to the label *possibly* upon negotiation.

Results For Facet 1. Potentially any kind of content can be represented by video: text, music, still images, and video proper. Text can be rehearsed, presented as running lines or a sequence of textual fragments (and such videos can be found on the Web in plenty). When labeling queries in this aspect, we tried to assess to which extent a video answer would be appropriate and helpful. To be marked with *yes* the query must relate to a real-life, tangible problem. The topic of the question might be abstract, as long as the answer can be shown on video. For example, the query how to solve absolute value inequalities relates to a rather abstract mathematical problem, but was labelled as allowing a video answer, taking into account proliferation of MOOCs and supported by plenty of relevant video results for this query. how to calculate profitability is an example of a 'non-video' query.

Results For Facet 2. Some queries are local – relate to national mobile network operators (MNO) how to remove a number from the blacklist megafon, locally used software how to work in 1C 7.7, taxation or legislation how to pay the vehicle tax, and customs how to dress on 1 september. This kind of questions was tagged as inappropriate for translation.

Table 4 shows the outcome of the manual labelling for the first two facets. The target subset of the queries for this study – for which both video results and

Table 4. Query labeling results, in percentages of the unique 1,000 queries (proportions accounting for log frequencies are similar).

Yes	Possibly	No	Hard to answer
Are video results potentially useful?			
74.5	12.8	11.1	1.7
Are English results potentially useful?			
83.6	1.3	14.8	0.4

results in other languages are potentially useful – constitutes 68.9 % of unique queries in our sample and 66.4 % in the corresponding query stream.

Results For Facet 3. As a starting point for query categorization, we took the YouTube channel topics.[3] The list consists of 16 items and is not an ideal flat taxonomy – in our case, almost all the queries could have been assigned to the *How-to* category, so we tried to choose the most specific category. In the course of labeling, we slightly modified the list of categories: (1) *Cooking & Health* was divided into two separate categories; (2) *Legal & Finance* and *Adult* were introduced, (3) *Tech* was renamed into *Computers, Internet and Cell phones.* The latter category became expectantly the largest one, but we did not divide it further, because many questions correspond simultaneously to several related concepts, e.g. how to download a photo from iphone to computer or how to setup Internet on MTS (MTS is a national MNO). Table 5 shows the breakdown of categories in our question set along with fractions of queries, for which video results and results in a language other than Russian are potentially useful in each category. It can be seen from the table that *Legal & Finance category* is the least suitable both for video and non-local results. Low figures in *Science & Education* are due to questions like how to translate... and how to spell.... Many questions from *Lifestyle & Social* are about relationships, dating, etc. that can be well *illustrated*, but hardly *answered* with video.

Manual investigation of questions allowed us for making several additional observations: About 2 % of questions contain spelling errors; 8 % contain slang (e.g. *бесплатка* for a free text service 'please call me') or transliterated names of software, computer games, or services (e.g. *фотошоп* for *photoshop*). Spelling errors can be seen as a lesser problem, since search engines are good at correcting misspelled queries; slang and transliteration can potentially harm translation quality to a larger extent.

In the sample, we saw that question queries starting with *how* followed by a verb can be divided in two groups: (1) a large group of question queries starting with *how + infinitive* that have a clear practical intent (equivalent to the English *how to*), e.g. how to cook stuffed peppers, and (2) a much smaller group of queries starting with *how + finite verb form* that have a more abstract curiosity intent,

---

[3] https://www.youtube.com/channels?gl=US.

e.g. how was the clock invented. The ratio of infinite/finite verbs following *как* is 16:1. Also note that not all Russian questions starting with *как* correspond to English *how* counterparts. For example, *как зовут X?*-questions – literally *how is X called* – correspond to *what is X's name?*

How-to questions are about actions that are usually described by verbs. Therefore it is interesting to note that some categories are very characteristic for their verb use in question, though most generic verb *do/make* is presented in all categories in different proportions. The most distinguished category is *Cooking*, which presents the entire range of culinary manipulations – *cook* (by a large margin), *bake, soak, pickle, cut, jerk, marinate*, etc. Another example – *Computers, Internet and Cell phones*, where leading *do/make* is followed by more specific *create, install, configure, download*, and *remove*.

These insights can be valuable for automatic analysis and categorization of *how-to* question queries.

4.2   Machine Translation

The 1,000 queries were machine translated using three free online services – Yandex[4], Google[5], and Bing[6] – to avoid bias in the gold standard translation: a professional translator post-edited randomly picked translations from the three MT engines' outputs. As a byproduct we obtained a comparative evaluation of three services.

We calculated two popular MT quality measures widely adopted by the MT community: BLEU (Bilingual Evaluation Understudy, [12]) and TER (Translation Error Rate, [15]) – using the post-edited translation as reference. Table 6 summarizes automatic translation quality scores for the three MT engines. While BLEU indicates the proportion of common n-grams in reference and machine translations (larger scores mean better translations), TER measures the number of edits required to change a system output into the reference (the lower the better). Both measures rank the three systems equivalently. The obtained BLEU scores are significantly higher than those by the best performing systems for Russian-English pair in the WMT'2015 evaluation campaign (around 0.29) [1]. This is expected, since reference translations were obtained as a result of post-editing, not as 'from scratch' translations.

For our retrieval evaluation experiments we took the output of Google Translate (the lowest score in our list) to be not overoptimistic.

4.3   Video Retrieval Evaluation

We used the YouTube search API[7] to retrieve videos for 100 queries. We sampled these queries from our *target* subset, i.e. queries for which we marked that both

---

[4] https://translate.yandex.com/.

[5] https://translate.google.com/.

[6] http://www.bing.com/translator.

[7] https://developers.google.com/youtube/v3/.

Table 5. Question category breakdown. To several categories (*Music, Comedy, Film & Entertainment, From TV, Animation, Causes & Non-profits, News & Politics*) only zero to two queries were assigned, so we do not cite figures for them in the Table. For reader's convenience, the table shows data for unique queries only. Category breakdown accounting for query frequencies is roughly the same with minor deviations. "Comp, Int & Phon" refers to the category "Computers, Internet and Cell phones"

Category	Share (%)	Video? (%)	Translate? (%)	Example
Gaming	5.9	89.2	95.4	How to save Mordin
Beauty & fashion	7.0	98.7	98.7	How to get rid of freckles
Automotive	2.7	89.7	79.3	How to improve sound in car
Sports	1.9	100.0	100.0	How to jump on a skateboard
How-to & DIY	18.7	94.6	95.1	How to fix hooklink
Comp, Int & Phon	26.6	86.3	82.1	How to change local disk icon
Science & education	7.6	45.8	72.3	How is beeswax made
Cooking	6.3	98.6	97.1	How to make puff pastry
Health	5.0	70.9	100.0	How to treat wound
Lifestyle & social	4.9	13.0	87.0	How to attract a guy
Legal & finance	5.0	3.6	20.0	How to calculate income tax
Adult	2.7	93.1	100.0	How to give erotic massage
Other	4.6	8.0	48.0	How to call to Thailand

video answers and answers in a different language could be useful. Thus, the evaluation results can be considered an upper limit of cross-lingual video retrieval, when no query analysis is performed. We retrieved 10 videos from YouTube for each original Russian query, and 10 videos for the query's English translation by Google Translate. We had each of the videos assessed by three workers on the crowd sourcing platform Amazon Mechanical Turk[8] — resulting in a total of 6,000 ($100 * (10 + 10) * 3$) HITs.

---

[8] https://www.mturk.com.

Table 6. Quality evaluation of the machine translation engines for query translation (1,000 unique *how-to* queries), using a professional post-edited translation as reference.

MT engine	BLEU	TER
Yandex	0.52	30.95
Google	0.44	37.18
Bing	0.49	34.17

Unfortunately, Russian native speakers are marginally presented on Mechanical Turk [14]. Therefore, we modelled cross-language video retrieval in a reverse direction: workers supposedly proficient in English – we set locale to US as qualification for the HITs – were presented with the reference query translation and had to evaluate videos retrieved both for original Russian query and its English machine translation. Note that this reverse setting is more rigorous than the true Ru→En direction: we can imagine that even an average Russian-speaking user possesses some elementary knowledge of English, whereas the odds are much lower that MTurk workers with US locale are proficient in Russian.

We set up an annotation interface in which we showed a question together with one retrieved video and the question "How well does the video answer the question?" Relevance labeling was done on a four-point scale: (3) Excellent answer; (2) Good answer; (1) May be good; (0) Not relevant. In order to validate that the MTurk labels by speakers of English are a good approximation for the assessments by Russian speakers, we recruited Russian volunteers through online social networks. The volunteers labeled the search results for 20 original Russian queries and their translations (10 results per query) in the same interface. Each question–video pair was assessed by two volunteers; 45 volunteers took part in the labeling.

We calculated the inter-rater agreement between the Russian volunteers and English-speaking MTurk workers as an indication for the validity of the MTurk labels. We found the following agreement scores in terms of weighted Cohen's κ:[9] the agreement among MTurkers was 0.448; the agreement among the Russian volunteers was 0.402 and the agreement between Russians and MTurkers was 0.414. Since the agreement between Russian volunteers and MTurk workers is not lower than the agreement among Russian volunteers, the MTurk annotations can be considered a good approximation for the assessments by Russian speakers.

Table 7 shows the results for the video retrieval evaluation in terms of Precision@10, Success@10, and DCG@10[10]. In case of DCG we averaged MTurk's scores for each query-video pair; for evaluation with binary relevance, we considered the scores 2 and 3 (good or excellent answer) as relevant and used the majority vote of the three workers as final relevance judgment. According to a paired

---

[9] Weighted κ is a variant of κ that takes into account that the labels are interval variables: 3 is closer to 2 than it is to 1.

[10] We opted for DCG, since it also reflects how many relevant results were retrieved, not only how well the retrieved results were ranked (as in case of nDCG).

Table 7. Evaluation of the video re for the original Russian how-questions and their English translations. Precision@10 is the proportion of relevant videos (assessed relevance ≥ 2) in the top-10 YouTube results. Success@10 is the proportion of questions that have at least one relevant video in the top-10. DCG uses averaged relevance scores by MTurk workers.

	Precision@10 (stderr)	Success@10	DCG@10
For original questions	0.643 (0.250)	0.98	3.45
For translations	0.638 (0.311)	0.96	3.39

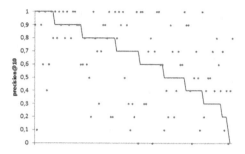

Fig. 3. Precision@10 for original queries (line) and corresponding translated queries (dots). The x-axis represents the individual queries, ordered by decreasing p@10 for original queries. All dots that occur above the line are queries that show improved p@10 when translated.

t-test the difference between DCG scores for original queries and their translations is not significant ($P = .73$, $n = 100$), neither is the difference between the Precision@10 scores ($P = .98$).

If we consider the proportions of relevance labels in the labelled videos, we see that 17 % of the assessed videos was labelled as (0) Not relevant; 19 % was labelled as (1) May be good; 29 % was labelled as (2) Good answer and 35 % was labelled as (3) Excellent answer. Figure 3 illustrates the differences in Precision@10 scores between original Russian queries and their English translations. In total, 48 queries show improved precision@10 for the translated query, in 39 cases the translated query gives worse results, and for 13 queries the results tie. Manual investigation of harmed queries reveals that the drop in quality is mainly due to translation flaws – either wrong translation for polysemic words or poor processing of Russian writings of English names such as *майнкрафт* for *minecraft*. In some cases the translation is fair, but either the topic is unpopular (e.g. how to clean white mink fur at home) or the search results are not precise (e.g. how to turn on flash player in chrome browser results in videos *how to install flash player in chrome, how to fix crash from flash player in chrome,* etc.). English content (or English queries submitted through the API) may be moderated more strictly, e.g. there is a relevant result for original query how to delay ejaculation, but no relevant results for its correct translation.

5   Conclusions

The main contribution of this study is that it shows the potential of cross-lingual video retrieval for *how-to* questions. We combined an in-depth manual analysis with evaluation by the crowd of the translation–retrieval pipeline. The result of the manual analysis was a set of questions for which we decided that videos in a different language are potentially useful answers. This claim was supported by our results: 98 % of the Russian queries in our selection had at least one relevant video answer in the top-10 from YouTube. Precision@10 is 0.638, which implies that on average, 6 out of the first 10 video results are relevant ('Good answer' or 'Excellent answer') to the query. The results show that *how-to* queries translated to English by off-the-shelf systems give the same video retrieval performance as the original Russian queries. Cross-lingual video search for *how-to* queries can improve recall and diversity of search results, as well as to compensate the shortage of original content in emerging markets.

The obtained results suggest the following directions of research in the future. First, it would be interesting to study the topics of *how-to* question queries that benefit most from cross-lingual video retrieval. A recent study [19] demonstrates that even rare questions can be categorized in topical categories with acceptable quality (recall that about one third of *how-to* questions is unique in a yearly log). Categorization of questions could be paired with video categorization based on metadata and user comments [4]. Second, a user study must be carried out to analyze the users' experience with video retrieval results in a foreign language.

The annotated data is available for research purposes.[11]

Acknowledgments. We thank Yandex for preparing the dataset and granting access. Pavel Braslavski's work was supported by RFBR, research project #14-07-00589-a. This publication was partially supported by the Dutch national program COMMIT (project P7 SWELL). We also thank all volunteers, who took part in the evaluation.

References

1. Bojar, O., et al.: Findings of the 2015 workshop on statistical machine translation. In: WMT (2015)
2. Cao, J., Nunamaker, J.F.: Question answering on lecture videos: a multifaceted approach. In: JCDL (2004)
3. Chua, T.S., Hong, R., Li, G., Tang, J.: From text question-answering to multimedia QA on web-scale media resources. In: LS-MMRM Workshop (2009)
4. Filippova, K., Hall, K.B.: Improved video categorization from text metadata and user comments. In: SIGIR (2011)
5. Giampiccolo, D., et al.: Overview of the CLEF 2007 multilingual question answering track. In: Peters, C., et al. (eds.) CLEF 2007. LNCS, vol. 5152, pp. 200–236. Springer, Heidelberg (2008)
6. Hong, R., Wang, M., Li, G., Nie, L., Zha, Z.J., Chua, T.S.: Multimedia question answering. IEEE Trans. Multimed. **19**(4), 72–78 (2012)

---

[11] http://kansas.ru/howto-video/.

7. Li, G., et al.: Video reference: question answering on youtube. In: MM (2009)
8. Li, G., Li, H., Ming, Z., Hong, R., Tang, S., Chua, T.S.: Question answering over community-contributed web videos. IEEE Trans. Multimed. **17**(4), 46–57 (2010)
9. Mitamura, T., et al.: Overview of the NTCIR-7 ACLIA tasks: advanced cross-lingual information access. In: NTCIR-7 Workshop (2008)
10. Nie, L., Wang, M., Gao, Y., et al.: Beyond text QA: multimedia answer generation by harvesting web information. IEEE Trans. Multimed. **15**(2), 426–441 (2013)
11. Pang, B., Kumar, R.: Search in the lost sense of query: question formulation in web search queries and its temporal changes. In: ACL, vol. 2 (2011)
12. Papineni, K., Roukos, S., Ward, T., Zhu, W.J.: BLEU: a method for automatic evaluation of machine translation. In: ACL (2002)
13. Parton, K., McKeown, K.R., Allan, J., Henestroza, E.: Simultaneous multilingual search for translingual information retrieval. In: CIKM (2008)
14. Pavlick, E., Post, M., Irvine, A., Kachaev, D., Callison-Burch, C.: The language demographics of amazon mechanical turk. TACL **2**, 79–92 (2014)
15. Snover, M., Dorr, B., Schwartz, R., Micciulla, L., Makhoul, J.: A study of translation edit rate with targeted human annotation. In: AMTA (2006)
16. Spink, A., Ozmultu, H.C.: Characteristics of question format web queries: an exploratory study. Inf. Process. Manage. **38**(4), 453–471 (2002)
17. Surdeanu, M., Ciaramita, M., Zaragoza, H.: Learning to rank answers to non-factoid questions from web collections. Comput. Linguist. **37**(2), 351–383 (2011)
18. Torrey, C., Churchill, E.F., McDonald, D.W.: Learning how: the search for craft knowledge on the internet. In: CHI (2009)
19. Völske, M., Braslavski, P., Hagen, M., Lezina, G., Stein, B.: What users ask a search engine: analyzing one billion russian question queries. In: CIKM (2015)
20. Weber, I., Ukkonen, A., Gionis, A.: Answers, not links: Extracting tips from yahoo! answers to address how-to web queries. In: WSDM (2012)
21. Wu, Y.C., Chang, C.H., Lee, Y.S.: CLVQ: cross-language video question/answering system. In: IEEE MMSE (2004)
22. Yang, H., Chaisorn, L., Zhao, Y., Neo, S.Y., Chua, T.S.: VideoQA: question answering on news video. In: MM (2003)

The CLEF Monolingual Grid of Points

Nicola Ferro and Gianmaria Silvello[✉]

Department of Information Engineering, University of Padua, Padua, Italy
{ferro,silvello}@dei.unipd.it

Abstract. In this paper we run a systematic series of experiments for creating a *grid of points* where many combinations of retrieval methods and components adopted by *MultiLingual Information Access (MLIA)* systems are represented. This grid of points has the goal to provide insights about the effectiveness of the different components and their interaction and to identify suitable baselines with respect to which all the comparisons can be made.

We publicly release a large grid of points comprising more than 4 K runs obtained by testing 160 IR systems combining different stop lists, stemmers, n-grams components and retrieval models on CLEF monolingual tasks for nine European languages. Furthermore, we evaluate such grid of points by employing four different effectiveness measures and provide some insights about the quality of the created grid of points and the behaviour of the different systems.

1 Introduction

Component-based evaluation, i.e. the ability of assessing the impact of the different components in the pipeline of an *Information Retrieval (IR)* system and understanding their interaction, is a long-standing challenge, as pointed out by [24]: "if we want to decide between alternative indexing strategies for example, we must use these strategies as part of a complete information retrieval system, and examine its overall performance (with each of the alternatives) directly".

This issue is even more exacerbated in the case of *MultiLingual Information Access (MLIA)*, where the combinations of components and languages grow exponentially, and even the more systematic experiments explore just a small fraction of them, basically hampering a more profound understanding of MLIA.

In Grid@CLEF [15], we proposed the idea of running a systematic series of experiments and creating a *grid of points*, where (ideally) all the combinations of retrieval methods and components were represented. This would have had two positive effects: first, to provide more insights about the effectiveness of the different components and their interaction; second, to identify *suitable baselines* with respect to which all the comparisons have to be made.

However, even if Grid@CLEF succeeded in establishing the technical framework to make it possible to create such grid of points, it did not delivered a grid big enough, due to the high technical barriers to implement it.

© Springer International Publishing Switzerland 2016
N. Fuhr et al. (Eds.): CLEF 2016, LNCS 9822, pp. 16–27, 2016.
DOI: 10.1007/978-3-319-44564-9_2

More recently, the wider availability of open source IR systems [26] made it possible to run systematic experiments more easily and we see a renewed interest in creating grid of points, which also allow for *reproducible baselines* [14,21]. Indeed, in the context the "Open-Source Information Retrieval Reproducibility Challenge"[1] [1], we provided several of these baselines for many of the CLEF Adhoc collections as well as a methodology for systematically creating and describing them [11].

In this paper, we move a step forward and we release as an open resource the first fine-grained grids of points for many of the CLEF monolingual Adhoc tasks over a range of several years. The goal of these grids is to facilitate research in the MLIA field, to provide a set of standard baseline on standard collections, and to offer the possibility of conducting deeper analyses on the interaction among components in multiple languages.

The paper is organized as follows: Sect. 2 provides an overview of the used CLEF collections; Sect. 3 describes how we created the different grids of points; Sect. 4 presents some analyses to assess the quality of the created grids of points and get an outlook of the behaviour of the different systems; finally, Sect. 5 wraps up the discussion and provides an outlook of future work.

2   Overview of CLEF Monolingual Tasks

We considered the CLEF Adhoc monolingual tasks from 2000 to 2007 [2–6,12,13] in nine languages: Bulgarian, German, Spanish, Finnish, French, Hungarian, Italian, Portuguese and Swedish. The main information about the corpora, topics and relevance judgments of considered tasks are reported in Table 1.

The CLEF corpora are formed by document sets in different European languages but with common features: the same genre and time period, comparable content. Indeed, the large majority of the corpora are composed by newspaper articles from 1994–1995 with the exception of the Bulgarian and Hungarian corpora composed of newspaper articles from 2002.

The French, German and Italian news agency dispatches – i.e. ATS, SDA and AGZ – are all gathered from the Swiss news agency and are the same corpus translated in different languages. The Spanish corpus is composed of news agencies (i.e. EFE) from the same time period as the Swiss news agency corpus and thus it is very similar in terms of structure and content.

CLEF topics follow the typical TREC structure composed of three fields: title, description and narrative. The topic creation process in CLEF has had to deal with specific issues related to the multilingualism as described in [19].

As far as relevance assessments are concerned, CLEF adopted they standard approach based on the pooling method and the assessment based on the longest, most elaborate formulation of the topic, i.e. the narrative [25]. Typical pool depths are between 60 and 100 documents.

---

[1] https://github.com/lintool/IR-Reproducibility.

Table 1. Employed CLEF monolingual tasks: used corpora; number of documents; number of topics; size of the pool; number of submitted runs. Languages are expressed as ISO 639:1 two letters code.

Task	Year	Corpora	Docs	Topics	Pool	Runs
AH Mono BG	2005	SEGA 2002 STANDART 2002	69,195	49	20,130	20
	2006			50	17,308	11
	2007			50	19,441	16
AH Mono DE	2000	FRANKFURTER 1994	139,715	49	11,335	22
	2001	FRANKFURTER 1994	225,371	49	16,726	22
	2002	SDA 1994		50	19,394	28
	2003	SPIEGEL 1994 & 1995		57	21,534	38
AH Mono ES	2001	EFE 1994	215,738	49	14,268	22
	2002			50	19,668	28
	2003	EFE 1994 & 1995	454,045	57	23,822	38
AH Mono FI	2002	AMULEHTI 1994 & 1995	55,344	30	9,825	11
	2003			45	10,803	13
	2004			45	20,124	30
AH Mono FR	2000	LEMONDE 1994	44,013	34	7,003	10
	2001	LEMONDE 1994	87,191	49	12,263	15
	2002	ATS 1994		50	17,465	16
	2003	LEMONDE 1994 ATS 1994 & 1995	129,806	52	16,785	35
	2004	LEMONDE 1995 ATS 1995	90,261	49	23,541	38
	2005	LEMONDE 1994 & 1995	177,452	50	23,999	38
	2006	ATS 1994 & 1995		49	17,882	27
AH Mono HU	2005	MAGYAR 2002	49,530	50	20,561	30
	2006			48	20,435	17
	2007			50	18,704	19
AH Mono IT	2000	AGZ 1994 LASTAMPA 1994	108,578	34	6,760	10
	2001			47	10,697	14
	2002			49	17,822	25
	2003	AGZ 1994 & 1995 LASTAMPA 1994	157,558	51	20,902	27
AH Mono PT	2004	PUBLICO 1994 & 1995	106,821	46	20,103	22
	2005	FOLHA 1994 & 1995	210,734	50	20,539	32
	2006	PUBLICO 1994 & 1995		50	20,154	34
AH Mono SV	2002	TT 1994 & 1995	142,819	49	12,580	7
	2003			54	15,975	18

Figure 1 reports the box plots of the selected CLEF monolingual tasks grouped by language. We can see that in most cases the data are evenly distributed within the quantiles and they are not particularly skewed. For the monolingual tasks there is only one system with MAP equal to zero (i.e., an outlier for the AH-MONO-ES task) and for 78 % of the monolingual tasks the first quantile is above 10 % of MAP. Note that even amongst the tasks on the same

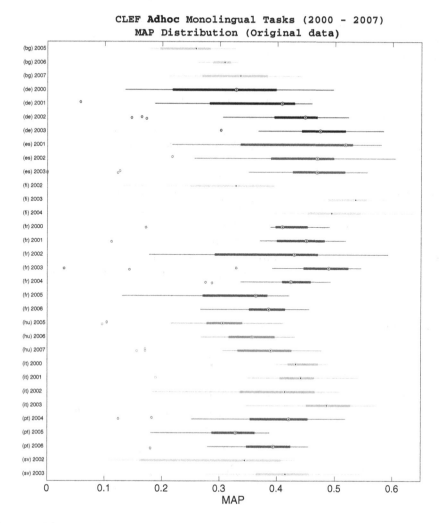

Fig. 1. MAP distribution of original runs submitted to the considered CLEF monolingual tasks.

language, the experimental collections differ from task to task and thus a direct comparison of performances across years is not possible; in [16] an across years comparison between CLEF monolingual, bilingual and multilingual tasks has been conducted by employing the standardization methodology defined in [28].

3   Grid of Points

We considered four main components of an IR system: stop list, stemmer, n-grams and IR model. We selected a set of alternative implementations of each component and by using the Terrier open source system [22] we created a run for each system defined by combining the available components in all possible ways. Note that stemmers and n-grams are mutually exclusive alternatives since either you can employ a stemmer or a n-grams component.

stop list: nostop, stop;
stemmer: nostem, weak stemmer, aggressive stemmer;
n-grams: nograms, 4grams, 5grams;
model: BB2, BM25, DFRBM25, DFRee, DLH, DLH13, DPH, HiemstraLM, IFB2, InL2, InexpB2, InexpC2, LGD, LemurTFIDF, PL2, TFIDF.

The specific language resources employed such as the stoplist and the stemmers depend by the language of the task at hand. All the stoplists have been provided by the University of Neuchâtel (UNINE)[2]; in the Table 2 we report the number of words composing each stoplist. The stemmers have been provided by University of Neuchâtel (UNINE in the table) and by the Snowball Stemming language and algorithms project[3] (snowball in the table). We chose to use these stop lists and stemmers due to their availability as open source linguistic resources.

Table 2. The linguistic resources employed for each monolingual task.

Language	Stoplist	Weak stemmer	Aggressive stemmer
Bulgarian (bg)	UNINE 258 words	UNINE light stemmer	UNINE stemmer
German (de)	UNINE 603 words	UNINE light stemmer	Snowball stemmer
Spanish (es)	UNINE 307 words	UNINE light stemmer	Snowball stemmer
Finnish (fi)	UNINE 747 words	UNINE light stemmer	Snowball stemmer
French (fr)	UNINE 463 words	UNINE light stemmer	Snowball stemmer
Hungarian (hu)	UNINE 737 words	UNINE light stemmer	Snowball stemmer
Italian (it)	UNINE 399 words	UNINE light stemmer	Snowball stemmer
Portuguese (pt)	UNINE 356 words	UNINE light stemmer	Snowball stemmer
Swedish (sv)	UNINE 386 words	UNINE light stemmer	Snowball stemmer

To obtain the desired grid of points, we employed Terrier ver. 4.1 which we extended to work with UNINE stemmers and n-grams. For each task we obtained 160 runs and we calculated four measures: AP, RBP, nDCG20 and ERR20 which capture different performance angles by employing different user models; we chose these measures due to their large use in IR evaluation. The measures have been calculated by employing the *MATlab Toolkit for Evaluation of information Retrieval Systems (MATTERS)* library[4].

---

[2] http://members.unine.ch/jacques.savoy/clef/index.html.
[3] https://github.com/snowballstem.
[4] http://matters.dei.unipd.it/.

Average Precision (AP) [8] represents the "gold standard" measure in IR, known to be stable and informative, with a natural top-heavy bias and an underlying theoretical basis as approximation of the area under the precision/recall curve. AP is the reference measure in this study for all CLEF tasks and it is the measure originally adopted by CLEF for evaluating the systems participating in the campaigns.

Rank-Biased Precision (RBP) [23] is built around a user model based on the utility a user can achieve by using a system: the higher, the better. The model it implements is that a user always starts from the first document in the list and then s/he progresses from one document to the next with a probability p. We calculated RBP by setting $p = 0.8$ which represent a good trade-off between a very persistent and a remitting user.

nDCG [18] is the normalized version of the widely-known *Discounted Cumulated Gain (DCG)* which is defined for graded relevance judgments. We calculated nDCG in a binary relevance setting by giving gain 0 to non-relevant documents and gain 1 to the relevant ones; furthermore, we used a log_{10} discounting function.

Expected Reciprocal Rank (ERR) [10] is a measure defined for graded relevance judgments and for evaluating navigational intent and it is particularly top-heavy since it highly penalizes systems placing not-relevant documents in high positions. We calculated ERR in a binary relevance setting as we have done for nDCG.

The calculated measures, the scripts used to run Terrier on the CLEF collections along with the property files required to correctly setup the system and the modified version of Terrier comprising UNINE stemmers and n-grams components are publicly available at the URL: http://gridofpoints.dei.unipd.it/.

4   Analysis of the Grid of Points

In Fig. 2 we can see the MAP distributions for the runs composing the grid of points for each considered monolingual task. Given that these runs have been produced by adopting comparable systems, we can conduct an across years comparison between the different editions of the same task. Furthermore, given a task, we can compare the performances obtained by the runs in the grid of points with the performances achieved by the original systems reported in Fig. 1.

By analysing the performances reported in Fig. 2 we can identify two main groups of tasks, the first one comprising languages achieving the highest median and best MAP values which are Spanish, Finnish, French, German and Italian; and, a second group with the Bulgarian, Hungarian, Portuguese and Swedish languages. This difference in performances between different languages can be in part explained by the quality of the linguistic resources employed; indeed, the systems in the grid points obtained better performances for languages introduced in the early years of CLEF – e.g., French and Spanish – and lower performances for the languages introduced in the latter years – e.g., Bulgarian and Hungarian.

By comparing the box plots in Figs. 1 and 2 we can see the distribution of runs in the two sets and we can see where the grid of points runs are a good

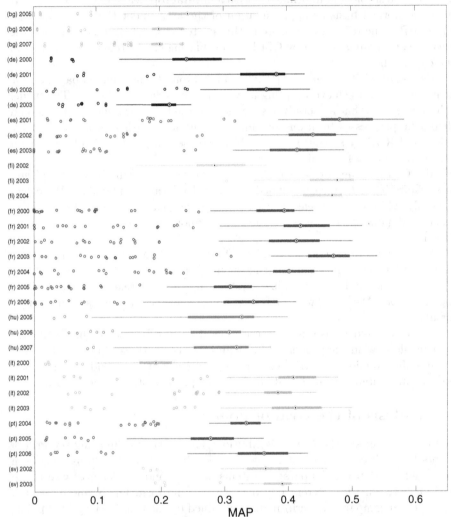

Fig. 2. Grid of points MAP distribution for the considered CLEF monolingual tasks.

representation of the original runs and where they differ one from the other. In the grid of points we have many more runs than in the original CLEF setting and this could explain the higher number of outliers we see in Fig. 2. If we focus on the median MAP values we can see several close correspondences between the original runs and the grid of points ones as for example for the Bulgarian 2005 task, the German 2001 task, the Spanish 2002 task, all Finnish tasks, French tasks from 2000 to 2004, the Italian 2001 task, the Portuguese 2006 task and all Swedish tasks. On the other hand, there are tasks that do not find a close correspondence between the two run sets as for example the Bulgarian 2006 and 2007 tasks and the Hungarian tasks. Generally, when there is no correspondence, the performances of the grid of points runs are lower than those of the original runs. It must be underlined that some languages, as German and Swedish, get benefit from the use of a word decompounder component [7] which has not been included in the current version of the gird of points; this could lead to worse results in the grid of points with respect to the original CLEF languages.

We employ the *Kernel Density Estimation (KDE)* [27] to estimate the *Probability Density Function (PDF)* of both the original runs submitted at CLEF and the various grids of points. Then, we compute the *Kullback–Leibler Divergence (KLD)* [20] between these PDFs in order to get an appreciation of how different are the grids of points from the original runs. Indeed, KLD $\in [0, +\infty)$ denotes the information lost when a grid of points is used to approximate an original set of runs [9]; therefore, 0 means that there is no loss of information and, in our settings, that the original runs and the grid of points are considered the same; $+\infty$ means that there is full loss of information and, in our settings, that the grid of points and the original runs are considered completely different.

The values of the KLD for all the considered tasks are reported in Fig. 3. In our setting, we assume the "true"/reference probability distribution to be the one associated to the original runs and the "reference" probability distribution to be the one associated to the grid of points runs.

In Fig. 3 we can see that most of the KLD values are fairly low showing the proximity between the original AP values distributions and the grid of points ones. The bigger differences between the distributions are found for the Bulgarian 2006 and 2007 tasks, the German 2000 and 2003 tasks and the Italian 2000 task; for Bulgarian and German, this fact can be checked also by looking at the box plots in Figs. 1 and 2.

In Fig. 4 we can see a comparison between the KDEs of the PDF of AP calculated from the original runs and the grid of points ones; for space reasons

Task	KL-Divergence							
Bulgarian (bg)						6.3642	18.8435	131.6713
Finnish (fi)			5.4461	4.3093	1.9777			
French (fr)	7.8072	5.1439	4.3669	2.1618	3.7242	6.1699	8.5966	
German (de)	14.9074	2.9264	5.5079	61.2449				
Hungarian (hu)						1.4365	8.5492	7.7116
Italian (it)	1633.5	2.3715	3.1710	8.7488				
Portuguese (pt)					7.8868	6.8498	4.3388	
Spanish (es)		4.1603	3.8043	3.4854				
Swedish (sv)			9.0646	3.9338				
	2000	2001	2002	2003	2004	2005	2006	2007

Fig. 3. KLD for all the considered tasks.

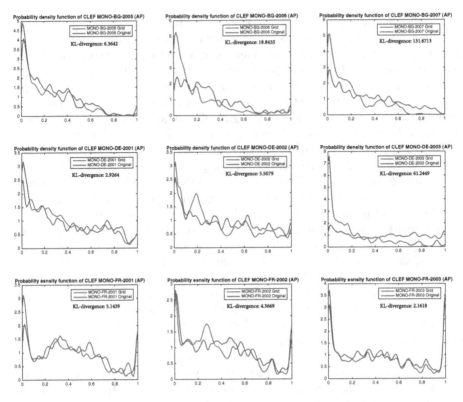

Fig. 4. The KDE of the PDF of AP calculated from the original runs and the grid of points ones.

we report the plots only for nine selected tasks – i.e. the 2005–2007 Bulgarian tasks, the 2001–2003 German tasks and the 2001–2003 French tasks. It is quite straightforward to see the correlation between the shape of the PDF curves and the KLD values reported in Fig. 4.

In Fig. 5 we present a multivariate plot for the CLEF 2003 Monolingual French task which reports the performances of the grid of points runs grouped by stop list, stemmer/n-grams and model. This figure shows a possible performance analysis allowed by the grid of points; indeed, we can see how the different components of the IR systems at hand contribute to the overall performances even though we cannot quantify the exact contribution of each component. For instance, by observing at Fig. 5 we can see that the effect of the stop list is quite evident for all the combinations of system components; indeed, the performances of the systems using a stop list are higher than those not using a stop list. The effect of the stemmer and n-grams components is also noticeable given that the lowest performing systems are consistently those employing neither a stemmer nor a n-grams component; we can also see that the employment of a n-grams component has a positive sizable impact on performances for the French language

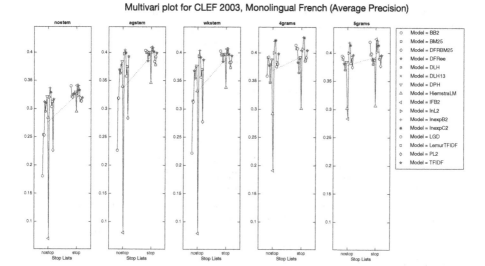

Fig. 5. Multivari plot grouped by stop list, stemmer/n-grams and model for the CLEF 2003 Monolingual French task.

and that it reduces the performance spread amongst the systems. Finally, we can also analyse the impact of different models and their interaction with the other components. For instance, we can see that the IFB2 model is always achieving the lowest performances of the group when the stop list is not employed, whereas it is among the best performing models when a stop list is employed. On the other hand, this model is not highly influenced by the use of stemmers and n-grams components.

5   Final Remarks

In this paper we presented a new valuable resource for MLIA research built over the CLEF Adhoc collections: a big and systematic grid of points combining various IR components – stop lists, stemmers, n-grams, IR models – for several European languages and for different evaluation measures – AP, nDCG, ERR, and RBP.

We assessed whether the produced grids of points are actually representative enough to allow for subsequent analyses and we have found that they have performance distributions similar to those of the runs originally submitted to the CLEF Adhoc tasks over the years.

Moreover, we have shown some of the analyses that are enabled by the grid of point and how they allow us to start understanding how components interact together.

These analyses are intended to show the potentialities of the grid of points that can be exploited to carry out deeper analyses and considerations.

For instance, the grid of points can be the starting point for determining the contribution of a specific component within the full pipeline of an IR system and to estimate the interaction of one component with the other. As a consequence, as far as future work is concerned, we will decompose system performance into components' ones according to the methodology we proposed [17] and we will try to generalize this decomposition across languages.

References

1. Arguello, J., Crane, M., Diaz, F., Lin, J., Trotman, A.: Report on the SIGIR 2015 workshop on reproducibility, inexplicability, and generalizability of results (RIGOR). SIGIR Forum **49**(2), 107–116 (2015)
2. Braschler, M.: CLEF 2000 - overview of results. In: Peters, C. (ed.) CLEF 2000. LNCS, vol. 2069, p. 89. Springer, Heidelberg (2001)
3. Braschler, M.: CLEF 2001 - overview of results. In: Peters, C., Braschler, M., Gonzalo, J., Kluck, M. (eds.) CLEF 2001. LNCS, vol. 2406, pp. 9–26. Springer, Heidelberg (2002)
4. Braschler, M.: CLEF 2002 – overview of results. In: Peters, C., Braschler, M., Gonzalo, J. (eds.) CLEF 2002. LNCS, vol. 2785, pp. 9–27. Springer, Heidelberg (2003)
5. Braschler, M.: CLEF 2003 – overview of results. In: Peters, C., Gonzalo, J., Braschler, M., Kluck, M. (eds.) CLEF 2003. LNCS, vol. 3237, pp. 44–63. Springer, Heidelberg (2004)
6. Braschler, M., Di Nunzio, G.M., Ferro, N., Peters, C.: CLEF 2004: ad hoc track overview and results analysis. In: Peters, C., Clough, P., Gonzalo, J., Jones, G.J.F., Kluck, M., Magnini, B. (eds.) CLEF 2004. LNCS, vol. 3491, pp. 10–26. Springer, Heidelberg (2005)
7. Braschler, M., Ripplinger, B.: How effective is stemming and decompounding for german text retrieval? Inf. Retr. **7**(3–4), 291–316 (2004)
8. Buckley, C., Voorhees, E.M.: Retrieval system evaluation. In: TREC: Experiment and Evaluation in Information Retrieval, pp. 53–78. MIT Press (2005)
9. Burnham, K.P., Anderson, D.R.: Model Selection and Multimodel Inference: A Practical Information-Theoretic Approach, p. 488. Springer, Heidelberg (2002)
10. Chapelle, O., Metzler, D., Zhang, Y., Grinspan, P.: Expected reciprocal rank for graded relevance. In: Proceedings of 18th International Conference on Information and Knowledge Management (CIKM), pp. 621–630. ACM Press (2009)
11. Di Buccio, E., Di Nunzio, G.M., Ferro, N., Harman, D.K., Maistro, M., Silvello, G.: Unfolding off-the-shelf IR systems for reproducibility. In: Proceedings of SIGIR Workshop on Reproducibility, Inexplicability, and Generalizability of Results (RIGOR) (2015)
12. Di Nunzio, G.M., Ferro, N., Jones, G.J.F., Peters, C.: CLEF 2005: ad hoc track overview. In: Peters, C., et al. (eds.) CLEF 2005. LNCS, vol. 4022, pp. 11–36. Springer, Heidelberg (2006)
13. Di Nunzio, G.M., Ferro, N., Mandl, T., Peters, C.: CLEF 2006: ad hoc track overview. In: Peters, C., et al. (eds.) CLEF 2006. LNCS, vol. 4730, pp. 21–34. Springer, Heidelberg (2007)
14. Ferro, N., Fuhr, N., Järvelin, K., Kando, N., Lippold, M., Zobel, J.: Increasing reproducibility in IR: findings from the Dagstuhl seminar on "reproducibility of data-oriented experiments in e-science". SIGIR Forum **50**(1), 68–82 (2016)

15. Ferro, N., Harman, D.: CLEF 2009: Grid@CLEF pilot track overview. In: Roda, G., Peters, C., Nunzio, G.M., Kurimo, M., Mandl, T., Mostefa, D., Peñas, A. (eds.) CLEF 2009. LNCS, vol. 6241, pp. 552–565. Springer, Heidelberg (2010)

16. Ferro, N., Silvello, G.: CLEF 15th birthday: what can we learn from ad hoc retrieval? In: Kanoulas, E., Lupu, M., Clough, P., Sanderson, M., Hall, M., Hanbury, A., Toms, E. (eds.) CLEF 2014. LNCS, vol. 8685, pp. 31–43. Springer, Heidelberg (2014)

17. Ferro, N., Silvello, G.: A general linear mixed models approach to study system component effects. In: Proceedings of 39th Annual International ACM SIGIR Conference on Research and Development in Information Retrieval (SIGIR). ACM Press (2016)

18. Järvelin, K., Kekäläinen, J.: Cumulated gain-based evaluation of IR techniques. ACM Trans. Inf. Syst. (TOIS) **20**(4), 422–446 (2002)

19. Kluck, M., Womser-Hacker, C.: Inside the evaluation process of the cross-language evaluation forum (CLEF): issues of multilingual topic creation and multilingual relevance assessment. In: Proceedings of 3rd International Language Resources and Evaluation Conference (LREC 2002) (2002)

20. Kullback, S., Leibler, R.A.: On information and sufficiency. Ann. Math. Stat. **22**(1), 79–86 (1951)

21. Lin, J., et al.: Toward reproducible baselines: the open-source IR reproducibility challenge. In: Ferro, N., et al. (eds.) ECIR 2016. LNCS, vol. 9626, pp. 408–420. Springer, Heidelberg (2016). doi:10.1007/978-3-319-30671-1_30

22. Macdonald, C., McCreadie, R., Santos, R.L.T., Ounis, I.: From puppy to maturity: experiences in developing terrier. In: Proceedings of OSIR at SIGIR, pp. 60–63 (2012)

23. Moffat, A., Zobel, J.: Rank-biased precision for measurement of retrieval effectiveness. ACM Trans. Inf. Syst. (TOIS) **27**(1), 2:1–2:27 (2008)

24. Robertson, S.E.: The methodology of information retrieval experiment. In: Jones, K.S. (ed.) Information Retrieval Experiment, pp. 9–31. Butterworths, London (1981)

25. Sanderson, M.: Test collection based evaluation of information retrieval systems. Found. Trends Inf. Retr. **4**(4), 247–375 (2010)

26. Trotman, A., Clarke, C.L.A., Ounis, I., Culpepper, J.S., Cartright, M.A., Geva, S.: Open source information retrieval: a report on the SIGIR 2012 workshop. ACM SIGIR Forum **46**(2), 95–101 (2012)

27. Wand, M.P., Jones, M.C.: Kernel Smoothing. Chapman and Hall/CRC, Boca Raton (1995)

28. Webber, W., Moffat, A., Zobel, J.: Score standardization for inter-collection comparison of retrieval systems. In: Proceedings of 31st Annual International ACM SIGIR Conference on Research and Development in Information Retrieval (SIGIR), pp. 51–58. ACM Press (2008)

A Test Collection for Research on Depression and Language Use

David E. Losada[1]($\boxtimes$) and Fabio Crestani[2]

[1] Centro Singular de Investigación en Tecnoloxías da Información (CiTIUS),
Universidade de Santiago de Compostela, Santiago de Compostela, Spain
david.losada@usc.es
[2] Faculty of Informatics, Università della Svizzera italiana, Lugano, Switzerland
fabio.crestani@usi.ch

Abstract. Several studies in the literature have shown that the words people use are indicative of their psychological states. In particular, depression was found to be associated with distinctive linguistic patterns. However, there is a lack of publicly available data for doing research on the interaction between language and depression. In this paper, we describe our first steps to fill this gap. We outline the methodology we have adopted to build and make publicly available a test collection on depression and language use. The resulting corpus includes a series of textual interactions written by different subjects. The new collection not only encourages research on differences in language between depressed and non-depressed individuals, but also on the evolution of the language use of depressed individuals. Further, we propose a novel early detection task and define a novel effectiveness measure to systematically compare early detection algorithms. This new measure takes into account both the accuracy of the decisions taken by the algorithm and the delay in detecting positive cases. We also present baseline results with novel detection methods that process users' interactions in different ways.

1 Introduction

Citizens worldwide are exposed to a wide range of risks and threats and many of these hazards are reflected on the Internet. Some of these threats stem from criminals such as stalkers, mass killers or other offenders with sexual, racial, religious or culturally related motivations. Other worrying threats might even come from the individuals themselves. For instance, depression may lead to an eating disorder such as anorexia or even to suicide.

In some of these cases appropriate action or intervention at early stages could reduce or minimise these problems. However, the current technology employed to deal with these issues is only reactive. For instance, some specific types of risks can be detected by tracking Internet users, but alerts are triggered when the victim makes his disorders explicit, or when the criminal or offending activities are actually happening. We argue that we need to go beyond this late detection technology and foster research on innovative early detection solutions.

N. Fuhr et al. (Eds.): CLEF 2016, LNCS 9822, pp. 28–39, 2016.
DOI: 10.1007/978-3-319-44564-9_3

Depression is a health problem that severely impacts our society. According to the World Health Organisation[1], more than 350 million people of all ages suffer from depression worldwide. Depression can lead to disability, to psychotic episodes, and even to suicide. However, depression is often undetected and untreated [16]. We believe it is crucial to develop tools and to compile data to shed light on the onset of depression.

Language is a powerful indicator of personality, social or emotional status, but also mental health. The link between language use and clinical disorders has been studied for decades [15]. For instance, depression has been associated with linguistic markers such as an elevated use of first person pronouns. Many studies of language and depression have been confined to clinical settings and, therefore, to analysing spontaneous speech or written essays. A stream of recent work has come from the area of Text and Social Analytics, where a number of authors have attempted to predict or analyse depression [3,4,13,14]. Some of them proposed innovative methodologies to gather textual contents shared by individuals diagnosed with depression. However, there are not publicly available collections of textual data. This is mainly because text is often extracted from social networking sites, such as Twitter or Facebook, that do not allow re-distribution. Another limitation of previous studies is that the temporal dimension has often been ignored. We strongly believe that tracking the evolution of language is crucial and, therefore, a proper sample collection strategy, which facilitates studying depression over time, should be designed.

In this paper we make four main contributions. First, we describe the methodology that we have applied to build a collection of text to foster research on the characteristics of the language of depressed people and its evolution. This methodology could be adopted by others to build collections in similar areas (for example, offensive or deceptive language). Second, we sketch the main characteristics of the collection and encourage other teams to use it to gain insights into the evolution of depression and how it affects the use of language. Third, we propose an early detection task and define a novel effectiveness measure to systematically compare early detection algorithms. This new measure takes into account both the accuracy of the decisions taken by the algorithm and the delay in detecting positive cases. Risk detection has been studied in other areas–e.g. privacy risks related to user's search engine query history [2] or suicidality risks on Twitter [11]–but there is a lack of temporal-aware risk detection benchmarks in the domain of health disorders. Four, we performed some experiments with baseline techniques and we report here their performance. These experiments provide an initial set of early risk detection solutions that could act as a reference for further studies.

2 Building a Textual Collection for Depression

Some authors have analysed mental health phenomena in publicly available Social Media [5,6,12]. These studies are often confined to understand language

---

[1] See http://www.who.int/mediacentre/factsheets/fs369/en/.

differences between people suffering from a given disorder and a control group (e.g., depressed vs non-depressed, bipolar vs non-bipolar). To the best of our knowledge, no one has attempted to build a dataset where a large chronological sequence of writings leading to that disorder is properly stored and analysed. This is precisely our main objective.

Time is a fundamental factor because appropriate action or intervention at early stages of depression can be highly beneficial. We want to instigate research on innovative early detection solutions able to identify the states of those at risk of developing major depression episodes, and want to stimulate the development of algorithms that computationally treat language as a meaningful tracker of the evolution of depression. These challenging aims can only be achieved with the help of solid evaluation methodologies and benchmarks.

The next section presents the data source selection process performed; Sect. 2.2 reports the method employed to extract a group of depressed individuals; Sect. 2.3 explains the method employed to create a control group of non-depressed individuals; Sect. 2.4 gives details on the submissions extracted from each individual; and, finally, Sect. 2.5 reports the main statistics of the collection built.

2.1   Selection of Data Source

We have studied the adequacy of different types of Internet repositories as data sources to create test collections for research on depression and language use. Within this process, the main aspects that we analysed were: (i) the size and quality of the data sources, (ii) the availability of a sufficiently long history of interactions of the individuals in the collection, (iii) the difficulty to distinguish depressed cases from non-depressed cases, and (iv) the data redistribution terms and conditions (this is important to make the collection available to others). The main sources considered were:

Twitter. Most previous works have focused on microblogs and, in particular, tweets. However, tweets provide little context about the tweet writer. It is therefore difficult to determine when a mention of depression is genuine. Another limitation for us is that Twitter is highly dynamic and only allows to retrieve a limited number of previous tweets per user (up to 3200). In many cases, this is only a few weeks of history. Clearly, this is not enough for collecting a sufficiently long history of previous interactions. Besides, Twitter is highly restrictive about data redistribution.

MTV's A Thin Line (ATL). ATL is a social network launched by the MTV channel in 2010. It is a platform designed to empower distressed teenagers to identify, respond to, and stop the spread of digital abuse. Within this campaign, information is given on how a teenager might cope with issues ranging from sexting to textual harassment and cyberbullying. Young people are encouraged to share their stories publicly and they get feedback, help and advise from the website's visitors. On the ATL platform, posted personal stories have 250 characters or less and other users can rate the story as "over the line" (i.e., inappropriate and rude), "on the line" (could go either way), or "under the line" (nothing to get uptight about). Dinakar and others [7] obtained a set of 7144 stories posted on ATL over a period of three years from 2010 to 2013 (along with their ratings, comments, the age and gender of posters) and analysed teenage distress language. The dataset, which contains no personally identifiable information of its participants, was obtained through a licensing agreement with Viacom (MTV's parent company). We also contacted Viacom, signed a similar agreement and got access to this collection of data. But there are some limitations that prevent us for using it for creating a benchmark. First, the data cannot be redistributed. Second, the subject identifiers are anonymous and untraceable (i.e., no uniquely identifiable) and, therefore, there is no way to obtain a previous history of interactions.

Reddit. Reddit is an open-source platform where community members (*redditors*) can submit content (posts, comments, or direct links), vote submissions, and the content entries are organised by areas of interests (*subreddits*). Reddit has a large community of members and many of the members have a large history of previous submissions (covering several years). It also contains substantive contents about different medical conditions, such as anorexia or depression. Reddit's terms and conditions allow to use its contents for research purposes[2]. Reddit fulfills all our selection criteria and, thus, we have used it for creating the depression test collection. In the following, we explain how we have used Reddit to create the collection.

2.2   Depression Group

A fundamental issue is how to determine subjects that have depression. Some studies, e.g. [4], have resorted to standard clinical depression surveys. But relying on self-reported surveys is a tedious process that requires to individually contact every participant. Besides, the quality and volume of data obtained in this way is limited. Coppersmith et al. [5] opted instead for an automatic method to identify people diagnosed with depression in Twitter. We have adapted Coppersmith et al.'s estimation method to Reddit as follows.

Self-expressions of depression diagnoses can be obtained by running specific searches against Reddit (e.g. "I was diagnosed with depression"). Next, we manually reviewed the matched posts to verify that they were really genuine. Our confidence on the quality of these assessments is high because Reddit texts are long and explicit. As a matter of fact, many of the matched posts came from the depression subreddit, which is a supportive space for anyone struggling with depression. It is often the case that redditors go there and are very explicit about their medical condition. Although this method still requires manual intervention, it is a simple and effective way to extract a large group of people that

---

[2] Reddit privacy policy states explicitly that the posts and comments redditors make are not private and will still be accessible after the redditor's account is deleted. Reddit does not permit unauthorized commercial use of its contents or redistribution, except as permitted by the doctrine of fair use. This research is an example of fair use.

explicitly declare having being diagnosed with depression. The manual reviews were strict. Expressions like "I have depression", "I think I have depression", or "I am depressed" did not qualify as explicit expressions of a diagnosis. We only included a redditor into the depression group when there was a clear and explicit mention of a diagnosis (e.g., "In 2013, I was diagnosed with depression", "After struggling with depression for many years, yesterday I was diagnosed").

2.3   Control Group

This initial set of (depressed) redditors was expanded with a large set of random redditors (control group). Besides random members, we also included in the control group a number of redditors who were active on the depression subreddit but had no depression. There is a variety of such cases but most of them are individuals interested in depression because they have a close relative suffering from depression. These individuals often talk about depression and including them in the control group helps to make the collection more realistic. We cannot rule out the possibility of having some truly depressed individual in the control group, and we cannot rule out the possibility of having some non-depressed individual into the depressed group (an individual's claim about his diagnosis might be false). Still, we expect that the impact of such cases would be negligible and, anyway, other screening strategies (e.g. based on questionnaires) are not noise-free either.

2.4   Texts Extracted

For each redditor, the maximum amount of submissions that we can retrieve is 1000 posts and 1000 comments (Reddit's API limit). We retrieved as many submissions as possible and, therefore, we have up to 2000 submissions from the most active redditors. This included textual contents (posts, comments to posts made by others, links) submitted to any subreddit. Redditors are often active on a variety of subreddits and we collected submissions to any subreddit. We are interested in tracking the redditor's language (regardless of the topic discussed). The collection therefore contains submissions from a wide range of subreddits (e.g., food, videos, news). We organised all these contents in chronological order. The resulting data cover a large time period for most redditors and, thus, enables to study not only the differences in language use between depressed and non-depressed users, but also the evolution of the written text.

We also stored the link to the post where the redditor made the explicit mention to the diagnosis. This information might be useful for further experiments. However, we removed this post from the user's chronology. Otherwise, depression text classifiers would be strongly centered on the specific phrases that we used to manually search for depression diagnosis.

The collection was created as a sequence of XML files, one file per redditor. Each XML file stores the sequence of the redditor's submissions (one entry per submission). Each submission is represented with the submission's title, the submission's text and the submission's date. No other metadata is available.

Table 1. Main statistics of the collection.

	Depressed	Control
Num. subjects	137	755
Num. submissions (posts & comments)	49,580	481,873
Avg num. of submissions per subject	361.9	638.2
Avg num. of days from first to last submission	578.3	625.3
Avg num. words per submission	27.4	36.7

Regarding diagnosis dates, we have a variety of cases. Sometimes, the diagnosis is recent (e.g. "Yesterday", "This week") and, therefore, most of the messages retrieved are *pre-diagnosis*. Other times, the diagnosis was a long time before ("In 2010", "3 years ago") and, therefore, most of the redditor's text is *post-diagnosis*. In other cases, retrieved texts contain both *pre-diagnosis* and *post-diagnosis* submissions. There is often some degree of uncertainty about the specific date of the diagnosis but this approximate information about the diagnosis date is still valuable and can be potentially used in a variety of ways.

The retrieval of submissions was done with Reddit's Python API[3] and all redditors with less than 10 submissions were removed, as we think there would be not enough history to be able to track the evolution of the depression.

2.5 Resulting Collection

The statistics of the resulting collection are reported in Table 1[4]. Following our strategy, we have been able to collect a reasonably high number of subjects and a large number of submissions. The average period of time between the redditor's first submission and the redditor's last submission covers more than a year. There is a high variance in the length of the submissions. Some submissions are short replies to an existing post (comments), while other submissions–typically posts–are lengthy. The average submission length is relatively low (around 30 words after pre-processing) because the number of submitted comments is higher than the number of submitted posts.

We have the firm intention to support research on these topics. The collection is available for research purposes under proper user agreements[5].

3   Early Prediction Task

In this section we present a task of detection of early traces of depression and propose a new metric to measure the effectiveness of early alert systems. Of course, these systems can never become substitutes of trained medical practitioners and, additionally, the widespread adoption of technologies for analysing

---

[3] https://praw.readthedocs.org/en/v3.1.0/.

[4] The number of terms per submission are counted after pre-processing the texts with the scikit-learn Python toolkit, *scikit-learn.org*. This was configured with no stopword processing and no vocabulary pruning based on document frequency.

[5] http://tec.citius.usc.es/ir/code/dc.html.

health-related publicly shared data has to be dictated by a legal framework. Still, we think it is important to bring the possibilities of such predictive technologies to the front and stimulate discussion on their role in enhancing public health.

The challenge consists of sequentially processing pieces of evidence and detect risk cases as soon as possible. Texts should be processed in the order they were created. In this way, we can simulate systems that monitor social media evidence as it appears online. Let us consider a corpus of documents written by p different individuals ($\{I_1, \ldots, I_p\}$). For each individual I_l ($l \in \{1, \ldots, p\}$), the n_l documents that he has written are provided in chronological order (from the oldest text to the most recent text): $D_{I_l,1}, D_{I_l,2}, \ldots, D_{I_l,n_l}$. Given these p streams of messages, we define the following early risk detection task:

- An early risk detection system (ERDS) has to process every sequence of messages (following the order in which the messages are produced). At some point k ($k \in \{1, \ldots, n_l\}$) the system has to make a binary decision on whether or not the individual might be a positive case of depression.
- It is desirable to detect positive cases as soon as possible. But there is a tradeoff between making early decisions and making *more informed* decisions (as we gain more evidence on the subjects, the system's estimations can be more accurate).

This task can be regarded as a new form of data stream classification where systems not only have to assign a class for the stream, but also have to decide when to make the assignment.

3.1   Evaluation Metric

Standard classification measures, such as the F-measure, could be employed to assess the system's output with respect to golden truth judgments that inform us about what subjects are really positive cases. However, standard classification measures are time-unaware and, therefore, we need to complement them with new measures that reward early alerts.

An early risk evaluation metric needs to take into account the correctness of the (binary) decision and the delay taken by the system to make the decision. The delay is measured here by counting the number (k) of distinct textual items seen before giving the answer. Another important factor is that, in many application domains, data are unbalanced (many more negative cases than positive cases). Hence, we also need to weight different errors in a different way.

Let us consider a binary decision d taken by a ERDS at point k. Given golden truth judgments, the prediction d can lead to one of the following cases: true positive (TP), true negative (TN), false positive (FP) or false negative (FN). Given these four cases, we propose and *early risk detection error* (ERDE) measure defined as:

$$ERDE_o(d, k) = \begin{cases} c_{fp} & \text{if } d = \text{positive AND ground truth} = \text{negative (FP)} \\ c_{fn} & \text{if } d = \text{negative AND ground truth} = \text{positive (FN)} \\ lc_o(k) \cdot c_{tp} & \text{if } d = \text{positive AND ground truth} = \text{positive (TP)} \\ 0 & \text{if } d = \text{negative AND ground truth} = \text{negative (TN)} \end{cases}$$

How to set c_{fp} and c_{fn} depends on the application domain and the implications of FP and FN decisions. We will often face detection tasks where the number of negative cases is several orders of magnitude greater than the number of positive cases. Hence, if we want to avoid building trivial classifiers that always say no, we need to have $c_{fn} >> c_{fp}$. For instance, we can fix c_{fn} to 1 and set c_{fp} according to the proportion of positive cases in the data (e.g. if the collection has 1 % of positive cases then we set c_{fp} to 0.01). The factor $lc_o(k)(\in [0,1])$ encodes a cost associated to the delay in detecting true positives. In domains where late detection has severe consequences we should set c_{tp} to c_{fn} (i.e. late detection is equivalent to not detecting the case at all). The function $lc_o(k)$ should be a monotonically increasing function of k. Inspired by the TREC temporal summarization track [1], which incorporated a latency discount factor (sigmoid function) to penalize late emission of relevant sentences, we propose the following cost function that grows with k:

$$lc_o(k) = 1 - \frac{1}{1 + e^{k-o}} \tag{1}$$

The function is parameterised by o, which controls the place in the X axis where the cost grows more quickly (Fig. 1 plots $lc_7(k)$ and $lc_{20}(k)$).

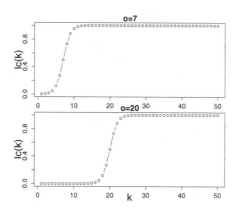

Fig. 1. Latency cost functions: $lc_7(k)$ and $lc_{20}(k)$

Observe that the latency cost factor was introduced only for the true positives. We understand that late detection is not an issue for true negatives. True negatives are non-risk cases that, in practice, would not demand early intervention. They just need to be effectively filtered out from the positive cases. Algorithms should therefore focus on early detecting risk cases and detecting non-risk cases (regardless of when these non-risk cases are detected).

According to the formulas above, if all cost weights are in $[0,1]$ then ERDE would also be in the range $[0,1]$. Since we have p unique individuals in the collection, systems would have to take p decisions (one for each subject, after analysing the subject's stream of submissions). The overall error would be the mean of the p ERDE values.

4   Baseline Experiments

We implemented several relatively simple early detection strategies and ran a series of experiments to evaluate their performance. These experiments aim to provide a pool of depression detection solutions that could be used by others as a reference for comparison.

First, we randomly split the collection into a training and a test set. The training set contained 486 users (83 positive, 403 negative) and the test set contained 406 users (54 positive, 352 negative). Some of the methods described below require a training stage, which consists of building a depression language classifier. To meet this aim, each training user was represented with a single document, consisting of the concatenation of all his writings. After vectorising these 486 documents[6], we built a depression language classifier as follows. We considered a Logistic Regression classifier with L1 regularisation as our reference learning method. This classification approach, which simultaneously selects variables and provides regularisation, has state-of-the-art effectiveness on a range of text categorisation tasks [8]. The resulting models are sparse (many variables are assigned a weight equal to 0). This improves human interpretability and reduces computational requirements at prediction time. Furthermore, this type of sparse models has shown to be superior to other regularised logistic regression alternatives [8].

We optimised the penalty parameter, C ($C > 0$), and the class weight parameter w ($w \geq 1$). C is the parameter associated to the error term of the optimisation formula of the L1-penalised Logistic Regression classifier. C controls the trade-off between the training error and the complexity of the resulting model. If C is large we have a high penalty for training errors and, therefore, we run the risk of overfitting. If C is small we may instead underfit. Another important issue is that our classification problem is unbalanced. When dealing with unbalanced problems, discriminative algorithms may result in trivial classifiers that completely ignore the minority class [10]. Adjusting the misclassification costs is a standard way to deal with this problem. We set the majority class ("non-depression") weight to $1/(1+w)$ and the minority class ("depression") weight to $w/(1+w)$. If $w = 1$ both classes have the same weight (0.5). As w grows, we give more weight to the minority class and, therefore, the learner will penalise more the errors of classifying a depression case as a non-depression case. Following standard practice [9], we applied a grid search on the tuning parameters, with exponentially growing sequences ($C = 2^{-10}, 2^{-4}, ..., 2^9$ and $w = 2^0, 2^1, ..., 2^9$). Model selection was done by 4-fold cross-validation on the training data (optimising F1 computed with respect to the minority class). $C = 16$ and $w = 4$ was the parameter configuration with the

---

[6] We employed sklearn library, version 0.16.1, for Python. Vectorisation was done with the TfidfVectorizer–with a standard stoplist and removing terms that appear in less than 20 documents–and classification was done with the LogisticRegression class.

highest F1 (avg 4-fold performances: $F1 = .66$, $Precision = .65$, $Recall = .67$). We finally proceeded to fix this parameter setting and built a depression language classifier from the whole training data.

We experimented with different strategies to process the stream of texts written by each user in the test split. Some strategies employ the depression language classifier described above and other strategies do not require a text classifier. More specifically, we implemented and tested the following methods:

- **Random.** This is a naïve strategy that emits a random decision ("depression"/"non-depression") for each user. It does not use the depression language classifier and it emits its random decision right after seeing the first submission from every user[7]. This method is therefore fast–delay equal to 1–but we expect it to have poor effectiveness. We include it here as a baseline for comparison.
- **Minority.** This is another naïve strategy that emits a "depression" decision for each user. It does not use the depression language classifier and it also emits its decision right after seeing the first submission from every user[8]. This method is also fast–delay equal to 1–but we expect it to have poor effectiveness. Observe that we do not include here the alternative strategy (majority, always "non-depression") because it does not find any depression case and, therefore, it would score 0 on all our effectiveness metrics.
- **First n.** This method consists of concatenating the first n texts available from each user (first n submissions written by the subject) and making the prediction–with the depression language classifier–based on this text. The delays are therefore fixed to n. If n is larger than the maximum number of submissions per user then the strategy is gonna be slow (it waits to see the whole sequence of submissions for every user) but it makes the decisions with all the available data (we label this particular instance as "All" in Table 2).
- **Dynamic.** The dynamic method does not work with a fixed number of texts for each user. Instead, it incrementally builds a representation of each user, passes this text to the depression language classifier, and only makes a "depression" decision if the depression language classifier outputs a confidence value above a given threshold (thresholds tested: 0.5, 0.75 and 0.9). Otherwise, it keeps concatenating more texts. If the stream of user texts gets exhausted then the dynamic method concludes with a "non-depression" decision.

Not surprisingly, random and minority are the worst performing methods in terms of F1 and ERDE. The fixed-length strategies score well in terms of F1 but their ERDE results show that they are perhaps too slow at detecting positive cases. The dynamic methods, instead, can make quicker decisions. Overall, the

---

[7] This strategy does not make any text analysis and, therefore, it does not make sense to wait any longer to make the decision.

[8] Again, this strategy does not make any text analysis and, therefore, it does not make sense to wait any longer to make the decision.

Table 2. Early risk classifiers

	F1	P	R	$ERDE_5$	$ERDE_{50}$
Random	.19	.12	.48	13.0 %	13.0 %
Minority	.23	.13	1	11.6 %	13.0 %
First 10	.31	.50	.22	11.1 %	10.9 %
First 100	**.62**	.64	.59	7.0 %	6.7 %
First 500	**.62**	.59	.65	6.6 %	6.2 %
All	.59	.55	.65	6.7 %	6.4 %
Dynamic 0.5	.53	.40	.78	**6.0 %**	**5.3 %**
Dynamic 0.75	.58	.57	.59	7.0 %	6.6 %
Dynamic 0.9	.56	.71	.46	8.1 %	7.8 %

results suggest that if we are only concerned about the correctness of the decisions (F1 measure) then we should go for a fixed-length strategy that analyses the first 100/500 messages. However, this fixed-length strategy is suboptimal in terms of ERDE. The dynamic method with the default threshold (Dynamic 0.5) is the best performing method when we want to balance between correctness and time. Anyway, there is substantial room for improvement and we expect that these results instigate others to design innovative and more effective early detection solutions.

5 Conclusions

In this paper, we presented a new test collection to foster research on depression and language use. We have outlined the methodology followed to build a test collection that includes a series of textual interactions written by depressed and non-depressed individuals. The new collection not only encourages research on differences in language between depressed and non-depressed people, but also on the evolution of the language use of depressed users.

We started working on a suitable evaluation methodology to accompany the collection. We also started working on baseline methods to detect early symptoms of depression and we provided an initial report on the effectiveness of these preliminary solutions.

Acknowledgements. This research was funded by the Swiss National Science Foundation (project "Early risk prediction on the Internet: an evaluation corpus", 2015). The first author also thanks the financial support obtained from "Ministerio de Economía y Competitividad" of the Goverment of Spain and FEDER Funds under the research project TIN2015-64282-R.

References

1. Aslam, J., Diaz, F., Ekstrand-Abueg, M., McCreadie, R., Pavlu, V., Sakai, T.: TREC temporal summarization track overview. In: Proceedings of the 23rd Text Retrieval Conference, Gaithersburg (2014)
2. Biega, J., Mele, I., Weikum, G.: Probabilistic prediction of privacy risks in user search histories. In: Proceedings of the First International Workshop on Privacy and Security of Big Data, PSBD 2014, pp. 29–36. ACM, New York (2014)
3. Choudhury, M.D., Counts, S., Horvitz, E.: Social media as a measurement tool of depression in populations. In: Davis, H.C., Halpin, H., Pentland, A., Bernstein, M., Adamic, L.A. (eds.) WebSci, pp. 47–56. ACM (2013)
4. Choudhury, M.D., Gamon, M., Counts, S., Horvitz, E.: Predicting depression via social media. In: Kiciman, E., Ellison, N.B., Hogan, B., Resnick, P., Soboroff, I. (eds.) ICWSM. The AAAI Press (2013)
5. Coppersmith, G., Dredze, M., Harman, C.: Quantifying mental health signals in Twitter. In: ACL Workshop on Computational Linguistics and Clinical Psychology (2014)
6. Coppersmith, G., Dredze, M., Harman, C., Hollingshead, K., Mitchell, M.: CLPsych: depression and PTSD on Twitter. In: NAACL Workshop on Computational Linguistics and Clinical Psychology (2015)
7. Dinakar, K., Weinstein, E., Lieberman, H., Selman, R.L.: Stacked generalization learning to analyze teenage distress. In: Adar, E., Resnick, P., Choudhury, M.D., Hogan, B., Oh, A. (eds.) ICWSM. The AAAI Press (2014)
8. Genkin, A., Lewis, D., Madigan, D.: Large-scale bayesian logistic regression for text categorization. Technometrics **49**(3), 291–304 (2007)
9. Hsu, C.-W., Chang, C.-C., Lin, C.-J.: A practical guide to support vector classification. Technical report, Department of Computer Science, National Taiwan University (2003)
10. Nallapati, R.: Discriminative models for information retrieval. In: Proceeding of ACM SIGIR Conference on Research and Development in Information Retrieval, pp. 64–71 (2004)
11. O'Dea, B., Wan, S., Batterham, P.J., Calear, A.L., Paris, C., Christensen, H.: Detecting suicidality on Twitter. Internet Interventions **2**(2), 183–188 (2015)
12. Park, M., Cha, C., Cha, M.: Depressive moods of users portrayed in Twitter. In: 18th ACM International Conference on Knowledge Discovery and Data Mining (SIGKDD) Workshop on Health Informatics (HI-KDD) (2012)
13. Park, M., McDonald, D.W., Cha, M.: Perception differences between the depressed and non-depressed users in Twitter. In: Kiciman, E., Ellison, N.B., Hogan, B., Resnick, P., Soboroff, I. (eds.) ICWSM. The AAAI Press (2013)
14. Paul, M.J., Dredze, M.: You are what you Tweet: analyzing Twitter for public health. In: Adamic, L.A., Baeza-Yates, R.A., Counts, S., (eds.) ICWSM. The AAAI Press (2011)
15. Pennebaker, J.W., Mehl, M.R., Niederhoffer, K.G.: Psychological aspects of natural language use: our words, our selves. Annu. Rev. Psychol. **54**(1), 547–577 (2003)
16. Saeb, S., Zhang, M., Karr, C., Schueller, S., Corden, M., Kording, K., Mohr, D.: Mobile phone sensor correlates of depressive symptom severity in daily-life behavior: an exploratory study. J. Med. Internet Res. **17**(7), e175 (2015). http://www.jmir.org/2015/7/e175/

Assessors Agreement: A Case Study Across Assessor Type, Payment Levels, Query Variations and Relevance Dimensions

Joao Palotti[1(✉)], Guido Zuccon[2], Johannes Bernhardt[3],
Allan Hanbury[1], and Lorraine Goeuriot[4]

[1] Vienna University of Technology, Vienna, Austria
{palotti,hanbury}@ifs.tuwien.ac.at
[2] Queensland University of Technology, Brisbane, Australia
g.zuccon@qut.edu.au
[3] Medical University of Graz, Graz, Austria
johannes.bernhardt@medunigraz.at
[4] Université Grenoble Alpes, Saint-Martin-d'Hères, France
lorraine.goeuriot@imag.fr

Abstract. Relevance assessments are the cornerstone of Information Retrieval evaluation. Yet, there is only limited understanding of how assessment disagreement influences the reliability of the evaluation in terms of systems rankings. In this paper we examine the role of assessor type (expert vs. layperson), payment levels (paid vs. unpaid), query variations and relevance dimensions (topicality and understandability) and their influence on system evaluation in the presence of disagreements across assessments obtained in the different settings. The analysis is carried out in the context of the CLEF 2015 eHealth Task 2 collection and shows that disagreements between assessors belonging to the same group have little impact on evaluation. It also shows, however, that assessment disagreement found across settings has major impact on evaluation when topical relevance is considered, while it has no impact when understandability assessments are considered.

Keywords: Evaluation · Assessments · Assessors agreement

1 Introduction

Traditional Information Retrieval (IR) evaluation relies on the Cranfield paradigm where a test collection is created including documents, queries, and, critically, relevance assessments [12]. Systems are then tested and compared on such test collections, for which evaluation measures are computed using the relevance assessments provided. This paradigm crucially relies on relevance assessments provided by judges or annotators.

Since the inception of the Cranfield paradigm and TREC, many other evaluation initiatives have emerged (e.g., CLEF and NTCIR) and many test collections

© Springer International Publishing Switzerland 2016
N. Fuhr et al. (Eds.): CLEF 2016, LNCS 9822, pp. 40–53, 2016.
DOI: 10.1007/978-3-319-44564-9_4

have been created. Although assessments are of paramount importance within this evaluation method, they are often not evaluated for their reliability and are not deeply analysed. The contribution of this paper is to shed some light on this overlooked issue. With this aim, we investigate in depth the assessments of one such test collection, the CLEF eHealth 2015 Task 2 collection [9]. This collection comprises of web pages and queries issued by laypeople to find information about certain health topics, primarily with the aim of self-diagnosis. This collection fully supports the investigation of the topic of this paper because: (i) it contains two types of assessments (topical relevance assessments and understandability assessments), (ii) it contains up to three query variations for each single topic, and (iii) assessments were collected so as to have pair-wise assessments from multiple people for a set number of queries. We further add to these resources additional assessments performed by unpaid medical students and laypeople, allowing us to analyse the reliability of assessments both in terms of payment associated to the assessment task and in terms of expertise.

While some previous work has shown that large disagreement between relevance assessments does not lead to differences in system rankings [7,11], other work has shown that system ranking stability is compromised in the presence of significant disagreement [4], or large variation in topic expertise [2]. In this paper we extend prior work by considering also assessments beyond those for topical relevance and assessments with respect to query variations. In particular, because of the presence of query variations, a large proportion of documents has been judged multiple times, both within and across assessors.

2 Related Work

Prior work has examined the agreement between judges for topical relevance assessment tasks. Lesk and Salton's work [7] is one of the earliest works on variations in relevance judgments. They found a low agreement among assessors: 31 % and 33 % in binary relevance assessment using Jaccard similarity to measure agreement. However, they also found that choosing one assessment or the other had little impact on systems ranking and thus rankings produced with one assessment were highly correlated to those produced with the alternative assessment. Their investigation put forward some hypotheses and reasons to justify the fact that the differences in relevance assessments did not lead to changes in system ordering. Among these were the fact that evaluation occurs over many queries and that disagreements involved mainly borderline documents.

Similar findings were reported by Voorhees [11], who studied differences in the assessments made for TREC-4 and TREC-6. For TREC-4, she used secondary assessors from NIST, while for TREC-6, she compared the assessments made by NIST with the ones made by the University of Waterloo. In both cases, the same trend unveiled by Lesk and Salton's work [7] was found: although the agreement among judges was weak, system ordering was stable, with Kendall correlations between rankings produced using relevance assessments from different assessors varying from 89 % to 95 %.

Bailey et al. [2] studied three sets of assessors: "gold standard" judges, who are topic originators and experts in the task, "silver standard", who are experts but did not create the topics, and "bronze standard", which are neither experts nor topic creators. They evaluated agreement among different assessment sets using conditional probability distributions and Cohen's k coefficient on 33 of the 50 topics from the TREC 2007 Enterprise Track. Similar to the studies above, they reported little agreement between judges and, at the same time, little difference in system ordering when gold or silver judgements were used ($\tau = 0.96$ and $\tau = 0.94$ for infAP and infNDCG, respectively). However, larger differences across system rankings were observed if gold and bronze standard judgements were used ($\tau = 0.73$ and $\tau = 0.66$). This prior work supports the use of test collections as a reliable instrument for comparative retrieval experiments.

Other work has examined the impact systematic assessment errors have on retrieval system evaluation. Carterette and Soboroff [4] modified the assessments of the TREC Million Query Track to inject significant and systematic errors within the assessments and found that assessor errors can have a large effect on system rankings.

In this paper we focus on the domain-specific task of finding health information from the Web. The assessment of medical information has been shown to be cognitively taxing [6] and, as we hypothesise below, this may be one reason for disagreement on relevance assessment between and across assessors.

3   Data

In this paper we use the CLEF 2015 eHealth Task 2 dataset [9]. The dataset comprises of a document collection, topics including query variations, and the corresponding assessments, including both topical relevance and understandability assessments. Documents were obtained through a crawl of approximately 1 million health web pages on the Web; these were likely targeted at both the general public and healthcare professionals. Queries aimed to simulate the situation of health consumers seeking information to understand symptoms or conditions they may be affected by. This was achieved by using imaginary or video stimuli that referred to 23 symptoms or conditions as prompts for the query creators (see [9,10,15] for more details on the query creation method). A cohort of 12 query creators was used and each query creator was given 10 conditions for which they were asked to generate up to 3 queries per condition (thus each condition/image pair was presented to more than one person). The task collected a total of 266 possible unique queries; of these, 66 queries (21 conditions with 3 queries, 1 condition with 2 queries, and 1 condition with 1 query) were selected to be used as part of the CLEF 2015 task. A pivot query was randomly selected for each condition, and the variations most and least similar to the pivot were also selected. Examples of queries, query variations and imaginary material used for the query creation are provided in Table 1.

The collection has graded relevance assessments on a three point scale: 0, "Not Relevant"; 1, "Somewhat Relevant"; 2, "Highly Relevant". These assessments were used to compute topical relevance based evaluation measures, such

Table 1. Example of queries from the CLEF 2015 eHealth Task 2.

Image	Information need	Query type	QueryId	Query variation
	Ringworm	Pivot	03	Dry red and scaly feet in children
		Most	38	Scaly red itchy feet in children
		Least	45	Dry feel with irritation
	Scabies	Pivot	04	Itchy lumps skin
		Most	43	Itchy raised bumps skin
		Least	21	Common itchy skin rashes
	Onycholysis	Pivot	61	Fingernail bruises
		Most	19	Bruised thumb nail
		Least	44	Nail getting dark
	Rocky Mountain Spotted Fever	Pivot	27	Return from overseas with mean spots on legs
		Most	01	Many red marks on legs after traveling from us
		Least	58	39 degree and chicken pox

as precision at 10 (P@10), MAP and RBP. In addition, the collection also contains understandability judgements, which have been used in the evaluation to inform understandability-biased measures such as uRBP[1] [13,14]. These assessments were collected by asking assessors whether they believed a patient would understand the retrieved document. Assessments were provided on a four point scale: 0, "It is very technical and difficult to read and understand"; 1, "It is somewhat technical and difficult to read and understand"; 2, "It is somewhat easy to read and understand"; 3, "It is very easy to read and understand".

All assessments in the CLEF collection were provided by paid medical students (paid at a rate of 20 Euros per hour). We further extend these assessments by undertaking a large re-assessment exercise using a pool of unpaid medical students and a pool of unpaid laypeople volunteers. Unpaid medical students were recruited through an in-class exercise that required them to assess documents for relevance. Laypeople were recruited in our research labs: although these participants have prior Information Retrieval knowledge, they do not have any specific medical training background. The collection of these additional sets

---

[1] uRBP is a variation of RBP [8] where gains depend both on the topical relevance label and the understandability label of a document. For more details, see [13]. In the empirical analysis of this paper, we set the persistence parameter ρ of all RBP based measures to 0.8 following [9,13].

of assessments allows us to study the impact of both payment levels and expertise levels (assessor type) on the reliability of the relevance assessment exercise and system evaluation. Within this analysis, assessments performed by the paid medical students are assumed to be the gold standard. Specifically, the following relevance assessment sets (qrels) are considered in our analysis:

Default: The original set of judgements from the CLEF 2015 collection. On average, 132 documents were judged per query. Assessments were provided by 5 paid medical students.

ICS (In Class Students): The set of assessments made by unpaid medical students as an in-class activity. This set has partial assessments for 44 queries, with on average 98 documents judged per query.

Default44: The subset of documents present in the ICS set, but with assessments extracted from the Default set. This set has therefore a complete alignment between Default and ICS and thus allows a direct comparison between paid and unpaid medical students judgements.

Laypeople: All documents of Default44 set, but judged by laypeople with respect to their topical relevance and understandability.

In the analysis reported below, we consider only the first three runs submitted by each participating team to CLEF eHealth 2015 (for a total of 42 runs), as these runs were fully assessed up to rank cutoff 10 [9].

Table 2. Comparing assessment means. Pairs that are significantly different ($p < 0.05$ using two-tailed t-test) are indicated with a star ($*$)

Comp.	#Top.	Asse.	Relevance	Understability	Comp.	#Top.	Asse.	Relevance	Understability
1–2	4	1	0.38 ± 0.69	$2.36 \pm 1.02*$	ICS-1	12	ICS	$0.56 \pm 0.75*$	$2.09 \pm 0.90*$
		2	0.33 ± 0.64	$1.20 \pm 0.88*$			1	$0.17 \pm 0.45*$	$2.33 \pm 1.06*$
2–3	3	2	$0.01 \pm 0.12*$	$1.45 \pm 0.74*$	ICS-2	7	ICS	$0.50 \pm 0.67*$	$1.82 \pm 0.94*$
		3	$0.27 \pm 0.46*$	$2.47 \pm 0.87*$			2	$0.02 \pm 0.15*$	$1.16 \pm 0.87*$
3–4	3	3	$0.62 \pm 0.62*$	2.36 ± 0.68	ICS-3	9	ICS	$0.52 \pm 0.67*$	$1.87 \pm 0.94*$
		4	$0.41 \pm 0.72*$	2.33 ± 0.72			3	$0.38 \pm 0.53*$	$2.21 \pm 0.99*$
4–5	3	4	$0.07 \pm 0.25*$	$1.87 \pm 1.07*$	ICS-4	13	ICS	$0.58 \pm 0.72*$	1.98 ± 0.94
		5	$0.18 \pm 0.38*$	$1.63 \pm 1.00*$			4	$0.21 \pm 0.55*$	1.99 ± 1.01
					ICS-5	12	ICS	$0.49 \pm 0.71*$	$1.98 \pm 1.06*$
							5	$0.22 \pm 0.46*$	$1.69 \pm 0.99*$

4   Agreements for Topical Relevance Assessments

Next we analyse the agreement between assessors with respect to topical relevance and what impact this has for system evaluation. In Sect. 5 we shall repeat the analysis but considering understandability assessments instead.

Section 4.1 studies inter-assessor agreement across the paid medical students using a limited number of queries for which two assessors from this group both provided judgements. Section 4.2 compares the original assessments (Default and Default44) with the assessments made by unpaid medical students as in-class activity (ICS) and the Laypeople set. Section 4.3 considers the query variations included in this collection and their implications for system evaluation.

4.1   Inter-assessor Agreement Among Paid Assessors

Thirteen randomly selected queries were assigned to two assessors from the paid medical student group: *4 queries* were assigned to both assessors 1 and 2, *3 queries* to assessors 2 and 3, *3 queries* to assessors 3 and 4, and finally *3 queries* to assessors 4 and 5.

The official CLEF eHealth 2015 qrels (Default) comprises of all assessments done for queries that were judged by one assessor only; for the thirteen queries with two assessments per document, relevance labels were assigned by selecting the labels from one assessor for half of the overlapping queries, and the labels from the other assessor for the remaining half of the overlapping queries.

The left part of Table 2 shows the mean and standard deviation for assessments made by each pair of assessors for queries assessed by multiple assessors. The means were calculated summing over all labels assigned to each document-query pair (e.g., label 2 if the document was highly relevant) and dividing the total by the number of documents in each set. Pairs that are significantly different ($p < 0.05$ using two-tailed t-test) are indicated with a star ($*$). From Table 2, assessors 2 and 3 exhibit a large mean difference in their assessments. This difference could be explained by the fact that the topics in common between the two assessors had very few highly relevant documents and, while Assessor 2 did not consider documents reporting differential diagnosis as "somewhat relevant", Assessor 3 did.

Most of the pairwise comparisons in Table 2 are significantly different: how does system evaluation change if the assessments of one assessors are used in place of those of another? That is, how reliable is the evaluation (for this test collection) with respect to assessor disagreement? We study three ways to combine assessments made by the paid medical students:

1. **Inverted:** we invert the labels for the assessments chosen when two assessments were available, e.g., by assigning the label given by the other assessor (see the beginning of this section);
2. **Max_Label:** we keep the highest relevance label for any query-document that was judged by two judges;
3. **Min_Label:** similar to Max_Label, but here we keep the lowest label for any assessment made by two judges.

Table 3 reports the Kendall's τ correlation for each of the three sets, compared to the default qrels used in CLEF eHealth 2015. The empirical results using judgements from paid medical students confirm the findings of previous studies [7,11]: assessors disagreement has little effect on system rankings and thus on their evaluation.

Table 3. Kendall's τ correlation between systems rankings when multiple assessments are compared.

Section	Comparison	P@10	MAP	RBP
Section 4.1	Default - Inverted	0.90	0.95	0.92
	Default - Max_Label	0.94	0.93	0.95
	Default - Min_Label	0.93	0.96	0.94
Section 4.2	Default44 - ICS	0.81	0.64	0.68
	Default44 - Laypeople	0.67	0.75	0.68
	Default44 - Random	0.42 ± 0.08	0.60 ± 0.01	0.32 ± 0.09
Section 4.3	Default - Pivot	0.79	0.82	0.75
	Default - Most	0.60	0.82	0.60
	Default - Least	0.75	0.80	0.75

4.2 Influence of Assessor Type and Payment Level

In this section we compare the influence of assessor type (medical expert and laypeople) and payment level (unpaid and paid medical students). The use of unpaid assessors and laypeople has the advantage of reducing the costs associated with building the test collection, however it may come at the expense of less reliable assessments and thus system evaluation. Next we aim to determine if this issue is actually present and, if it is, how to quantify the possible error.

Unpaid and laypeople assessors used the same system used in CLEF eHealth 2015 to collect relevance assessments (Relevation [5]) and the same information displayed to paid assessors was displayed to the other assessors. However unpaid medical students had no training to use the interface (although note that the interface is intuitive) and were subjected to strict time constraints as assessments were done as an in-class activity. Laypeople had training and no time constraints.

The right part of Table 2 reports the results of the comparison between assessments in the Default set (paid medical students) and those in the ICS set (unpaid medical students). We observe that, unlike paid assessors, unpaid assessors had a strong bias towards judging documents based on their relevance to the query, rather than their relevance to the case description, which goes beyond the query and requires assessors to evaluate whether the document supports the correct diagnosis, rather than just relating to the aspects mentioned in the queries. Comparison between paid assessors and laypeople are omitted due to space constraints and are available as an online appendix; they show a similar trend to those for unpaid students.

Table 3 reports the correlation of system rankings across different evaluation measures between the Default44 assessments and: (1) ICS, (2) Laypeople, and (3) the mean correlation of 1,000 random assignment of relevance labels for all pairs of documents and queries (this represents a lower bound for disagreements and evaluation errors).

Comparing Default44 and ICS, we observe that a strong correlation (> 0.8) is found only when P@10 is used, while correlations are weaker when other evaluation measures are considered. This suggests that ICS assessments are not adequate to replace Default assessments. That is: unpaid assessors largely disagree with paid assessors with respect to relevance labels and, unlike when considering paid inter-assessor disagreement, these differences have a noticeable impact on system ranking and evaluation. This result is in line with those reported by Bailey et al. [2] when comparing gold standard assessments with the bronze standard assessments collected through crowdsourcing. We hypothesise that in our case, the consistent assessor disagreements between the two groups are due to the lack of training of the unpaid cohort for the relevance assessment task (rather than interface); a task that, for the medical domain, is rather complex [6]. Note that similar findings are observed when comparing Default44 and Laypeople assessments, with correlations between these two groups being even lower than when ICS was used (although higher than when using Random). This result further stresses the complexity of the medical assessment task and that relying on laypeople to individuate relevant documents to health-related queries can bias system evaluation, rendering it unreliable.

4.3   Assessor Agreement Across Query Variations

Next we study the overlap between the assessments made for a document but with respect to different query formulations (called query variations [3,9]) collected for the same information need (case description).

First, however, we examine the distribution of documents across types of query variation (Fig. 1): pivot queries, most related query (most), and least related query (least) (see [9] for details). Query variations largely contributed new documents to the pool: every query variation was responsible for roughly a one-fold increase in the number of documents in the pool. This finding resonates with what is reported in [3].

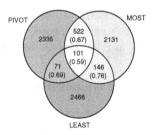

Fig. 1. Distribution of assessments for the three query variations and the agreement across pairwise types of variation.

To further quantify the role that query variations had on system evaluation, we contrast the values of mean P@10 and MAP obtained by the submitted systems on the whole set of queries, with the corresponding values obtained if only one type of query variation was used instead. Results of this analysis are reported in Fig. 2 and system ranking correlations between the different settings are shown in Table 3. The highest correlation (0.82) is measured when MAP and Pivot or Most are used, while the lowest (0.60) is measured when P@10 or RBP and Most are used. For example, the plot in Fig. 2 for P@10 shows that if only the Pivot variations are used, the KISTI_3 run would be ranked as 2nd best, while, when all variations are used, this run is only ranked 8th. Similarly, when only the Least variations are used, KISTI_3 is ranked 20th. These results suggest that using only one type of query variation does lead to noticeable different system rankings and thus the use of multiple query variations is an important aspect for system evaluation, as it more realistically captures the use of search systems than considering one type of query variation only.

There are many ways to experiment with assessments derived from query variations. Given all queries for one type of query variation, we first measure system effectiveness using the assessments for this query variation and compare with those for other variations. In Table 4, we examine whether qrels for one type of query variation can be used to assess another type of variation, e.g., use qrels for Pivot to evaluate document rankings created in response to queries from the Most variations. Given the limited document intersection between different types of queries (see Fig. 1), it is expected that the correlations across different variations are small. Similar to Sect. 4.1, we evaluate the Min_Label and Max_Label; however, now the min and max functions are applied to the three types of query variation. Due to the larger coverage of Min_Label and Max_Label, correlations are high in most of cases.

5   Agreements for Understandability Assessments

In this section we analyse the agreement between assessors with respect to assessments of the understandability of information contained within documents and its impact on system evaluation. Understandability assessments are used to inform the understandability-biased evaluation and compute uRBP and its graded version, uRBPgr [13]. The analysis proceeds on a similar path to that in the previous section about topical relevance assessments.

5.1   Inter-assessor Agreement Among Paid Assessors

We analyse the understandability assessments for the queries for which assessments were collected from two paid assessors; we further use the Max_Label and Min_Label from Sect. 4.1 to combine labels. To compute understandability-biased measures, we use the topical relevance assessments from the Default set (the original CLEF 2015 labels). Statistics about the amount of disagreement between paid assessors in terms of assessments of understandability are reported in Table 2 and, overall, demonstrate similar levels of disagreement between assessors as for the topical relevance labels. Correlations between system rankings

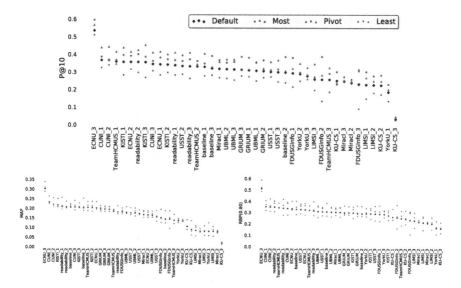

Fig. 2. System performance using queries and assessments for only one single query variant.

are reported in Table 5. Regardless of the specific label aggregation method and understandability measure, there is high correlation between system rankings produced with differing understandability assessments, suggesting system rankings are stable despite assessor disagreements. This is in line with the findings reported in Sect. 4.1 for topical relevance assessments.

5.2 Influence of Assessor Type and Payment Level

Next, we study differences due to assessor type (medical student vs. layperson) and payment level (paid vs. unpaid medical students). Table 2 reports the disagreements between the group of unpaid medical students and the 5 paid students, when assessing understandability. Overall they demonstrate close mean assessments, with the largest differences occurring due to Assessor 2, who tended to assess documents with a stricter view about understandability. The smallest differences are instead observed due to Assessor 4; however this did not show statistically significant differences ($p > 0.05$). Disagreement statistics among laypeople are available as an online appendix; they show a similar trend to those for unpaid students.

Table 5 reports the correlations between system rankings obtained when using the Default assessments and those with the ICS group and the laypeople group. These results demonstrate that, regardless of who performs the understandability assessments, high correlations across values of understandability-biased measures are obtained. This suggests that the use of either unpaid medical students or unpaid laypeople to assess understandability in place of paid medical students does not negatively influence the reliability of system rankings and evaluation.

Table 4. Kendall-τ rank correlations for comparison of system ranking when different qrels are used.

Run set	Qrel comparison	P@10	MAP	RBP(0.8)
Pivot	Pivot - Most	0.74	0.79	0.64
	Pivot - Least	0.59	0.54	0.58
	Most - Least	0.66	0.58	0.63
	Max - Pivot	0.89	0.90	0.88
	Min - Pivot	0.87	0.93	0.84
Most	Pivot - Most	0.51	0.80	0.57
	Pivot - Least	0.41	0.63	0.42
	Most - Least	0.36	0.57	0.33
	Max - Most	0.82	0.90	0.84
	Min - Most	0.64	0.88	0.62
Least	Pivot - Most	0.67	0.88	0.66
	Pivot - Least	0.44	0.72	0.42
	Most - Least	0.60	0.77	0.53
	Max - Least	0.87	0.87	0.85
	Min - Least	0.90	0.86	0.90

Thus, neither payment levels nor expertise influence the abilities of assessors to judge understandability: while there are assessment disagreements, these have limited impact on evaluation. This is unlike the results obtained in Sect. 4.2 when examining topical relevance.

Table 5. Kendall-τ rank correlation for comparison of system ranking for understandability measures.

Section	Topical set	Understandability set	uRBP(0.8)	uRBPgr(0.8)
Section 5.1	Default	Default - Max_Scores	0.91	0.96
	Default	Default - Min_Scores	0.97	0.98
Section 5.2	Default44	Default44 - ICS	0.82	0.85
	ICS	ICS - Default44	0.83	0.86
	Default44	Layperson - Default44	0.82	0.87
	Default44	Layperson - ICS	0.85	0.90
Section 5.3	Default	Default - Pivot	0.77	0.75
	Default	Default - Most	0.74	0.71
	Default	Default - Least	0.72	0.71

5.3   Assessors Agreement Across Query Variations

Here we study how understandability assessments vary across query variations for the same information need and what is the impact of potential disagreements on the evaluation based on understandability-biased measures. Figure 2 reports the uRBP values (with $\rho = 0.8$) for each system across the three types of query variations (Pivot, Most and Least); Table 5 lists the correlations between each type of query variation and the default system ranking. Results here are similar to those obtained when investigating topical relevance (see Sect. 4.3) and support the importance of query variations for system evaluation.

6   Conclusions

In this paper we have examined assessment agreement between annotators across a number of different facets, including domain expertise, payment level, query variations, and assessment type (i.e., topical relevance and understandability).

Our analysis shows that there are often assessment disagreements both among assessors of the same type (e.g., among paid medical students) and among assessors of different types (e.g., among paid and unpaid medical students). Neither payment level, nor domain expertise and assessment type had significant influence in reducing the amount of disagreement across assessors.

We show that while assessor disagreement within the same type of assessor does not influence system rankings and evaluation, assessor disagreement with respect to topical relevance across types of assessors lead to lower correlations between system rankings. This results in unreliable system comparisons and thus evaluation if unpaid assessors or assessors with lower expertise are used in place of gold (paid, expert) assessors. This finding confirms results of previous research [2,4]. However, we also show that this is not the case when assessments of understandability, rather than of topical relevance, are sought. Our results in fact demonstrate that correlations between system rankings obtained with understandability-biased measures are high, regardless of payment levels and expertise. This is a novel finding and suggests that (1) Laypeople understandability assessments of health information on the web can be used in place of those of experts; and (2) The adoption of a two-stage approach to gather multi-dimensional relevance assessments where assessments are gathered from different types of assessors (both due to payment and expertise) may be viable, in particular if the assessment of dimensions beyond topicality requires additional time. In the first stage of such a method, assessor time from highly-paid, expert assessors is focused on assessing topical relevance. Labels produced by these assessments are to be used as a basis for both topical relevance measures (P@10, MAP, RBP, etc.) and understandability-biased measures. In the second stage, understandability assessments are acquired employing less expert or less expensive assessors, e.g., laypeople or through inexpensive graduate in-class activities. The use of such a two-stage approach for collecting assessments has the potential of reducing the overall cost of evaluation, or, with a fixed certain assessment-budget, of allowing to assess more documents. In addition, this approach may reduce the implicit dependencies assessors have between judging the different dimensions of relevance.

Finally, our results add to the recent body of work showing the importance of query variations for increasing the reliability and veracity of Information Retrieval evaluation [1,2]. We show, in fact, that the availability of query variations for an information need contribute great diversity to the pool and that system rankings obtained with only one of the three types of variation considered here are unstable when compared with the rankings obtained with all variations (both for topical relevance and understandability). The data and code used in this research is available online at https://github.com/ielab/clef2016-AssessorAgreement.

Acknowledgements. This work has received funding from the European Union's Horizon 2020 research and innovation programme under grant agreement No. 644753 (KConnect), and from the Austrian Science Fund (FWF) projects P25905-N23 (ADmIRE) and I1094-N23 (MUCKE).

References

1. Azzopardi, L.: Query side evaluation: an empirical analysis of effectiveness and effort. In: Proceedings of SIGIR, pp. 556–563 (2009)
2. Bailey, P., Craswell, N., Soboroff, I., Thomas, P., de Vries, A.P., Yilmaz, E.: Relevance assessment: are judges exchangeable and does it matter. In: Proceedings of SIGIR, pp. 667–674 (2008)
3. Bailey, P., Moffat, A., Scholer, F., Thomas, P.: User variability and IR system evaluation. In: Proceedings of SIGIR, pp. 625–634 (2015)
4. Carterette, B., Soboroff, I.: The effect of assessor error on IR system evaluation. In: Proceedings of SIGIR, pp. 539–546 (2010)
5. Koopman, B., Zuccon, G.: Relevation!: an open source system for information retrieval relevance assessment. In: Proceedings of SIGIR, pp. 1243–1244. ACM (2014)
6. Koopman, B., Zuccon, G.: Why assessing relevance in medical IR is demanding. In: Medical Information Retrieval Workshop at SIGIR 2014 (2014)
7. Lesk, M.E., Salton, G.: Relevance assessments and retrieval system evaluation. Inform. Storage Retrieval **4**(4), 343–359 (1968)
8. Moffat, A., Zobel, J.: Rank-biased precision for measurement of retrieval effectiveness. ACM Trans. Inform. Syst. (TOIS) **27**(1), 2 (2008)
9. Palotti, J., Zuccon, G., Goeuriot, L., Kelly, L., Hanbury, A., Jones, G.J., Lupu, M., Pecina, P.: CLEF eHealth evaluation lab: retrieving information about medical symptoms. In: CLEF (2015)
10. Stanton, I., Ieong, S., Mishra, N.: Circumlocution in diagnostic medical queries. In: Proceedings of SIGIR, pp. 133–142. ACM (2014)
11. Voorhees, E.M.: Variations in relevance judgments and the measurement of retrieval effectiveness. Inform. Process. Manage. **36**(5), 697–716 (2000)
12. Voorhees, E.M., Harman, D.K.: TREC: Experiment and Evaluation in Information Retrieval, vol. 1. MIT Press, Cambridge (2005)

13. Zuccon, G.: Understandability biased evaluation for information retrieval. In: Ferro, N., Crestani, F., Moens, M.F., Mothe, J., Silvestri, F., Di Nunzio, G.M., Hauff, C., Silvello, G. (eds.) ECIR 2016. LNCS, vol. 9626, pp. 280–292. Springer, Heielberg (2016)

14. Zuccon, G., Koopman, B.: Integrating understandability in the evaluation of consumer health search engines. In: Medical Information Retrieval Workshop at SIGIR 2014, p. 32 (2014)

15. Zuccon, G., Koopman, B., Palotti, J.: Diagnose this if you can: on the effectiveness of search engines in finding medical self-diagnosis information. In: Hanbury, A., Kazai, G., Rauber, A., Fuhr, N. (eds.) ECIR 2015. LNCS, vol. 9022, pp. 562–567. Springer, Heidelberg (2015)

Reranking Hypotheses of Machine-Translated Queries for Cross-Lingual Information Retrieval

Shadi Saleh[(✉)] and Pavel Pecina

Institute of Formal and Applied Linguistics, Faculty of Mathematics and Physics,
Charles University, Prague, Czech Republic
{saleh,pecina}@ufal.mff.cuni.cz

Abstract. Machine Translation (MT) systems employed to translate queries for Cross-Lingual Information Retrieval typically produce a single translation with maximum translation quality. This, however, might not be optimal with respect to retrieval quality and other translation variants might lead to better retrieval results. In this paper, we explore a method using multiple translations produced by an MT system, which are reranked using a supervised machine-learning method trained to directly optimize retrieval quality. We experiment with various types of features and the results obtained on the medical-domain test collection from the CLEF eHealth Lab series show significant improvement of retrieval quality compared to a system using single translation provided by MT.

1 Introduction

The growing amounts of information available on-line and its language diversity give rise to the task of Cross-Lingual Information Retrieval (CLIR), where queries are formulated in one language to search for information available in another language. To allow this, queries and documents must be mapped (translated) to a single space (language). This is typically realized by Machine Translation (MT); recently mainly by Statistical MT (SMT). Translating documents into the query language is computationally expensive. Most CLIR systems thus follow the query-translation approach, although document translation can be of a better quality (given the larger context available). User queries are usually short, with free word order and no additional context. Generic MT systems have difficulties to translate such text; they are tuned to translate complete and grammatically correct sentences rather than ungrammatical sequences of terms.

The way how MT is employed to translate queries for CLIR is usually very trivial: A source-language query is fed to a generic MT system and a single best output is used to query the document collection. Such an approach has several shortcomings: First, the system is not aware of the fact that the input is not a complete grammatical sentence but attempts to translate it as such. Second, the MT system (usually statistical) is often able to produce much richer output, including multiple translation hypotheses, provided with various scores from the decoding process, which is ignored. Third, the MT system produces translations

© Springer International Publishing Switzerland 2016
N. Fuhr et al. (Eds.): CLEF 2016, LNCS 9822, pp. 54–66, 2016.
DOI: 10.1007/978-3-319-44564-9_5

in the traditional human-readable form although this is not necessary. If MT is more tightly integrated with IR it can construct the output as a more complex structure (e.g., with translation alternatives or stemmed words).

In this paper, we build on some of the previously published methods and enhance them by several new ideas. We employ our own SMT system specifically adapted to translate user search queries rather than fluent sentences. This system produces several translation alternatives (hypotheses) which are reranked to select the translation maximizing retrieval quality. The reranking method combines various kinds of features (including internal SMT features and features extracted from external resources) in a linear model that is optimized directly towards retrieval quality. The experiments are conducted on the medical-domain data from the CLEF 2013–2015 eHealth Lab series. The document collection is in English and queries in Czech, French, and German.

2   Related Work

The query-translation and document-translation approaches were studied and compared by Oard [20] already in 1998. Oard showed that the latter was more effective (in terms of retrieval quality, especially for longer queries) but less efficient (in terms of computational resources required to perform the translation). Although the current MT techniques are more advanced, the document-translation approach is still much less practical and the query-translation approach has been predominant. However, hybrid methods combining both approaches were proposed too. McCarley [17], for instance, exploited query-translation and document-translation systems in parallel and combined their outputs by averaging document scores obtained by both. Fujii and Ishikawa [6] employed two-step method where the query-translation approach was used to retrieve a limited number of documents which were then translated into the query language and reranked according to relevance to the original query.

Query translation often suffers from the problem of ambiguity and lexical selection (i.e., multiple translation equivalents of query terms) due to the limited context available. Hull [12] improved the initial (dictionary-based) approaches exploiting all possible translations by using a weighted boolean model to remove translations which are spurious (in the context of other terms). Hiemstra and de Jong [10] investigated several strategies of disambiguation in the target language (including a manual approach) but none outperformed the method using all possible translations. The authors suggested that if search algorithms are sophisticated enough, disambiguation is done implicitly during search.

Lexical processing in the target language can also be performed to expand query translations. Choi and Sungbin [2], who placed first in the multilingual CLEF eHealth 2014 Task 3 [7], identified UMLS concepts [13] in translations provided by Google Translate[1] and enriched them by adding (weighted) alternative concept labels. A similar approach was used by Liu and Nie [15] in the monolingual task of CLEF eHealth 2015 [8], who expanded the queries not only

---

[1] http://translate.google.com/.

through the UMLS concepts but also by terms extracted from Wikipedia articles. Herbert et al. [9] exploited Wikipedia in a different way. They mined the redirect and cross-language links to enriched query translation obtained via Google Translate directly based on the source side.

Ture et al. [30] were among the firsts who exploited multiple query translations provided by SMT (often called n-best-list). They improved the previous work on probabilistic structured queries [4], where query terms were represented by a probability distribution over its translations, by estimating the term translation probabilities extracted from the n-best-lists.

The first attempt to rerank SMT n-best-lists w.r.t. the retrieval quality was published by Nikoulina et al. [19]. To select the best translation, they employed MIRA (Margin Infused Relaxed Algorithm) [3] trained directly towards Mean Average Precision (MAP) and reported an improvement between 1 % and 2.5 % absolute on the CLEF AdHocTEL 2009 task (French to German) [16]. They used internal features from the SMT decoder plus syntax-based features extracted from the source queries and the translation hypothesis. They also reported that trivial concatenating top 5 translation hypotheses (5-best-list) of each query improved the unadapted baseline too. Ture and Boschee [29] employed a similar approach. They used a set of binary classifiers to produce *query-specific* weights of various different features to select optimal translations from the n-best-lists. They reported significant improvements on several English-Arabic and English-Chinese tasks. Sokolov et al. [26] attempted to directly optimized an SMT decoder to output the best translation by tuning the SMT model weights towards the retrieval objective. They reported "small but stable improvements" on the BoostCLIR task of Japanese-English patent CLIR [27].

3   Experimental Setting

3.1   Data

The data collection in our experiments is adopted from the CLEF eHealth Lab series 2013–2015, which consists of web pages automatically crawled from medical-domain websites. Specifically, we used the version from 2015 eHealth Task 2: User-Centred Health Information Retrieval [8], which is almost identical to the collections used in the two preceding years of the CLEF eHealth Lab and the relevance assessments against this collection are available for queries from all the three years. The collection contains 1,096,879 documents comprising a total of 1,111,711,884 tokens (after removing the HTML markup using the HTML-Strip Perl module[2]). The average length of a document is 6,316 tokens.

The query set consists of 50 queries from 2013, 50 queries from 2014, and 66 queries from 2015. The queries were originally constructed in English and then translated to Czech, French and German. For 2014 and 2015 queries, the translations were provided by the CLEF eHealth Lab organizers. Translation of the 2013 queries was conducted for the purpose of this work afterwards, following

---

[2] http://search.cpan.org/dist/HTML-Strip/Strip.pm.

the same guidelines as used to translation the 2014 and 2015 queries (translation was done by medical professionals and reviewed). The 2013 and 2014 queries were generated from patients' discharge summaries and often include language of medical experts. The 2015 queries were constructed to mimic queries of lay people (patients) that are confronted with a sign, symptom, or condition and attempt to find out more about the condition they may have. The queries were re-split into a set of 100 queries for training and a set of 66 queries for testing. The queries are equally distributed in the two sets in terms of the year of origin (2013–2015), length (number of words in title), and number of relevant documents.

The relevance assessments provided by the CLEF eHealth organizers included 6,873 documents judged as relevant (41.40 per query on average) and 23,565 documents judged as non-relevant (141.95 per query on average). To ensure a complete assessment coverage in our experiments, we conducted an additional assessment of the unjudged documents appearing among the top 10 documents for each query in all our experiments. We followed the original assessment guidelines and processed a total of 2,114 documents – 422 of them were judged to be relevant (2.54 per query on average) and 1,692 as not relevant (10.19 per query on average). This helped to better evaluate our methods – without the additional assessment, all the unjudged documents would be treated as non-relevant.

3.2   Retrieval System

Our system is based on Terrier, an open source search engine [21], and its implementation of the language model with Bayesian smoothing and Dirichlet prior [25] with the default value of the smoothing parameter ($\mu = 2500$, tuning this parameter by grid search did not improve the result).

Terrier was used to index the cleaned document collection (exploiting the in-domain stopword list by PubMed[3]) and to perform the retrieval experiments. For each non-English query (title), we constructed its equivalent in English (using the SMT system described below), which was used to query the collection by Terrier to retrieve top 1000 ranked documents. The results were evaluated by the standard `trec_eval` tool[4] using three evaluation metrics (P@10, NDCG@10 and MAP), all reported as percentages in the range $\langle 0, 100 \rangle$. Precision at top 10 documents was used as the main evaluation measure. The significance tests were performed using the paired Wilcoxon signed-rank test [11], with $\alpha = 0.05$.

3.3   Translation System

The SMT system employed in our experiments was developed within the Khresmoi project[5] [5] as a part of a large-scale multi-lingual multi-modal search and access system for biomedical information and documents. The SMT system is built on Moses, a state-of-the-art phrase-based SMT system [14], and adapted to

---

[3] http://www.ncbi.nlm.nih.gov/.
[4] http://trec.nist.gov/trec_eval.
[5] http://www.khresmoi.eu/.

translate texts from the medical domain. It is available for three language pairs (Czech–English, French–English and German–English) and supports translation of standard sentences and search queries.

In a phrase-based SMT, the output translation is constructed from possible translations of subsequences of consecutive words (phrases) in the input sentence. The best translation is searched for by maximizing the probability of the output given the input formulated as a log-linear combination of several feature functions. These features play an important role in the reranking method presented in this paper. They include scores of the following models: *phrase translation model* ensuring that the individual phrases correspond to each other, the *target language model* estimating the fluency of the output sentence, the *reordering model* capturing different phrase order in the two languages, and *word penalty* penalizing translations that are too long or too short.

The models of the Khresmoi SMT system were trained on a combination of general-domain data (e.g., EuroParl, JRC Acquis, or News Commentary corpus) and medical-domain data (e.g., EMEA, PatTR, COPPA, or UMLS), see [23] for details. The query translation system was designed to translate short and rather ungrammatical sequences of terms typical for search queries. The feature weights were not optimized towards the traditional translation quality measured by BLEU (Bilingual Evaluation Understudy [22]) but towards PER (Position-independent word Error Rate [28]), which does not penalize word order and was shown to be more adequate for tuning SMT for search queries [23].

4   Method

Our method employs SMT to translate queries (in Czech, German, French) into the language of documents (English). However, we do not rely on the SMT system to select the best translation variant. Instead, we obtain multiple top-scored hypotheses (*n*-best-list) and rerank then w.r.t. the retrieval objective. The highest-ranked hypothesis is then used to query the document collection.

Formally, for each query q_i, each its translation hypothesis $q_{i,j}$ is represented by a vector of features (predictors). For training queries, each hypothesis is assigned a score (response) equal to $1-(O_j-P_{i,j})$, where $P_{i,j}$ is P@10 score of top 10 documents retrieved by the translation hypothesis $q_{i,j}$ and O_j is the maximum (oracle) P@10 of all the translation hypotheses of the query q_i. The response values are in the range of $\langle 0, 1 \rangle$, where 1 indicates a good query translation and 0 a bad translation.

The reranker is trained by fitting a generalized linear regression model (GLM) with logit as the link function (ensuring the response to be in the $\langle 0, 1 \rangle$ interval) [18]. For testing, translation hypotheses of the test queries are scored by this model and the highest-scored hypothesis is selected as the translation. We employed the GLM implementation in R[6] which optimizes the model parameters by the iteratively reweighted least squares algorithm.

The features are extracted from various different sources and include:

---

[6] https://www.r-project.org/.

SMT The main set of features are the eight scores from the SMT models plus the final translation score (see Sect. 3.3).

RANK Two features extracted from the original ranking – the rank itself and a binary feature indicating the top-ranked hypothesis.

IDF To distinguish translations containing informative terms, each hypothesis is scored by the sum and average of inverse document frequency of the terms.

BRF Motivated by the blind-relevance feedback approach for query expansion, a single best translation provided by SMT for each query is used to retrieve the 10 highest-ranked documents and each hypothesis is scored by the sum and average of term frequencies extracted from the retrieved documents.

TP Hypotheses of each query (n-best-list) are merged and each is scored by the sum and average of term frequencies extracted from the merged n-best-list.

WIKI Each hypothesis is scored by the sum and average of term frequencies extracted from abstracts of 10 Wikipedia articles retrieved as a response to the single best query translation provided by SMT (using our own index of abstracts of all English Wikipedia articles and the Terrier search engine).

UMLS Two features based on the UMLS Metathesaurus [24]: the number of UMLS concepts identified in each hypothesis by MetaMap [1] (with word sense disambiguation and part-of-speech tagging on); the number of unigrams and bigrams which match entries in the UMLS Metathesaurus.

RSV Retrieval Status Value, a score assigned to the highest-ranked document by the retrieval system in the response to the query translation hypothesis.

5   Experiments and Results

For each query (both in the training and test sets) we considered up to 15 best translation hypotheses (without duplicities). Queries with oracle P@10 = 0 were excluded from training. The training data then included 1,249 items for Czech, 1,181 for German, and 1,246 for French which were merged into a single training data set used totrained one language-independent model which proved to be a better solution than to train a specific model for each language. The training set included a total of 3,676 items of query translation hypotheses of the 100 original queries (each translated from Czech, German and French).

Prior training, the data was normalized to have sample mean equal to 0 and sample variance equal to 1. The test data was normalized using the coefficients estimated on the training data.

The training data was first used in a leave-one-query-out-cross-validation fashion to tune the hyperparameters (such as the type of the learning algorithm, the n-best-list size, and parameters of all the features). Then, all the training data was used to train a single model which was then applied to the 15-best-lists of the 66 test queries for each language.

In the remainder of this section, we first present some complementary experiments for comparison and then the main results of our method. We comment on the main evaluation measure (P@10) but the main results (Table 1) also include scores of other measures (NDCG@10, MAP).

5.1   Monolingual Performance

It is generally useful to compare CLIR results to monolingual results obtained by using ground truth (manual) translations of the queries into the document language. This also sets a "soft upper bound" of the cross-lingual results. The "monolingual" P@10 score is 47.10 % for the training queries and 50.30 % for the test queries. In the cross-lingual experiments, we would like to get as close to this value as possible for all languages. The complete monolingual results on the test set are shown in Table 1 (row denoted as *Mono*).

5.2   Baseline

Our baseline is the system which accepts a single best translation as provided by the Khresmoi SMT system. Results of the baseline systems are presented in Table 1 (row *Baseline*). On the training queries, the baseline P@10 values are 41.90 for German to, 45.30 for French, and 46.00 for Czech. On the test queries, the P@10 values range from 42.42 for German to 47.73 for French, with Czech in between with 45.61. We should emphasize that the baseline is quite strong. Compared to generic translation systems, the Khresmoi system is specifically adapted to the medical domain and tuned to translate queries for CLIR [23]. Therefore, the relative performance w.r.t. the monolingual results is as high as 84 %–94 % (depending on the source language).

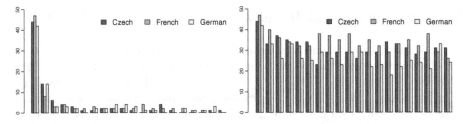

Fig. 1. Histograms of ranks of translation hypotheses with the highest P@10 for each training query: the first such ranks only (left), all such ranks (right).

5.3   Oracle Results

To confirm the hypothesis that reranking of SMT n-best-lists can improve CLIR quality, we performed the following experiment: For each query in the training data we selected the translation hypothesis with the highest P@10 and averaged those values to get the maximum (oracle) score of P@10 achievable if the reranking method always selects the best translation. On the training data, the oracle score is 55.10 for Czech, 58.90 for French, and 52.70 for German. This result is very encouraging and confirms that there is enough space for improvement. The baseline scores could be improved by 11.67 on average.

A deeper analysis of this observation is illustrated in Fig. 1. The two plots visualize distribution of the best translations (highest P@10) in the 20-best-lists for all training queries (for each language). The first plot shows histograms of the *highest* ranks with the best translations. Here, for about 45 % of the queries, the best translations are ranked as first. For the remaining 55 % queries, the first best translations are ranked lower. Those are the cases, which can be improved by better ranking. The second plot displays the histogram for *all* hypotheses with the highest P@10 (not just the top ones). For each query there are multiple such translations and any of them can be selected to achieve the best performance.

5.4   *n*-best List Merging

Nikoulina et al. [19] presented a method combining *n*-best-list translations by trivial concatenation of 5 top translations as produced by SMT. This approach completely failed on our data (all languages) and did not improve the baseline for any value of *n* from 0 to 20 (on the training data and the test data). Results of the 5-best-list concatenation on the test data are shown in Table 1 (row *5-best*).

Table 1. Complete results of the final evaluation on the test set queries

System	Czech			French			German		
	P@10	NDCG@10	MAP	P@10	NDCG@10	MAP	P@10	NDCG@10	MAP
Mono	50.30	49.95	29.97	50.30	49.95	29.97	50.30	49.95	29.97
Baseline	45.61	38.57	23.58	47.73	41.11	25.72	42.42	36.47	22.74
5-best	38.94	33.01	22.30	41.06	37.20	23.05	30.45	30.16	17.28
SMT	44.70	37.92	24.77	48.79	42.85	25.81	42.73	37.88	22.65
+RANK	48.64	**41.63**	**25.73**	48.48	43.83	26.07	44.55	**40.76**	24.09
++IDF	48.03	41.06	25.22	48.64	43.83	26.10	44.39	40.71	**24.11**
++BRF	47.27	40.52	24.99	49.70	44.12	26.64	43.64	39.81	23.76
++TP	45.76	39.92	23.74	48.48	43.88	26.26	44.39	40.41	24.07
++WIKI	48.64	**41.63**	**25.73**	49.24	44.00	26.36	43.64	39.81	23.76
++UMLS	48.64	**41.63**	**25.73**	49.09	44.10	26.09	44.55	**40.76**	24.09
++RSV	48.64	**41.63**	25.66	48.94	43.84	25.95	43.03	39.20	23.55
ALL	**50.15**	40.72	**25.73**	**51.06**	**46.49**	**27.86**	**45.30**	39.47	23.71
Google	50.91	39.98	26.93	49.70	43.88	26.36	49.39	42.77	26.87
Bing	47.88	40.51	25.22	48.64	42.75	26.43	46.52	41.69	25.04

5.5   Reranking

The reranking method described in Sect. 4 was tested with several combinations of features. The complete results are displayed in the middle section of Table 1. The figures in bold denote the best scores for each language and evaluation metric. All of those are statistically significantly better than the respective baselines (tested by Wilcoxon signed-rank test, $\alpha = 0.05$). For comparison, we also provide

results of systems based on translation by two on-line translation tools: Google
Translate and Bing Translator[7] (rows Google and Bing, respectively).

The system based only on the SMT features did not bring any substantial
improvement over the baseline (row SMT) for any language. P@10 improved
by more than 1 point only for French. For Czech, the score decreased and for
German, the difference was negligible. However, none of these differences was
statistically significant. The traditional way of SMT tuning towards translation
quality seems sufficient if no additional features are available. However, adding
the explicit features derived from the SMT rankings helped a lot (row +RANK)
for Czech and German. Measured by NDCG@10, the increase was statistically
significant w.r.t. the baseline. The effect of the other features was studied by
adding those features independently to the model with the SMT+RANK features. However, in terms of P@10, none of them brought any notable improvement. Although the BRF, WIKI, and UMLS features improved the results for
French, they were not statistically significant even compared to the baseline.

The baseline, however, was outperformed by a statistically significant difference by systems combining all the features (row ALL). P@10 increased by 3.58
on average (7.90 % relative) In comparison with the monolingual results, the
ALL system performed at 101.51 % for French, 99.70 % for Czech, and 90.05 %
for German. For French the system even outperformed the one based on translations by Google Translate. These results are very positive and show that our
mehtod is able to push the CLIR performance very close to monolingual performance.

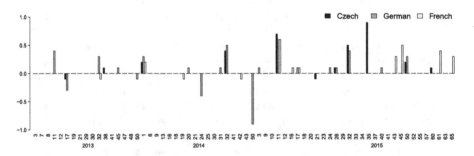

Fig. 2. Per-query results on the test set. The bars represent absolute difference of P@10
of the best system (ALL) and the baseline system for each query and each language.

In Fig. 2, we present detailed comparison of the baseline results and the
results of the best system (ALL). For each query in the test set, the plot displays
the difference of P@10 obtained by the best system and the baseline system.
Positive values denote improvement which was observed for a total of 9 queries
in Czech, 15 queries in German, and 8 queries in French. Negative values denote
degradation, which was observed in 2 cases for Czech, 4 cases for German, and 3

[7] https://www.bing.com/translator/.

cases for French. A good example of a query whose translation was improved is 2015.11 (reference translation: *white patchiness in mouth*). The Czech baseline translation *white coating mouth* improved to *white coating in oral cavity* (P@10 increased from 10.00 to 80.00) and the French baseline *white spots in the mouth* improved to *white patches in the mouth* (P@10 increased from 10.00 to 70.00). More examples illustrating the effect of our methods can be found in Table 2.

Table 2. Examples of translations of training queries including reference (*ref*), oracle (*ora*), baseline (*base*) and best (*best*) translations (system using all features). The scores in parentheses refer to query P@10 scores.

Query: 2013.02 (German)
ref: facial cuts and scar tissue (30.00)
ora: cut face scar tissue (80.00)
base: cut face scar tissue (80.00)
best: face cuts and scar tissue (80.00)
Query: 2013.42 (French)
ref: copd (70.00)
ora: disease copd (90.00)
base: copd (70.00)
best: disease copd (90.00)

Query: 2014.5 (German)
ref: bleeding after hip operation (60.00)
ora: bleeding after hip surgery (80.00)
base: bleeding after hip surgery (80.00)
best: hemorrhage after hip operation (50.00)
Query: 2015.53 (Czech)
ref: swollen legs (10.00)
ora: leg swelling (80.00)
base: swollen lower limb (40.00)
best: swollen lower limb (40.00)

6   Conclusions

In this paper, we explored the reranking-based approach to query translation selection for Cross-Lingual Information Retrieval in the medical domain. We employed the Khresmoi SMT system for medical query translation to obtain multiple highest-scored translation hypotheses. A detailed analysis showed that the best translation as provided by the SMT system is optimal (w.r.t. retrieval quality) for less than 50 % of our queries. For the remaining queries, the optimal translations are ranked lower, most often within top 15 options. In our method, we took 15-best translation hypotheses of each query which were then reranked and the top-ranked translation used to query the collection.

The reranking model is based on generalized linear regression with logit as the link function and trained to predict, for each query, which translation hypothesis gives the highest P@10. The features exploited by the model include the internal scores provided by the SMT system for each hypothesis plus additional features extracted from the n-best-list translation, document collection, retrieval system, Wikipedia articles, UMLS Metathesaurus, and other sources.

The SMT features were not sufficient to beat the baseline based on single best translations as provided by the SMT system for any of the source languages. A substantial improvement was observed after adding features derived from the original rankings. Other features did not bring any significant improvement when added independently. However, in combination, the model exploiting all the features improved the baseline substantially for all the languages. For French, surprisingly, the system combining all the features produced results better than those obtained by using manual translations of the queries into English and also the results obtained using translations by Google Translate. The Czech system outperformed the results obtained using Bing translations and was very close to the monolingual performance. German turned to be harder to get closer to the results obtained using translation by the commercial systems probably due to the linguistic properties (e.g., word compounding) which make translation from such a language (and in such a domain) more difficult.

Acknowledgments. This research was supported by the Czech Science Foundation (grant no. P103/12/G084) and the EU H2020 project KConnect (contract no. 644753).

References

1. Aronson, A.R., Lang, F.M.: An overview of MetaMap: historical perspective and recent advances. J. Am. Med. Inform. Assoc. **17**(3), 229–236 (2010)
2. Choi, S., Choi, J.: Exploring effective information retrieval technique for the medical web documents: SNUMedinfo at CLEFeHealth2014 Task 3. In: Proceedings of the ShARe/CLEF eHealth Evaluation Lab, pp. 167–175 (2014)
3. Crammer, K., Singer, Y.: Ultraconservative online algorithms for multiclass problems. J. Mach. Learn. Res. **3**, 951–991 (2003)
4. Darwish, K., Oard, D.W.: Probabilistic structured query methods. In: Proceedings of the 26th Annual International ACM SIGIR Conference on Research and Development in Informaion Retrieval, pp. 338–344. ACM, New York (2003)
5. Dušek, O., Hajič, J., Hlaváčová, J., Novák, M., Pecina, P., Rosa, R., et al.: Machine translation of medical texts in the Khresmoi project. In: Proceedings of the Ninth Workshop on Statistical Machine Translation, Baltimore, USA, pp. 221–228 (2014)
6. Fujii, A., Ishikawa, T.: Applying machine translation to two-stage cross-language information retrieval. In: White, J.S. (ed.) AMTA 2000. LNCS (LNAI), vol. 1934, pp. 13–24. Springer, Heidelberg (2000)
7. Goeuriot, L., Kelly, L., Li, W., Palotti, J., Pecina, P., Zuccon, G., Hanbury, A., Jones, G., Mueller, H.: ShARe/CLEF eHealth evaluation lab 2014, Task 3: user-centred health information retrieval. In: Proceedings of CLEF 2014 (2014)
8. Goeuriot, L., Kelly, L., Suominen, H., Hanlen, L., Névéol, A., Grouin, C., Palotti, J., Zuccon, G.: Overview of the CLEF eHealth evaluation lab 2015. In: Mothe, J., Savoy, J., Kamps, J., Pinel-Sauvagnat, K., Jones, G.J.F., SanJuan, E., Cappellato, L., Ferro, N. (eds.) CLEF 2015. LNCS, vol. 9283, pp. 429–443. Springer, Heidelberg (2015)
9. Herbert, B., Szarvas, G., Gurevych, I.: Combining query translation techniques to improve cross-language information retrieval. In: Clough, P., Foley, C., Gurrin, C., Jones, G.J.F., Kraaij, W., Lee, H., Mudoch, V. (eds.) ECIR 2011. LNCS, vol. 6611, pp. 712–715. Springer, Heidelberg (2011)
10. Hiemstra, D., de Jong, F.: Disambiguation strategies for cross-language information retrieval. In: Abiteboul, S., Vercoustre, A.-M. (eds.) ECDL 1999. LNCS, vol. 1696, pp. 274–293. Springer, Heidelberg (1999)
11. Hull, D.: Using statistical testing in the evaluation of retrieval experiments. In: Proceedings of the 16th Annual International ACM SIGIR Conference on Research and Development in Information Retrieval, Pittsburgh, USA, pp. 329–338 (1993)

12. Hull, D.A.: Using structured queries for disambiguation in cross-language information retrieval. In: AAAI Symposium on Cross-Language Text and Speech Retrieval, California, USA, pp. 84–98 (1997)
13. Humphreys, B.L., Lindberg, D.A.B., Schoolman, H.M., Barnett, G.O.: The unified medical language system. J. Am. Med. Inform. Assoc. **5**(1), 1–11 (1998)
14. Koehn, P., Hoang, H., Birch, A., Callison-Burch, C., Federico, M., Bertoldi, N., et al.: Moses: open source toolkit for statistical machine translation. In: Proceedings of the 45th Annual Meeting of the Association for Computational Linguistics. Demo and Poster Sessions, Czech Republic, Prague, pp. 177–180 (2007)
15. Liu, X., Nie, J.: Bridging layperson's queries with medical concepts - GRIUM @CLEF2015 eHealth Task 2. In: Working Notes of CLEF 2015 Conference and Labs of the Evaluation forum, Toulouse, France, vol. 1391 (2015)
16. Macdonald, C., Plachouras, V., He, B., Lioma, C., Ounis, I.: University of Glasgow at WebCLEF 2005: experiments in per-field normalisation and language specific stemming. In: Peters, C., et al. (eds.) CLEF 2005. LNCS, vol. 4022, pp. 898–907. Springer, Heidelberg (2006)
17. McCarley, J.S.: Should we translate the documents or the queries in cross-language information retrieval? In: Proceedings of the 37th Annual Meeting of the Association for Computational Linguistics on Computational Linguistics, College Park, Maryland, pp. 208–214 (1999)
18. McCullagh, P., Nelder, J.: Generalized Linear Models. Chapman & Hall/CRC Monographs on Statistics & Applied Probability. Taylor & Francis, New York (1989)
19. Nikoulina, V., Kovachev, B., Lagos, N., Monz, C.: Adaptation of statistical machine translation model for cross-lingual information retrieval in a service context. In: Proceedings of the 13th Conference of the European Chapter of the Association for Computational Linguistics, Avignon, France, pp. 109–119 (2012)
20. Oard, D.W.: A comparative study of query and document translation for cross-language information retrieval. In: Farwell, D., Gerber, L., Hovy, E. (eds.) AMTA 1998. LNCS (LNAI), vol. 1529, pp. 472–483. Springer, Heidelberg (1998)
21. Ounis, I., Amati, G., Plachouras, V., He, B., Macdonald, C., Lioma, C.: Terrier: a high performance and scalable information retrieval platform. In: Proceedings of Workshop on Open Source Information Retrieval, Seattle, WA, USA (2006)
22. Papineni, K., Roukos, S., Ward, T., Zhu, W.J.: BLEU: a method for automatic evaluation of machine translation. In: Proceedings of the 40th Annual Meeting on Association for Computational Linguistics, Philadelphia, USA, pp. 311–318 (2002)
23. Pecina, P., Dušek, O., Goeuriot, L., Hajič, J., Hlaváčová, J., Jones, G.J., et al.: Adaptation of machine translation for multilingual information retrieval in the medical domain. Artif. Intell. Med. **61**(3), 165–185 (2014)
24. Schuyler, P.L., Hole, W.T., Tuttle, M.S., Sherertz, D.D.: The UMLS Metathesaurus: representing different views of biomedical concepts. Bull. Med. Libr. Assoc. **81**(2), 217 (1993)
25. Smucker, M.D., Allan, J.: An investigation of Dirichlet prior smoothing's performance advantage. Technical report, University of Massachusetts (2005)
26. Sokolov, A., Hieber, F., Riezler, S.: Learning to translate queries for CLIR. In: Proceedings of the 37th International ACM SIGIR Conference on Research & Development in Information Retrieval, Gold Coast, Australia, pp. 1179–1182 (2014)
27. Sokolov, A., Jehl, L., Hieber, F., Riezler, S.: Boosting cross-language retrieval by learning bilingual phrase associations from relevance rankings. In: Proceedings of the Conference on Empirical Methods in NLP, Seattle, USA (2013)

28. Tillmann, C., Vogel, S., Ney, H., Zubiaga, A., Sawaf, H.: Accelerated DP based search for statistical translation. In: European Conference on Speech Communication and Technology, Rhodes, Greece, pp. 2667–2670 (1997)
29. Ture, F., Boschee, E.: Learning to translate: a query-specific combination approach for cross-lingual information retrieval. In: Proceedings of the Conference on Empirical Methods in Natural Language Processing, Qatar, pp. 589–599 (2014)
30. Ture, F., Lin, J., Oard, D.W.: Looking inside the box: context-sensitive translation for cross-language information retrieval. In: Proceedings of the 35th International ACM SIGIR Conference on Research and Development in Information Retrieval, Portland, Oregon, USA, pp. 1105–1106 (2012)

Classification, Profiling and Suggestion

Two-Way Parsimonious Classification Models for Evolving Hierarchies

Mostafa Dehghani[1]([✉]), Hosein Azarbonyad[2], Jaap Kamps[1], and Maarten Marx[2]

[1] Institute for Logic, Language and Computation,
University of Amsterdam, Amsterdam, The Netherlands
{dehghani,kamps}@uva.nl
[2] Informatics Institute, University of Amsterdam, Amsterdam, The Netherlands
{h.azarbonyad,maartenmarx}@uva.nl

Abstract. There is an increasing volume of semantically annotated data available, in particular due to the emerging use of knowledge bases to annotate or classify dynamic data on the web. This is challenging as these knowledge bases have a dynamic hierarchical or graph structure demanding robustness against changes in the data structure over time. In general, this requires us to develop appropriate models for the hierarchical classes that capture all, and only, the essential solid features of the classes which remain valid even as the structure changes. We propose *hierarchical significant words language models* of textual objects in the intermediate levels of hierarchies as robust models for hierarchical classification by taking the hierarchical relations into consideration. We conduct extensive experiments on richly annotated parliamentary proceedings linking every speech to the respective speaker, their political party, and their role in the parliament. Our main findings are the following. First, we define hierarchical significant words language models as an iterative estimation process across the hierarchy, resulting in tiny models capturing only well grounded text features at each level. Second, we apply the resulting models to party membership and party position classification across time periods, where the structure of the parliament changes, and see the models dramatically better transfer across time periods, relative to the baselines.

Keywords: Significant words language models · Evolving hierarchies

1 Introduction

Modern web data is highly structured in terms of containing many facts and entities in a graph or hierarchies, making it possible to express concepts at different levels of abstraction. However, due to the dynamic nature of data, their structure may evolve over time. For example, in a hierarchy, nodes can be removed or added or even transfer across the hierarchy. Thus, modeling objects in the evolving structures and building robust classifiers for them is notoriously

© Springer International Publishing Switzerland 2016
N. Fuhr et al. (Eds.): CLEF 2016, LNCS 9822, pp. 69–82, 2016.
DOI: 10.1007/978-3-319-44564-9_6

hard and requires employing a set of solid features from the data, which are not affected by these kinds of changes.

For example, assume we would build a classifier for the "US president" over recent data, then a standard classifier would not distinguish the role in office from the person who is the current president, leading to obvious issues after the elections in 2016. In other words, if we can separate the model of the function from the model of the person fulfilling it, for example by abstracting over several presidents, that more general model would in principle be robust over time.

These challenges are ubiquitous in dealing with any dynamic data annotated with concepts from a hierarchical structure. We study the problem in the context of parliamentary data, as a particular web data. Parliamentary proceedings in public government are one of the fully annotated data with an enriched dynamic structure linking every speech to the respective speaker, their role in the parliament and their political party.

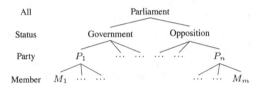

Fig. 1. Hierarchical relations in parliament.

Consider a simple hierarchy of a multi-party parliament as shown in Fig. 1, which determines different categories relevant to different layers of membership in the parliament. Also assume that all speeches of members of the parliament are available and each object in the hierarchy is represented using all the speeches given by members affiliated by the object. It is desirable to use text classification approaches to study how speeches of politicians relate to ideology or other factors such as party membership or party status as government or opposition, over different periods of parliament. To this end, we need models representing each object in the intermediate levels of the hierarchy as a category representing all its descendant objects. However, in the parliament hierarchy, since members and parties can move in the hierarchy over different periods, it is challenging to estimate models that transfer across time. For instance, after elections, governments change and prior opposition parties may form the new government, and prior government parties form the new opposition. Thus, if the model of, say, status in terms of government and opposition, is affected by terms related to the parties' ideology, they will not be valid in the next period. This requires making these models less dependent on the "accidental" parties and members forming the government in a particular period and capture the essential features of the abstract notion of status.

In order to estimate a robust model for an object in an evolving hierarchy, we need to explicitly take all the relations between the object and other objects in other layers into account and try to capture essential features by removing features that are better explained by other objects in different layers. This way, by estimating independent models for related objects, we can assure that the models remain valid even if the relational structure of the hierarchy changes over time.

Based on this, we propose *hierarchical significant words language models* (HSWLM) of hierarchical objects, which are highly robust against structural changes by capturing, all, and only the significant terms as stable set of features. Our inspiration comes from the early work on information retrieval by Luhn [13], in which it is argued that in order to establish a model consisting of *significant words*, we need to eliminate both common words and rare words. Based on this idea, with respect to the structure of the hierarchy, we propose to define general terms as terms already explained by ancestor models, and specific terms as terms already explained by models of descendants, and then employ the parsimonization technique [10] to hierarchically eliminate them as non-essential terms from the models, leading to models that capture permanent significant words.

The main aim of this paper is *to develop appropriate language models for classification of objects in the evolving hierarchies.* We break this down into a number of concrete research questions:

1. How to estimate robust language models for objects in the evolving hierarchies, by explicitly taking relations between the levels into account?
2. How effective are hierarchical significant words language models for classifying textual objects regarding different levels of the hierarchy across time periods?
3. Do the resulting hierarchical significant words language models capture common characteristics of classes in different levels of hierarchy over time?

The rest of the paper is structured as follows. Next, in Sect. 2, we discuss related work. Section 3 introduces our approach to estimate hierarchical significant words language models. In Sect. 4 we apply our models to the parliamentary proceedings, and show how effective are HSWLMs to model party status and party membership across different government periods. Furthermore, we investigate the ability of models for capturing similar and stable features of parliamentary objects over time. Finally, Sect. 5 concludes the paper and discusses extensions and future work.

2   Related Work

There is considerable research related to our work in terms of using the same type of data, or focusing on the problem of hierarchical text classification or aiming on improving transferability of models over time, which we discuss them in this section.

There is a range of work on political data which is related to our research in terms of using the same type of data and hierarchical structure. The recent study of Hirst et al. [11] is the closest to our work. They presented an analytical study on the effectiveness of classifiers on political texts. Using Canadian parliamentary data they demonstrated that although classifiers may perform well in terms of accuracy on party classification in the parliamentary data, they pick the expressions of opposition and government, of attack and defence, or of questions and answers, and not of ideology. They also showed that using classic approach for categorization fails in extracting ideology by examining the models over different government periods. In our paper, we examine our method also with the evaluation strategy of Hirst et al., and in contrast to the failure of classic categorization methods on parliamentary data reported before, we demonstrate that our proposed method performs well under these difficult conditions.

Although our research problem differs from issues in typical hierarchical text classification problems using a topical hierarchy [8,9,19,20], we review some research in this area and will use effective approaches like SVM as baselines in our experiments. McCallum et al. [15] proposed a method for modeling an object in the hierarchy, which tackles the problem of data sparseness for low layered objects. They used shrinkage estimator to smooth the model of each leaf object with the model of its ancestors to make them more reliable. Ogilvie and Callan [16] and Oh et al. [17] extended the McCallum et al.'s idea by including the models of children as well as parents, and controlling the level of information that is needed to be gathered from ancestors. Recently, Song and Roth [21] tackled the problem of representing hierarchical objects with the lack of training data by embedding all objects in a semantic space to be able to compute a meaningful semantic similarity between them. Although the general problem in these papers is similar to ours, they address the problem of *train data sparseness* [15,21] or present techniques for *handling large scale data* [17].

In terms of modeling hierarchical objects, there are similarities with work on hierarchical topic modeling. Kim et al. [12] used Hierarchical Dirichlet Process (HDP) [22] to construct models for objects in the hierarchies using their own models as well as the models of their ancestors. Also Zavitsanos et al. [26] used HDP to construct the model of objects in a hierarchy employing the models of its descendants. These research try to bring out precise topic models using the structure of the hierarchy, but they do not aim to capture a model which keeps its validity over the time even while changes occur in the structural relations. The longitudinal changes in the data in our problem, relate it to the works on constructing dynamic models for data streams [1,24]. In this line of research, they first discovered the topics from data and then tried to efficiently update the models as data changes over the time, while our method aims to identify tiny precise models that remain valid over time. Research on domain adaptation [2,23] also tried to tackle the problem of missing features when very different vocabulary are used in test and train data. This differs from our approach first in terms of considering the hierarchical relations, and also the fact that we aim to estimate models that are robust against changes in the structural relations, not the corpus vocabulary.

3   Hierarchical Significant Words Language Models

In this section, we address our first research questions: "How to estimate robust language models for objects in the evolving hierarchies, by explicitly taking relations between the levels into account?" We propose to extract hierarchical significant words language models (HSWLM) as models estimated for objects in evolving hierarchies that are robust and *persistent* even by changing the structural relations in the hierarchy over time. Each object in the hierarchy is assumed to be a textual document, representing the corresponding concept of that object in the hierarchy.

Basically, our proposed approach, two-way parsimonization, tries to iteratively re-estimate the models by discarding non-essential terms from them. This pruning for each object is accomplished using parsimonization technique toward both the ancestors of the object and its descendants. One of the main components of the process of estimating HSWLM is the procedure of *Model Parsimonization*, which we will discuss first.

3.1   Model Parsimonization

Model parsimonization is a technique that was introduced by Hiemstra et al. [10] in which given a raw probabilistic estimation, the goal is to re-estimate the model so that non-essential terms are eliminated with regard to the background estimation.

To do so, each term t in the object model, θ_o, assumed to be drawn from a two-component mixture model, where the first component is the background language model, θ_B, and the other is the latent parsimonious model of the object, $\tilde{\theta}_o$. With regard to the generative models, when a term t is generated using this mixture model, first a model is chosen and then the term is sampled using the chosen model. Thus, the probability of generating term t can be shown as follows:

$$p(t|\theta_o) = \alpha p(t|\tilde{\theta}_o) + (1 - \alpha)p(t|\theta_B), \tag{1}$$

where α is the standard smoothing parameter that determines the probability of choosing the parsimonious model to generate the term t. The log-likelihood function for generating all terms in the whole object o is:

$$\log p(o|\tilde{\theta}_o) = \sum_{t \in o} c(t, o) \log \left(\alpha p(t|\tilde{\theta}_o) + (1 - \alpha)p(t|\theta_B) \right), \tag{2}$$

where $c(t, o)$ is the frequency of occurrence of term t in object o. With the goal of maximizing this likelihood function, the maximum likelihood estimation of $p(o|\tilde{\theta}_o)$ can be computed using the Expectation-Maximization (EM) algorithm by iterating over the following steps:

E-step:

$$p[t \in \mathcal{T}] = c(t|o) \cdot \frac{\alpha p(t|\tilde{\theta}_o)}{\alpha p(t|\tilde{\theta}_o) + (1 - \alpha)p(t|\theta_B)}, \tag{3}$$

M-step:

$$p(t|\tilde{\theta}_o) = \frac{p[t \in \mathcal{T}]}{\sum_{t' \in \mathcal{T}} p[t' \in \mathcal{T}]} \tag{4}$$

where $\mathcal{T}$ is the set of all terms with non-zero probability in the initial estimation. In Eq. 3, θ_o is the maximum likelihood estimation. $\tilde{\theta}_o$ represents the parsimonious model, which in the first iteration, is initialized by the maximum likelihood estimation, similar to θ_o.

Model Parsimonization

1: **procedure** PARSIMONIZE(o,B)
2:     **for all** term t in the vocabulary **do**
3:         $p(t|\theta_B) \leftarrow \Sigma_{b_i \in B}\left(p(t|\theta_{b_i}) \prod_{\substack{b_j \in B \\ j \neq i}}(1 - p(t|\theta_{b_j}))\right)$
4:     **repeat**
5:         E-Step: $p[t \in \mathcal{T}] \leftarrow p(t|\theta_o) \cdot \frac{\alpha p(t|\tilde{\theta}_o)}{\alpha p(t|\tilde{\theta}_o)+(1-\alpha)p(t|\theta_B)}$
6:         M-Step: $p(t|\tilde{\theta}_o) \leftarrow \frac{p[t \in \mathcal{T}]}{\sum_{t' \in \mathcal{T}} p[t' \in \mathcal{T}]}$
7:     **until** $\tilde{\theta}_o$ becomes stable
8:     **end for**
9: **end procedure**

(a) Pseudo-code for EM procedure of parsimonization.

Estimating SWLM

1: **procedure** ESTIMATESWLMS
    Initialization:
2:     **for all** object o in the hierarchy **do**
3:         $\theta_o \leftarrow$ standard estimation for o using MLE
4:     **end for**
5:     **repeat**
6:         SPECIFICATION
7:         GENERALIZATION
8:     **until** models do not change significantly anymore
9: **end procedure**

(b) Pseudo-code for procedure of estimating SWLM.

Specification Stage

1: **procedure** SPECIFICATION
2:     Queue ← all objects in BFS order
3:     **while** Queue is not empty **do**
4:         $o \leftarrow$ Queue.pop()
5:         $l \leftarrow o$.Depth();
6:         **while** $l > 0$ **do**
7:             $A \leftarrow o$.GETANCESTOR(l)
8:             PARSIMONIZE(o,A)
9:             $l \leftarrow l - 1$
10:        **end while**
11:     **end while**
12: **end procedure**

(c) Procedure of Specification. o.GETANCESTOR(l) gives the ancestor of object o with l edges distance from it.

Generalization Stage

1: **procedure** GENERALIZATION
2:     Stack ← all objects in BFS order
3:     **while** Stack is not empty **do**
4:         $o \leftarrow$ Stack.pop()
5:         $l \leftarrow o$.Height();
6:         **while** $l > 0$ **do**
7:             $D \leftarrow o$.GETDECEDENTS(l)
8:             PARSIMONIZE(o,D)
9:             $l \leftarrow l - 1$
10:        **end while**
11:     **end while**
12: **end procedure**

(d) Procedure of Generalization. o.GETDECEDENTS(l) gives all the decedents of object o with l edges distance from it.

Fig. 2. Pseudocode of Estimating hierarchical significant words language models.

Modified Model Parsimonization. In the original model parsimonization [10], the background model is explained by the estimation of the *collection language model*, i.e. the model representing all the objects. So, according to Eq. 3, parsimonization penalizes raw inference of terms that are better explained by the collection language model, as the background model, and continuing the iterations, their probability is adjusted to zero. This eventually results in a model with only the specific and distinctive terms of the object that makes it distinguishable from other objects in the collection.

However, with respect to the hierarchical structure, and our goal in two-way parsimonization for removing the effect of other layers in the object model, we need to use parsimonization technique in different situations: (1) toward ancestors of the object (2) toward its descendants. Hence, besides parsimonizing toward a single parent object in the upper layers, as the background model, we need to be able to do parsimonization toward multiple descendants in lower layers.

We propose the following equation for estimating the background model, which supports multiple background object, to be employed in the two-way model parsimonization:

$$p(t|\theta_B) \xleftarrow{normalized} \sum_{t_i \in B} \left(p(t|\theta_{b_i}) \prod_{\substack{b_j \in B \\ j \neq i}} (1 - p(t|\theta_{b_j})) \right) \qquad (5)$$

In this equation, B is the set of background objects—either one or multiple, and θ_{b_i} demonstrates the model of each background object, b_i, which is estimated using MLE. We normalize all the probabilities of the terms to form a distribution.

In two-way parsimonization, regarding the abstraction level in the hierarchy, when the background model represents an ancestor object in the upper layers of the hierarchy, it is supposed to reflect the generality of terms, so that parsimonaizing toward this model brings "specification" for the estimated model by removing general terms. On the other hand, when the background model represents multiple descendants from lower layers, it is supposed to reflect the specificity of terms, so that parsimonaizing toward this model brings "generalization" for the estimated model by discarding specific terms.

According to the aforementioned meanings of background model in these situations, Eq. 5 provides a proper estimation: In the multiple background case, it assigns a high probability to a term if it has a high probability in one of the background (descendant) models but not others, marginalizing over all the background models. This way, the higher the probability is, the more specific the term will be. In the single background case, i.e. having only one background object in the set B, $p(x|\theta_B)$ would be equal to $p(x|\theta_b)$, i.e. MLE of background object b. Since this single background object is from upper layers that are more general, this model reflects generality of terms.

Figure 2a presents pseudo-code of Expectation-Maximization algorithm which is employed in the modified model parsimonization procedure. In general, in the E-step, the probabilities of terms are adjusted repeatedly and in the M-step, adjusted probability of terms are normalized to form a distribution.

Model parsimonization is an almost parameter free process. The only parameter is the standard smoothing parameter α, which controls the level of parsimonization, so that the lower values of α result in more parsimonious models. The iteration is repeated a fixed number of times or until the estimates do not change significantly anymore.

3.2 Estimating HSWLM

We now investigate the question: How hierarchical significant words language models provide robust models by taking out aspects explained at other levels? In order to estimate HSWLM, in each iteration, there are two main stages: a

Specification stage and a *Generalization stage*. In loose terms, in the specification stage, the model of each object is specified relative to its ancestors and in generalization stage, the model of each object is generalized considering all its descendants. The pseudo-code of overall procedure of estimating HSWLM is presented in Fig. 2b. Before the first round of the procedure, a standard estimation like maximum likelihood estimation is used to construct the initial model for each object in the hierarchy. Then, in each iteration, models are updated in specification and generalization stages. These two stages are repeated until all the estimated models of all objects become stable.

In the specification stage, the parsimonization method is used to parsimonize the model of an object toward its ancestors, from the root of the hierarchy to its direct parent, as background estimations. The top-down order in the hierarchy is important here. Because when a model of an ancestor is considered as the background estimation, it should demonstrate the "specific" properties of that ancestor. Due to this fact, it is important that before considering the model of an object as the background estimation in specification stage, it should be already specified toward its ancestors. Pseudo-code for the recursive procedure of specification of objects' model is shown in Fig. 2c.

After specification stage, unless the root object, the models of all the objects are updated and the terms related to general properties are discarded from all models. In the generalization stage, again parsimonization is exploited but toward descendants. In the hierarchy, descendants of an object are usually supposed to represent more specific concepts compared to the object. Although the original parsimonization essentially accomplishes the effect of specification, parsimonizing the model of an object toward its descendants' models means generalizing the model. Here also, before considering the model of an object as background estimation, it should be already generalized toward its ancestors, so generalization moves bottom up. Figure 2d presents the pseudo-code for the recursive procedure of generalization of objects' model. It is noteworthy that the order of the stages is important. In the generalization, the background models of descendants are supposed to be specific enough to show their extremely specific properties. Hence, generalization stages must be applied on the output models of specification stages as shown in Fig. 2b where specification precedes generalization.

It is noteworthy that although the process of estimating HSWLM is an iterative method, it is highly efficient. This is because of the fact that in the first iteration of the process, model parsimonization in specification and generalization stages results in tiny effective models which do not contain unessential terms. Therefore, in the next iterations, the process deals with sparse distributions, with very small numbers of essential terms.

In this section, we proposed to iteratively use of parsimonization to take out general aspects explained at higher levels and estimate more specific and precise models as well as eliminating specific aspects of lower layers, to make models more general, — resulting in hierarchical significant words language models.

4   HSWLM for Evolving Hierarchies

This section investigates our second research question: "How effective are hierarchical significant words language models for classifying textual objects regarding different levels of the hierarchy across time periods?" We first explain the data collection we used as well as our experimental settings. Then we discuss how the estimation method addresses the requirement outlined in the introduction.

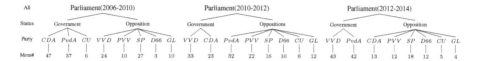

Fig. 3. Composition of Dutch parliament in 3 periods. *VVD*:People's Party for Freedom and democracy, *PvdA*:Labour Party, *CDA*:Christian Democratic Appeal, *PVV*:Party for Freedom, *SP*:The Socialist Party, *D66*:Democrats 66, *GL*:Green-Left, *CU*:Christian-Union.

4.1   Data Collection and Experimental Settings

In this research, we have made use of the Dutch parliamentary data. The data are collected and annotated as the part of *PoliticalMashup* project [18] to make semantically enriched parliamentary proceedings available as open data [14].

As a brief background, Dutch parliamentary system is a multi-party system, requiring a coalition of parties to form the government. We have chosen three interesting periods of parliament, from March 2006 to April 2014, in which eight main parties have about 95 % of seats in the parliament. The coalition in the first period is between a left-wing party and a centrism party, in the second period between a right-wing party and centrism party, and in the third, between a right-wing and left-wing party. Figure 3 shows the hierarchical structure of Dutch parliament in these three different periods.

In order to model parliamentary objects, first of all, we prepare the data. In the proceedings, there are series of parliamentary speeches by different MPs following the debate structure. We invert the data matrix so that for each speaker we collect their speeches as a single document, which represents the features of that member. Then, for representing the internal objects in the parliament's hierarchy, we first consider members as the leaf objects and then concatenate all leaf documents below internal objects as a single document which textually represent them: first over parties, and then parties into government and opposition, etc. The whole corpus consists of 14.7 million terms from 240,501 speeches, and contains 2.1 million unique terms. No stemming and no lemmatization is done on the data and also stop words and common words are not removed in data preprocessing. After data preparation, we estimate HSWLM for all objects in the hierarchy as it is explained in Sect. 3.

4.2 Classification Across Periods

As an extrinsic evaluation of the estimated models, we investigate the question: "How hierarchical significant words language models provide robust models by taking out aspects explained at other levels?" In the parliament, the composition of parties and statuses changes over different periods (Fig. 3) and hence the speeches related to different objects can vary dramatically. Due to this fact, cross period classification is notoriously challenging [11,25]. We show that our proposed approach tackles the problem of having non-stable models when the composition of parliament evolves during the time, by capturing the essence of language models of parliamentary objects at aggregate levels.

Tables 1b and 2b show the performance of employing HSWLM on status and party classification respectively. As a hard baseline, we have employed SVM classifier on parliamentary data like experiments done in [7] and also examined it on the cross period situation. Tables 1a and 2a indicate the results of SVM classifier on status and party classification respectively. Comparing the results in Tables 1b and a, we see that the accuracy of SVM in within period experiments is sometimes slightly better, but in cross period experiments, classifier which uses HSWLM of statuses achieves better results. This is also observed in the results in Table 2b compare to the results in Table 2a.

For party classification, employing HSWLM results more significant improvement over the baseline. Hirst et al. [11] discuss that since the status of members in parliament, compare to their party, has more effect on the content of their speeches, classifiers tend to pick features related to the status, not the party ideologies. So, SVM performs very well in terms of accuracy in the within-period experiments, but this performance is indebted to the separability of parties due

Table 1. Results on the task of status classification.

(a) Accuracy of SVM classifier

Period	Test			
	2006-10	2010-12	2012-14	All
2006-10	84.14	68.83	87.24	-
2010-12	68.29	78.57	87.91	-
2012-14	68.90	75.97	88.59	-
All	-	-	-	79.87

(b) Accuracy of classifier uses SWLM

Period	Test			
	2006-10	2010-12	2012-14	All
2006-10	82.32	80.51	89.29	-
2010-12	79.87	74.66	88.58	-
2012-14	78.65	77.27	93.28	-
All	-	-	-	86.98

Table 2. Results on the task of party classification.

(a) Accuracy of SVM classifier

Period	Test			
	2006-10	2010-12	2012-14	All
2006-10	47.56	29.22	26.84	-
2010-12	29.87	40.90	35.57	-
2012-14	31.09	30.51	44.96	-
All	-	-	-	39.18

(b) Accuracy of classifier uses SWLM

Period	Test			
	2006-10	2010-12	2012-14	All
2006-10	44.51	46.10	43.62	-
2010-12	40.85	40.25	39.59	-
2012-14	40.24	38.96	42.28	-
All	-	-	-	49.94

to their status. Hence, changing the status in cross period experiments, using trained model on other periods fails to predict the party so the accuracies drop down. This is exactly the point which the strengths of our proposed method kicks in. Since for each party, the HSWLM is less affected by the status of the party in that period, the model remains valid even when the status is changed. In other words, eliminating the effect of the status layer in the party model in the specification stage ensures that party model captures the essential terms related to the party ideology, not its status. Thereby, it is a stable model which is transferable through the time. We conducted the one-tailed t-test on the results. In both party and status classification, in all cases which HSWLM performs better than the SVM, the improvement is statistically significant (p-value < 0.005).

To get a better intuition of the procedure of estimating HSWLM, consider the hierarchical relations of Dutch parliaments in the period of *2006–2010* which is depicted in Fig. 3. Assume that the goal is modeling language usage of "Christian-Union (CU)" as an object in the party layer. In the speeches from the members of this party, words like *"Chairman"* or *"Agree"* might occur repeatedly. However, they are not a good point of reference for the party's ideological language usage. In the procedure of estimating HSWLM of the "Christian-Union", these words are removed from the initial estimated standard language model in the specification stages, since *"Chairman"* is a general term in the parliamentary domain and is only able to explain the root object and *"Agree'* is somehow an indicator of language usage of all the "Government" parties. On the other side, consider the goal is to model language usage of "Government" as an object in the status layer. Speeches from "Christian-Union" members, which are also counted as "Government" members, may contain words like *"Bible"* or *"Charity"*. It is trivial that involving these party-specific words in the constructed model for the "Government" in an individual period demolishes the comprehensiveness. In the procedure of estimating HSWLM for the "Government", in the generalization stages, these words are discarded from the model. This way, "Government" model does not lose its validity on other periods where the "Christian-Union" is not in a Government party.

As another indicator of the effectiveness of HSWLM, it outperforms the SVM bringing all the data together from three different periods in both party and status classification. This is because it gets the chance of having a more rich train data which leads to more precise models. While in SVM, changes in the parliamentary composition make speeches diverse and this makes it not to be able to learn a concrete model.

4.3   Invariance of Models

This section investigates our third research question: "Do the resulting hierarchical significant words language models capture common characteristics of classes in different levels of hierarchy over time?" As an intrinsic evaluation of the models, we evaluate the invariance of models over different periods—how similar are models of a particular object in the hierarchy when trained on data from different periods. Since HSWLM is supposed to captures the essence of objects, not

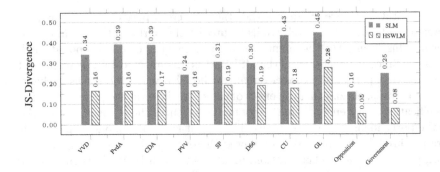

Fig. 4. Average of JS-Divergence of standard language models and HSWLMs for parliamentary entities in three different periods.

only HSWLM of an object learned using an individual period should be valid for representing the object on other periods, but also models of the same object learned on data from different periods should be invariant.

To assess this, we use the diversity of objects' models in different periods to measure their (in)variance over time. First, all HSWLM from different periods of each party and each status is smoothed using Jelinek-Mercer smoothing [27] considering all parliamentary speeches in the corresponding period as the background collection and with the same value of the smoothing parameter. Then, we use the Jensen-Shannon divergence as the diversity metric to measure dissimilarities between each two HSWLMs learned from different periods and then calculate the average of values for each object. As the baseline, the same calculation is done for the standard language models of objects, i.e. language models estimated using maximum likelihood estimation. Figure 4 shows the diversity of models in different periods. As can be seen, in all objects in both party and status layers, diversity of HSWLM of different periods is lower than diversity of standard language models, which shows the extracted HSWLMs are more invariant over different periods.

In this section, we examined classification accuracy over time using HSWLM and saw significantly better results across different government periods. This suggest that HSWLM captures the essential and permanent features of parliamentary objects. Moreover, we looked at the divergence of models from different periods, and observed that HSWLMs from different periods are more invariant compared to the standard models.

5   Conclusions

In this research, we dealt with the problem of modeling hierarchical objects for building classifiers in different levels of evolving hierarchies. To address this problem, inspired by parsimonious language models used in information retrieval, we proposed *hierarchical significant words language models* (HSWLM).

Our first research question was: *How to estimate robust language models for objects in the evolving hierarchies, by explicitly taking relations between the levels into account?* We proposed the iteratively use of parsimonization to take out general aspects explained at higher levels and eliminate specific aspects of lower levels—resulting in HSWLM. Our second question was: *How effective are hierarchical significant words language models for classifying textual objects regarding different levels of the hierarchy across time periods?* We utilized HSWLM for the task of party and status classification in the parliament over time. The results showed that since the models capture the essential and permanent features of parliamentary objects, they lead to significantly better classification accuracy across different government periods. Our third question was: *Do the resulting hierarchical significant words language models capture common characteristics of classes in different levels of hierarchy over time?* We designed an experiment in which divergence of models from different periods is measured for all objects. We observed that HSWLMs from different periods are more consistent compared to the standard models.

The general idea of HSWLM is to estimate models possessing separation property [6] and it is generally applicable in other problems [3–5]. Besides, we are currently extending the work in this paper in several directions. First, we apply the approach to other kinds of web data in particular social network data. Second, we investigate the effectiveness of the models for various other hierarchical classification tasks, in particular those over dynamic or stream data, and develop variants dealing with data sparsity. Third, we further develop new variants of topic models building on the specialization and generalization outlined in this paper.

Acknowledgments. This research is funded in part by Netherlands Organization for Scientific Research through the *Exploratory Political Search* project (ExPoSe, NWO CI # 314.99.108), and by the Digging into Data Challenge through the *Digging Into Linked Parliamentary Data* project (DiLiPaD, NWO Digging into Data # 600.006.014).

References

1. Blei, D.M., Lafferty, J.D.: Dynamic topic models. In: ICML, pp. 113–120 (2006)
2. Chen, M., Weinberger, K.Q., Blitzer, J.: Co-training for domain adaptation. In: NIPS '24, pp. 2456–2464 (2011)
3. Dehghani, M.: Significant words representations of entities. In: SIGIR 2016 (2016)
4. Dehghani, M., Azarbonyad, H., Kamps, J., Marx, M.: Generalized group profiling for content customization. In: CHIIR 2016, pp. 245–248 (2016)
5. Dehghani, M., Azarbonyad, H., Kamps, J., Hiemstra, D., Marx, M.: Luhn revisited: significant words language models. In: The Proceedings of The ACM International Conference on Information and Knowledge Management (CIKM'16) (2016)
6. Dehghani, M., Azarbonyad, H., Kamps, J., Marx, M.: On horizontal and vertical separation in hierarchical text classification. In: The Proceedings of ACM SIGIR International Conference on the Theory of Information Retrieval (ICTIR'16) (2016)
7. Diermeier, D., Godbout, J.-F., Yu, B., Kaufmann, S.: Language and ideology in congress. Br. J. Polit. Sci. **42**(1), 31–55 (2012)

8. Dumais, S., Chen, H.: Hierarchical classification of web content. In: SIGIR, pp. 256–263 (2000)
9. Frank, J.R., Kleiman-Weiner, M., Roberts, D.A., Voorhees, E.M., Soboroff, I.: Evaluating stream filtering for entity profile updates in trec 2012, 2013 and 2014. In: TREC 2014 (2012)
10. Hiemstra, D., Robertson, S., Zaragoza, H.: Parsimonious language models for information retrieval. In: SIGIR 2004, pp. 178–185 (2004)
11. Hirst, G., Riabinin, Y., Graham, J., Boizot-Roche, M.: Text to ideology or text to party status? From Text Polit. Positions: Text Anal. Across Disciplines **55**, 93–116 (2014)
12. Kim, D.-K., Voelker, G., Saul, L.K.: A variational approximation for topic modeling of hierarchical corpora. In: ICML, pp. 55–63 (2013)
13. Luhn, H.P.: The automatic creation of literature abstracts. IBM J. Res. Dev. **2**(2), 159–165 (1958)
14. Marx, M., Schuth, A.: Dutchparl: a corpus of parliamentary documents in dutch. In: DIR Workshop, pp. 82–83 (2010)
15. McCallum, A., Rosenfeld, R., Mitchell, T.M., Ng, A.Y.: Improving text classification by shrinkage in a hierarchy of classes. In: ICML 1998, pp. 359–367 (1998)
16. Ogilvie, P., Callan, J.: Hierarchical language models for XML component retrieval. In: Fuhr, N., Lalmas, M., Malik, S., Szlávik, Z. (eds.) INEX 2004. LNCS, vol. 3493, pp. 224–237. Springer, Heidelberg (2005)
17. Oh, H.-S., Choi, Y., Myaeng, S.-H.: Text classification for a large-scale taxonomy using dynamically mixed local and global models for a node. In: Clough, P., Foley, C., Gurrin, C., Jones, G.J.F., Kraaij, W., Lee, H., Mudoch, V. (eds.) ECIR 2011. LNCS, vol. 6611, pp. 7–18. Springer, Heidelberg (2011)
18. PoliticalMashup. Political mashup project (2015). http://search.politicalmashup. nl/. Netherlands Organization for Scientific Research
19. Sebastiani, F.: Machine learning in automated text categorization. ACM Comput. Surv. **34**(1), 1–47 (2002)
20. Silla Jr., C.N., Freitas, A.A.: A survey of hierarchical classification across different application domains. Data Min. Knowl. Discov. **22**(1–2), 31–72 (2011)
21. Song, Y., Roth, D.: On dataless hierarchical text classification. In: AAAI, pp. 1579–1585 (2014)
22. Teh, Y.W., Jordan, M.I., Beal, M.J., Blei, D.M.: Hierarchical dirichlet processes. J. Am. Stat. Assoc. **101**(476), 1566–1581 (2006)
23. Xue, G.-R., Dai, W., Yang, Q., Yu, Y.: Topic-bridged plsa for cross-domain text classification. In: SIGIR 2008, pp. 627–634 (2008)
24. Yao, L., Mimno, D., McCallum, A.: Efficient methods for topic model inference on streaming document collections. In: SIGKDD, pp. 937–946 (2009)
25. Yu, B., Kaufmann, S., Diermeier, D.: Classifying party affiliation from political speech. J. Inf. Technol. Politics **5**(1), 33–48 (2008)
26. Zavitsanos, E., Paliouras, G., Vouros, G.A.: Non-parametric estimation of topic hierarchies from texts with hierarchical dirichlet processes. J. Mach. Learn. Res. **12**, 2749–2775 (2011)
27. Zhai, C., Lafferty, J.: A study of smoothing methods for language models applied to ad hoc information retrieval. In: SIGIR 2001, pp. 334–342 (2001)

Effects of Language and Terminology on the Usage of Health Query Suggestions

Carla Teixeira Lopes[(✉)] and Cristina Ribeiro

DEI, Faculdade de Engenharia, Universidade do Porto and INESC TEC,
Rua Dr. Roberto Frias, s/n, 4200-465 Porto, Portugal
{ctl,mcr}@fe.up.pt

Abstract. Searching for health information is one of the most popular activities on the Web. In this domain, users frequently encounter difficulties in query formulation, either because they lack knowledge of the proper medical terms or because they misspell them. To overcome these difficulties and attempt to retrieve higher-quality content, we developed a query suggestion system that provides alternative queries combining the users' native language and English language with lay and medico-scientific terminology. To assess how the language and terminology impact the use of suggestions, we conducted a user study with 40 subjects considering their English proficiency, health literacy and topic familiarity. Results show that suggestions are used most often at the beginning of search sessions. English suggestions tend to be preferred to the ones formulated in the users' native language, at all levels of English proficiency. Medico-scientific suggestions tend to be preferred to lay suggestions at higher levels of health literacy.

Keywords: Health information retrieval · Query suggestion · English proficiency · Health literacy · Topic familiarity

1 Introduction

Searching for health information is the third most popular online activity after email and using a search engine, being performed by 80 % of U.S. Internet users [2]. This domain poses specific challenges to health consumers, who frequently encounter additional difficulties in finding the correct terms to include in their queries [6,16] because they lack knowledge of the proper medical terms [14,17]. The misspelling of medical terms is another common problem [5,11]. For these reasons, support in query formulation may contribute to an improved retrieval experience. Considering this is a domain in which the quality of the retrieved content is crucial, and considering that quality depends on the language used to conduct the search [7], support for query translation may also be useful.

Our goal is to improve the health search experience of users, particularly users for whom English is not their primary language. The importance of query

© Springer International Publishing Switzerland 2016
N. Fuhr et al. (Eds.): CLEF 2016, LNCS 9822, pp. 83–95, 2016.
DOI: 10.1007/978-3-319-44564-9_7

formulation support in health searches, the lack of such support and the findings of previous studies motivated the development of a system that, based on an initial user query, suggests 4 different queries combining two languages (English and Portuguese) and two bodies of terminology (lay and medico-scientific). To the best of our knowledge, no previous works have explored cross-language query suggestions in the health domain.

To assess users' receptivity to query suggestions in a language that not their native and to suggestions using different types of terminologies, we conducted a user study and, based on clicks, analysed the effective use of the proposed suggestions. It is important to note that, although it has been proved that some of these suggestions contribute to improve the retrieval performance [7,8], this will only be the case if users have the willingness to take the recommendations.

Previous studies have concluded that search assistance should be personalized to achieve its maximal outcome [4]. Yet, little attention has been paid to how people perform query reformulations across different user groups. Therefore, we have considered users' English proficiency, health literacy and topic familiarity.

2   Related Work

In consumer health information retrieval, there is an awareness that several difficulties can emerge due to the terminology gap between medical experts and lay people [18]. To overcome these difficulties in query formulation, some authors have proposed query expansion approaches. The Health Information Query Assistant proposed by Zeng et al. [16] suggests terms based on their semantic distance from the original query. To compute this distance, the authors use co-occurrences in medical literature and log data as well as the semantic relations in medical vocabularies. A user study with 213 subjects randomized into 2 groups, one receiving suggestions and the other not receiving them, showed that recommendations resulted in higher rates of successful queries, i.e., queries with at least one relevant result among the top 10, but not in higher rates of satisfaction. Two proposed search engines for health information retrieval — iMed [9] and MedSearch [10] — provide suggestions of medical phrases to assist users in refining their queries. The phrases are extracted and ranked based on MeSH (Medical Subject Headings), the collection of crawled webpages, and the query.

Zarro and Lin [15] presented a search system that uses social tagging and MeSH to provide users with peer and professional terms. To evaluate the impact of these suggestions, the authors conducted a user study with 10 lay subjects and 10 expert subjects. Both groups preferred MeSH terms because their quality was considered superior to the quality of social tags. Also in the health domain, Fattahi et al. [1] proposed a query expansion method that uses non-topical terms (terms that occur before or after topical terms to represent a specific aspect of the theme, such as 'about' in 'about breast cancer') and semi-topical terms (terms that do not occur alone, such as 'risk of' in 'risk of breast cancer') in conjunction with topical terms (terms that represent the subject content of documents, such as 'breast cancer'). The authors found that web searches can be enhanced by the combination of these three types of terms.

Although not in the specific area of health information retrieval, we identified only one work involving the proposal of query suggestions in a language different from the original query's language, namely, a study performed by Gao et al. [3]. The authors proposed a method to translate generalist queries using query logs and then estimate the cross-lingual query similarity using information such as word translation relations and word co-occurrence statistics. The evaluation was performed on French-English and Chinese-English tasks. They found that these suggestions, when used in combination with pseudo-relevance feedback, improved the effectiveness of cross-language information retrieval.

Since 2014, the Conference and Labs of the Evaluation Forum (CLEF) eHealth lab began to propose a multilingual information user-centred health retrieval task, incorporating queries in several languages in its dataset.

3   Suggestion Tool

We designed and developed a prototype for a suggestion tool that can be integrated into IR systems. Given a health query, our tool suggests alternative queries in two languages, Portuguese (PT) and English (EN), using medico-scientific (MS) and lay terminology. In Fig. 1, we present the architecture of the suggestion tool, which will be further detailed in the following paragraphs.

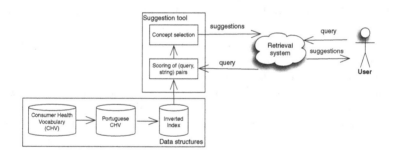

Fig. 1. Architecture of the suggestion tool.

We created an inverted index using the Portuguese translation of the Consumer Health Vocabulary (CHV), an open-access and collaborative vocabulary that maps technical terms to consumer friendly language [12]. In the index, each stemmed term is associated with an inverse string frequency (isf_t) and a postings list, i.e., a list of the strings in which the stemmed term appears. The computation of the inverse string frequency is similar to the computation of the inverse document frequency that is traditionally performed in IR, that is, $isf_t = log(N/sf_t)$, where sf_t is the number of strings in which the term appears and N is the total number of strings. Because strings are typically small, the probability of finding multiple occurrences of the same term in a string is very small. For this reason, we decided to weight each term based only on its isf_t, ignoring its frequency in each string $(tf_{t,s})$. To determine the vocabulary of terms, namely, the list of terms in our inverted index, the strings were tokenized and stop words were removed. In the terms, all letters were converted to lower case and the accents were removed, and the terms were also stemmed.

The score assigned to each (query, string) pair is defined by $score(q, s) = \sum_{t \in q} isf_t$. Because the length of strings and queries has a very small variance, we found that the additional computational power required to normalize the above score formula would not be justified by the gains thus achieved.

In this stage of the prototype development, to limit the number of suggestions, we decided to select only the string with the maximum score for each input query. For this string, we identify the associated concept and then return its CHV and Unified Medical Language System (UMLS) preferred names in English and Portuguese. If a suggestion is identical to the query or to any other suggestion, it will not be presented, i.e., the output of the system will contain only unique suggestions different from the query. This results in a maximum of 4 suggestions for each query.

The CHV vocabulary was translated into Portuguese using the Google Translator API (Application Programming Interface). We manually evaluated 1 % of the total number of translated strings and concluded that 84.2 % (95 % CI: [82.3 %, 85.9 %]) of the translations were correct, a very satisfactory outcome.

Our retrieval system used the Bing Search API to obtain web results for users' queries. To increase the usability of the interface with regard to learning, we decided to keep the interfaces very simple and similar to those used in the most popular search engines. All the suggestions are presented in a single line above the list of retrieved documents. As an example, a set of suggestions could be: "colectomia", "remoção do cólon", "colectomy" and "colon removal".

All types of suggestions might be useful after any type of query. Imagine, for example, an initial query in English. Portuguese query suggestions might be useful for an user that is not proficient in the English language and prefers to retrieve documents in his native language. On the other hand, if he is proficient in English he might just want to switch terminology, keeping the same language.

4 Experiment

We conducted a user study with 40 participants (24 female; 16 male), with a mean age of 23.48 years (standard deviation (sd) = 7.66). Portuguese was the native language of every participant. The study had two within-subject independent variables: language and terminology; three quasi-independent variable: English proficiency, health literacy and topic familiarity; and one major dependent variable: clicks on query suggestions.

English proficiency was evaluated using an instrument developed by the European Council that grades English proficiency in the Common European Framework of Reference for Languages (CEFR), a widely accepted European standard for this purpose. To evaluate the users' health literacy, we have used the Medical Term Recognition Test (METER), an instrument proposed by Rawson et al. [13]. The users' familiarity with each topic was self-assessed on a five-level scale.

Each user was assigned a set of 8 tasks, each associated with one of 8 simulated work task situations. To define the simulated situations, we selected 20 persons with no medical expertise and spanning a wide range of ages (from 30 to 68) and education levels (from high school to PhD degrees). These individuals were asked to state the health topic for which they had most recently searched on the Web. From these topics, we randomly selected 8 and created a scenario for each. The situations were described to the users in Portuguese. The following situation, presented as an example, was one of them: "Two weeks ago, someone from your family was diagnosed with shingles. To understand what characterizes this disease, you decided to search on the Web for its causes and symptoms. Find out what causes the disease and identify two common symptoms".

In each task the user had to formulate 3 queries and assess the relevance of the top 10 results for each query. In the first query, the user had to formulate the query without any help from the system. Users did not have any type of restrictions in query formulation. Users used their preferred language and terminology. Based on the initial query, the system presents suggestions that can, or not, be used for the formulation of the second query. The same happens when the user is moving from the second to the third iteration. The set of 3 iterations constituted a search session. The usefulness of the suggestions was assessed in a post-search questionnaire.

Our experiment was motivated by the following research questions: (1) In which stage of the search process are suggestions used, and considered useful, more often? (2) To which type of suggestions are users most receptive? (3) To which language are users most receptive and how does this change with the users' English proficiency? (4) To which terminology are users most receptive and how does this change with the users' health literacy and topic familiarity?

5   Data Analysis

To evaluate the usage given to suggestions, we considered that users might use them as suggestions, clicking or not on them, and as source of terms they can use in the following queries. Considering this last scenario, for each type of suggestion, we computed the proportion of suggestion's terms that were used in the subsequent query (termsUsed) and the proportion of the suggestion's terms that were used in the following query and were not used in the previous query (newTermsUsed). The former is useful to assess the quality of suggestions' terms and the latter is also useful to assess the utility of the suggestions for the users. Let Q_{it} be the set of unique stemmed terms belonging to the query of the iteration it and S_{it} the set of unique stemmed terms belonging to the suggestion presented in the iteration it, these proportions are computed as follows: $termsUsed_{it} = \frac{|Q_{it} \cap S_{it}|}{|S_{it}|}$ and $newTermsUsed_{it} = \frac{|(Q_{it} \cap S_{it}) \backslash Q_{it-1}|}{|S_{it}|}$.

We used the test of equal proportions with the chi-squared value to compare proportions between groups. To compare the means of termsUsed and newTermsUsed between groups we used the Student's t-test. When the variances were found to be not homogeneous, we applied the Welch t-test. In comparisons involving more than two groups (e.g.: comparing levels of English proficiency in terms of suggestion usage), we applied the one-way ANOVA and the Tukey's test to assess the location of the differences, whenever significant differences were found. When reporting our results, we use a * to mark significant results at $\alpha = 0.05$ and a ** to mark significant results at $\alpha = 0.01$.

6   Use of Suggestions

As explained in Sect. 3, all types of suggestions were generated through the same algorithm. Moreover, the translation of the CHV was considered very good with almost 85 % of correct translations. Consequently, we don't expect quality differences between types of suggestions that might have affect user behaviour.

During the experiments, in the second and third iterations, the suggestion system did not present suggestions in only 4.7 % of the iterations. Note that the system generates suggestions based on the query just inserted by the user, what means the first query has to be formulated without any help. All these initial queries were formulated using the Portuguese language and lay terminology.

Almost 55 % of the sessions presenting suggestions had one or more clicks in suggestions. Of the 40 participants in the study, 5 did not click on any suggestion during their tasks. Suggestions were used in 86.9 % of the iterations and the participants tended to find the suggestions useful more often in the initial iterations than in the final ones (Table 1). This is also supported by the proportions presented in the two last lines of Table 1, showing that initial iterations have more suggestions' clicks and use suggestions as a source of terms more often.

Table 1. Use of suggestions by iteration. "Proportion of iterations where..."

	Iteration		
	2	3	2 versus 3
Suggestions were not presented	1.9 %	7.5 %	$\chi^2(1) = 4.5$, p $= 0.02$*
Suggestions were not considered useful	10.0 %	16.3 %	$\chi^2(1) = 3.7$, p $= 0.07$
Users used terms from 1 suggestion	30.6 %	37.5 %	$\chi^2(1) = 1.39$, p $= 0.12$
Users used terms from several suggestions	57.5 %	38.8 %	$\chi^2(1) = 10.5$, p $= 6e-4$**
Suggestions were clicked	41.4 %	24.3 %	$\chi^2(1) = 9.3$, p $= 0.002$**

After iterations with suggestions, participants used, in average, 1.34 terms from the suggestions. Considering only the new terms, that is, the terms that did not belong to the previous query, this value falls to 0.66. In the analysis by iteration (Table 2), we see that the number of suggestions' terms, new or not, used in the subsequent query is higher in earlier iterations. This is in line with what was described above.

Table 2. Means of terms used by iteration. One sided significant differences.

	It2	It3	It2 vs It3
termsUsed	1.89	0.76	$t(302.2) = 8.7$, p $= 2.2e-16$**
newTermsUsed	0.82	0.49	$t(301) = 3.1$, p $= 0.002$**

Users employ all terms from suggestions in 56.7 % of the iterations where suggestions were presented. The above tendency is still true, that is, complete suggestions are used more in the initial iterations as shown in Table 1.

If, instead of entire suggestions, we consider clicks, the proportion of iterations with clicked suggestions falls to 33.1 % and is also significantly higher in the initial iterations as shown in Table 1. Still regarding clicks, we found that 54.7 % of the sessions had at least one click and 8.8 % of the sessions had two clicks. We found that a large proportion of users (87.5 %) have clicked at least once in the proposed suggestions. A lower proportion of users (27.5 %) have clicked on suggestions in the two iterations where they were presented.

As shown in Table 3, users extract the larger number of terms from Portuguese/medico-scientific suggestions. In terms of significant differences, we found that the mean number of terms extracted from this type of suggestions is larger than the mean number of terms extracted from English suggestions (Tukey's adjusted p $= 0$ for EN/Lay; Tukey's adjusted p $= 1.7e-6$ for EN/MS). Moreover, as can be seen in Table 4, Portuguese/Lay suggestions are also preferred to both types of English suggestions. Regarding the use of new terms, the English/medico-scientific suggestions are the ones with the greatest contribution to the expansion of terms in users' queries. This difference is explained by users' lack of habit to begin their searches with an English query. English/medico-scientific suggestions are also the ones with a higher proportion of clicks. On the other hand, Portuguese/Lay suggestions are the ones with lower proportion of clicks and lower proportion of new terms, showing that users consider these suggestions the least useful ones. In fact, this type of suggestions has a significantly lower mean of new terms and a significantly lower proportion of clicks with respect to all the other types of suggestions (Table 4).

6.1 Analysis by Language

In terms of CEFR classes, 16 users had *basic* English proficiency, 17 were *independent*, and 7 were *proficient* users. In Table 5, we present an analysis of the users' preferred language, in general and by English proficiency. If we consider all the used terms, we can see that *basic* and *independent* English proficiency users prefer to use terms from Portuguese suggestions. In the *proficient* group, users tend to prefer English suggestions but this is not a significant difference. If we only consider the newly introduced terms or clicks, users preferred English suggestions. In the *independent* group, the users also tended to prefer English suggestions but not significantly.

Table 3. termsUsed and newTermsUsed: mean and standard deviation (SD) by type of suggestion. Proportion of clicks by type of suggestion. Boldface indicates the maximum per column.

	termsUsed		newTermsUsed		Clicks
	Mean	SD	Mean	SD	Proportion
EN/Lay	0.24	0.38	0.16	0.33	14 %
EN/MS	0.30	0.41	**0.19**	0.37	**18 %**
PT/Lay	0.40	0.40	0.08	0.20	5 %
PT/MS	**0.46**	0.43	0.16	0.33	14 %

Table 4. Tukey's adjusted p-value for one-sided significant comparisons of the termsUsed and newTermsUsed. Holm adjusted p-value for one-sided significant comparison of proportions of clicks.

PT/Lay vs:	PT/MS	EN/Lay	EN/MS
TermsUsed ($>$)	-	5e$-$6	0.01
NewTermsUsed ($<$)	0.002	0.002	1e$-$5
clicks ($<$)	0.009	0.009	8e$-$6

Table 5. Means, proportions and one-sided significant differences of termsUsed, new-TermsUsed and clicks by language and English proficiency (EP). Boldface identifies the row's maximum.

	EN	PT	English vs Portuguese	
			test value	p value
termsUsed				
All	0.27	**0.43**	$t(1214.7) = -6.9$	3.3e$-$12**
Basic EP users	0.25	**0.45**	$t(483.5) = -5.38$	6e$-$06**
Independent EP users	0.24	**0.44**	$t(511.4) = -6.0$	2.4e$-$09**
newTermsUsed				
All	**0.18**	0.12	$t(1153.7) = 3.2$	5e$-$04**
Basic EP users	**0.18**	0.12	$t(455.8) = 2.1$	0.01*
English proficient users	**0.25**	0.10	$t(171.7) = 3.3$	5e$-$04**
clicks				
All	**15.9 %**	9.7 %	$\chi^2(1) = 10.1$	7.6e$-$04**
Basic EP users	**16.8 %**	8.2 %	$\chi^2(1) = 0.15$	0.003**
English proficient users	**23.6 %**	13.2 %	$\chi^2(1) = 1.5$	0.04*

In addition to testing the differences between languages, we also tested the differences between levels of English proficiency. We found that *proficient* users clicked on English suggestions more often than *independent* users

Table 6. Means, proportions and one-sided significant differences of termsUsed and newTermsUsed and clicks by terminology, health literacy (HL) and topic familiarity. Boldface identifies the row's maximum.

	Lay	MS	Lay vs Medico-scientific	
			test value	p value
termsUsed				
All	0.14	**0.46**	$t(275.1) = -7.0$	9e−10**
Marginal HL	0.14	**0.47**	$t(204.6) = -6.3$	7e−08**
Functional HL	0.06	**0.70**	$t(27.1) = -5.8$	1.7e−06**
Not familiar	0.12	**0.51**	$t(136.4) = -6.3$	1.8e−09**
Familiar	0.16	**0.48**	$t(55.3) = -3.0$	0.001**
Extremely familiar	0.16	**0.36**	$t(80.8) = -2.3$	0.01*
newTermsUsed				
All	0.09	**0.32**	$t(247.2) = -5.5$	9.5e−06**
Marginal HL	0.07	**0.32**	$t(176) = -5.0$	6e−05**
Functional HL	0.06	**0.48**	$t(24.5) = -3.3$	0.001**
Not familiar	0.00	**0.31**	$t(27) = -5.3$	7e−04**
Familiar	0.15	**0.35**	$t(57) = -2.1$	0.02*
Extremely familiar	0.14	**0.30**	$t(79.9) = -1.8$	0.03*
clicks				
All	5.3 %	**24.3 %**	$\chi^2(1) = 20.4$	3e−06**
Marginal HL	4.5 %	**21.4 %**	$\chi^2(1) = 12.8$	2e−04**
Functional HL	5.6 %	**55.5 %**	$\chi^2(1) = 8.4$	0.002**
Not familiar	2.6 %	**22.4 %**	$\chi^2(1) = 11.8$	3e−04**
Familiar	9.4 %	**37.5 %**	$\chi^2(1) = 5.6$	0.009**

(Tukey's adjusted p = 0.012*). *Proficient* users are also associated with a higher mean of *termsUsed* than *independent* (Tukey's adjusted p = 0.001**) and *basic* users (Tukey's adjusted p = 0.006**). Excluding the previously used terms (*newTermsUsed*), *proficient* users employ more terms from English suggestions than *independent* users (Tukey's adjusted p = 0.01*).

6.2 Analysis by Terminology

The distribution of the users among the health literacy (HL) classes was as follows: *low* (7 users), *marginal* (28 users) and *functional* (5 users). In Table 6 we can observe that, in general, the users preferred medico-scientific suggestions to lay suggestions. However, if we consider the users' health literacy, we see that this statement only holds for the *marginal* and *functional* groups.

In addition to the differences presented in Table 6, we also found that the use of terms from medico-scientific suggestions significantly increases with the health literacy of the users. In fact, the *low* health literacy group uses fewer terms than the *marginal* (Tukey's adjusted p = 0.01*) and *functional* literacy group (Tukey's adjusted p = 5e−04**). In addition, the *marginal* health literacy group uses fewer terms than the *functional* one (Tukey's adjusted p = 0.05*). Regarding clicks, the *functional* group clicked more often on medico-scientific suggestions than did the *low* (Tukey's adjusted p = 0.013**) and *marginal* groups (Tukey's adjusted p = 0.008**).

The users' familiarity with each topic depends on the theme of the task. The pairs "user, topic" were distributed as follows: *not familiar* (86 pairs), *familiar* (114 pairs) and *extremely familiar* (120 pairs). In Table 6, we can see that, with one exception, users significantly prefer medico-scientific suggestions, disregarding their familiarity with the topic. The only exception occurs among users *extremely familiar* with the topic where we could not find a significant difference between the terminologies. When comparing the several levels of familiarity, we found that users *extremely familiar* with a topic use more newTerms from lay suggestions than *non-familiar* users (Tukey's adjusted p = 0.05*).

7   Discussion

We found that suggestions were used more often at the beginning of the search sessions. In the initial iterations, users not only click more often but they also use more terms from suggestions. Almost 55 % of the sessions with suggestions had at least one click and almost 87 % had a query with, at least, one of the suggestions' terms. Of the 40 participants in the study, 5 did not click on any suggestion during their tasks. These findings indicate a good acceptance rate of the suggestions, similar to that found by Jansen and McNeese [4]. In the initial iterations, users tend to found suggestions useful more often, but this difference is not significant.

The suggestions formulated in the Portuguese language and lay terminology had a smaller proportion of clicks than other types of suggestions. The average number of new terms extracted from these suggestions is also lower. This indicates that the users found these suggestions to be the least useful, which is not surprising considering that queries formulated by lay people without assistance will, most probably, use their native language and lay terminology. In this experiment, all the queries in the first iteration were formulated with Portuguese language and lay terminology.

Users from the lowest and highest levels of English proficiency clicked more often on English suggestions and extract a larger number of new terms from English suggestions than from Portuguese ones. These findings regarding *basic* proficiency users surprised us because we expected that suggestions in a language in which they were not proficient would not attract them. This might have occurred because these suggestions had a great degree of novelty, which may have aroused their curiosity. Ignoring the terms used in previous queries, both types of

Portuguese suggestions are preferred to both types of English suggestions. Yet, this only happens in the lower levels of English proficiency, advanced proficiency users tend to prefer terms from English suggestions. As expected, the preference for English suggestions is more notorious in proficient users than in *independent* users, in clicks and in number of extracted terms.

In general, the users preferred medico-scientific suggestions to lay suggestions. However, if we consider the users' health literacy, we see that this is true only in the *marginal* and *functional* groups. The *functional* group exhibited a larger proportion of clicks on medico-scientific suggestions compared with the *low* and *marginal* groups. Topic familiarity was not found to be a discriminating factor in terms of lay versus medico-scientific terminology use.

8   Conclusion

In this study we assessed users' acceptance to health query suggestions proposed in two languages, Portuguese and English, using two types of terminologies, lay and medico-scientific. In this analysis we also considered if and how users' English proficiency, health literacy and topic familiarity affect their preference. The usage analysis takes into account the utility of the suggestions as new whole queries and as sources of terms.

Suggestions were found to be used more often and, when contributing to query expansion, in a larger quantity, in the initial stages of a search session. In general, suggestions had a good acceptance by the users and the novelty aspect seems to be important in the choice of suggestions to use. Excluding the scenario in which terms from suggestions are used, useful to assess the quality of suggestions' terms but not so useful to assess their utility to the users, English suggestions tend to be preferred to the ones in Portuguese in all levels of English proficiency, a significant preference in the *basic* and *proficient* users. On the other hand, medico-scientific suggestions tend to be preferred to lay ones in the higher levels of health literacy and the extraction of new terms from these suggestions increases with health literacy.

The good acceptance of the suggestions is an indicator of their quality, as perceived by users during query formulation. Nonetheless, as future work, we will analyse the impact of suggestions in retrieval effectiveness through users' relevance assessments.

Acknowledgments. This work was partially funded by project "NanoSTIMA: Macro-to-Nano Human Sensing: Towards Integrated Multimodal Health Monitoring and Analytics/NORTE-01-0145-FEDER-000016", financed by the North Portugal Regional Operational Programme (NORTE 2020), under the PORTUGAL 2020 Partnership Agreement, and through the European Regional Development Fund (ERDF).

References

1. Fattahi, R., Wilson, C.S., Cole, F.: An alternative approach to natural language query expansion in search engines: text analysis of non-topical terms in web documents. Inf. Process. Manage. **44**(4), 1503–1516 (2008). http://dx.doi.org/10.1016/j.ipm.2007.09.009

2. Fox, S.: Health topics. Technical report, Pew Internet & American Life Project (2011)

3. Gao, W., Niu, C., Nie, J.Y., Zhou, M., Wong, K.F., Hon, H.W.: Exploiting query logs for cross-lingual query suggestions. ACM Trans. Inf. Syst. **28**(2), 1–33 (2010). http://dx.doi.org/10.1145/1740592.1740594

4. Jansen, B.J., McNeese, M.D.: Evaluating the effectiveness of and patterns of interactions with automated searching assistance. J. Am. Soc. Inf. Sci. **56**(14), 1480–1503 (2005). http://dx.doi.org/10.1002/asi.20242

5. Kogan, S., Zeng, Q., Ash, N., Greenes, R.A.: Problems and challenges in patient information retrieval: a descriptive study. In: Proceedings AMIA Symposium, pp. 329–333 (2001). http://www.ncbi.nlm.nih.gov/pmc/articles/PMC2243602/

6. Kriewel, S., Fuhr, N.: Evaluation of an adaptive search suggestion system. In: Gurrin, C., He, Y., Kazai, G., Kruschwitz, U., Little, S., Roelleke, T., Rüger, S., van Rijsbergen, K. (eds.) ECIR 2010. LNCS, vol. 5993, pp. 544–555. Springer, Heidelberg (2010)

7. Lopes, C.T., Ribeiro, C.: Measuring the value of health query translation: an analysis by user language proficiency. J. Am. Soc. Inf. Sci. Technol. **64**(5), 951–963 (2013). http://dx.doi.org/10.1002/asi.22812

8. Lopes, C.T., Ribeiro, C.: Effects of Terminology on Health Queries: An Analysis by User's Health Literacy and Topic Familiarity, vol. 39, chap. 10, pp. 145–184. Emerald Group Publishing Limited (2015). http://www.emeraldinsight.com/doi/abs/10.1108/S0065-283020150000039013

9. Luo, G., Tang, C.: On iterative intelligent medical search. In: SIGIR 2008: Proceedings of the 31st Annual International ACM SIGIR Conference on Research and Development in Information Retrieval, pp. 3–10. ACM, New York (2008). http://dx.doi.org/10.1145/1390334.1390338

10. Luo, G., Tang, C., Yang, H., Wei, X.: MedSearch: a specialized search engine for medical information retrieval. In: CIKM 2008: Proceeding of the 17th ACM Conference on Information and Knowledge Mining, pp. 143–152. ACM, New York (2008). http://dx.doi.org/10.1145/1458082.1458104

11. McCray, A.T., Tse, T.: Understanding search failures in consumer health information systems. In: AMIA Annual Symposium Proceedings, pp. 430–434 (2003). http://www.ncbi.nlm.nih.gov/pmc/articles/PMC1479930/

12. NLM: 2012AA consumer health vocabulary source information (2012). http://www.nlm.nih.gov/research/umls/sourcereleasedocs/current/CHV/index.html

13. Rawson, K.A., Gunstad, J., Hughes, J., Spitznagel, M.B.B., Potter, V., Waechter, D., Rosneck, J.: The METER: a brief, self-administered measure of health literacy. J. Gen. Intern. Med. **25**(1), 67–71 (2010). http://dx.doi.org/10.1007/s11606-009-1158-7

14. Toms, E.G., Latter, C.: How consumers search for health information. Health Inform. J. **13**(3), 223–235 (2007). http://dx.doi.org/10.1177/1460458207079901

15. Zarro, M., Lin, X.: Using social tags and controlled vocabularies as filters for searching and browsing: a health science experiment. In: The Fifth Workshop on Human-Computer Interaction and Information Retrieval, October 2011

16. Zeng, Q.T., Crowell, J., Plovnick, R.M., Kim, E., Ngo, L., Dibble, E.: Assisting consumer health information retrieval with query recommendations. J. Am. Med. Inform. Assoc. JAMIA **13**(1), 80–90 (2006). http://dx.doi.org/10.1197/jamia.m1820

17. Zhang, Y.: Contextualizing consumer health information searching: an analysis of questions in a social Q&A community. In: Proceedings of the 1st ACM International Health Informatics Symposium, pp. 210–219 (2010)

18. Zielstorff, R.: Controlled vocabularies for consumer health. J. Biomed. Inform. **36**(4–5), 326–333 (2003). http://dx.doi.org/10.1016/j.jbi.2003.09.015

Predicting Contextually Appropriate Venues in Location-Based Social Networks

Jarana Manotumruksa[✉], Craig Macdonald, and Iadh Ounis

School of Computing Science, University of Glasgow, Glasgow G12 8QQ, UK
j.manotumruksa.1@research.gla.ac.uk,
{craig.macdonald,iadh.ounis}@glasgow.ac.uk

Abstract. The effective suggestion of venues that are appropriate for a user to visit is a challenging problem, as the appropriateness of a venue can depend on particular contextual *aspects*, such as the duration of the user's visit, or the composition of the user's travelling group (e.g. alone, with friends, or with family). This paper proposes a supervised approach that predicts appropriateness of venues to particular contextual aspects, by leveraging user-generated data in Location-Based Social Networks (LBSNs) such as Foursquare. Our approach learns a binary classifier for each dimension of three considered contextual aspects. A set of discriminative features are extracted from the comments, photos and website of venues. Using a dataset from the TREC 2015 Contextual Suggestion track, supplemented by venue annotations generated by crowdsourcing, we conduct a comprehensive experimental study to identify the set of features appropriate for our problem and to evaluate the effectiveness of our proposed approach. Our results demonstrate both the accuracy of our classification approach in predicting suitable contextual aspects for a venue, and its effectiveness at making better venue recommendations than the best performing system in TREC 2015.

1 Introduction

Making effective venue recommendations that a user may wish to visit relies on contextual information about the user, such as the user's location, time of visit, and previous venues visited. Dey *et al.* [7] defines context as *"any information that can be used to characterize the situation of an entity that is considered relevant to the interaction between a user and an application"*. In the *context-aware venue recommendation* (CAVR) task, the involved entity is the user, whose context can be explicitly provided by the user or implicitly detected by sensing devices (e.g. GPS location). Moreover, CAVR is a challenging task, as users may not have visited a city before, rendering collaborative filtering approaches less useful. Therefore, to suggest venues to the users, approaches for effective personalised CAVR can encompass venue features (e.g. the number of people visiting the venue (check-ins) in an LBSN), user features (e.g. the user's rating of similar venues) and contextual features (e.g. the user's location and the time of the day).

© Springer International Publishing Switzerland 2016
N. Fuhr et al. (Eds.): CLEF 2016, LNCS 9822, pp. 96–109, 2016.
DOI: 10.1007/978-3-319-44564-9_8

In this paper, we argue that by considering new aspects of context, e.g. the duration of trip, the season of the year and the group of people the users are intending to visit the venue with, we can improve the effectiveness of a personalised CAVR system. However, unlike information about a venue's category or the number of check-ins, which are easy to obtain from LBSNs, identifying the appropriateness of venues to various contextual dimensions may not be directly made from the existing metadata of the venue in the LBSNs. We propose a personalised CAVR system that can account for contextual preferences explicitly provided by users, and which operates in two phases: firstly, leveraging user-generated data from a LBSN to predict appropriate contextual dimensions for each venue, using a supervised approach; and secondly adapting a state-of-the-art venue recommendation system to account for each venue's predicted dimensions when ranking venue suggestions. Moreover, as a venue can be appropriate for multiple dimensions of a contextual aspect, e.g. a restaurant is suitable to visit at day time and night time, this problem can be addressed as a *multi-label classification* problem. Indeed, we develop classifiers for the dimensions of three contextual aspects used in the recent TREC 2015 Contextual Suggestions track: (1) *Duration*, how long a trip the user is on? (2) *Season*, when is the most suitable season the user should visit the venue? and (3) *Group*, who is the venue suitable to visit with (e.g. with family)? In particular, to the best of our knowledge, the prediction of contextual dimensions for the Group aspect for a venue is a new problem that has not been addressed in previous works. Later, we show how to effectively integrate the proposed dimension classifiers as features within a CAVR system based upon learning-to-rank. In tackling this problem, this paper's contributions are as follows: (1) a learned approach that can predict appropriate contextual dimensions for a venue, based on different types of features, namely *temporal features* extracted from the venue's comments and photos on the LBSN, as well as *term-based features* extracted from the comments about the venue and the textual contents of the venue's website; (2) a demonstration of the usefulness of taking contextual aspects into account during venue ranking, based upon a TREC 2015 dataset. Indeed, the experimental results demonstrate the accuracy of our classification approach in predicting suitable contextual aspects for a venue and its effectiveness at making better venue recommendations than the best performing systems participating in TREC 2015.

2   Related Work

Various existing works have shown that leveraging user-generated data in LBSNs can significantly enhance the effectiveness of context-aware venue recommendation (CAVR) systems (e.g. [5,6,14]). Yuan *et al.* [14] developed a collaborative *time-aware venue recommendation* that suggests venues to users at a specific time of the day. In particular, they mined historical check-ins of users in LBSNs to enable personalised venue recommendations using a time-aware collaborative filtering approach. Deveaud *et al.* [6] made time-aware venue recommendations by forecasting the popularity of nearby venues in the immediate future. However, all these approaches only considered the user's location and the time of the day as context when making venue recommendations. Recently, Hashem *et al.* [9] proposed an approach that recommends a sequence of venues to visit to users, which aims to optimise recommendation quality based on constraints (i.e. number of people, travelling time and distances). In contrast, we propose an approach that applies a learning to rank technique to recommend venues to users by considering multiple contextual aspects such as duration of the trip and type of the group the user like to travel with, rather than the number of users who are joining the trip.

Previous works on CAVR [13,14] used check-in data from LBSNs to evaluate the effectiveness of their recommendation systems, by assuming that users implicitly like the venues they visited. However such data may not be appropriate to evaluate CAVR systems because check-in data do not explicitly express the users' contextual preferences. Indeed, research into CAVR has been boosted by the TREC Contextual Suggestion track [4]. This track aims to investigate search techniques for complex information needs that are highly dependent on the users' contexts and interests. In particular, the task addressed by the track is as follows: given the user's preferences (ratings of venues) and context (user's location), produce a ranked list of venue suggestions for each user-context pair. Moreover, in TREC 2015 [4], new contextual aspects were proposed. Additional contextual dimensions are provided by each user for each aspect: namely the duration and season of their trip, the type of trip (holiday, business etc.) and type of group the user is travelling with. Our work directly proposes an accurate modelling of the appropriateness of venues w.r.t. the aspects proposed in TREC 2015.

A few participants in TREC 2015 attempted to explicitly model the contextual appropriateness of the venues. Indeed, as the best performing participant, Aliannejadi *et al.* [2] proposed a system that learns the user's positive and negative profiles for the venues in the user's preferences, based on the positive and negative comments and categories defined by different LBSNs of the venues. However, they do not explicitly model the user's preferences in terms of aspects of contextual preference. McCreadie *et al.* [10] is the most similar to our own work in that they also examine the timestamps of photos and comments from an LBSN, but without using such evidence to predict the appropriate dimensions of context for a venue. In contrast, we propose to predict the contextual appropriateness of a venue (Sect. 3), by leveraging the photos and comments about the venue, as well as the content of the venue's website (Sect. 4). We later show how this can be used in making better context-aware venue recommendations (Sect. 6).

3   Problem Statement

We now define the problem of predicting the appropriate contextual dimensions for a venue. Firstly, let V be a set of venues $\{v_1, \ldots, v_n\}$ and A be a set of contextual aspects about which users may express explicit requirements for relevant venue suggestions. In this work, we focus upon three contextual aspects proposed within the TREC 2015 Contextual Suggestions track [4], namely the *Duration* and *Season* of the user's visit, and the *Group* that the user intends to visit the

Table 1. The 10 dimensions of the contextual aspects that we consider in this work.

Aspect	Dimension	Description
Duration	Day Time	Is a venue suitable to visit between 6:00 AM – 6:00 PM?
	Night Time	Is a venue suitable to visit between 6:00 PM – 6:00 AM?
	Weekend	Is a venue suitable to visit on weekend?
Season	Spring	Is a venue suitable to visit between March and May?
	Summer	Is a venue suitable to visit between June and August?
	Autumn	Is a venue suitable to visit between September and November?
	Winter	Is a venue suitable to visit between December and February?
Group	Alone	Is a venue suitable to visit alone?
	Friends	Is a venue suitable to visit with friends?
	Family	Is a venue suitable to visit with family?

venue with. Associated with each contextual aspect $a \in A$ is a set of dimensions, $a = \{d_{a,1} \ldots d_{a,m}\}$. Table 1 describes the dimensions for each of the contextual aspects. Therefore, the problem of predicting the appropriate contextual dimensions for a venue can be defined as follows: for a given venue v_i, predict the members of the set D_i, where D_i is the set of all contextual dimensions that the venue is appropriate for, i.e. $D_i = \{d|d \in a, \forall a \in A\}$. Indeed, each venue may be appropriate to multiple dimensions for a given contextual aspect, e.g. for the Season and Duration aspects, a park might be suitable to visit in the Spring or Summer, and only during the day time. We assume that each dimension is independent, e.g. a bar can be open both during the day and at night. Therefore, we formulate our problem as a *multi-label classification* problem and apply the most widely-used method by considering the prediction of each dimension as an independent binary classification problem, i.e. for a venue v_i, each $d \in D_i$ is identified by a binary classifier $h_d : v_i \rightarrow \{d, \neg d\}$.

4   Contextual Aspect Features

In this section, we describe our proposed approach that predicts the dimensions of contextual aspects that are appropriate for each venue. Our approach is based upon the definition and extraction of categorical and temporal features (Sect. 4.1) as well as textual features (Sect. 4.2) that are suitable for training the 10 binary classifiers, i.e. one for each dimension of the contextual aspects in Table 1.

4.1   Categorical and Temporal Features

Intuitively, due to the different activities offered by each venue, different venues generally exhibit different temporal characteristics e.g. a venue such as a bar is more suitable to be visited at night time, while a venue such as a park is more suitable to visit during the day. Such intuitions can be used to extract *temporal features* for each venue. In LBSNs, users can upload photos taken at a venue they are visiting or write a comment to review the venue they have visited. The timestamps of comments (photos) and the venue's metadata (e.g. venue's categories) can be leveraged to extract discriminative features for each venue, which will be used to train our binary classifiers.

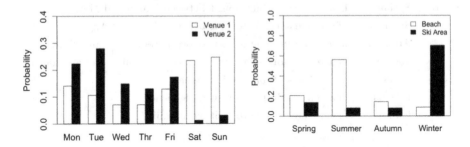

Fig. 1. Distribution of timestamps over different time patterns

In terms of notation, each venue v_i has a set of associated comments $R_i = \{r_1 \ldots r_n\}$, and photos $P_i = \{p_1 \ldots p_m\}$, as well as a set of categories $\Theta_i = \{\tau_1 \ldots \tau_n\}$ and a website W_{v_i}. Both a photo p_j and a comment r_k are represented as a tuple $\langle u, v, t, content \rangle$, indicating that the photo or comment is generated by user u at venue v at time t, where *content* represents the actual image of the photo or the text of the comment. The time t (e.g. "2015-02-15 15:45:22") that either the photo or comment was generated is represented as a *time-slot*, for instance as a specific hour of the day (15:00), a day of the week (Sunday) or a month of the year (February). $TS_m(t)$ is a function that returns *time-slot* w.r.t. the specific *time-slot* granularity m, e.g. this function can be chosen to produce a time slot for each hour of the day, i.e. $TS_{hour}(t) \in \{0, 1, \ldots, 23\}$. From now on, the term timestamps is equally applicable to the timestamps of comments or photo, unless otherwise specified. Next, we propose to extract *category features* and *temporal features* for the Duration and Season aspects, based on the venue's metadata and the timestamps of photos or comments uploaded by LBSN users.

Category Features ($f1$, $f2$): Intuitively, venues belonging to a similar category likely share similar contextual appropriateness to each other. $f1$ is a feature indicating the category membership of a venue within the 10 top-level Foursquare categories[1]. Similarly $f2$ represents the membership of the 147 low-level Foursquare categories.

Temporal Venue-based Feature ($f3$): The timing of visits by users to venues differs and can be indicative of its appropriateness to different contexts, e.g. a venue mostly visited at weekend is less likely to be appropriate for a weekday. Figure 1(a) provides an example of the distribution of timestamps of 2 venues

---

[1] https://developer.foursquare.com/categorytree.

over the days of the week, demonstrating that the venues exhibit different temporal characteristics. Hence, for a given venue v_i, we calculate the maximum likelihood probability of observing comments (or photos) with a timestamp that is appropriate for a dimension d of a time-based aspect (Duration or Season), $p(v_i|d) = \frac{\sum_{j \in R_i}^n AT(TS_d(j),d)}{|R_i|}$, where R_i (P_i) is the set of comments (photos) for venue v_i, and $AT(.)$ is a function that returns 1 if timestamp j is appropriate to a given contextual dimension d, 0 otherwise, based on the time descriptions listed in Table 1.

Temporal Category-based Features ($f4,f5$): $f3$ suffers from a sparsity problem – as most venues in our dataset have a small number of comments/photos in the LBSN – thereby hindering the accuracy of a classifier using this feature. To alleviate this problem, we assume that similar venues share similar contextual behaviour, e.g. all ski park venues are more likely to be appropriate to visit in winter rather than in summer, while all beaches are more suitable to visit in summer (this can be seen in Fig. 1(b)). In particular, we calculate the likelihood at the level of a category τ, $P(c|\lambda) = \frac{\sum_{v_i \in V} P(v_i|\tau) \cdot P(v_i|\lambda)}{\sum_{v_i \in V} P(v_i|\tau)}$, where $P(v_i|\tau)$ is a binary function denoting if venue v_i belongs to the given category τ (1 if true, 0 otherwise). Note that we consider as separate features the distribution of top-level ($f4$) and low-level ($f5$) Foursquare categories.

4.2   Term-Based Features

Unlike the *temporal features* described above, we cannot use timestamps to infer the appropriateness of a venue for dimensions of the Group aspect. In this section, we describe our term-based features for the Group aspect that score occurrences of appropriate terms within two sources of evidence, the websites and the comments of venues.

Web-based Term Feature ($f6$): Intuitively, if a venue wishes to attract a particular audience, its website will contains terms related to the corresponding dimension(s) of the Group aspect. For instance, a restaurant website that contains "family deals" in its menu section is likely to be appropriate to visit with family. To illustrate this, Fig. 2 shows how terms relating to each dimension of the Group aspect occur within two venues that we have identified as suitable for Family and Friends respectively. Indeed, from the figure, it can be seen that the website of a venue suitable for a family group exhibits a higher frequency of terms relating to that dimension than a venue suitable for friends does, and vice versa. Therefore, the occurrence of terms corresponding to each dimension of the Group aspect in a venue's website is likely to be a useful feature for predicting the appropriate Group dimensions of venues. To extract discriminative features for the dimensions of the Group aspect, we collect terms related to each dimension from an external web resource[2]. We then index the websites of venues (extracted from the venue metadata using a standard IR system, and issue to the

---

[2] http://www.enchantedlearning.com/wordlist/.

system a query Q_d consisting of a set of terms corresponding to the dimension of context d. Finally, we use the system's retrieval score of each venue's website for each dimension of context as a single feature, $P_{term}(v_i|d) \propto score(Q_d, W_{v_i})$, where Q_d is a query consisting of the set of terms related to the given dimension d of the Group aspect, W_{v_i} is the website of venue v_i and $score(.)$ is a standard retrieval model. Hence, the higher score the more likely the venue is suitable for the dimension of contextual aspect.

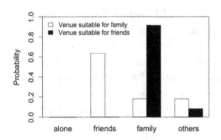

Fig. 2. The distribution of term frequency of two venues on the Group aspect.

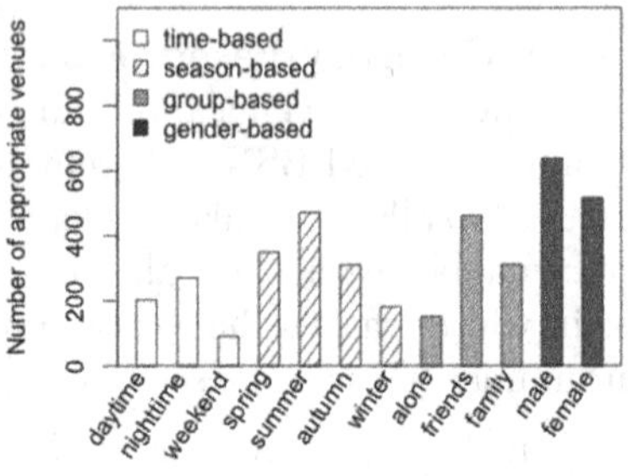

Fig. 3. The distribution of appropriate venues for each dimension of contextual aspects in crowdsourcing dataset.

Comment-based Term Features $(f7, f8)$**:** These features are defined similarly to $f6$, except that the comments for each venue are indexed, instead of the venue's website. However, users may vary in the sentiments they express in their comments about venues they have visited. Ignoring these sentiments may hinder the classification performance. For instance, a venue that contains a negative comment like *"I was disappointed that there were no small chairs for children"* will obtain a high retrieval score since its comment contains family-related terms, although this venue is likely not appropriate to the Family dimension. To tackle this limitation, we use the SentiStrength [12] sentiment analysis tool, which was developed for short user-generated content such as tweets, to classify all of the comments of the venues into three different classes: positive, negative, and neutral. We then separately index the positive and negative comments for each venue, while ignoring the neutral comments. Features $f7$ and $f8$ are calculated as for $f6$, but for the the positive and negative comments, respectively. Next, we evaluate the accuracy of our proposed contextual dimension classifiers (Sect. 5). Later, in Sect. 6, we show that learned ranking approach with contextual features generated from our proposed classifiers can significantly outperform the best TREC participants.

5   Venue Dimension Classification Evaluation

In this section, we evaluate the accuracy of the classifiers through answering two research questions: **(RQ1)** Can we exploit the distribution of timestamps of photos or comments to predict appropriate contextual aspects for venues for the Duration and Season aspects? **(RQ2)** Can we leverage the terms occurring in either the venue's website or comments to predict the appropriate dimensions of the Group aspect for venues?

5.1 Crowdsourcing Venue Annotations

We use crowdsourcing to obtain ground truth data by asking workers to annotate the dimensions of context suitable to venues. We randomly select 746 venues from the TREC Contextual Suggestion 2015 test collection. We use the Crowd-Flower[3] crowdsourcing platform, asking workers to annotate the applicable contextual dimensions for each venue, based upon representative information of each venue extracted from the Foursquare LBSN. In particular, for each venue, the worker views the venue's title, category, an image and two randomly-selected comments, and uses check-boxes to indicate appropriateness for each contextual dimension. Following best practices for crowdsourcing [1], and to ensure the quality of the obtained ground truth data, we ask three different workers to label each venue, resulting in 2,238 judgements, for a total cost of US$31[4]. The distribution of judgements for each dimension is shown in Fig. 3. The final annotations are derived by choosing the dimensions of context that the maximum number of workers agreed upon, e.g. if 2 workers agree that a venue is suitable to visit in Spring and Summer while 1 worker considers that the venue is suitable to visit in Winter, the final ground truth dimensions for that venue are Spring and Summer.

5.2 Experimental Setup

Learning Algorithms. We use the Weka machine learning software [8] for training and predicting contextual dimensions. We explore the effectiveness of our classifiers using 3 classification algorithms: Naive Bayes, J48, and SVM. All classification experiments are conducted using a 10-fold cross-validation on the crowdsourcing dataset.

Retrieval Models. To extract the *term-based features* $f6 - f8$, we index the venues' websites and comments using v4.0 of the Terrier platform[5] and use BM25 for calculating $score(.,.)$. While other standard weighting models can be used, initial experiments found that our conclusions are not changed by the choice of weighting models.

Evaluation Measure and Baseline. We report the accuracy of our contextual dimension classifiers for each dimension in terms of the F_1 classification measure. As the problem of contextual dimension classification has never been addressed before, and as the nature of our dataset is imbalanced across the class labels of each

---

[3] http://crowdflower.com.

[4] Our crowdsourced venue annotations are freely available from http://dx.doi.org/10.5525/gla.researchdata.325.

[5] http://terrier.org/.

dimension, we compare our proposed approach with a baseline that classifies each venue as the majority class for each dimension (denoted as Majority), i.e. for all dimensions except weekend, the majority class would be 'appropriate' (see Fig. 3).

5.3   Experimental Results

Firstly, Table 2 reports the accuracy, in term of F_1, of contextual dimension classification using different classification algorithms learned with all features across the Duration, Season and Group aspects. For brevity, we report mean F_1 across all dimensions for a given aspect. Recall that our Majority baseline is where all instances in the test set for a given dimension are classified as the majority class. For this table, we use a default experimental setting, which we vary below: we use timestamps from the comments to extract the time-based features ($f4$ & $f5$). Indeed, Table 2 shows that Naive Bayes significantly outperforms both J48 and SVM in predicting the appropriate dimensions for venues across all aspects. The high effectiveness of Naive Bayes when trained with a small dataset is also supported by the literature, e.g. [3]. Hence, in the remainder of our analysis and experiments, we focus solely upon the Naive Bayes classifier.

Table 2. F_1 accuracy of contextual dimension classification using different classification algorithms. Δ differences denoted by ** exhibit significant decreases (McNemar's test, $p < 0.01$) compared to Naive Bayes.

F_1	Duration	Season	Group	Mean	Δ
Majority	0.481	0.488	0.541	0.503	
Naive Bayes	**0.680**	**0.573**	**0.574**	**0.609**	
J48	0.602	0.542	0.548	0.564	-7.88 %**
SVM	0.482	0.489	0.542	0.504	-11.97 %**

Next, Table 3 reports the classification accuracy in terms of F_1 for each dimension of the Duration and Season aspects, for each source of evidence (comments or photos). The top part of the table reports effectiveness when using only the Majority class (our baseline) as well as when all features ($f1$–$f5$) are used for these aspects (denoted All). On analysing this part of the table, we note firstly that the F_1 scores are markedly higher than the Majority class baseline. Moreover, while effectiveness is slightly higher when using the timestamps of photos for the Duration aspect, the timestamps of comments are overall more effective, providing more valuable evidence for the Season aspect. This fits with our intuition of the mobile-phone based use of the Foursquare LBSN: users are likely to upload photos when they are currently attending the venue. In contrast, comments are often left after the user has visited the venue, perhaps reflecting on a good or bad time he/she had at the venue. This makes the timestamps of comments less useful for accurately predicting the appropriate dimensions of the Duration aspect.

Table 3. Classification accuracy in terms of F_1, for each source of evidence (comments or photos), for each dimension of the Duration and Season contextual aspects. Majority denotes classification using only the majority class, while All denotes all features. Feature groups from All are ablated. Best performances for each dimension are highlighted in bold. Values denoted by * and ** exhibit significant differences (McNemar's test where $p < 0.05$ and 0.01 resp.) compared to All features for each source of evidence.

F_1		Duration			Season					
		day time	night time	weekend	spring	summer	autumn	winter	Mean	Δ
Majority		0.342	0.465	0.638	0.382	0.642	0.342	0.588	0.486	
All	comments	0.628	0.689	**0.723**	**0.532**	**0.656**	**0.563**	**0.604**	**0.627**	
	photos	**0.644**	**0.695**	0.72	0.502	0.538	0.532	0.525	0.595	
Ablation										
-$f1$	comments	0.615	0.691	0.717	0.521	0.652	0.530	0.598	0.618	-1.59 %
	photos	0.635	0.700	0.725	0.496	0.536	0.531	0.517	0.591	-0.670 %**
-$f2$	comments	0.598	0.676	0.711	0.514	0.649	0.530	0.612	0.613	-2.39 %**
	photos	0.634	0.699	0.722	0.462	0.493	0.518	0.451	0.568	-4.54 %**
-$f3$	comments	0.611	0.696	0.720	0.527	0.664	0.549	0.609	0.625	-0.48 %
	photos	0.653	0.687	0.732	0.494	0.513	0.509	0.486	0.582	-2.18 %**
-$f4$	comments	0.645	0.672	0.720	0.541	0.649	0.491	0.61	0.618	-1.59 %
	photos	0.630	0.687	0.724	0.519	0.661	0.547	0.529	0.614	3.19 %*
-$f5$	comments	0.619	0.690	0.701	0.505	0.643	0.578	0.604	0.620	-1.27 %
	photos	0.644	0.693	0.729	0.504	0.649	0.571	0.638	0.633	6.39 %**

The second part of Table 3, denoted Ablation, reports F_1 when groups of features are ablated (removed) from All features, with the column Δ reporting the mean increase or decrease compared to the corresponding classifier using All features. In general, the largest decreases in effectiveness are obtained when the low-level category information $f2$ is removed from the features used by the dimension classifiers, showing that detailed knowledge of the venue category can be informative in accurately predicting the appropriate dimensions for venues. Features $f3$ (for photos) and $f4 - f5$ (for comments) are also shown to be important, but comparatively less so.

For the Group aspect, Table 4 follows a similar layout to Table 3. In the top part of the table, we report the F_1 classification effectiveness for All applicable features for this aspect (namely $f1$, $f2$, $f6$, $f7$, $f8$). Recall that $f6 - f8$ are *term-based features*, extracted from venue's website, positive comments and negative comments, respectively. In Table 4, we observe that this contextual aspect represents a more difficult classification problem, where the majority class is comparatively strong (Mean F_1 0.542 over the three dimensions). The results show that, on average, our classifiers are more effective than the majority in predicting the appropriateness of venues for the group aspect.

Next, the second part of Table 4 reports different combinations of features, starting with the categorical features $f1$ & $f2$ alone, and then adding $f6 - f8$ (each calculated using BM25) in turn. We observe that the F_1 scores for the combination of features are overall higher than for the All features, suggesting that more data would be required to obtain the most effective model. Moreover, among the *term-based features* $f6 - f8$, $f7$, which is calculated using the positive comments offers the highest improvement over $f1$ & $f2$ for the alone dimension. For

Table 4. For the Group aspect, the table reports F_1 for different feature combinations, as well as Δ w.r.t. F_1 score of All, where * exhibit significant increase (McNemar's test, $p < 0.01$).

Features	Alone	Friends	Family	Mean	Δ
Majority	0.576	0.667	0.382	0.542	
All	0.600	0.564	0.557	0.574	
$f1$ & $f2$	0.644	0.700	**0.594**	0.65	11.20 %*
+ $f6$	0.661	**0.709**	0.590	**0.653**	12.19 %*
+ $f7$	**0.671**	0.695	0.575	0.647	11.33 %*
+ $f8$	0.668	0.673	0.580	0.640	10.41 %*

friend dimension, the textual contents of the website, $f6$, offers the largest margin of improvement. Overall, the general trend across all rows in the bottom part of Table 4 is that the textual evidence from the websites is more important than the positive comments ($f7$), which is in turn more important than the negative comments ($f8$). This surprising result can be explained in that the comments are sparse in comparison with venues' websites. Indeed, the number of tokens indexed from websites and comments index are 17,138,495 and 1,515,640, respectively.

To summarise, our findings for research question **RQ1** were that the *temporal features* - based on the timestamps of the comments and photos for each venue - can be useful for creating accurate classifiers for the Duration and Season aspects (as shown in Table 3). For **RQ2**, we find that textual evidence found on the websites of the venues is the most useful on average for predicting the appropriate dimensions of the Group aspect.

6   Ranking Contextually Appropriate Venues

In this section, we describe how we improve the effectiveness of a CAVR system using our contextual dimension classifiers trained on *temporal features* extracted from the timestamps of comments and *term-based features* extracted from venue websites.

Firstly, we formally describe the venue recommendation scenario of the TREC 2015 Contextual Suggestion track [4] in which our evaluation is conducted. Rankings in the Contextual Suggestion track are created in response to a user-context pair, denoted $\langle U_j, C_j \rangle$ (and which can be thought as a "query"). A user's profile consists of a set of venue preferences, denoted as $U_j = \{v_i \rightarrow p_{i,j}, \ldots\}$, where $p_{i,j}$ is the user's preference rating (1 to 5) for venue v_i. The context C_j contains a number of contextual preferences in terms of the dimensions of interest to this work: $C_j = \{d\}$. As only one dimension can be expressed for each of the aspects listed in Table 1, $|C_j| = |A| \leq 3$.

Given a set of dimensions preferences C_j (e.g. $\{Weekend, Summer, Alone\}$) expressed by the user, we now describe how we integrate the outcome of our dimension classifiers into the ranking approach of a CAVR system. Firstly, following recent work in creating personalised venue suggestions [5], we adopt a learning to rank approach to take into account different sources of evidence when ranking venues, by making use of features about the venue, $\mathcal{F}(v_i)$ and features representing how the venue matches the users interests, $\mathcal{F}(v_i, U_j)$, (e.g. a cosine similarity between the categories of the venue v_i and the categories of the venues rated positively in U_j). Moreover, we encompass the expressed contextual preferences as one numerical feature for each aspect, denoting the confidence of classifier that the venue is appropriate for dimension $d \in C_j$:

$$\mathcal{F}(v_i, C_j) = \bigcup_{a \in A} \begin{cases} h_d(v_i) & \text{if } d \in C_j \wedge d \in a, \\ 0 & \text{otherwise} \end{cases} \tag{1}$$

where $h_d(v_i)$ is the *confidence* of the classifier for dimension d that venue v_i is appropriate for d. Note that not all user-context pairs express a contextual dimension for each aspect. Hence, when no dimensions of contextual aspect a are present in C_j, the classifier confidence for that aspect a is replaced by 0, therefore $\forall C_j, |\mathcal{F}(v_i, C_j)| = 3$.

6.1   Experimental Setup

In the following, we address a final research question: (**RQ3**) Can our proposed dimension classifiers improve the effectiveness of a state-of-the-art CAVR system? Our experiments make use of the TREC 2015 Contextual Suggestion track test collection. As our venue ranking features rely on information about the venue from Foursquare, we only consider venues in the TREC test collection that originated from Foursquare. Our baselines are the two best approaches from TREC 2015, mentioned in Sect. 2 (namely uogTr [10], USI [2]). For a fair comparison, we also remove venues suggested by these TREC participants that did not originate from Foursquare, as well as any users in the test collection who did not explicitly express any contextual preferences (i.e. $|C_j| = 0$). This results in 194 user-context pairs in the collection (down from 211 pairs).

As a basis for our experiments, we use a personalised CAVR system based upon learning to rank – similar to that of Deveaud *et al.* [5] – building upon the Automatic Feature Selection (AFS) [11] technique that creates a linear learned model. This model is trained on the 60 venue preferences of all users – as these are separate from the test venues, this represents a clear separation between training and test environments. We report the effectiveness using the measures reported in the track overview paper [4], namely Precision@5 (P@5) and mean reciprocal rank (MRR). For each venue, we calculate a total of 11 venue ranking features, namely 6 venue features ($\mathcal{F}(v_i)$): number of check-ins, number of likes, number of comments, number of photos, average Foursquare rating, unique number of users - all obtained from the Foursquare API, 2 user-venue features ($\mathcal{F}(v_i, U_j)$): cosine similarity between the categories of the venue v_i and the categories of the venues rated by the user in his/her profile U_j – one feature for positive-rated venues, and one for negative-rated venues, and 3 contextual features ($\mathcal{F}(v_i, C_j)$): Classifier confidences for the dimensions expressed by the user in C_j.

6.2 Experimental Results

Table 5 indicates the sources of evidence considered by each of the systems in terms of user-venue preferences (denoted as User), venue information (Venue), and contextual sources of evidence (Context). The first part of Table 5 shows the effectiveness of the learned model obtained from AFS using all 11 venue ranking features (denoted All), as well as when different feature groups have been ablated. In this table, we observe that the best overall results are achieved by the model trained with All features. Moreover, ablating the contextual features generated by our 10 dimension classifiers causes a decrease in P@5 (-2.45 %), showing the importance of these features in an effective ranking model. We also observe the same significant decrease in effectiveness (upto 11 %) when venue features are removed, also reported by Deveaud *et al.* [5].

Table 5. The effectiveness of learned CAVR using different features, in comparison with the 2 best TREC 2015 Contextual Suggestion track systems. The performances denoted * exhibit significant decreases in effectiveness (paired t-test, $p < 0.05$) compared to the All feature.

	User	Venue	Context	P@5	Δ	MRR	Δ
TREC Median	-	-	-	0.5090		0.6716	
AFS (All)	✓	✓	✓	**0.6020**		**0.7858**	
AFS (VC)	×	✓	✓	0.6010	-0.17 %	0.7827	-0.40 %
AFS (UC)	✓	×	✓	0.5443*	-10.60 %	0.7394*	-6.28 %
AFS (UV)	✓	✓	×	0.5876	-2.45 %	0.7800	-0.74 %
uogTr	✓	✓	✓	0.5742*	4.84 %	0.7584	3.61 %
USI	✓	✓	×	0.5722	5.21 %	0.7494	4.86 %

Next, we compare the effectiveness of the learned CAVR models with the two best performing systems in the TREC 2015 Contextual Suggestion track. We find that the AFS model trained with All features outperforms the best TREC 2015 participants, for both P@5 and MRR. Note that without our proposed contextual features (AFS (UV)), our CAVR system would have not significantly outperformed uogTr approach. Indeed, while the uogTr is similar to ours, it does not deployed learned classifiers for identifying contextual appropriateness of venues. Hence, for **RQ3**, we find that our proposed classifiers can markedly enhance an CAVR system and can significantly outperform the best participating TREC 2015 system in terms of P@5 and MRR.

7 Conclusions

In this paper, we proposed classifiers that can predict the appropriateness of venues to contextual dimensions, and showed how they could be successfully integrated into a state-of-the-art CAVR system. Our results showed not only that dimensions can be accurately predicted, but that by considering the new dimensions of context, the quality of venue recommendation can be significantly enhanced. Moreover, we found that textual contents of venue's website is more suitable than comments about the venue on an LBSN for identifying if the venue is suitable to visit under different dimensions of the Group aspect, while the temporal characteristics of venues can be successfully captured using the timestamps of comments or photos. A direction for future research will encapsulate the modelling of dependencies between aspects of contextual dimensions.

References

1. Aker, A., El-Haj, M., Albakour, M.D., Kruschwitz, U.: Assessing crowdsourcing quality through objective tasks. In: Proceedings of LREC. ELRA (2012)
2. Aliannejadi, M., Bahrainian, S.A., Giachanou, A., Crestani, F.: Univ of Lugano at TREC 2015: contextual suggestion and temporal summarization tracks. In: Proceedings of TREC (2015)
3. Brain, D., Webb, G.: The need for low bias algorithms in classification learning from large data sets. In: Proceedings of PKDD (2002)
4. Dean-Hall, A., Kamps, J., Kiseleva, J., Voorhees, E.: Overview of the TREC 2015 contextual suggestion track. In: Proceedings of TREC (2015)
5. Deveaud, R., Albakour, M.D., Macdonald, C., Ounis, I.: On the importance of venue-dependent features for learning to rank contextual suggestions. In: Proceedings of CIKM (2014)
6. Deveaud, R., Albakour, M.D., Macdonald, C., Ounis, I.: Experiments with a venue-centric model for personalised and time-aware venue suggestion. In: Proceedings of CIKM (2015)
7. Dey, A.K., Abowd, G.D., Salber, D.: A conceptual framework and a toolkit for supporting the rapid prototyping of context-aware applications. Hum. Comput. Interact. **16**(2–4), 97–166 (2001)
8. Hall, M., Frank, E., Holmes, G., Pfahringer, B., Reutemann, P., Witten, I.H.: The WEKA data mining software: an update. ACM SIGKDD Explor. Newsl. **11**(1), 10–18 (2009)
9. Hashem, T., Barua, S., Ali, M.E., Kulik, L., Tanin, E.: Efficient computation of trips with friends and families. In: Proceedings of CIKM (2015)
10. McCreadie, R., Vargas, S., Macdonald, C., Ounis, I., Mackie, S., Manotumruksa, J., McDonald, G.: Univ of Glasgow at TREC 2015: experiments with Terrier in contextual suggestion, temporal summarisation and dynamic domain tracks. In: Proceedings of TREC (2015)
11. Metzler, D.A.: Automatic feature selection in the markov random field model for information retrieval. In: Proceedings of CIKM (2007)
12. Thelwall, M., Buckley, K., Paltoglou, G.: Sentiment strength detection for the social web. JASIS&T **63**(1), 163–173 (2012)
13. Yao, L., Sheng, Q.Z., Qin, Y., Wang, X., Shemshadi, A., He, Q.: Context-aware point-of-interest recommendation using tensor factorization with social regularization. In: Proceedings of SIGIR (2015)
14. Yuan, Q., Cong, G., Ma, Z., Sun, A., Thalmann, N.M.: Time-aware point-of-interest recommendation. In: Proceedings of SIGIR (2013)

I, Me, Mine: The Role of Personal Phrases in Author Profiling

Rosa María Ortega-Mendoza[1,2(✉)], Anilú Franco-Arcega[1],
Adrián Pastor López-Monroy[3], and Manuel Montes-y-Gómez[3]

[1] Universidad Autónoma del Estado de Hidalgo (UAEH), Pachuca, Mexico
{or300944,afranco}@uaeh.edu.mx, mortega@itesa.edu.mx
[2] Instituto Tecnológico Superior del Oriente del Estado de Hidalgo (ITESA),
Apan, Mexico
[3] Instituto Nacional de Astrofísica, Óptica y Electrónica (INAOE), Cholula, Mexico
{pastor,mmontesg}@inaoep.mx

Abstract. The Author Profiling (AP) task aims to distinguish between groups of authors labeled by a common demographic characteristic such as gender or age by studying the language usage. In this work we studied the role of personal phrases (i.e., sentences containing first person pronouns) for the AP task. We support the idea that people better expose their personal interests and writing style when they talk about themselves and, consequently, that words near to a personal pronoun reveal valuable information for the classification of authors. The evaluation using different social media data showed that phrases containing *singular first person pronouns* are highly valuable for predicting the age and gender of users. Considering only these phrases we obtained reductions of up to 60 % of the information in the user documents and a comparable classification performance than using all available data. In addition, the results obtained by personal phrases considerably outperformed those from non-personal sentences, indicating their greater suitability for the AP task. We consider these findings could be further applied in the design of strategies for the construction of AP corpora, novel feature selection methods, as well as new feature and instance weighting schemes.

Keywords: Author profiling · Personal pronouns · Topics · Writing style

1 Introduction

In Natural Language Processing, the Author Profiling (AP) task consists in analyzing texts in order to extract as much information as possible from their authors [11]. Its aim is to predict general or demographic attributes that integrate authors' profiles such as: gender [2,11,12,31], age [2,12,20,31], personality [1,32], native language [2], political orientation [21], among others. Recently, because of the variety of its applications, AP has gained a lot of interest. For example, in marketing, companies leverage online reviews to improve targeted

© Springer International Publishing Switzerland 2016
N. Fuhr et al. (Eds.): CLEF 2016, LNCS 9822, pp. 110–122, 2016.
DOI: 10.1007/978-3-319-44564-9_9

advertising, and in forensics, the linguistic profile of authors could be used as valuable additional evidence.

AP is supported on the idea that documents are the major medium by which people communicate their knowledge and express their thoughts and opinions. It also considers that word usage patterns extracted from these documents expose people interests and writing style, which in turn, could reveal valuable information for their automatic profiling. Broadly speaking, AP has been approached as a single-label classification problem using machine learning algorithms [33]. In this context, most of the work has been devoted to determine useful textual features to model the writing profile of authors [1,11,28,31]. According to the literature two kinds of features are the most relevant: thematic features, mainly captured by nouns, verbs and adjectives, and stylistic features, e.g., function words, punctuation marks, and POS tags [14].

In this work, rather than define a suitable set of features for AP, we focus on studying the relevance of sentences containing first person pronouns, which we refer as *personal phrases*. Our interest in this kind of phrases is motivated by recent works in social psychology, which have demonstrated that pronouns and prepositions reveal important information about the linguistic profile of an author [22], and also people tend to be more honest when they write about themselves [19]. Based on these findings, we hypothesize that words around personal pronouns better expose the thematic interests and writing style of authors, and therefore that they could reveal valuable information for their classification. Accordingly, the research questions we aim to answer are:

- Are all the information in a document equally relevant for AP? Particularly, are personal phrases more discriminating than others?
- Are the personal phrases containing singular and plural first person pronouns equally useful for AP? Are they complementary or redundant?
- Do personal phrases better expose the writing style or the thematic interests of authors?
- Are personal phrases equally relevant in different social media domains?

To answer these questions we evaluated the prediction of users' age and gender in different social media domains. Our study shows that personal phrases can be considered the *essence of documents*[1] for the AP task [16]. We mainly found that focusing on the subset of personal phrases, it is possible to get reductions of up to 60 % of the information in the user documents, while maintaining the classification performance. Our findings have significant implications for future work in AP, since they can lead to the design of new feature selection and weighting methods as well as to the development of alternative strategies for the construction of AP corpora.

The rest of the paper is organized as follows. Section 2 describes some previous works in AP, making special emphasis on psychological motivated

---

[1] In this context, documents are commonly referred to as *user profiles* or *user histories*, and they correspond to all textual information generated by a user, for example, all posts from her blog or the set of tweets from her account.

approaches. Section 3 presents the corpora used in the experiments, whereas Sect. 4 describes our experimental methodology. Section 5 presents the experiments and results in different social media. Finally, Sect. 6 depicts our conclusions and some future work directions.

2   Related Work

There are several works for AP in social media [21,31,32]. These works have mainly proposed different document representations, which combine several kinds of features [24]. For example, Argamon et al. [2] used content and style features to identify the age, gender, native language and neuroticism level of authors. Mukherjee and Liu [17] studied the classification of blogs by gender using POS patterns as features. Other proposals include the use of stylometrics characteristics. For example, Goswami et al. [9] predicted age and gender of blogs' authors by means of slang words and the length of sentences. Rangel and Rosso [25] used style features such as the frequency of capital letters, words length, and number of words with flooded characters (e.g. Heeeellooo). Meina et al. [15] have studied structural features such as the number of sentences, words, paragraphs, special characters, among others. On the other hand, there are some works that have also explored the use of sociolinguistic features to determine the age and gender of authors [29]. This kind of features aims to capture, for example, the communication behavior (e.g. retweet frequency) and the network characteristics (e.g. number of followers and friends) of social media users.

From a psychological perspective, some recent works have shown that language carries information about our feelings, emotions [26,27], and opinions [34], and that function words are the most revealing [4,22]. For example, the frequent use of singular first person pronouns is related to: young people [23], female [2,18], low social status [10], and depression [30]. Furthermore, it has been found that people tend to use this kind of pronouns when they tell the truth [19]. In other words, the use of self-references such as "I", "me", "my" and "mine" are strongly related to the expression of people's feelings, concerns and opinions.

These previous works have demonstrated the usefulness of pronouns as features for characterizing the author of a document. This paper goes a step forward by studying the role of personal phrases in AP across different social media domains. We consider that words around personal pronouns better expose the thematic interests and writing style of social media users, and that this subset of phrases could be considered as the essence of the documents for the AP task.

3   Social Media Datasets

For the majority of the experiments we used the corpus gathered by Schler et al. [31][2]. This corpus is a collection of blogs from blogger.com, written in English and collected in August 2004. This corpus is widely used in AP due to its large

---

[2] http://u.cs.biu.ac.il/~koppel/BlogCorpus.htm.

Table 1. Distribution of the Schler corpus.

Age (age range)	Gender		
	Female	Male	Total
10s (13–17)	4,120	4,120	8,240
20s (23–27)	4,043	4,043	8,086
30s (33–47)	1,497	1,497	2,994
Total	9,660	9,660	19,320

number of documents (i.e., user profiles) as well as its balanced distribution regarding the number of men and women for each age group. Table 1 shows some numbers about this corpus.

For evaluating the generality of the proposed approach, we used English corpora from different social media domains. For this purpose we considered the corpus from the AP task of PAN-2014[3], referred as PAN-AP-2014, which include data from blogs, reviews, social media and Twitter. As shown in Table 2, all these corpora are balanced regarding gender, but imbalanced regarding age. It is also important to notice that these collections have very different sizes, varying from 147 blog users to 7746 social media profiles.

Table 2. Data distribution of the PAN-AP-2014 corpus.

Corpus	Gender	Age					
		18–24	25–34	35–49	50–64	65 o more	Total
Blogs	Female	3	30	27	11	2	73
	Male	3	30	27	12	2	74
	Total	6	60	54	23	4	147
Twitter	Female	10	44	65	30	4	153
	Male	10	44	65	30	4	153
	Total	20	88	130	60	8	306
Reviews	Female	180	500	500	500	400	2080
	Male	180	500	500	500	400	2080
	Total	360	1000	1000	1000	800	4160
Social media	Female	775	1049	1123	919	7	3873
	Male	775	1049	1123	919	7	3873
	Total	1550	2098	2246	1838	14	7746

---

[3] http://pan.webis.de/clef14/pan14-web/author-profiling.html.

4   Experimental Methodology

This section presents the experimental methodology devised to investigate the relevance of the personal phrases in the AP task. Basically, the central idea of our experiments is to compare the classification performance when using only these phrases vs. the entire documents. Section 4.1 describes the process followed to filter the personal phrases of a document. Then, Sect. 4.2 details the configuration settings of the classification process used in all the experiments.

4.1   Filtering Process

We define a personal phrase as a sentence which includes a first person pronoun. We considered the following lists of pronouns: subjective (I, we), objective (me, us), possessive (my, mine, our, ours) and reflexive (myself, ourselves). Second and third person pronouns were not considered because they suggest that the writer is talking about something/someone else without including herself.

The filtering process considers the extraction of all the personal phrases appearing in each document (user history) of a given corpus. As shown in Fig. 1, it first splits documents into sentences, and then it selects the sentences which include a first person pronoun. The rest of the sentences, which does not have any personal pronoun, is discarded. In our experiments we refer to these subsets of phrases as the *filtered corpus* and the *complement corpus* respectively. It is important to notice that there could exist documents with no personal phrases, which would lead to empty filtered files. In such situations we decided using the original document instead of the empty filtered file.

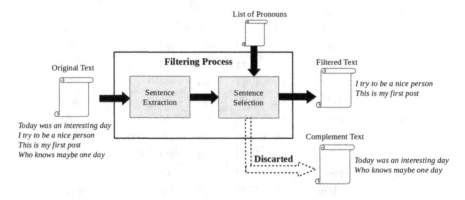

Fig. 1. Filtering process

4.2   Classification Process

For all the experiments we considered a standard classification framework for AP: we used a combination of content and style features, and a Support Vector

Machine as learning algorithm [31]. Following we describe the main configuration settings for the classification and evaluation processes.

Features: we used the set of features described in [13,31]: 1000 content words with the highest information gain, stopwords and punctuation marks, slang words, out-of-dictionary terms like emoticons and POS tags[4].

Representation: based on all these features, we build a standard BOW representation. The weighting of terms corresponds to their normalized frequency with respect to the total number of terms in the document.

Classifier: To classify the documents, we used the SVM classifier from the LIBLINEAR library [7] without any parameter optimization.

Evaluation: we applied a stratified 10 cross fold validation (10CFV) on each corpus, and used the accuracy as main evaluation measure, which represents the percentage of users that were correctly classified. To assess the statistical differences among the different corpora configurations (original, filtered and complement), we applied a 10CFV paired t test [5,6].

5   Results and Discussion

5.1   Experiment 1: The Relevance of Personal Phrases for AP

The aim of this experiment was to determine the value of the personal phrases for the AP task. Based on the idea that people better expose their interests and writing style when they talk about themselves, this first experiment focused on evaluating the role of the phrases which contain *singular first person pronouns*.

For carrying out this evaluation we used the Schler corpus (refer to Sect. 3). First, we filtered the personal phrases that contain one of the following pronouns: I, me, mine, my, myself, as well as the string "im", because it is commonly used in social media documents. Table 3 shows some numbers from the resulting corpora. The obtained filtered corpus represents 48.12 % of the information of the original collection, and it is smaller than the complement corpus.

To assess the relevance of the personal phrases in AP, we compared the classification accuracy in the age and gender prediction tasks when using the three different corpora. The last two columns of Table 3 show the obtained results. It is worth noting that results obtained using the filtered corpus are significantly better than those corresponding to the complement corpus, even thought there is less information in the former one. This indicates that self-information is indeed more useful for AP than general impersonal information. Furthermore, these results also show that using only the personal phrases it is possible to achieve a very similar performance than using the complete documents. In fact, for the gender prediction there is no statistically significant difference between the results using the filtered and the original corpora. On the one hand, these

---

[4] POS tags were obtained using Stanford tagger: http://nlp.stanford.edu/software/tagger.shtml.

Table 3. Data and accuracy results from the first experiment. The filtered corpus is the subset of sentences including singular first person pronouns from the Schler corpus.

	Sentences	Empty files	Age	Gender
Original corpus	9,155,301	0	77.49	80.07
Filtered corpus	4,405,783	69	76.09	79.63
Complement corpus	5,510,302	131	69.98	72.59

results confirm the relevance of the personal phrases for the AP task, and on the other hand, they support our hypothesis that these phrases can be considered as the essence of the documents for this task.

5.2   Experiment 2: The Added Value of Plural Personal Phrases

The purpose of this experiment was to examine the role of the phrases with *plural first person pronouns* in the AP task. Particularly, it focused on investigating if these phrases, which have inclusive nature and they express information about the user as part of a group, could enrich the representation of users, and consequently could improve their automatic classification.

As in the previous experiment, we used the Schler corpus as reference collection. However, in this case, we considered personal phrases not only containing singular pronouns but also plural first person pronouns. Accordingly, in the filtering process we extracted sentences containing one of the following pronouns: we, us, our, ours, ourselves. Some numbers from the obtained corpora are shown in Table 4. It is worth noting that there are considerably less phrases with plural first person pronouns than with singular first person pronouns, which could be explained by the kind of information shared in blogs. In addition, it can be noticed that their combination only caused an increment of 537,607 phrases (5.9 %) over the singular filtered corpus, indicating the frequent co-occurrence of singular and plural first person pronouns in social media posts.

Table 4 shows the accuracy results obtained by the different configurations of the filtered corpus. One first thing to notice is that results corresponding to the use of only singular personal phrases considerably outperformed those obtained by the plural personal phrases. The differences were of 9.1 % and 9.3 % for age and gender respectively. These differences could be attributed to the difference in the sizes of the corpora, but they also suggest that plural personal phrases change their focus from the user particular interests to the group's concerns.

On the other hand, the test of statistical significance indicated that the observed accuracy differences between the singular/plural filtered corpus and the singular filtered corpus were not statistically significant for both, age and gender, prediction tasks. These results allow us to conclude that plural personal phrases have no special relevance for the AP. Moreover, they also corroborate the outstanding usefulness of the singular personal phrases for this task.

Table 4. Accuracy results using singular and plural personal phrases.

	Sentences	Empty files	Age	Gender
Original corpus	9, 155, 301	0	77.49	80.07
Singular/plural filtered corpus	4, 943, 390	33	76.99	79.82
Plural filtered corpus	908, 815	1075	67.00	70.35
Singular filtered corpus	4, 405, 783	69	76.09	79.63

5.3   Experiment 3: Content and Style Information in Personal Phrases

Previous experiments have shown the important role of personal phrases for the AP task. The purpose of this experiment was to understand the discrimination power of these phrases. Particularly, we wanted to determine the contribution of content and style information from these phrases for the profiling of authors.

For this experiment we divided the features (refer to Sect. 4.2) into three disjoint sets: *words*, which represent content information, and *function words* and *POS* that represent style information. To assess the relevance of each feature type we compared their classification accuracy when using the singular filtered and complement corpora. Table 5 shows the obtained results.

Results from Table 5 confirm conclusions from previous works [31], which have pointed out that content information is more relevant than style information for AP. They also show that the performance difference between the original and filtering corpora is lower in the word space, demonstrating that thematic interests are adequately captured in personal phrases. On the other hand, by comparing the results from the filtered and complement corpora, it is possible to observe an average difference of 6.7 % in favor of the filtered corpus when

Table 5. Accuracy results for feature type. The filtered corpus is the subset of sentences including a singular person pronoun from the Schler corpus.

Type of feature	Corpus	Accuracy	
		Age	Gender
Words	Original	76.06	78.12
	Filtered	75.04	78.08
	Complement	68.49	71.19
Function words	Original	68.56	73.05
	Filtered	67.00	70.78
	Complement	61.31	67.56
POS	Original	63.09	68.11
	Filtered	62.87	66.35
	Complement	59.79	65.68

words were used as features, whereas the differences were around 4.4 % and 1.9 % when using function words and POS features respectively. These results suggest that the value of personal phrases lies mostly in the content aspect rather than in the style information. Hence, we can conclude that style information from authors could be equally well captured from personal and non-personal phrases, nonetheless, topics of interest are better extracted from personal phrases.

5.4 Experiment 4: Personal Phrases in Different Social Media

The purpose of this experiment was to evaluate the relevance of personal phrases for AP across different social media domains. Mainly, we aimed to corroborate the generality of our previous findings and check their degree of domain independence. For this experiment we used the PAN-AP-2014 corpus. We built the filtered corpus by selecting the posts that contain singular personal pronouns as detailed in Sect. 5.1. Table 6 shows some numbers on the obtained corpora.

Table 7 shows the results across different social media domains. For all the collections we approached two classification problems: age prediction with five classes (18–24, 25–34, 35–49, 50–64, 65 o more), and gender classification with two classes (male and female). The results are very interesting since they present similar accuracy values when using the filtered and the original corpus, although the filtered corpora only represent a small subset (ranging from 15 % to 36 %) of the original corpora. Particularly, the statistical significance test indicated that results for age prediction were comparable across all considered domain, whereas for the gender classification we found a statistically significant difference for the Twitter and Blog domains. However, it is important to notice that for these two collections we obtained better age prediction results using the filtered corpus than using the original corpus, which causes a comparable overall performance.

Table 7 shows the results across different social media domains. For all the collections we approached two classification problems: age prediction with five classes (18–24, 25–34, 35–49, 50–64, 65 o more), and gender classification with two classes (male and female). The results are very interesting since they present similar accuracy values when using the filtered and the original corpora, although the first only represent a small subset (ranging from 15 % to 36 %) of the original corpora. Particularly, the statistical significance test indicated that results for age prediction were comparable across all considered domains. This is a very

Table 6. Data from the PAN-AP-2014 corpus. The filtered corpora correspond to the subsets of posts containing a firs person pronoun.

Collection	Posts in original corpus	Posts in filtered corpus	Empty files
Blogs	22, 994	5, 565	10
Twitter	318, 691	49, 540	7
Reviews	52, 833	19, 248	1, 377
Social media	3, 207, 509	736, 615	1, 349

Table 7. Accuracy results at PAN 2014 collections.

Collection	Corpus conf.	Accuracy		% kept in filtered corpus
		Age	Gender	
Blogs	Original	36.56	68.42	24.20 % (from 22,944 posts)
	Filtered	43.92	62.14	
Twitter	Original	35.33	71.33	15.54 % (from 318,691 posts)
	Filtered	37.49	59.55	
Reviews	Original	30.84	67.24	36.43 % (from 52,833 posts)
	Filtered	29.21	65.21	
Social media	Original	34.84	53.64	22.97 % (from 3,207,509 posts)
	Filtered	33.99	52.68	

encouraging result since age prediction in these collections considers five age categories with consecutive values and, therefore, it represents a harder classification problem than that from the Schler corpus. On the other hand, for the gender classification we found a statistically significant difference for the Twitter and Blog domains. However, it is important to notice that for these two collections we obtained better age prediction results using the filtered corpus than using the original corpus, which causes a comparable overall performance. In general, these results support the relevance of the personal phrases as well as their role as the essence of the documents for the AP task.

6   Conclusions and Future Work

Inspired on the idea that people best reflect their personal characteristics and writing style when they talk about themselves, in this work we investigated the relevance of personal phrases for the author profiling task. The experiments carried out clearly indicated that personal phrases have a huge value for predicting age and gender of social media users, since considering only this kind of phrases we obtained reductions of up to 60 % of the information in the user documents and a comparable performance than using all available data. Hence, personal phrases can be considered as the *essence of documents* for the AP task.

Throughout the paper, we answered the research questions outlined in the introduction, finding that: (1) not all the information from a document is equally relevant for this task, personal phrases are more discriminating than non-personal phrases; (2) although plural personal phrases have inclusive nature, they have not a special relevance for the AP task, and their information is not complementary to that from the singular personal phrases; (3) personal phrases better capture content information (user interests), whereas style information can be equally extracted from both personal and non-personal phrases; (4) the relevance of personal phrases is a general characteristic that was observed in different social media domains.

The achieved results motivate us to evaluate the proposed approach in other profiling tasks such as personality identification, as well as to evaluate its appropriateness in other languages, particularly in those where the use of subjective pronouns is uncommon (pronoun-dropping languages). On the other hand, the obtained conclusions encourage us to explore new ideas for taking advantage of the information from personal phrases in the AP task. In particular, we consider that our findings could be applied to design new strategies for constructing corpora, a task highly expensive in terms of effort and time. They also could help the design of novel feature selection methods, as well as new terms and instances weighting schemes.

Acknowledgments. This work was supported under CONACYT project no. 247870 and scholarship 243957.

References

1. Argamon, S., Dhawle, S., Koppel, M., Pennebaker, J.W.: Lexical predictors of personality type. In: Joint Annual Meeting of the Interface and the Classification Society of North America, St. Louis, MI (2005)
2. Argamon, S., Koppel, M., Pennebaker, J.W., Schler, J.: Automatically profiling the author of an anonymous text. Commun. ACM **52**(2), 119–123 (2009)
3. Cappellato, L., Ferro, N., Jones, G., San-Juan, E. (eds.): CLEF 2015 Labs and Workshops, Notebook Papers, Toulouse, France, September 2015
4. Chung, C.K., Pennebaker, J.W.: The psychological functions of function words. In: Fiedler, K. (ed.) Social Communication: Frontiers of Social Psychology, pp. 343–359. Psychology Press, New York (2007)
5. Demšar, J.: Statistical comparisons of classifiers over multiple data sets. J. Mach. Learn. Res. **7**, 1–30 (2006)
6. Dietterich, T.: Approximate statistical tests for comparing supervised classification learning algorithms. Neural Comput. **10**, 1895–1923 (1998)
7. Fan, R.E., Chang, K.W., Hsieh, C.J., Wang, X.R., Lin, C.J.: LIBLINEAR: a library for large linear classification. J. Mach. Learn. Res. **9**, 1871–1874 (2008)
8. Forner, P., Navigli, R., Tufis, D. (eds.): Notebook Papers of CLEF 2013 LABs and Workshops (CLEF-2013), Valencia, Spain, September 2013
9. Goswami, S., Sarkar, S., Rustagi, M.: Stylometric analysis of bloggers' age and gender. In: Third International ICWSM Conference, pp. 214–217 (2009)
10. Kacewicz, E., Pennebaker, J.W., Davis, M., Moongee, J., Graesser, A.C.: Pronoun use reflects standings in social hierarchies. J. Lang. Soc. Psychol. **33**, 125–143 (2013)
11. Koppel, M., Argamon, S., Shimoni, A.R.: Automatically categorizing written texts by author gender. Literary Linguist. Comput. **17**(4), 401–412 (2002)
12. López-Monroy, A.P., Montes-y-Gómez, M., Escalante, H.J., Villaseñor-Pineda, L., Villatoro-Tello, E.: INAOE's participation at PAN'13–Notebook for PAN at CLEF 2013: author profiling task. In: Forner et al. [8]
13. López-Monroy, A.P., Montes-y-Gómez, M., Escalante, H.J., Villaseñor-Pineda, L., Stamatatos, E.: Discriminative subprofile-specific representations for author profiling in social media. Knowl. Based Syst. **89**, 134–147 (2015)

14. Maharjan, S., Solorio, T.: Using wide range of features for author profiling–notebook for PAN at CLEF 2015. In: Cappellato et al. [3]
15. Meina, M., Brodzínska, K., Celmer, B., Czoków, M., Patera, M., Pezacki, J., Wilk, M.: Ensemble-based classification for author profiling using various features-notebook for PAN at CLEF 2013. In: Forner et al. [8]
16. Mihalcea, R., Hassan, S.: Using the essence of texts to improve document classification. In: RANLP 2005, Borovetz, Bulgaria (2005)
17. Mukherjee, A., Liu, B.: Improving gender classification of blog authors. In: Conference on Empirical Methods in Natural Language Processing (EMNLP 2010), Stroudsburg, PA, USA, pp. 207–217. Association for Computational Linguistics (2010)
18. Newman, M.L., Groom, C.J., Handelman, L.D., Pennebaker, J.W.: Gender differences in language use: an analysis of 14,000 text samples. Discourse Process. **45**, 211–236 (2008)
19. Newman, M., Pennebaker, J., Berry, D., Richards, J.: Lying words: predicting deception from linguistic styles. Pers. Soc. Psychol. Bull. **29**, 665–675 (2003)
20. Nguyen, D., Smith, N.A., Rosé, C.P.: Author age prediction from text using linear regression. In: 5th ACL-HLT Workshop on Language Technology for Cultural Heritage, Social Sciences and Humanities, pp. 115–123. Association for Computational Linguistics (2011)
21. Pennachiotti, M., Popescu, A.M.: Democrats, republicans and starbucks afficionados: user classification in Twitter. In: 17th ACM SIGKDD International Conference on Knowledge Discovery and Data Mining, New York, USA, pp. 430–438 (2011)
22. Pennebaker, J.: The Secret Life of Pronouns: What Our Words Say About Us. Bloomsbury, London (2011)
23. Pennebaker, J., Stone, L.: Words of wisdom: language use over the life span. J. Pers. Soc. Psychol. **85**, 291–301 (2003)
24. Rangel, F., Celli, F., Rosso, P., Potthast, M., Stein, B., Daelemans, W.: Overview of the 3rd author profiling task at PAN 2015. In: Cappellato et al. [3]
25. Rangel, F., Rosso, P.: Use of language and author profiling: identification of gender and age. In: Workshop on Natural Language Processing and Cognitive Science (NLPCS-2013), Marseille, France (2013)
26. Rangel, F., Rosso, P.: On the multilingual and genre robustness of emographs for author profiling in social media. In: Mothe, J., et al. (eds.) Experimental IR Meets Multilinguality, Multimodality, and Interaction. LNCS, vol. 9283, pp. 274–280. Springer, Heidelberg (2015)
27. Rangel, F., Rosso, P.: On the impact of emotions on author profiling. Inf. Process. Manage. **52**(1), 73–92 (2016)
28. Rangel, F., Rosso, P., Koppel, M., Stamatatos, E., Inches, G. Overview of the author profiling task at PAN 2013. In: Forner et al. [8]
29. Rao, D., Yarowsky, D., Shreevats, A., Gupta, M.: Classifying latent user attributes in Twitter. In: Proceedings of SMUC 2010, pp. 710–718 (2010)
30. Rude, S., Gortner, E.M., Pennebaker, J.W.: Language use of depressed and depression-vulnerable college students. Cogn. Emot. **18**, 1121–1133 (2004)
31. Schler, J., Koppel, M., Argamon, S., Pennebaker, J.W.: Effects of age and gender on blogging. In: AAAI Spring Symposium: Computational Approaches to Analyzing Weblogs, pp. 199–205. AAAI (2006)

32. Schwartz, H.A., Eichstaedt, J.C., Dziurzynski, L., Kern, M.L., Blanco, E., Kosinski, M., Stillwell, D., Seligman, M.E.P., Ungar, L.H.: Toward personality insights from language exploration in social media. In: AAAI Spring Symposium: Analyzing Microtext. AAAI (2013)
33. Sebastiani, F.: Machine learning in automated text categorization. ACM Comput. Surv. **34**(1), 1–47 (2002)
34. Sidorov, G., Miranda Jiménez, S., Viveros Jiménez, F., Gelbukh, A., Castro Sánchez, N., Velásquez, F., Díaz Rangel, I., Suárez Guerra, S., Treviño, A., Gordon, J.: Empirical study of opinion mining in spanish tweets. LNAI, pp. 7629–7630 (2012)

Improving Profiles of Weakly-Engaged Users
With Applications to Recommender Systems

Gaurav Singh[1]([⊠]), Amin Mantrach[2], and Fabrizio Silvestri[2]

[1] UCL, London, UK
gaurav.singh.15@ucl.ac.uk
[2] Yahoo! Research, Sunnyvale, CA, USA

Abstract. The majority of online users do not engage highly with services that are offered via Web. This is a well-known fact and it is also one of the main issues that personalization algorithms try to overcome. A popular way of personalizing an online service is to record users' actions into *user profiles*. Weakly-engaged users lead to sparsely populated user profiles, or *weak profiles* as we name them. Such *weak profiles* constitute a source of potential increase in user engagement and as a consequence, windfall profits for Internet companies. In this paper, we define the novel problem of enhancing weak profiles in positive space and propose an effective solution based on learning collective embedding space in order to capture a low-dimensional manifold designed to specifically reconstruct sparse user profiles. Our method consistently outperforms baselines consisting of kNN and collective factorization without constraints on user profile. Experiments on two datasets, news and video, from a popular online portal show improvements of up to more than 100% in terms of MAP for extremely weak profiles, and up to around 10% for moderately weak profiles. In order to evaluate the impact of our method on learned latent space embeddings for users and items, we generate recommendations exploiting our user profile constrained approach. The generated recommendations outperform state-of-the-art techniques based on low-rank collective matrix factorization in particular for users that clicked at most four times (78–82% of the total) on the items published by the online portal we consider.

Keywords: Weak profiles reconstruction · Weak profiles enrichment · Collective matrix factorization · Learning embeddings

1 Introduction

Personalization is a popular technique to increase effectiveness of an online web service by tailoring it to the specific characteristics of each user (or group of users). To this extent, a *user profile* is built and maintained for each user in the system and it is subsequently used in the various services the portal offers.

G. Singh was intern in Yahoo at the time of the work.

N. Fuhr et al. (Eds.): CLEF 2016, LNCS 9822, pp. 123–134, 2016.
DOI: 10.1007/978-3-319-44564-9_10

For example, a large search company might host a user profile that is used to personalize for search results, product search, advertising, online news shown, etc.

There is a major shortcoming, though, in this approach. Online users of web services can often be divided into a minority of active users who interact on a regular basis with the system and a majority of users that rarely connect to the service. This global user behavior has been measured for different kinds of online activities: daily activities on Facebook [6], user behavior in sponsored search [2]. These weakly-engaged users are of particular interest to internet businesses as they represent a potential direction of expansion and growth in revenue. Making *weakly-engaged users* churn to active users is particularly challenging due to the limited information we have about them. For instance, on a popular online news provider tested in this work, when considering all users that clicked at least once on the front page, about 40 % of them did not interact more than once with the system. In practice, the problems caused by weakly-engaged users are due to the fact that their user profiles are *"sparse"*. In other words, little or no historical information is available for sparse user profiles but, still, an effective personalization mechanism should be able to exploit every single bit of information available in the best possible way.

Therefore, in this paper we consider a very important problem in personalized online service: *"completing"* sparse user profiles. It is worth being remarked that solutions to this problem are immensely important for various reasons and are of particular interest in real case scenarios. For instance, most effective recommender systems make use of user profiles in their pipelines. While such a system can be costly to change as it requires a complete overhaul of the workflow, an improved user profile can easily be delivered as an input to any state-of-the-art recommendation algorithm without requiring any additional change. The contribution of this paper is to do a *user-profile constrained* collective factorization in positive space and study its effectiveness for reconstructing user profiles.

2 Related Work

Our method provides a novel approach to constructing the user profile from implicit feedback, which means that the recommender system does not need to collect external information about users in order to enrich their profile. In some cases, the external factors can work well due to the presence of a direct correlation with the items, but such an information is not always available. [8] proposes collaborative filtering using latent model from implicit feedback, but does not attempt to improve the user profiles. Similarly, [13] proposes a unified collaborative and content-based recommender system. As there have been very few direct attempts at implicit improvement of user profiles (especially, in strictly positive space), most of the related work with respect to user profile enrichment are based on explicit feedback. In [5], the authors enrich user profiles using the tags that are directly defined by the user. The proposed idea consists of improving the profile by using explicit feedback and is specific to search systems where explicit feedback corresponds to input queries. Another approach in [12] exploits the genre-information associated with multimedia content to enrich the user profiles.

As explicit information for enhancing user profile is not always available, we focus our attention on the user profile enhancement from the implicit feedback. One of the approaches widely used for matrix completion is singular value decomposition (SVD), which is based on decomposition of a given matrix $X \approx U \Sigma V$ where $X \in \mathbb{R}^{n \times m}$, $U \in \mathbb{R}^{n \times k}$, $V \in \mathbb{R}^{k \times m}$ and Σ is the diagonal matrix of singular values, usually $k \ll min(n, m)$. Recently, in [4], the authors use SVD for matrix completion. Although widely popular, SVD has problems in the interpretation of the results since the values in the factorized and reconstructed matrix can be negative. Also, the orthogonality constraints can lead to overfitting of latent space in some cases. For example, topical distribution of documents does not need to be orthogonal as a document can belong to different topics.

In this work, we make the hypothesis that user profiles are made only from implicit positive (or negative) feedbacks given by the user (for instance, a click on a news article). To deal with the natural non-negative aspect of the implicit feedback considered in this study, we build on the non-negative matrix factorization framework (NMF). In the recent past, a number of publications have focused their attention on low rank matrix factorization based on NMF [9,16]. [7,10] discuss online versions of NMF for large scale and streaming data. The results from NMF can be interpreted more easily as the elements are nonnegative and therefore user profile construction can be believed to benefit from such an approach.

In cases where there is availability of both content and collaborative information, collective matrix factorization (CMF) techniques have shown to perform better [3,15]. Since a collective matrix factorization technique uses a given item-feature relation to factorize the user-item relation and vice-versa, it can be interpreted as hybrid of both content and collaborative filtering. It has been shown that CMF performs better than purely collaborative or content based approaches for recommendation [15]. In that work, authors provide a theoretical framework for collective matrix factorization. They also provide empirical results to prove the effectiveness of the method. More recently, [3] presented a convex formulation of the collective matrix factorization approach. The algorithm, based on an eigen decomposition, suffers from two major drawbacks. First, the eigen decomposition step has a high complexity and cannot be used on large matrices. Second, the eigen decomposition and re-composition step increases the density of the originally sparse input matrices. Existing methods of collective matrix factorization are not specifically designed for user profile completion. In this paper, we extend the traditional collective factorization loss function, by forcing the embedding space to reconstruct well user profiles. Other CMF based approaches have been designed for item cold-start recommendations: [17] addressed the item cold-start by making use of the social network information, while [14] addressed the same problem by introducing a graph-based regularization. In this last work, it has been shown that CMF based approaches outperform the fLDA [1] probabilistic framework when recommending fresh news to engaged users.

3 Proposed Model

In this section, we are going to formulate our proposed model based on the problem as defined in the previous sections. For the sake of clarity, let us consider the practical example of an online news service provider. Each news article is associated with a textual description that is the set of words its headline contains and a set of users consume those items. Furthermore, let us assume we record for each news the set of users who click on it. This information is then represented with two matrices, a document-term matrix $X_s \in \mathbb{R}^{d \times N_w}$, and a document-user matrix $X_u \in \mathbb{R}^{d \times n}$, where d is the number of documents, N_w is the vocabulary size and n is the number of users. The document-term matrix (X_s) may be a boolean matrix or may represent the *tf-idf* scores of the words in the document. On the other hand, the entries of the document-user matrix (X_u) reflects whether a given user clicked on a given article.

A user profile consists of non-negative weights indicating the contribution of terms to the profile. Hence, a non-negative matrix factorization (NMF) based approach for reconstructing user profiles naturally adapts to our problem. Adopting this definition we can model our problem as follows:

$$\operatorname*{Min}_{H_u, H_s, W} J = \frac{1}{2}(\alpha||X_p - H_u^T H_s||^2 + (1-\alpha)||X_u - WH_u||^2$$
$$+ (1-\alpha)||X_s - WH_s||^2 + \lambda(||H_u||^2 + ||H_s||^2 + ||W||^2)) \tag{1}$$

Subject to $H_u, H_s, W \geq 0$

X_p is the user profile matrix where each row represents an observed user profile, and H_s, H_u are the latent factors associated to each term and each user, respectively. W is a latent shared variable making the bridge between items' content (X_s), and users' feedback (X_u). α and λ are hyper parameters that control the weight of different components of the loss function J and the regularization of different parameters respectively. Below mentioned multiplicative updates for learning each variable can be derived from the derivatives of the loss function (see [11]).

$$H_u \leftarrow H_u \odot \frac{[(1-\alpha)W^T X_u + \alpha H_s X_p^T]}{[(1-\alpha)W^T W H_u + \lambda H_u + \alpha H_s H_s^T H_u]} \tag{2}$$

$$H_s \leftarrow H_s \odot \frac{[(1-\alpha)W^T X_s + \alpha H_u X_p^T]}{[(1-\alpha)W^T W H_s + \lambda H_s + \alpha H_u H_u^T H_s]} \tag{3}$$

$$W \leftarrow W \odot \frac{[(1-\alpha)X_s H_s^T + (1-\alpha)X_u H_u^T]}{[(1-\alpha)W H_s H_s^T + (1-\alpha)W H_u H_u^T + \lambda W]} \tag{4}$$

In this model, each factor can be described by a set of words (i.e., a topic) but also by a set of users (i.e., a community). This is achieved by collectively factorizing X_s and X_u while enforcing a low-dimensional representation in a common space (using the shared variable W). One advantage of our proposed joint factorization relies on its ability to approximate the user profiles directly from the latent factors by computing the following product: $H_u^T H_s$, which is different from other collective factorization techniques. The proposed model creates a common latent space for all 3 entities (i.e. users, items, features), which is important in the case of users that are extremely sparse and require more regularization in order to learn better features for them. It means that we learn a common latent space that not only learns the X_u and X_s, but X_p as well. Intuitively, it means that if a user likes a number of items that have similar features then the contribution of user to the topic to which these features belong should increase even more. This constraint differentiates it from other applications of collective matrix factorization, where usually a common latent space is learned using shared variable (like W) without an explicit constraint on user profile (X_p).

4 Experimentation

In this section we conduct experiments to evaluate the performance of our approach for completing profiles of sparse users on two use cases. Firstly, we evaluate how accurate is the profile generated by our algorithm -referred to as Collective Embedded User Profiles (CEUP)- against a simple aggregation of the k nearest neighbors profiles computed from the collaborative matrix. To evaluate the performance of the approaches, we consider loyal users (non weak profiles) that we artificially churn to weakly-engaged users after sparsifying their profiles. Then, we measure the extent to which we can recover their original profile. The experimental setup is detailed in Sects. 4.2 and 4.3. Secondly, we test how well CEUP can recommend news and videos to the same set of users whose profiles have been sparsified. We compare CEUP against two states-of-the-art techniques for recommendation based on low rank collaborative matrix factorization. Namely, we test SVT proposed recently by Bouchard et al. [3], and CMF proposed by Singh and Gordon [15].

4.1 Dataset

We collected two datasets, one each from a Yahoo news and Yahoo video portal. As expected, the user engagement on both datasets exhibits a long tail distribution.

- **News Dataset:-** The news dataset consists of the set of the news articles displayed to the users along with their feedback. For the purpose of the study, we only use as content headline's features of the article, as this is the piece of information viewed by the user on the front page leading him to click on the article or to skip it. For each article, we also record all the users that clicked on it during the studied period. From these three months data, we randomly select (in order to respect the long tail distribution) 200, 000 users. We then add to them 20, 000 loyal users selected from the distribution peak. More precisely, we randomly select them from the top 5 % (i.e. users that clicked at least 25 times) of the users that have been mostly engaged during three month. This constitutes the final set of users that are studied for both experiments: user profile completion and news recommendation. These users have clicked on total of around 48, 527 news articles during three months.

- **Video Dataset:**- The video dataset is collected in similar fashion consisting of videos viewed by users and features of the videos. We collect as features the title and description of the video that a user reads before clicking it. A click on the video refers to an intentional play of the video. For these videos, we record all the users that clicked on it during a period of 3 months. We select 130, 000 random users (original distribution) and add to it 20, 000 loyal users (i.e. users that clicked at least 8 times). These users have clicked on a total of around 116, 926 videos during 3 month period.

4.2 User Profile Completion

In this set of experiments, we compare our user profile completion approach against the three following baselines.

- **No Enrichment:**- We estimate the performance of the sparse user profile without doing any enrichment. It serves as a baseline in order to ensure that the tested methods are not degrading the profiles.
- k **Nearest Neighbor:**- kNN is the most commonly used algorithm for personalization of results based on the neighborhood of the user's profile. It could be assumed as the simplest approach to enhance the user profile. We implement a weighted kNN approach where the user profile is generated using a weighted aggregation of the nearest neighbors' profiles and tuned it for the best value of k using a validation set.
- **Simple Matrix Reconstruction:**- We try to reconstruct the user profile using NMF based matrix reconstruction $X_p = H_u^T H_s$ without collective constraints on X_u and X_s.

Experimental Setup. Our goal is to evaluate the extent to which the different methods are able to complete the weakly-engaged user's profile (i.e. majority users in the long tail distribution). To do so, we convert a loyal-user to a weakly-engaged user by artificially sparsifying his profile (more precisely, clicks in the *user-item* matrix are randomly deleted). To evaluate the performance of the different methods for increasing level of sparsity, we test the different completion methods on user profiles going from 1 up to 5 clicks (this is the case for more than 80 % of the users in the original dataset). After completion, the generated user profile is evaluated using the original user profile as ground-truth. We plot results as the average over 5 different test sets randomly sampled from the data.

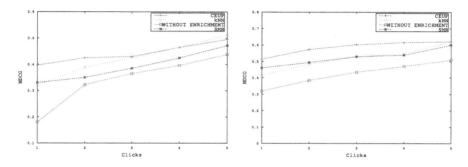

Fig. 1. NDCG for different user profile construction methods at different levels of sparsity for news (left) and video (right) dataset. The given results are statistically significant for a confidence level of 99 % using a t-test.

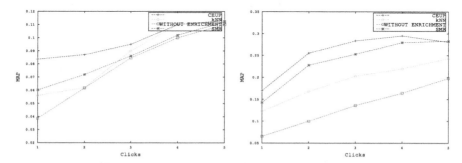

Fig. 2. MAP for different user profile construction methods at different levels of sparsity for news (left) and video (right) dataset. The given results are statistically significant for a confidence level of 99 % using a t-test.

User Profile Evaluation Metrics. The user profile completion process produces a ranking of the words in the vocabulary where each word comes with a positive weight. The ground-truth is constructed from the original user profile after applying a *tf-idf* function and selecting the top 20 words. Notice that we did not observe any significant difference when considering the top 10 or top 50 words. For evaluating the performance of the ranking, we use state-of-the-art evaluation metrics used in IR: nDCG (Normalized Discounted Cumulative Gain) and MAP (Mean Average Precision). These are metrics used to evaluate ranked lists. We use them because we want to be able to reconstruct profiles so that recovering words with higher weights should be given more importance.

Results. We report the performance achieved by the different methods in completing sparse profiles for various levels of sparsity going from 1 to 5 clicks (Figs. 1 and 2). Our approach, referred to as CEUP, outperforms *k*NN for sparse users when predicting both the correct words in the user profile (as measured by the MAP), but also predicting the correct ranking of most important words (as measured by NDCG). We perform better or equal to *k*NN when we have up to 4

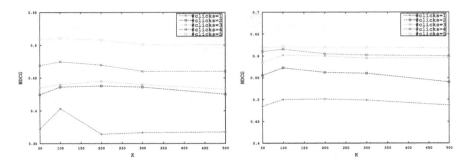

Fig. 3. Variations in NDCG for different number of latent dimensions for news (left) and video (right) dataset.

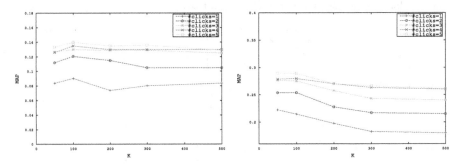

Fig. 4. Variations in MAP for different number of latent dimensions for news (left) and video (right) dataset.

clicks for the news dataset and for up to 5 clicks in the case of video dataset. The results are statistically significant according to a t-test with a p-value lower than 0.01. When sparsity decreases kNN reaches closer to CEUP performance as kNN is able to find better neighbors in case of non weak-users. Notice that by considering users that clicked at most 4 times, we can improve the user completion for 78–82% of the total number of users, while for the remaining (loyal) users we can use kNN.

Parameter Analysis

– **User Profile Reconstruction Parameter:**- The importance of the user profile reconstruction constraint is given by the parameter α. We measure the performance of CEUP for different values of the parameter α across both datasets (Fig. 5). The best performance for the method is achieved for a value of $\alpha = 0.1$ across all different sparsity levels, which means that our constraint on user profile definitely works better than a collective matrix factorization without the user profile constraint (confirmed by t-test with p-value lower than 0.01).

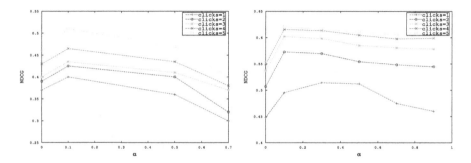

Fig. 5. NDCG for different values of parameter α at different levels of sparsity for news (left) and video (right) dataset. α is the weight of the user profile constraint in the Eq. (1).

- **Latent Dimensions**:- We report the NDCG and MAP measure for different number of latent dimensions at a given sparsity level for both datasets (Figs. 3 and 4). We observe that the results are more or less stable across different number of latent dimensions for both datasets, but we attain the best results when using 100 latent dimensions. Results do not drop significantly for higher number of dimension (up to 500 tested). These results are for α fixed to 0.1.

Running Time Analysis. We analyze the average running time for all the collective matrix factorization techniques. We observe that the running time for the CEUP approach is comparable to CMF, but SVT was extremely slow even on a smaller dataset as it involves eigen decomposition.

4.3 Recommendations

The ultimate goal of a profile reconstruction algorithm is that of producing an improved user profile that can replace the existing one in recommender systems explicitly exploit user profiles (e.g., content-based recommender sytems). It is not difficult to argue that it is likely that an improved user profile returns better (or equal, to say the least) recommendations in the above-mentioned settings. Nonetheless, we have run experiments using a content-based recommender system and by replacing the sparse user profiles with our enriched ones. We have measured the performance of the two systems using weak and improved user profiles, and observed improvements of around 100 % for both MAP and NDCG metrics in such simple content-based setting (cosine similarity between item and user in feature space). In order to increase our understanding on the possible limits in the reconstructing power of our algorithm, we compared two state-of-the-art recommender algorithms against a recommender algorithm *directly* exploiting the loss function we propose in this work. We call this algorithm CEUP. The two recommender systems we compare to are: SVT [3] and CMF [15]. The research question we want to answer in this part is the following: Do we

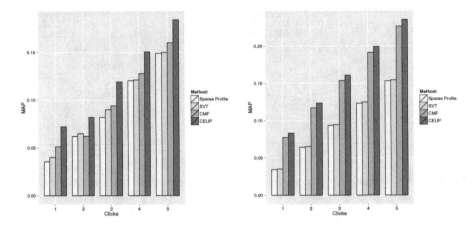

Fig. 6. Mean Average Precision for different methods at varying levels of sparsity for news (left) and video (right) dataset. The given results are statistically significant for a confidence level of 99 % using a t-test.

learn better latent representations of users and items (the H_u and H_s matrices) by exploiting our user profile constrained objective compared to state-of-the-art algorithms?

SVT: Singular Value Thresholding. Singular Value Thresholding (SVT)[3] is a state-of-the-art method for collective matrix factorization. The method involves creating a symmetric block matrix out of all given relations and factorizing them jointly.

CMF: Collective Matrix Factorization. In [15], the authors proposed a general framework for collective matrix factorization. The method involves approximating the original matrices with low rank approximations, such that one of the relations in the factorization is common.

Experimental Setup. Our goal is to evaluate the extent to which CEUP recommend better news article and videos to the weakly-engaged user than state-of-the-art recommender systems based on a collective matrix factorization. The hypothesis being that CEUP, by enforcing user profiles reconstruction, would get benefit (as a side effect) of better recommendations. To recommend items to users, we compute for a given user the similarity between his latent user profile (h_u) and the items' latent features (W). This procedure produces a ranking of all items for a given user. We apply exactly same procedure for CEUP, CMF and SVT except that for each approach we use the respective learned representations. All hyper-parameters have been tuned on an independent validation set extracted from the same news portal on another time period. We conduct the experiments on the same set of users tested during the user profile completion task (Sect. 4.2), i.e. loyal-users converted to weakly-engaged users by artificially sparsifying the clicks in their profile. The recommendations for a given user is evaluated using as ground-truth all the news articles and videos clicked by this user before sparsification. We remark that we used a smaller dataset of $5,000$ users for SVT, since SVT can't scale to large number of users.

Results and Analysis. We can see in Fig. 6 that CEUP outperforms (in a statistically significant way) CMF and SVT (according to t-test with p-value lower than 0.01) in terms of MAP for both news and video dataset. We see an improvement of about 20–30 % in terms of MAP for extremely sparse users in comparison to the nearest competitor.

5   Conclusions

We proposed a novel application of collective matrix factorization for constructing user profiles from implicit feedback in positive space. This method improves the profiles of the users that can be used as an input to any state-of-the-art content-based method for recommendations. The fact that the proposed method can be used as a preprocessing step with any state-of-the-art recommendation algorithm using user profiles is a great advantage. It basically means that the method is practical and can have huge amounts of empirical advantages without requiring overhaul of production system implementing novel recommendation algorithms. We show that our method outperforms kNN and NMF in user profile reconstruction. We also show that added user profile constraint improves recommendations compared to simple collective factorization. In the future, we will focus on learning common latent space representations for different multi-modal problems that have more than 3 entities and observe its effect on performance.

References

1. Agarwal, D., Chen, B.: Regression-based latent factor models. In: Proceedings of the 15th ACM SIGKDD International Conference on Knowledge Discovery and Data Mining, Paris, France, 28 June–1 July 2009, pp. 19–28 (2009)
2. Attenberg, J., Pandey, S., Suel, T.: Modeling and predicting user behavior in sponsored search. In: Proceedings of the 15th ACM SIGKDD international conference on Knowledge Discovery and Data Mining, pp. 1067–1076. ACM (2009)
3. Bouchard, G., Yin, D., Guo, S.: Convex collective matrix factorization. In: AISTATS, vol. 31. JMLR Proceedings, pp. 144–152 (2013). JMLR.org
4. Cai, J.-F., Candès, E.J., Shen, Z.: A singular value thresholding algorithm for matrix completion. SIAM J. Optim. **20**(4), 1956–1982 (2010)
5. De Meo, P., Quattrone, G., Ursino, D.: A query expansion and user profile enrichment approach to improve the performance of recommender systems operating on a folksonomy. User Model. User-Adap. Inter. **20**(1), 41–86 (2010)
6. Gjoka, M., Sirivianos, M., Markopoulou, A., Yang, X.: Poking facebook: characterization of osn applications. In: Proceedings of the first workshop on Online social networks, pp. 31–36. ACM (2008)

7. Guan, N., Tao, D., Luo, Z., Yuan, B.: Online nonnegative matrix factorization with robust stochastic approximation. IEEE Trans. Neural Networks Learn. Syst. **23**(7), 1087–1099 (2012)
8. Hu, Y., Koren, Y., Volinsky, C.: Collaborative filtering for implicit feedback datasets. In: Eighth IEEE International Conference on Data Mining, ICDM 2008, pp. 263–272. IEEE (2008)
9. Lee, D.D., Seung, H.S.: Algorithms for non-negative matrix factorization. In: Advances in neural information processing systems, pp. 556–562 (2000)
10. Lefevre, A., Bach, F., Févotte, C.: Online algorithms for nonnegative matrix factorization with the itakura-saito divergence. In: IEEE Workshop on Applications of Signal Processing to Audio and Acoustics (WASPAA), pp. 313–316. IEEE (2011)
11. Lin, C.-J.: On the convergence of multiplicative update algorithms for nonnegative matrix factorization. IEEE Trans. Neural Networks **18**(6), 1589–1596 (2007)
12. Manzato, M.G., Goularte, R.: A multimedia recommender system based on enriched user profiles. In: Proceedings of the 27th Annual ACM Symposium on Applied Computing, SAC 2012, pp. 975–980. ACM, New York (2012)
13. Popescul, A., Pennock, D.M., Lawrence, S.: Probabilistic models for unified collaborative and content-based recommendation in sparse-data environments. In: Proceedings of the Seventeenth Conference on Uncertainty in Artificial Intelligence, pp. 437–444. Morgan Kaufmann Publishers Inc. (2001)
14. Saveski, M., Mantrach, A.: Item cold-start recommendations: learning local collective embeddings. In: Eighth ACM Conference on Recommender Systems, RecSys 2014, Foster City, 06–10 October 2014, pp. 89–96 (2014)
15. Singh, A.P., Gordon, G.J.: Relational learning via collective matrix factorization. In: Proceedings of the 14th ACM SIGKDD International Conference on Knowledge Discovery and Data Mining, KDD 2008, pp. 650–658. ACM, New York (2008)
16. Xu, W., Liu, X., Gong, Y.: Document clustering based on non-negative matrix factorization. In: Proceedings of the 26th Annual International ACM SIGIR Conference on Research and Development in Informaion Retrieval, pp. 267–273. ACM (2003)
17. Yin, D., Guo, S., Chidlovskii, B., Davison, B.D., Archambeau, C., Bouchard, G.: Connecting comments and tags: improved modeling of social tagging systems. In: Sixth ACM International Conference on Web Search and Data Mining, WSDM 2013, Rome, 4–8 February 2013, pp. 547–556 (2013)

Best of CLEF 2015 Labs

Kronecker Decomposition
for Image Classification

Sabrina Fontanella[1,2]([✉]), Antonio J. Rodríguez-Sánchez[1], Justus Piater[1],
and Sandor Szedmak[3]

[1] Intelligent and Interactive Systems, Department of Computer Science,
University of Innsbruck, Innsbruck, Austria
fontanellasabrina@gmail.com,
{antonio.rodriguez-sanchez,justus.piater}@uibk.ac.at
[2] Department of Computer Science, University of Salerno, Fisciano, Italy
[3] Department of Computer Science, Aalto University, Espoo, Finland
sandor.szedmak@aalto.fi

Abstract. We propose an image decomposition technique that captures
the structure of a scene. An image is decomposed into a matrix that
represents the adjacency between the elements of the image and their
distance. Images decomposed this way are then classified using a maximum margin regression (MMR) approach where the normal vector of
the separating hyperplane maps the input feature vectors into the outputs vectors. Multiclass and multilabel classification are native to MMR,
unlike other more classical maximum margin approaches, like SVM. We
have tested our approach with the ImageCLEF 2015 multi-label classification task, Pascal VOC and Flickr dataset.

Keywords: ImageCLEF · Kronecker decomposition · Maximum
margin · MMR · SVM · Multi-label classification · Medical images

1 Introduction

Automatic image classification is a fundamental part of computer vision. An
image is classified according to the visual content it contains. Image classification
spans several decades from the first character or digit recognition challenges, such
as the MNIST dataset [1] to more recent, challenging image classification tasks,
such as the Pascal [2], Imagenet [3] or ImageCLEF [4,5] challenges.

One of the central problems in exploring the general structure of an image is
to recognize the relations between the objects appearing in the image. The task
is not really the recognition of the objects but rather building a model on the
structure: what belongs to what and how they can be related.

One of the most popular streams of machine learning research is to find efficient methods for learning structured outputs. Several researchers introduced
similar approaches to these kind of problems [6–10]. Those methods directly
incorporate the structural learning into a specially chosen optimization framework. It is generally assumed that to learn a discriminating function when the

© Springer International Publishing Switzerland 2016
N. Fuhr et al. (Eds.): CLEF 2016, LNCS 9822, pp. 137–149, 2016.
DOI: 10.1007/978-3-319-44564-9_11

output space is a labeled hierarchy is a much more complex problem than binary classification. In this paper we show that the complexity of this kind of problem can be detached from the optimization model and can be expressed by an embedding into Hilbert space. This allows us to apply a universal optimization model, processing inputs and outputs represented in a properly chosen Hilbert space which can solve the corresponding optimization task without tackling with the underlying structural complexity. The optimization model is an implementation of a certain type of maximum margin regression, an algebraic generalization of the well-known Support Vector Machine. The computational complexity of the optimization scales only with the number of input-output pairs and it is independent from the dimensions of both spaces. Furthermore its overall complexity is equal to a binary classification. Our approach can be easily extended towards other structural learning problems without giving up efficiency on the basic optimization framework.

We will make use of the following mathematical notation conventions in the rest of the paper: $\mathcal{X}$ stands for the space of the input objects, $\mathcal{Y}$ for the space of the outputs. $\mathcal{H}_\phi$ is a Hilbert space comprising the feature vectors, the images of the input vectors with respect to the embedding $\phi()$. $\mathcal{H}_\psi$ is a Hilbert space comprising the image of label vectors with respect to the embedding $\psi()$. $\mathbf{W}$ is a matrix representing the linear operator projecting the feature space $\mathcal{H}_\phi$ into $\mathcal{H}_\psi$. $\langle .,. \rangle_{\mathcal{H}_z}$ denotes the inner product in Hilbert space $\mathcal{H}_z$, $\|.\|_{\mathcal{H}_z}$ is the norm defined in Hilbert space $\mathcal{H}_z$. $\mathbf{tr}(\mathbf{W})$ is the trace of matrix $\mathbf{W}$. $\mathbf{dim}(\mathcal{H})$ is the dimension of the space $\mathcal{H}$. $\mathbf{x}_1 \otimes \mathbf{x}_2$ denotes the tensor product of the vectors $\mathbf{x}_1 \in \mathcal{H}_1$ and $\mathbf{x}_2 \in \mathcal{H}_2$. $\langle \mathbf{A}, \mathbf{B} \rangle_F$ is the Frobenius inner product of a matrix represented by the linear operators $\mathbf{A}$ and $\mathbf{B}$ and it is defined by $\mathbf{tr}(\mathbf{A}'\mathbf{B})$. $\|\mathbf{A}\|_F$ stands for the Frobenius norm of a matrix represented by the linear operator $\mathbf{A}$ and defined by $\sqrt{\langle \mathbf{A}, \mathbf{A} \rangle_F}$. $\mathbf{A} \cdot \mathbf{B}$ is the element-wise(Schur) product of the matrices $\mathbf{A}$ and $\mathbf{B}$. $\mathbf{A}'$, $\mathbf{a}'$ is the transpose of any matrix $\mathbf{A}$ or any vector $\mathbf{a}$.

2   Image Feature Generation via Decomposition

Let us consider a real 2D image decomposition, where we can expect that the points close to each other within continuous 2D blocks relate more strongly than only considering their connection in 1D rows and columns. To represent the image decomposition, the Kronecker product is applied, which can be expressed as

$$\mathbf{X} = \mathbf{A} \otimes \mathbf{B} \begin{bmatrix} A_{1,1}\mathbf{B} & A_{1,2}\mathbf{B} & \cdots & A_{1,n_A}\mathbf{B} \\ A_{2,1}\mathbf{B} & A_{2,2}\mathbf{B} & \cdots & A_{2,n_A}\mathbf{B} \\ \vdots & \vdots & \ddots & \vdots \\ A_{m_A,1}\mathbf{B} & A_{m_A,2}\mathbf{B} & \cdots & A_{m_A,n_A}\mathbf{B} \end{bmatrix} \tag{1}$$

$$\mathbf{A} \in \mathbb{R}^{m_A \times n_A}, \mathbf{B} \in \mathbb{R}^{m_B \times n_B}, \; m_X = m_A \times m_B, n_X = n_A \times n_B$$

In the Kronecker decomposition the second component ($\mathbf{B}$) can be interpreted as a 2D filter of the image represented by the matrix $\mathbf{X}$. We can try to find a sequence of filters by the following procedure:

1. $k = 1$
2. $\mathbf{X}^{(k)} = \mathbf{X}$
3. DO
4. $d(A^{(k)}, B^{(k)}) = \min_{\mathbf{A}_k, \mathbf{B}_k} \|\mathbf{X}^{(k)} - \mathbf{A}^{(k)} \otimes \mathbf{B}^{(k)}\|^2$
5. IF $d(A^{(k)}, B^{(k)}) \leq \epsilon$ STOP
6. $\mathbf{X}^{(k+1)} = \mathbf{X}^{(k)} - \mathbf{A}^{(k)} \otimes \mathbf{B}^{(k)}$
7. $k = k + 1$
8. Goto 3

The question is, if $\mathbf{X}$ is given, how do we compute $\mathbf{A}$ and $\mathbf{B}$? It turns out that the Kronecker decomposition can be carried out by Singular Value Decomposition (SVD) working on a reordered representation of the matrix $\mathbf{X}$.

For an arbitrary matrix $\mathbf{X}$ with size $m \times n$ the SVD is given by $\mathbf{X} = \mathbf{USV}^T$ where $\mathbf{U} \in \mathbb{R}^{m \times m}$ is an orthogonal matrix, $\mathbf{UU}^T = \mathbf{I}_m$, of left singular vectors, $\mathbf{V} \in \mathbb{R}^{n \times n}$, is an orthogonal matrix, $\mathbf{VV}^T = \mathbf{I}_n$, of right singular vectors, and $\mathbf{S} \in \mathbb{R}^{m \times n}$, is a diagonal matrix containing the singular values with nonnegative components in its diagonal.

2.1   Reordering of the Matrix

Since the algorithm solving the SVD problem does not depend directly on the order of the elements of the matrix [11], any permutation of the indexes, i.e. reordering the columns and(or) rows, preserves the same solution.

2.2   Kronecker Decomposition as SVD

The solution to the Kronecker decomposition via the SVD can be found in [11]. This approach considers the aforementioned observation regarding the invariance of the SVD on the reordering of the matrix elements.

In order to show how the reordering of matrix $\mathbf{X}$ can help to solve the Kronecker decomposition problem we present the following example. The matrices in the Kronecker product

$$\mathbf{X} = \mathbf{A} \otimes \mathbf{B}$$

$$\begin{bmatrix} x_{11} & x_{12} & x_{13} & x_{14} & x_{15} & x_{16} \\ x_{21} & x_{22} & x_{23} & x_{24} & x_{25} & x_{26} \\ x_{31} & x_{32} & x_{33} & x_{34} & x_{35} & x_{36} \\ x_{41} & x_{42} & x_{43} & x_{44} & x_{45} & x_{46} \\ x_{51} & x_{52} & x_{53} & x_{54} & x_{55} & x_{56} \\ x_{61} & x_{62} & x_{63} & x_{64} & x_{65} & x_{66} \end{bmatrix} = \begin{bmatrix} a_{11} & a_{12} & a_{13} \\ a_{21} & a_{22} & a_{23} \\ a_{31} & a_{32} & a_{33} \end{bmatrix} \otimes \begin{bmatrix} b_{11} & b_{12} \\ b_{21} & b_{22} \end{bmatrix},$$

can be reordered into

$$\tilde{\mathbf{X}} = \tilde{\mathbf{A}} \otimes \tilde{\mathbf{B}} = \begin{bmatrix} x_{11} & x_{13} & x_{15} & x_{31} & x_{33} & x_{35} & x_{51} & x_{53} & x_{55} \\ x_{12} & x_{14} & x_{16} & x_{32} & x_{34} & x_{36} & x_{52} & x_{54} & x_{56} \\ x_{21} & x_{23} & x_{25} & x_{41} & x_{43} & x_{45} & x_{61} & x_{63} & x_{65} \\ x_{22} & x_{24} & x_{26} & x_{42} & x_{44} & x_{46} & x_{62} & x_{64} & x_{66} \end{bmatrix}$$

$$= \begin{bmatrix} b_{11} \\ b_{12} \\ b_{21} \\ b_{22} \end{bmatrix} \otimes \begin{bmatrix} a_{11} & a_{12} & a_{13} & a_{21} & a_{22} & a_{23} & a_{31} & a_{32} & a_{33} \end{bmatrix},$$

where the blocks of $\mathbf{X}$ and the matrices $\mathbf{A}$ and $\mathbf{B}$ are vectorized in row wise order.

We can recognize that $\tilde{\mathbf{X}} = \tilde{\mathbf{A}} \otimes \tilde{\mathbf{B}}$ can be interpreted as the first step in the SVD algorithm where we might apply the substitution $\sqrt{s}\mathbf{u} = \tilde{\mathbf{A}}$ and $\sqrt{s}\mathbf{v} = \tilde{\mathbf{B}}$. The proof that this reordering generally provides the correct solution to the Kronecker decomposition can be found in [11].

We can summarize the main steps of the Kronecker decomposition in the following steps:

1. Reorder(reshape) the matrix,
2. Compute the SVD decomposition,
3. Compute the approximation of $\tilde{\mathbf{X}}$ by $\tilde{\mathbf{A}} \otimes \tilde{\mathbf{B}}$
4. Invert the reordering.

This kind of Kronecker decomposition is often referred to as Nearest Orthogonal Kronecker Product as well [11].

3   Learning Task

The learning task that we are going to solve is the following: there is a set, called sample, of pairs of output and input objects $\{(y_i, x_i) : y_i \in \mathcal{Y}, x_i \in \mathcal{X}, i = 1, \ldots, m, \}$ independently and identically chosen out of an unknown multivariate distribution $\mathcal{P}(Y, X)$. The input and the output objects can be arbitrary (graphs, matrices, functions, probability distributions etc.). To these objects, let's consider two functions $\phi : \mathcal{X} \to \mathcal{H}_\phi$ and $\psi : \mathcal{Y} \to \mathcal{H}_\psi$ mapping the input and output objects respectively into linear vector spaces, called from now on, the feature space in case of the inputs and the label space when the outputs are considered.

The objective is to find a linear function acting on the feature space

$$f(\phi(x)) = \mathbf{W}\phi(x) + \mathbf{b}, \tag{2}$$

that produces a prediction of every input object in the label space and in this way could implicitly give back a corresponding output object. Formally we have

$$y = \psi^{-1}(\psi(y)) = \psi^{-1}(f(\phi(x))). \tag{3}$$

4   Optimization Model

4.1   The "Classical" Scheme of Support Vector Machine (SVM)

In the framework of the SVM the outputs represent two classes and the labels are chosen out of the set $y_i \in \{-1, +1\}$. The aim is to find a separating hyperplane, via its normal vector, such that the distance between the elements of the two classes, called margin, is the largest one measured in the direction of this normal vector. This learning scenario can be formulated as an optimization problem:

$$
\begin{aligned}
\min \quad & \tfrac{1}{2}\|\mathbf{w}\|_2^2 + C\mathbf{1}'\boldsymbol{\xi} \\
\text{w.r.t.} \quad & \mathbf{w} : \mathcal{H}_\phi \to \mathbb{R}, \text{ normal vector} \\
& b \in \mathbb{R}, \text{ bias}, \boldsymbol{\xi} \in \mathbb{R}^m, \text{ error vector} \\
\text{s.t.} \quad & y_i(\mathbf{w}'\phi(\mathbf{x}_i) + b) \geq 1 - \xi_i \\
& \boldsymbol{\xi} \geq \mathbf{0}, \ i = 1, \ldots, m.
\end{aligned}
$$

4.2   Reinterpretation of the Normal Vector w

The normal vector $\mathbf{w}$ formally behaves as a linear transformation acting on the feature vectors whose capabilities can be even further extended. This extension can be characterized briefly in the following way

SVM	ExtendedView
– $\mathbf{w}$ is the normal vector of the separating hyperplane.	– $\mathbf{W}$ is a linear operator projecting the feature space into the label space.
– $y_i \in \{-1, +1\}$ binary outputs.	– $y_i \in \mathcal{Y}$ arbitrary outputs
– The labels are equal to the binary objects.	– $\psi(y_i) \in \mathcal{H}_\psi$ are the labels, the embedded outputs in a linear vector space

To summarize the learning task, we end up in the following optimization problem when compared to the original primal form of the SVM:

Primal problems for maximum margin learning

	Binary class learning Support Vector Machine(SVM)	Vector label learning Maximum Margin Regression(MMR)
min	$\frac{1}{2}\|\mathbf{w}\|_2^2 + C\mathbf{1}'\boldsymbol{\xi}$	$\frac{1}{2}\|\mathbf{W}\|_F^2 + C\mathbf{1}'\boldsymbol{\xi}$
w.r.t.	$\mathbf{w} : \mathcal{H}_\phi \to \mathbb{R},$ normal vector	$\mathbf{W} : \mathcal{H}_\phi \to \mathcal{H}_\psi,$ linear operator,
	$b \in \mathbb{R},$ bias,	$\mathbf{b} \in \mathcal{H}_\psi,$ translation(bias),
	$\boldsymbol{\xi} \in \mathbb{R}^m,$ error vector	
s.t.	$y_i(\mathbf{w}'\phi(\mathbf{x}_i) + b) \geq 1 - \xi_i,$	$\langle \psi(y_i), \mathbf{W}\phi(\mathbf{x}_i) + \mathbf{b}\rangle_{\mathcal{H}_\psi} \geq 1 - \xi_i,$
	$\boldsymbol{\xi} \geq \mathbf{0}, \; i = 1, \ldots, m.$	

In the extended formulation we exploit the fact that the Frobenius norm and inner product correspond to the linear vector space of matrices with dimension equal to the number of elements of the matrices, hence it gives an isomorphism between the space spanned by the normal vector of the hyperplane occurring in the SVM and the space spanned by the linear transformations.

4.3   Dual Problem

The dual problem of MMR presented in Sect. (4.2) is given by

$$\min \; \sum_{i,j=1}^m \alpha_i \alpha_j \overbrace{\langle \phi(\mathbf{x}_i), \phi(\mathbf{x}_j)\rangle}^{\kappa_{ij}^\phi} \overbrace{\langle \psi(\mathbf{y}_i), \psi(\mathbf{y}_j)\rangle}^{\kappa_{ij}^\psi} - \sum_{i=1}^m \alpha_i,$$

w.r.t. $\alpha_i \in \mathbb{R},$

s.t. $\sum_{i=1}^m (\psi(\mathbf{y}_i))_t \alpha_i = 0, \; t = 1, \ldots, \dim(\mathcal{H}_\psi),$

$0 \leq \alpha_i \leq C, \; i = 1, \ldots, m,$ (4)

where κ_{ij}^ϕ kernel items correspond to the feature vectors, and κ_{ij}^ψ kernel items correspond to the label vectors.

The symmetry of the objective function is clearly recognizable showing that the underlying problem without bias is completely reversible. The explicit occurrences of the label vectors can be transformed into implicit ones by exploiting that the feasibility domain covered by the constraints: $\sum_{i=1}^{m}(\psi(\mathbf{y}_i))_t\alpha_i = 0$, $t = 1,\ldots,\dim(\mathcal{H}_\psi)$, coincides with the domain of $\sum_{i=1}^{m}\kappa_{ij}^{\psi}\alpha_i = 0$, $j = 1,\ldots,m$ involving only inner products of the label vectors.

In the case of the original SVM κ_{ij}^{ψ} collapses into the product y_iy_j of the binary labels $+1$ and -1.

4.4   Prediction

After solving the dual problem with the help of the optimum dual variables we can write up the optimal linear operator

$$\mathbf{W} = \sum_{i=1}^{m}\alpha_i\psi(\mathbf{y}_i)\phi(\mathbf{x}_i)'. \tag{5}$$

We can solve this expression by comparing it to the corresponding formula which gives the optimal solution to the SVM, i.e. $\mathbf{w} = \sum_{i=1}^{m}\alpha_iy_i\phi(\mathbf{x}_i)$. The new part includes the vectors representing the output items which in the SVM were only scalar values but we could say in the new interpretation that they are one-dimensional vectors. With the expression of the linear operator $\mathbf{W}$ at hand, the prediction to a new input item $\mathbf{x}$ can be written as

$$\psi(\mathbf{y}) = \mathbf{W}\phi(\mathbf{x}) = \sum_{i=1}^{m}\alpha_i\psi(\mathbf{y}_i)\underbrace{\langle\phi(\mathbf{x}_i),\phi(\mathbf{x})\rangle}_{\kappa^\phi(\mathbf{x}_i,\mathbf{x})}, \tag{6}$$

which involves only the input kernel κ^ϕ and provides the implicit representation of the prediction $\psi(\mathbf{y})$ to the corresponding output $\mathbf{y}$.

Because only the implicit image of the output is given, we need to invert the function ψ to obtain its corresponding $\mathbf{y}$ (pre-image problem). We mention here a scheme that can be applied when the set of all possible outputs is finite with a reasonably small cardinality. At the conditions mentioned we can follow this scenario

$$\mathbf{y}^* = \arg\max_{\mathbf{y}\in\tilde{\mathcal{Y}}}\psi(\mathbf{y})'\mathbf{W}\phi(\mathbf{x})$$
$$= \arg\max_{\mathbf{y}\in\tilde{\mathcal{Y}}}\sum_{i=1}^{m}\alpha_i\overbrace{\langle\psi(\mathbf{y}),\psi(\mathbf{y}_i)\rangle}^{\kappa^\psi(\mathbf{y},\mathbf{y}_i)}\overbrace{\langle\phi(\mathbf{x}_i)'\phi(\mathbf{x})\rangle}^{\kappa^\phi(\mathbf{x}_i,\mathbf{x})} \tag{7}$$
$$\text{where } \mathbf{y}\in\tilde{\mathcal{Y}} = \{\mathbf{y}_1,\ldots,\mathbf{y}_N\} \Leftarrow \text{is the set of the possible outputs.}$$

The main advantage of this approach is that it requires only the inner products in label space. It is also independent from the representation of the output items and can be applied in any complex structural learning problem, e.g. on graphs.

4.5   Hierarchy Learning

As mentioned above in this paper we focus on the case where the output space is a labeled hierarchy. The hierarchy learning is realized via an embedding of each path going from a node to the root of the tree. Let V be the set of nodes in the tree. A path $p(v) \subset V$ is defined as a shortest path from the node v to the root of the tree and its length is equal to $|p(v)|$. The set $I = 1, \ldots, |V|$ gives an indexing of the nodes. The embedding is realized by a vector valued function $\psi : V \rightarrow \mathbb{R}^{|V|}$, and the components of $\psi(v)$ are given by

$$\psi(v)_i = \begin{cases} r & \text{if } v_i \notin p(v), \\ sq^k & \text{if } v_i \in p(v) \text{ and } k = |p(v)| - |p(v_i)|, \end{cases} \tag{8}$$

where r, q, s are the parameters of the embedding. The parameter q expresses the diminishing weight of the nodes being closer to the root. If $q = 0$, assuming $0^0 = 1$, then the intermediate nodes and the root are disregarded, thus we have a simple multiclass classification problem. The value of r can be 0 but some experiments show it may help to improve the classification performance. We might conjecture that the best choice of parameters are those which minimize the correlation between all pairs of the label vectors.

4.6 Input and Output Kernels

For the concrete learning task we need to construct the input and output kernels. To build the input kernel, the second component of the Kronecker decomposition of each image - the matrix $\mathbf{B}$ in (1) - is used. The inner product between those matrices is computed by applying the Frobenius inner product. The output kernel is created from the inner products of the vectors representing the path in the hierarchy in (8).

5 Experimental Evaluation

5.1 Methods

In the computation of the prediction results, a 5-fold cross-validation procedure is applied. In the learning procedure, first, a kernel is computed from the corresponding features. Parameters corresponding to each kernel are found by cross validation restricted to the training data, namely it is divided into validation test and validation training parts. Then the learner is trained only on the validation training items. The values of the parameters are chosen which maximize the $F1$ score on the validation test. We, indeed, used three different evaluation measures that are popular in multi-label classification, namely precision (P), recall (R) and F1. They are given by a combination of the true positives T_p, false positives F_p and false negatives F_n:

$$P = \frac{T_p}{T_p + F_p}, \quad R = \frac{T_p}{T_p + F_n}, \quad F1 = \frac{2PR}{P + R} \tag{9}$$

Here, the perfect case has a precision value of 1 for any recall. Also the results will report here on two types of kernels: polynomial and Gaussian.

5.2 ImageCLEF Multi-label Classification [4,5]

Description. The challenge we participated was the characterization of compound figures. The task consists of labeling the compound figures with 30 different classes without knowing where the separation lines are. The training set consists of 1,071 figures, the test set consists of 927 figures.

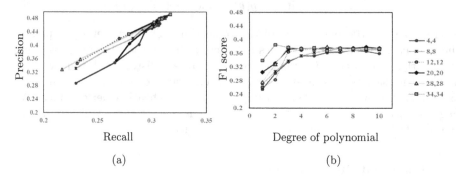

Fig. 1. Results for six filter sizes: 4, 8, 12, 20, 18 and 32, training with a polynomial kernel of degrees 1 to 10. (a) Precision and Recall, (b) F1 score.

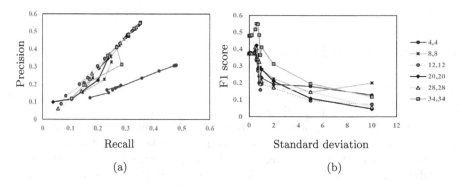

Fig. 2. Results for six filter sizes: 4, 8, 12, 20, 18 and 32, training with a Gaussian kernel with *stdev* 0.01 to 10. (a) Precision and Recall, (b) F1 score.

Results. We used a third degree polynomial kernel, the only factor changing at each run was the random selection in the 5-fold cross-validation. The ImageCLEF organisers provided the Hamming loss, that evaluates the fraction of wrong labels to the total number of labels. The perfect case would have a Hamming loss of 0. In our case the values were exceptionally low (very close to 0) and ranged from

0.0671 to 0.0817. Precision-Recall curves for six different Kronecker 2D filter sizes are given in Fig. 1a for polynomial kernels of different degrees and in Fig. 2a for Gaussian kernels having different standard deviations. Their respective F1 scores are in Figs. 1b and 2b. The parameter for the Precision-Recall curve (and the F1 plot) in the polynomial kernel was the degree of the polynomial, from 1 to 10. The parameter that was varied in the Gaussian kernel to generate its Precision-Recall curve (and the F1 plot) was the standard deviation of the Gaussian: 0.01, 0.02, 0.05, 0.1, 0.2, 0.5, 0.6, 0.7, 0.8, 0.9, 1, 2, 5 and 10.

These results show that larger filter sizes provide better results. Regarding kernels, when using a polynomial kernel, there is a dramatically increase in F1 scores when using a cubic kernel as compared to a linear or quadratic one. In the case of a Gaussian kernel, the best scores happen at standard deviations smaller than 1, although values in the middle (e.g. 0.5, 0.6) provide better results than very small values (e.g. 0.01, 0.05). The best F1 score using a polynomial kernel was 0.38, in the case of a Gaussian kernel, the highest F1 score was 0.43.

5.3   Pascal and Flickr

Description. Our approach has also been tested on the dataset Pascal VOC 07 and Flickr. The Pascal VOC [12] dataset is provided as part of the PASCAL Visual Object Classes challenge of which the main tasks are: classification, detection and segmentation. For our experiments we chose the dataset of the year 2007 containing 11.472 images for training, 10.358 for test and 20 categories. The Mir Flickr [13] dataset is composed of images downloaded from the

Table 1. Description of the 14 visual features.

Feature	Dimension	Source	Descriptor
Hsv	4096	color	HSV
Lab	4096	color	LAB
Rgb	4096	color	RGB
HsvV3H1	5184	color	HSV
LabV3H1	5184	color	LAB
RgbV3H1	5184	color	RGB
DenseHue	100	texture	hue
HarrisHue	100	texture	Hue
DenseHueV3H1	300	texture	hue
HarrisHueV3H1	300	texture	Hue
DenseSift	1000	texture	sift
HarrisSift	1000	texture	sift
DenseSiftV3H1	3000	texture	sift
HarrisSiftV3H1	3000	texture	sift

Gaussian kernel			
Feature	P(%)	R(%)	F1(%)
TD	**0.4158**	**0.2877**	**0.3400**
HarrisSiftV3H1	0.4623	0.4491	0.4552
HarrisSift	0.4202	0.4895	0.4522
DenseSiftV3H1	0.4189	0.4886	0.4510
DenseSift	0.3750	0.5044	0.4302
LabV3H1	0.3911	0.3366	0.3618
DenseHueV3H1	0.3884	0.3282	0.3558
HarrisHueV3H1	0.3274	0.3884	0.3552
RgbV3H1	0.3907	0.3224	0.3533
HsvV3H1	0.4080	0.3048	0.3489
Hsv	0.3911	0.3085	0.3449
Lab	0.4135	0.2920	0.3423
Rgb	0.3857	0.2985	0.3350
HarrisHue	0.3930	0.2887	0.3328
DenseHue	0.3962	0.2828	0.3299

Polynomial kernel			
Feature	P(%)	R(%)	F1(%)
TD	**0.3931**	**0.2855**	**0.3308**
HarrisSiftV3H1	0.4002	0.5520	0.4640
HarrisSift	0.3728	0.5523	0.4449
DenseSiftV3H1	0.3592	0.5663	0.4396
DenseSift	0.3442	0.5337	0.4184
HsvV3H1	0.3815	0.3295	0.3536
RgbV3H1	0.3479	0.3551	0.3515
LabV3H1	0.3106	0.3868	0.3434
HarrisHueV3H1	0.3110	0.3894	0.3417
DenseHueV3H1	0.3166	0.3607	0.3363
Hsv	0.3390	0.3232	0.3309
HarrisHue	0.3037	0.3597	0.3241
Rgb	0.2906	0.3420	0.3135
Lab	0.2800	0.3389	0.3031
DenseHue	0.2808	0.3329	0.2995

Fig. 3. Results for Pascal07 dataset with polynomial and Gaussian kernel.

Gaussian kernel			
Feature	P(%)	R(%)	F1(%)
TD	**0.3164**	**0.3780**	**0.3118**
HarrisSiftV3H1	0.5470	0.3842	0.4512
DenseSift	0.5438	0.3862	0.4515
HarrisSift	0.5368	0.3780	0.4435
DenseSiftV3H1	0.5475	0.3807	0.4491
LabV3H1	0.4693	0.3200	0.3806
HarrisHueV3H1	0.4368	0.3288	0.3752
DenseHueV3H1	0.4221	0.3333	0.3723
HsvV3H1	0.4570	0.3062	0.3667
HarrisHue	0.3753	0.3435	0.3587
RgbV3H1	0.4150	0.3089	0.3542
Lab	0.4153	0.3016	0.3494
DenseHue	0.3854	0.3187	0.3477
Rgb	0.4181	0.2824	0.3371
Hsv	0.4152	0.2762	0.3317

Polynomial kernel			
Feature	P(%)	R(%)	F1(%)
TD	**0.2311**	**0.2615**	**0.2453**
HarrisSiftV3H1	0.5289	0.4646	0.4940
DenseSiftV3H1	0.5328	0.4415	0.4828
HarrisSift	0.5260	0.4447	0.4819
DenseSift	0.5132	0.4316	0.4688
LabV3H1	0.4508	0.3533	0.3961
HsvV3H1	0.3961	0.3655	0.3798
HarrisHueV3H1	0.4115	0.3490	0.3777
DenseHueV3H1	0.4086	0.3445	0.3737
RgbV3H1	0.3996	0.3460	0.3704
Lab	0.2717	0.5600	0.3658
DenseHue	0.2698	0.5249	0.3564
HarrisHue	0.3294	0.4159	0.3561
Hsv	0.3603	0.3602	0.3540
Rgb	0.3495	0.3406	0.3443

Fig. 4. Results for Flickr dataset with polynomial and Gaussian kernel.

social network Flickr through its public API. For these experiments, the 2008 version has been chosen: it contains 12.500 training images, 12.500 test images and 38 categories.

Features for Comparison. For these datasets, in addition to the features extracted with tensor decomposition, we worked with other 14 visual features [14,15] summarized in Table 1. These include six global color histograms and eight local bag-of-visual-words features. Readers are referred to [14] for more detail on extracting these features.

Results. We compared Pascal and Flickr with other descriptors described in [14]. The decomposition used for Pascal is 3 components with a Kronecker 2D filter size of 22, while for Flickr is 4 components with filter size of 10. Parameters where chosen using cross-validation for Gaussian and polynomial kernels. Results are shown in Fig. 3 for the Pascal dataset and Fig. 4 for the Flickr dataset. Our results show that the Kronecker decomposition is in line with other features in these datasets when considered separately. When it is compared with combinations of features (e.g. HarrisSiftHV3), the Kronecker decomposition is clearly outperformed on both datasets. Future work would include a more extensive evaluation in order to improve our decomposition results by combing it with other features, such as color and texture.

6   Discussion

We can capture the structure of a scene by considering images as matrices that can be decomposed into two matrices, whose Kronecker product results in the original image. The question is how to obtain those two matrices. Our solution involved the use of Singular Value Decomposition and the reordering of the original matrix values (i.e. the pixels in the image). This solution leads to an accurate approximation of the Kronecker decomposition. Our results show that we can obtain filters (one of the decomposed matrices) that can be used for image classification. We showed the validity of this approach in the image classification challenge outperforming competition at this task. We further tested this approach on more classical object recogntion tasks using the Pascal and Flickr datasets. At these tasks, the Kronecker decomposition was on par with most features but it was also outperformed by others. There is still a number of issues that need to be solved when considering our approach that needs further evaluation, which was not included here due to time constraints:

1. Choosing the proper parameters for the Kronecker decomposition and the learning approach. Our experimental evaluation shows that the size of the filters is critical in order to obtain good results (Figs. 1 and 2). The type of learning kernel and their parameters are also very important. The search space is then quite large, we hope than in future work we can learn the best parameters for at least the Kronecker decomposition.
2. The Kronecker decomposition maybe better suited to scene recognition than object recognition. This is the case of many others features (e.g. Gist). We think that this may be also the case for the Kronecker decomposition since it showed a lower than expected performance in the Pascal and Flickr datasets for object classification, while at the CLEF image classification, results were very promising. We would need to further test the Kronecker decomposition in larger scene datasets (e.g. Sun) to confirm this point.
3. We used a learning scheme due to being better suited to the structure of the ImageCLEF dataset architecture than other learning approaches. It would be interesting to see how the decomposition behaves in other more classical tasks using a more classical learning approach (e.g. SVM, Random forests, etc.).

To summarize, the Kronecker decomposition provided very good results at the ImageCLEF classification task. For this work, we extended that experimental evaluation with other classification datasets. Unfortunately, even though the results were in par with many other features to which we compared, the Kronecker decomposition was not in the high ranks. We think that we would need further improvements and evaluation to show its capabilities.

7   Conclusions

By decomposing the image matrix into a similar structure, e.g. into a sequence of Kronecker products, the structure behind the scene could be captured. For classification we have applied a version of a maximum margin based regression (MMR) technique [16]. The evaluation of our methodology in the ImageCLEF 2015 [4,5], Pascal and Flickr provided promising results. For furture work, we need to further test our decomposition with other decomposition values as well as the results when combined with other features.

Acknowledgement. The research leading to these results has received funding from the EU seventh Framework Programme FP7/2007-2013 under grant agreement no. 270273, Xperience.

References

1. LeCun, Y., Bottou, L., Bengio, Y., Haffner, P.: Gradient-based learning applied to document recognition. Proc. IEEE **86**(11), 2278–2324 (1998)
2. Everingham, M., Eslami, S.A., Van Gool, L., Williams, C.K., Winn, J., Zisserman, A.: The pascal visual object classes challenge: a retrospective. Int. J. Comput. Vision **111**(1), 98–136 (2014)
3. Russakovsky, O., Deng, J., Su, H., Krause, J., Satheesh, S., Ma, S., Huang, Z., Karpathy, A., Khosla, A., Bernstein, M., Berg, A.C., Fei-Fei, L.: ImageNet large scale visual recognition challenge. Int. J. Comput. Vision **115**(3), 211–252 (2015)
4. Villegas, M., et al.: General overview of ImageCLEF at the CLEF 2015 Labs. In: Mothe, J., Savoy, J., Kamps, J., Pinel-Sauvagnat, K., Jones, G., San Juan, E., Capellato, L., Ferro, N. (eds.) CLEF 2015. LNCS, vol. 9283, pp. 444–461. Springer, Heidelberg (2015). doi:10.1007/978-3-319-24027-5_45
5. Seco, G., de Herrera, A., Müller, H., Bromuri, S.: Overview of the ImageCLEF 2015 medical classification task. In: Working Notes of CLEF 2015. CEUR Workshop Proceedings (2015). CEUR-WS.org
6. Taskar, B., Guestrin, C., Koller, D.: Max-margin Markov networks. In: NIPS (2003)
7. Altun, Y., Tsochantaridis, I., Hofmann, T.: Hidden markov support vector machines. In: ICML 2003, pp. 3–10 (2003)
8. Tsochantaridis, I., Joachims, T., Hofmann, T., Altun, Y.: Large margin methods for structured and interdependent output variables. J. Mach. Learn. Res. (JMLR) **6**, 1453–1484 (2005)
9. Rousu, J., Saunders, C., Szedmak, S., Shawe-Taylor, J.: Learning hierarchical multi-category text classification models. In: ICML (2005)
10. Bakir, G.H., Hofmann, T., Scholkopf, B., Smola, A.J., Taskar, B., Vishwanathan, S.V.N. (eds.): Predicting Structured Data. MIT Press, Cambridge (2007)
11. Loan, C.: The ubiquitous kronecker product. J. Comput. Appl. Math. **123**, 85–100 (2000). The nearest Kronecker product

12. Everingham, M., Van Gool, L., Williams, C.K.I., Winn, J., Zisserman, A.: The PASCAL Visual Object Classes Challenge 2007 (VOC2007) Results (2007). http://www.pascal-network.org/challenges/VOC/voc2007/workshop/index.html

13. Huiskes, M.J., Lew, M.S.: The MIR flickr retrieval evaluation. In: MIR 2008: Proceedings of the 2008 ACM International Conference on Multimedia Information Retrieval. ACM, New York (2008)

14. Guillaumin, M., Mensink, T., Verbeek, J., Schmid, C.: Tagprop: Discriminative metric learning in nearest neighbor models for image auto-annotation. In: International Conference on Computer Vision, pp. 309–316, September 2009

15. INRIA: Inria features for image annotation and classification data sets. http://lear.inrialpes.fr/people/guillaumin/data.php

16. Xiong, H., Szedmak, S., Piater, J.: Scalable, accurate image annotation with joint SVMs and output kernels. Neurocomputing **169**, 205–214 (2015)

A Two-Step Retrieval Method
for Image Captioning

Luis Pellegrin[1]([⊠]), Jorge A. Vanegas[2], John Arevalo[2], Viviana Beltrán[2],
Hugo Jair Escalante[1], Manuel Montes-y-Gómez[1], and Fabio A. González[2]

[1] Instituto Nacional de Astrofísica, Óptica y Electrónica (INAOE),
Tonantzintla, Mexico
pellegrin@inaoep.mx
[2] MindLab Research Group, Universidad Nacional de Colombia (UNAL),
Bogotá, Colombia

Abstract. Image captioning is the task of assigning phrases to images describing their visual content. Two main approaches for image captioning are commonly used. On the one hand, traditional approaches assign the captions from the most similar images to the image query. On the other hand, recent methods generate captions by sentence generation systems that learn a joint distribution of captions-images relying on a training set. The main limitation is that both approaches require a great number of manually labeled captioned images. This paper presents a unsupervised approach for image captioning based in a two steps image-textual retrieval process. First, given a query image, visually related words are retrieved from a multimodal indexing. The multimodal indexing is built by using a large dataset of web pages containing images. A vocabulary of words is extracted from web pages, for each word is used the visual representation of images to learn a feature model, in this way we can match query images with words by simply measuring visual similarity. Second, a query is formed with the retrieved words and candidate captions are retrieved from a reference dataset of sentences. Despite the simplicity of our method, it is able to get rid of the need of manually labeled images and instead takes advantage of the noisy data derived from the Web, e.g. web pages. The proposed approach has been evaluated on *Generation of Textual Descriptions of Images Task* at ImageCLEF 2015. Experimental results show the competitiveness of the proposed approach. In addition we report preliminary results on the use of our method for the auto-illustration task.

Keywords: Image captioning · Auto-illustration · Image retrieval · Multimodal indexing · Visual prototypes

1 Introduction

Every day, millions of images are shared through the Internet by using hosting services, however, most of these images are not properly organized, and hence it

© Springer International Publishing Switzerland 2016
N. Fuhr et al. (Eds.): CLEF 2016, LNCS 9822, pp. 150–161, 2016.
DOI: 10.1007/978-3-319-44564-9_12

is not straightforward getting access to them. One practical way to ease the accessibility to these images is by associating text to them, so they can be retrieved by using textual queries. However, it is rather uncommon for people to manually assign textual descriptions to images. In this line, the goal of automatic image captioning is to develop systems that can automatically generate textual descriptions depicting the visual content of images. Two main approaches for image captioning have been adopted. On the one hand, traditional approaches assign (transfer) the captions from the most similar images to the query image. On the other hand, recent methods rely on sentence generation systems that learn a joint distribution over training pairs of images and their captions. Both approaches require of manually labeled datasets of captioned images, where a large amount of images are available. Although, these approaches have proved to be competitive, they can only generate captions similar to those that were seen during training, and, of course, gathering manually labeled data is time consuming and expensive.

This paper presents an alternative approach to generate textual descriptions for images that does not require labeled data at all. Motivated by the large number of images that can be found and gathered from the Internet, covering a wide diversity of topics and being easily accessible, the proposed method relies on the use of the textual-visual information derived from web pages containing images. Although the relatedness of an image with the text in the web page varies greatly, the proposed method is able to take advantage of multimodal redundancy. In this regard, our strategy relies on a multimodal indexing of words, where for every word in the vocabulary we have a visual representation associated to it, in this way we can match query images with words by simply measuring visual similarity. The multimodal indexing is built by using a large dataset of web pages containing images. Hence, the proposed method does not depend on manually captioned images for training. The proposed image captioning method can be seen as a two-step information retrieval (IR) process: given a query image, first, visually related words are retrieved from the multimodal indexing, second, a query is formed with the retrieved words and candidate captions are retrieved from a reference dataset of sentences. An important remark about our method is that it is unsupervised, and in principle it can describe images using any word from the extracted vocabulary. The proposed method was evaluated in the ImageCLEF2015's Scalable Concept Image Annotation dataset. Experimental results show the competitiveness of our method when compared with representative approaches from the state of the art that use more complex processes to image captioning, motivating further research on the proposed methodology.

The remainder of the paper is organized as follows. Section 2 reviews relevant and recent work on image captioning; Sect. 3 provides a detailed description of the proposed method; Sect. 4 describes the experimental settings; Sect. 5 reports experimental results; finally, in Sect. 6 some conclusions of this work are presented.

2   Related Work

Image captioning methods can be organized in two main approaches: traditional methods based on content-based image retrieval (CBIR) and methods based on model learning. In the latter, recent methods based on deep learning have gotten more attention due to their good performance on image annotation [1].

In the traditional group, the task is posed as a retrieval problem: the image is used as query and the most similar images from a training set transfer their description to it [2,3]. An important drawback of this approach is that a great variety of images are necessary to have enough coverage in terms of the captions that can be generated, besides, each time an image will be captioned, it is necessary to estimate the similarity between query image and all images stored in the dataset.

The second approach is more elaborated, and is based on models learned from data (usually, classifiers) instead of a CBIR step. The task is commonly performed in two steps: first, given an image to describe, supervised models are used to detect objects or concepts in the image; then the labels associated to objects/concepts are used to generate sentences. Sentences can be generated by applying predefined rules or language templates on the detected objects/concepts or relying on sentence generation models (e.g., language models) [4–6]. A limitation of these models is the number of different objects/concepts that a model can recognize, and the need of labeled data to build the models. More recent approaches in this category use deep learning techniques to generate sentences. The general idea is to learn a joint distribution over images and captions, see e.g. [7], here the method allows to assign short phrases. More complex approaches have been capable to generate new phrases by means of Recurrent Neural Network models [8,9].

Progress in the generation of sentences for images is remarkable, but still remains a scalability challenge. Also, image captioning methods rely on manually labeled data for learning models, an expensive and subjective labor due to the great variety of images. Unlike state of the art approaches in image captioning, our method uses images contained in web pages to generate a (synthetic) visual representation (a visual prototype) for every word in the annotation vocabulary. Thus, visual prototypes are then used to detect objects/concepts, similarly as classifiers, but not requiring labeled data and of supervised learning methodologies. In this way, our method is not restricted to the set of objects a classifier can recognize. On the other hand, the second step of our method retrieves candidate captions from a sentences dataset, however, please note that we do not need these captions or phrases to necessarily be associated with the images. The details of the proposed method are described in the next section.

3   A Two-Step Retrieval Method for Image Captioning

The proposed image captioning method is divided into two IR stages (see Fig. 1): **word-retrieval** that receives as input a query image and generates words as outputs (the words associated to concepts present in the image); and **caption-retrieval** that takes as input the words detected in the previous step and generates a sentence as output. In the following we describe both steps in detail, please note that in order to perform these two IR steps, two reference collections are needed. On the one hand, a *reference image collection*, composed of images that have an associated free-text (in our case, a dataset of web pages containing images). Please note that it is not necessary that the free-text is entirely related to the image. On the other hand, the method also requires a *reference textual description* dataset that is composed of sentences or phrases. The phrases may or may not be related to the images from the reference image collection.

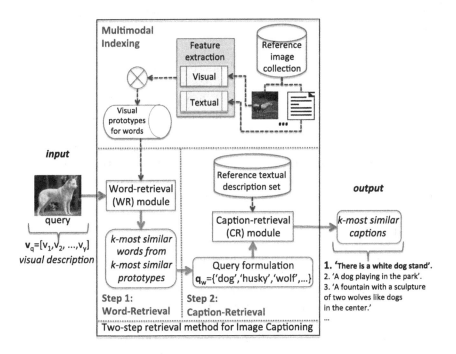

Fig. 1. Diagram of the proposed approach for image captioning.

Figure 1 summarizes the proposed method, it uses a query image as input, then the image is processed by the two retrieval steps mentioned above, finally a caption is generated as output. The first stage matches a query image with words using a CBIR (word-retrieval step) module. The CBIR is applied on top of a multimodal indexing (MI) that relates words with visual descriptors. The second stage uses the output of the first stage for building a query and searching for a caption in the reference sentences dataset. The final output is a caption that describes the input image. The remainder of section describes in detail the main processes associated to our method.

3.1   Feature Extraction

Images and texts from the reference image collections are represented in a feature space in order to apply the proposed method, in the following we describe the feature extraction process for both modalities.

Visual Feature Extraction. Each image is represented by a numerical vector that somehow describes the content of the image, e.g., color histogram, surface orientation, edge histograms, etc. Each image representation is associated to the representation of its corresponding text. When extracting features for images in the reference image collection we obtain $\mathbf{V}$, a matrix of dimensions $n \times |Y|$, where n is the number of images in the reference collection and $|Y|$ is the dimensionality of the considered descriptors.

Textual Feature Extraction. Documents (text in web pages) are represented with a *bag-of-words* representation. Each document under this representation is associated to its corresponding image. When processing the n documents in the collection we obtain $\mathbf{T}$, a matrix of dimensions $n \times |X|$, where, again, n is the number of texts in the reference image collection and $|X|$ is the size of the vocabulary that was used to build the bag-of-words. Likewise, textual feature extraction is also applied to the reference sentence dataset. In this case we obtain $\mathbf{C}$, a $m \times |X|$ matrix, where m is the number of the indexed sentences from the reference textual description dataset, and $|X|$ as before.

3.2   Multimodal Indexing

This section describes the MI that is used in the first retrieval stage. The MI makes possible the mapping of a visual representation (query image) into a textual representation (candidate words/concepts). In a nutshell, the MI is matrix that relates every word in the vocabulary with a visual representation, that is, we have for every word a prototypical image that somehow summarizes the visual appearance of a word across a set of web pages. In this way, any query image can be compared with prototypes and we can determine what words are more related to the query. The main idea behind this representation is that both the textual view $\mathbf{T}$ as the visual view $\mathbf{V}$ of an image have a salience in the same objects represented by the two different features. In other words, if in a web page the main topic is about 'dogs' then there exists a likelihood that the image in the web page is also about a 'dog'.

For the construction of the MI we rely on term-occurrence statistics that are the product of both textual and visual features. Our multimodal representation $\mathbf{M}$ is obtained as follows:

$$\mathbf{M} = \mathbf{T}^T \cdot \mathbf{V} \tag{1}$$

we can see that $\mathbf{M}_{i,j} = \sum_{k=1}^{n} \mathbf{T}_{i,k} \cdot \mathbf{V}_{k,j}$ is a scalar value that expresses the degree of association between word i and visual feature j, across the whole collection of documents[1]. In this way, each row of the matrix $\mathbf{M}$ can be seen as a visual prototype for the corresponding word from the vocabulary. Therefore, the MI is a matrix $\mathbf{M}$ of size $|X| \times |Y|$, that is, their dimensions are determined by the sizes of the textual vocabulary and the visual features.

3.3   Step 1: Word-Retrieval (WR)

The first retrieval stage aims at associating images with candidate words/concepts, the MI is used for this purpose. Specifically, the query image and visual prototypes are used in a similar way to a CBIR task. As is depicted in Fig. 1: first, given an image $\mathcal{I}_q$, its visual representation $\mathbf{v}_q$ is used as query, next, the word-retrieval module measures the similarity between $\mathbf{v}_q$ and the visual prototypes corresponding to every word $\mathcal{W}_i$ from the MI. The word-retrieval module gives a score to every word using the cosine as similarity measure defined by:

$$score(\mathcal{W}_i) = cosine(\mathbf{v}_q, \mathbf{M}_i) = \frac{\mathbf{v}_q * \mathbf{M}_i}{||\mathbf{v}_q||||\mathbf{M}_i||} \qquad (2)$$

where $\mathbf{M}_i$ is the ith row of the MI matrix $\mathbf{M}$, that is, the visual prototype for the ith word. Finally, the k words associated to the most similar prototypes are used in the next stage to generate the caption for the input image.

3.4   Step 2: Caption-Retrieval (CR)

This second retrieval stage aims at generating the caption for the image. As shown in Fig. 1, the k words retrieved by the WR module are used to formulate a second query $\mathbf{q}_w$, which is used as input to the caption-retrieval module. $\mathbf{q}_w$ is a vector of length $|X|$ that contains values different to zero only for the elements of the vector associated to the k retrieved words. The caption-retrieval module measures the cosine similarity between $\mathbf{q}_w$ and each indexed caption $\mathcal{C}_i$ from the indexed matrix $\mathbf{C}$ of the reference sentences set. Hence, for each caption $\mathcal{C}_i$, the caption-retrieval module gives a score using:

$$score(\mathcal{C}_i) = cosine(\mathbf{q}_w, \mathbf{C}_i) = \frac{\mathbf{q}_w * \mathbf{C}_i}{||\mathbf{q}_w||||\mathbf{C}_i||} \qquad (3)$$

where $\mathbf{C}_i$ is the ith row of matrix $\mathbf{C}$, associated to the ith sentence/caption $\mathcal{C}_i$, and $\mathbf{q}_w$ is the query vector formed with the words obtained from the first retrieval step. Finally, the s captions that maximize the cosine similarity can be used to describe the image $\mathcal{I}_q$. In this work we used the caption with the highest similarity as textual description.

---

[1] Both representations require to be normalized, in this work we used L1 normalization.

4   Experimental Settings

For the evaluation of the proposed method, we used the ImageCLEF2015's Scalable Concept Image Annotation dataset [10]. This dataset is composed of 500,000 images extracted from a database of millions of images downloaded from the Internet. Every image in the dataset has an associated text, i.e. the web pages where the images were found. A subset of 1,979 images is used as development set, every image in this subset has assigned at least five captions generated by a human. Images in the development set contain at least one of 251 predefined concepts [10], that were chosen to be visually concrete and localizable in the images. Additionally, there exists a testing dataset comprising 3,070 images, this dataset is only used for evaluation. Please note that the ground truth for this latter dataset has not been released.

In our case, we use the entire training dataset of 500,000 web pages for multimodal indexing.

For the visual representation of images, we experimented with several visual features, including: color histograms, a variety of SIFT descriptors, and activations of a CNN model. At the end, ReLU7 layer (activations in a CNN model of 16-layer) were chosen due to its better performance in the retrieval stage.

For the textual representation of reference collections, basically, metadata and *stopwords* were removed, next a stemming procedure is applied, after which the vocabulary is obtained. We consider that to express the visual content of the images, it is appropriate to use nouns rather to use pronouns or verbs, so we eliminated these in a further step. We use two different reference sentence sets for the generation of the textual descriptions:

- **Set A.** The set of sentences from the development set of ImageCLEF 2015, with ≈19,000 sentences for 1,979 images.
- **Set B.** Set of sentences used in the evaluation of MS-COCO 2014 dataset [11], with ≈200,000 sentences.

It is important to clarify that we do not use images from MS-COCO or development set of ImageCLEF 2015, just only the captions.

4.1   Settings for Query Formulation (from WR Step to CR Step)

As we mentioned before, a query $\mathbf{q}_w$ is formulated with the output of the WR step, then, $\mathbf{q}_w$ is used in the CR step to retrieve possible captions. We considered three aspects in the query formulation:

1. Types of terms: for this case we have experimented with two types to formulate $\mathbf{q}_w$, using the k words (from the whole vocabulary) associated to the most similar prototypes (from the output of the WR step), and using only the k-most related concepts taken from the predefined list of 251 concepts used in [10]. Our insight is that using words give us a general description, and concepts rather a controlled description.

2. Number of terms: using the images in the development set, we noted that the sparsity on the visual representation of these images could be used to choose a threshold in the number of terms to use. This threshold can be seen as indicator of generality or specificity for sentence generation. Images with high sparsity use few words, and images with low sparsity use more data:
   - Concepts c: three concepts for $>40\%$ sparsity; and five concepts for $<40\%$ sparsity.
   - Words w (all the extracted from vocabulary): 10 words for $>50\%$ sparsity; 30 words between 40% and 50% sparsity, and 50 words for $<40\%$ sparsity.
3. Weighting of terms: the last aspect to consider was the weighting of terms, this can use binary values, as well as the similarity scores obtained from the WR module.

Table 1 summarizes the settings of six runs/configurations we evaluated for the proposed method. Row 1 shows the reference sentence set used (see beginning of the section for more details), row 2 indicates the type of terms used for $\mathbf{q}_w$ (these terms are w for words and c for concepts), finally, row 3 indicates the type of weighting for terms (b for binary and r for real scores).

Table 1. Settings of evaluated runs.

	Runs →					
↓ Settings	1	2	3	4	5	6
1. Sentences set used	A	A	A	A	B	B
2. Data used	c	w	c	w	c	c
3. Query representation	r	r	b	b	r	b

5   Experimental Results

This section reports experimental results obtained with the proposed method. Table 2 shows the results obtained by the six different settings in the test set (as evaluated by the creators of the dataset). For comparison, we show results of state of the art techniques that have used the same dataset [10]: RUC's method [8] uses a deep learning based CNN for image encoding and an RNN-LSTM (Long- Short Term Memory based Recurrent Neural Network) for sentence encoding; UAIC's method [6] uses a template-based approach, and a human upper-bound evaluation that measure one description against the other descriptions. The reported scores correspond to the Meteor Score[2] [12], which is an F-measure of word overlaps with a fragmentation penalty on gaps and word order. Columns of Table 2 indicate the average, median, min and max of Meteor scores.

---

[2] For this case, it uses five human-authored textual descriptions as the gold standard reference.

According to the mean and median performance, it can be seen that when we used only concepts in $\mathbf{q}_w$ (runs 1, 3, 5 and 6) we obtained better results than when using words (runs 2 and 4), we believe this is because of the confidence of the detected concept and also due to the existence of sentences that describe the concept. The best mean score was obtained when using the set A (sentences of evaluation of ImageCLEF dataset) in run 3, we think this is because the set A contains sentences that are similar to those sentences for images in test set than the sentences from the set B, which come from a different dataset (MSCOCO dataset). Another characteristic of run 3 is that it uses binary values for building the query, we believe that a relationship exists between the amount of data used in the textual query and the retrieved captions, and short textual queries are beneficial to a binary representation.

Table 2. METEOR scores of our method and state of the art results.

Run	Mean (Stddev)	Median	Min	Max
run1	0.125 (0.065)	0.114	0.019	0.568
run2	0.114 (0.055)	0.103	0.017	0.423
run3	*0.140 (0.056)*	*0.134*	*0.026*	*0.374*
run4	0.123 (0.053)	0.115	0.022	0.526
run5	0.119 (0.052)	0.110	0.000	0.421
run6	0.126 (0.058)	0.117	0.000	0.406
RUC [8]	**0.180 (0.088)**	**0.168**	**0.019**	**0.570**
UAIC [6]	0.081 (0.051)	0.077	0.014	0.323
Human [10]	0.338 (0.156)	0.335	0.000	0.000

It also can be seen that, in spite of the simplicity of our method, all runs obtained better results than the UAIC method. This is because UAIC method generates sentences from a certain number of concepts obtained by classifiers, instead our method considers more words that are extracted from web pages. On the other hand, the RUC method obtains better results than our method. However, one should note that our method is advantageous in that it is simpler, it does not rely on a training dataset of manually captioned images, and it can detect any word extracted from web pages. Finally, the difference of performance in comparison with human upper-bound makes clear that there is scope for future work.

Figures 2 and 3 show the words (WR step) and captions (CR step) generated by our method for two sample images. They show outputs corresponding to different settings of the proposed method. Their comparison indicates that the use of concepts (as opposed to words) allow to generate more general captions, whereas the use of words allow to generate more specific captions.

As we can see in the output of WR step in Fig. 2, there are many related words, consequently, the generated sentences for the image description are

WR step:
[c]: *helicopter, airplane, tractor, truck, tank, ...*
[w]: *airbus, lockhe, helicopter, airforce, aircraft, warship, biplane, refuel, seaplane, amphibian, ...*

CR step:
[c_b]: *A helicopter hovers above some trees.*
[c_r]: *A helicopter that is in flight.*
[w_b]: *A large vessel like an aircraft carrier is sat stationary on a large body of water.*
[w_r]: *A helicopter that is in flight.*

Fig. 2. Query image 1 and its generated description using set A under different settings.

WR step:
[c]: *drum, piano, tractor, telescope, guitar, ...*
[w]: *sicken, drummer, cymbal, decapitate, remorse, conga, snare, bassist, orquesta, vocalist, ...*

CR step:
[c_b]: *A band is playing on stage, they are playing the drums and guitar and singing, a crowd is watching the performance.*
[c_r]: *Two men playing the drums.*
[w_b]: *A picture of a drummer drumming and a guitarist playing his guitar.*
[w_r]: *A picture of a drummer drumming and a guitarist playing his guitar.*

Fig. 3. Query image 2 and its generated description using set A under different settings.

acceptable. In this case, the use of concepts [c] achieves better sentences for the image description than the use of words [w].

On the other hand, Fig. 3 shows some sentences that describe the image content correctly, but in this case the use of words [w] achieves better sentences for image description than the use of concepts [c].

5.1 Auto-illustration

Auto-illustration is a closely related task to image captioning. The goal is to find an image that best illustrates a given sentence (i.e., the inverse captioning problem). Due to nature of our MI, it is possible to change the direction of the retrieval process, that is, it can be used to illustrate a sentence with images. In this case, a sentence is taken as query and used to retrieve images from a reference image collection. First, keywords are extracted from the given query sentence, then, using the visual prototypes that correspond to the extracted keywords, an average visual prototype is formed that is used to retrieve related images:

$$score(\mathcal{S}_q, \mathcal{I}_i) = cosine(\mathbf{M}_{avg}, \mathbf{v}_i) = \frac{\mathbf{M}_{avg} * \mathbf{v}_i}{||\mathbf{M}_{avg}|| ||\mathbf{v}_i||} \qquad (4)$$

where $\mathbf{M}_{avg}$ is the average visual prototype formed by the words extracted from the input sentence $\mathcal{S}_q$, and $\mathbf{v}_i$ is the visual representation of an image from

Fig. 4. Given the phrase *'Some people are standing on a crowd crowded sidewalk'*, the top five images retrieved by using the average visual prototype formed by *'crowd'*, *'people'*, *'sidewalk'* and *'stand'*.

Fig. 5. Given the phrase *'A grilled ham and cheese sandwich with egg on a plate'*, the top five images retrieved by using the average visual prototype formed by *'cheese'*, *'egg'*, *'grill'*, *'ham'*, *'plate'* and *'sandwich'*.

the reference image collection. The query is compared with every image of **V**. Finally, the k most similar images are used to illustrate the sentence.

Figures 4 and 5 show the retrieved images for two example sentences. Figure 4 shows top five retrieved images for the sentence *'Some people are standing on a crowded sidewalk'*, from this list of images we can see that not all include the mentioned words in the sentence, but all images are related to the main concepts of the sentence, thus these images can be useful to illustrate it.

On the other hand, Fig. 5 shows the top five retrieved images for the sentence *'A grilled ham and cheese sandwich with egg on a plate'*. These results are interesting because all retrieved images are not far from correct to illustrate the sentence. However, none of these images can completely illustrate the sentence, that is, all words from the sentence need to be illustrated in an image.

6   Conclusions

We have presented a method for generation of textual descriptions for images that is formulated as two-step IR process. Our method works in an unsupervised way using the information of textual and visual features in a multimodal indexing. With the resulting multimodal representation it is possible to generate descriptions for images, and retrieve images to illustrate phrases. Our method is flexible and can be applied with different visual features encouraging us to explore visual features learned by using different approaches. The experimental results show the competitiveness of the proposed method in comparison with state of the art methods that are more complex and require more resources. As future work, we plan to evaluate our method in an auto-illustration task, we will focus on improving our method of multimodal indexing, and also including refined reference sentences for the textual description.

Acknowledgments. This work was supported by CONACYT under project grant CB-2014-241306 (Clasificación y recuperación de imágenes mediante técnicas de minería de textos). The first author was supported by CONACyT under scholarship No. 214764.

References

1. Krizhevsky, A., Sutskever, I., Hinton, G.E.: Imagenet classification with deep convolutional neural networks. In: Pereira, F., Burges, C., Bottou, L., Weinberger, K. (eds.) Advances in Neural Information Processing Systems 25, pp. 1097–1105. Curran Associates Inc. (2012)
2. Ordonez, V., Kulkarni, G., Berg, T.L.: Im2text: describing images using 1 million captioned photographs. In: NIPS, pp. 1143–1151 (2011)
3. Hodosh, M., Young, P., Hockenmaier, J.: Framing image description as a ranking task: data, models and evaluation metrics. J. Artif. Int. Res. **47**, 853–899 (2013)
4. Farhadi, A., Hejrati, M., Sadeghi, M.A., Young, P., Rashtchian, C., Hockenmaier, J., Forsyth, D.: Every picture tells a story: generating sentences from images. In: Daniilidis, K., Maragos, P., Paragios, N. (eds.) ECCV 2010, Part IV. LNCS, vol. 6314, pp. 15–29. Springer, Heidelberg (2010)
5. Kulkarni, G., Premraj, V., Dhar, S., Li, S., Choi, Y., Berg, A.C., Berg, T.L.: Baby talk: understanding and generating image descriptions. In: Proceedings of the 24th CVPR (2011)
6. Calfa, A., Iftene, A.: Using textual and visual processing in scalable concept image annotation challenge. In: CLEF 2015 Evaluation Labs and Workshop, Online Working Notes (2015)
7. Srivastava, N., Salakhutdinov, R.: Multimodal learning with deep boltzmann machines. J. Mach. Learn. Res. **15**, 2949–2980 (2014)
8. Li, X., Jin, Q., Liao, S., Liang, J., He, X., Huo, Y., Lan, W., Xiao, B., Lu, Y., Xu, J.: Ruc-tencent at imageclef 2015: concept detection, localization and sentence generation. In: CLEF 2015 Evaluation Labs and Workshop, Online Working Notes (2015)
9. Karpathy, A., Li, F.: Deep visual-semantic alignments for generating image descriptions. In: IEEE Conference on Computer Vision and Pattern Recognition, CVPR 2015, Boston, MA, USA, 7–12 June, pp. 3128–3137 (2015)
10. Villegas, M., et al.: General overview of ImageCLEF at the CLEF 2015 labs. In: Mothe, J., Savoy, J., Kamps, J., Pinel-Sauvagnat, K., Jones, G., San Juan, E., Capellato, L., Ferro, N. (eds.) CLEF 2015. LNCS, vol. 9283, pp. 444–461. Springer, Heidelberg (2015). doi:10.1007/978-3-319-24027-5_45
11. Lin, T., Maire, M., Belongie, S.J., Bourdev, L.D., Girshick, R.B., Hays, J., Perona, P., Ramanan, D., Dollár, P., Zitnick, C.L.: Microsoft COCO: common objects in context. CoRR abs/1405.0312 (2014)
12. Denkowski, M., Lavie, A.: Meteor universal: language specific translation evaluation for any target language. In: Proceedings of the EACL 2014 Workshop on Statistical Machine Translation (2014)

Concept Recognition in French Biomedical Text Using Automatic Translation

Zubair Afzal, Saber A. Akhondi, Herman H.H.B.M. van Haagen,
Erik M. van Mulligen, and Jan A. Kors[✉]

Department of Medical Informatics, Erasmus University Medical Center,
Rotterdam, The Netherlands
{m.afzal,s.ahmadakhondi,h.vanhaagen,e.vanmulligen,j.kors}@erasmusmc.nl

Abstract. We describe the development of a concept recognition system for French documents and its application in task 1b of the 2015 CLEF eHealth challenge. This community challenge included recognition of entities in a French medical corpus, normalization of the recognized entities, and normalization of entity mentions that had been manually annotated. Normalization had to be based on the Unified Medical Language System (UMLS). We addressed all three subtasks by a dictionary-based approach using Peregrine, our open-source indexing engine. To increase the coverage of our initial French terminology, we explored the use of two automatic translators, Google Translate and Microsoft Translator, to translate English UMLS terms into French. The corpus consisted of 1665 titles of French Medline abstracts and 6 French drug labels of the European Medicines Agency (EMEA). The corpus was manually annotated with concepts from the UMLS, and split in an equally-sized training and test set. The best performance on the training set was obtained with a terminology that contained the intersection of the translated terms in combination with several post-processing steps to reduce the number of false-positive detections. When evaluated on the test set, our system achieved F-scores of 0.756 and 0.665 for entity recognition on the EMEA documents and Medline titles, respectively. For subsequent entity normalization, the F-scores were 0.711 and 0.587. Entity normalization given the manually annotated entity mentions resulted in F-scores of 0.872 and 0.671. Our system obtained the highest F-scores among the systems that participated in the challenge.

Keywords: Entity recognition · Concept identification · Term translation · French terminology

1 Introduction

Large amounts of biomedical information are only available in textual form, such as in scientific publications, electronic health records, and patents [1]. The extraction of biomedical entities, e.g., diseases and drugs, and their relationships is important for many areas of biomedical research, such as pharmacovigilance

© Springer International Publishing Switzerland 2016
N. Fuhr et al. (Eds.): CLEF 2016, LNCS 9822, pp. 162–173, 2016.
DOI: 10.1007/978-3-319-44564-9_13

and drug repositioning [2,3]. Text-mining systems hold promise for facilitating the cumbersome and expensive manual information extraction process, or even for automatically generating new hypotheses and other insights [4,5]. An important step in the information extraction task is the recognition and normalization of relevant terms in a text [6]. Term recognition aims at finding text strings that refer to entities or concepts, and marking each term with a semantic type, like disorder, drug, or procedure. Term normalization or concept recognition is more complex than term recognition only. It assigns a unique identifier to the recognized term, which links it to a source that contains further information about the concept, such as its definition, its preferred name and synonyms, and its relationships with other concepts.

While many such terminological resources are available in English, other languages are covered much less well or not at all. For example, in the Metathesaurus of the Unified Medical Language System (UMLS) [7], one of the largest biomedical terminological resources, only a few percent of the English terms are also available in French [8]. Furthermore, to develop and evaluate text-mining methods, manually annotated (gold-standard) corpora are necessary. There are several biomedical corpora that provide concept annotations, but almost all are in English and provide annotations for only one or a limited set of semantic types [9–13]. Notable exceptions are the Mantra Gold Standard Corpus (GSC) [14], with concept annotations of many semantic types in English, French, German, Spanish and Dutch parallel biomedical texts, and the Quaero French Medical Corpus [15], with concept annotations in French biomedical text.

In this paper, we describe the development of a concept recognition system for French medical text and its application in task 1b of the 2015 CLEF eHealth challenge [16,17]. The task consisted of three subtasks: recognition of relevant entities in an updated version of the Quaero French Medical Corpus, normalization of the recognized entities, and normalization of entity mentions that had been manually annotated. The entities covered a wide variety of semantic groups. The normalization had to be based on the UMLS, and involved assigning UMLS concept unique identifiers (CUIs) to the entities that were recognized or provided. Each subtask should be performed fully automatically.

We addressed all three subtasks. Central in our approach to entity recognition and normalization are French terminologies based on the UMLS and postprocessing steps to reduce the number of false-positive detections. The UMLS already contains a number of French vocabularies, but their coverage is rather limited. We therefore explored the possibility to expand the coverage by automatic translation of English UMLS terms into French. For this purpose, we utilized two automatic translators.

2   Methods

2.1   Corpora

We used two corpora in our experiments: the Quaero medical corpus, a French annotated resource for medical entity recognition and normalization [15], which was the basis for the training and test sets provided in task 1b; and the Mantra corpus, a large multilingual biomedical corpus developed as part of the Mantra project [18], which we used to determine the terms for term translation and to create a term exclusion list. Each corpus is briefly described below.

Quaero Corpus. The Quaero corpus consists of three subcorpora: titles from French Medline abstracts, drug labels from the European Medicines Agency (EMEA), and patents from the European Patent Office (EPO). For the task 1b challenge, only Medline titles and EMEA documents were made available. The training set consisted of 833 Medline titles and 3 full EMEA documents; the test set contained 832 Medline titles and another 3 EMEA documents.

The annotations in the Quaero corpus are based on a subset of the UMLS [7]. Briefly, the UMLS is a metathesaurus integrating more than 150 biomedical terminologies. Each concept in the UMLS is assigned a concept unique identifier (CUI), a set of corresponding terms, and one or more semantic types, which are mapped to one of 15 semantic groups (SGs) [19]. Typically, each concept belongs to one semantic group. An entity in the Quaero corpus was only annotated if the concept belonged to the UMLS and the corresponding SG was any of the following ten SGs: Anatomy, Chemicals and drugs, Devices, Disorders, Geographic areas, Living beings, Objects, Phenomena, Physiology, and Procedures. Nested or overlapping entities were all annotated, as were ambiguous entities (i.e., if an entity could refer to more than one concept, all concepts were annotated). Also discontinuous spans of text that refer to a single entity could be annotated, but this occurred in less than 1 % of the annotations. Table 1 shows the total number of annotations in the training and test sets.

Table 1. Annotated terms and concepts in the Quaero training and test sets

Annotation	Medline		EMEA	
	Training	Test	Training	Test
Terms	2,994	2,977	2,695	2,260
Unique terms	2,296	2,288	923	756
Concepts	1,860	1,848	648	523

Mantra Corpus. The Mantra corpus was compiled as part of the Mantra project [18], aimed at providing multilingual resources in English, French, German, Spanish, and Dutch. The corpus consists of 1.6 million bilingual Medline titles (always in English and one of the other languages), 130 k sentences of EMEA drug labels (available in all five languages), and 155 k sentences of EPO patents (in English, French, and German in parallel). The texts in the Quaero corpus are a subset of the French texts in the Mantra corpus. The Mantra corpus is supplied with automatically generated silver-standard annotations, and recently multilingual gold-standard annotations have become available for a small subset of the Mantra corpus [14], but none of these resources were used in the current work.

2.2   Term Translation

The UMLS version 2014AB contains 178,860 unique French terms from 88,986 concepts, mainly stemming from MedDRA and MeSH, and only covering a few percent of the more than 5 million English terms and 2.6 million concepts in the UMLS. To expand the number of French terms, we used the web services application programming interface from Google Translate (GT) [20] and Microsoft Translator (MT) [21] to automatically translate English terms into French. Initially, we considered the translation of all English terms in the UMLS, but dismissed this approach as being too expensive and time-consuming. Instead, we reasoned that only the concepts that are found in a large English corpus that is representative of the task domain, may also be found in the Quaero corpus. We therefore indexed all English Medline titles and EMEA sentences from the Mantra corpus with our indexing system Peregrine [22], using the full English UMLS, and found 133,246 unique concepts. The 745,158 English terms corresponding with these concepts were translated into French using the automatic translators.

2.3   Terminologies

In our experiments on the Quaero corpus we used five French terminologies:

- Baseline: all French terms in UMLS version 2014AB. Only terms belonging to concepts in the ten SGs listed above were considered.
- GT: all terms from Google Translate and the baseline terminology.
- MT: all terms from Microsoft Translator and the baseline terminology.
- Union: all terms from Google Translate, Microsoft Translator, and the baseline terminology.
- Intersection: all terms that had the same translation by Google Translate and Microsoft Translator, supplemented with the baseline terminology.

The English terminology for indexing the Mantra corpus consisted of all English terms in UMLS version 2014 AB, filtered for the ten relevant SGs.

Both on the English terminology and the French baseline terminology we applied a set of term rewrite and suppression rules [23]. Briefly, the rewrite rules generated additional synonyms and spelling variants that correspond to the meaning of the original terms. For example, a syntactic inversion rule reverses the order of words if the term contains a comma or semicolon followed by a space (e.g., "abdomen; acute" is rewritten to "acute abdomen"), and a semantic type rule removes expressions within parentheses that represent the semantic type of the term (e.g., "Acetazolamide (substance)" is rewritten to "Acetazolamide"). The suppression rules suppress undesired terms that may affect the precision of the entity recognition. For example, a short-token rule removes terms that after tokenization only consist of numbers or single characters. In a separate step (explained below), we supplemented the French terminologies with the concepts and terms in the training data.

Table 2 shows the number of concepts and terms in the various French terminologies.

Table 2. Sizes of the five French terminologies

Terminology	No. of concepts	No. of terms
Baseline	77,995	161,910
Google Translate	159,825	785,301
Microsoft Translator	159,802	806,203
Union	160,467	1,069,113
Intersection	136,127	386,617

2.4   Entity Recognition and Entity Normalization

The processing for the entity recognition and the entity normalization included an indexing and a post-processing step, which are described below.

Indexing. The corpora were indexed with Peregrine, our dictionary-based concept recognition system [22]. Peregrine employs a user-supplied dictionary and splits the terms in the dictionary into sequences of tokens. When such a sequence of tokens is found in a document, the term and the concept associated with that term, is recognized in the document. Peregrine removes stopwords (we used a small list of (in)definite articles and, for French, partitive articles) and tries to match the longest possible text phrase to a concept. It uses the Lexical Variant Generator tool of the National Library of Medicine to reduce a token to its stem before matching [24]. Peregrine is freely available [25].

Peregrine can find partially overlapping concepts, but it cannot detect nested concepts (it only returns the concept corresponding with the longest term). We therefore implemented an additional indexing step. For each term found by Peregrine and consisting of n words ($n > 1$), all subsets of 1 to $n-1$ words were generated, under the condition that for subsets consisting of more than one word, the words had to be adjacent in the original term. All word subsets were then also indexed by Peregrine. For example, Peregrine recognized the term "décollements de rétine" (detachment of the retina). Of the generated word subsets ("décollements", "de", "rétine", "décollements de", "de rétine"), Peregrine correctly recognized the term "rétine". We did not try to find discontinuous terms since there frequency was very low.

Post-processing. To reduce the number of false-positive detections that resulted from the indexing, we applied several post-processing steps. First, we removed terms that were part of an exclusion list. The list was manually created by indexing the French Mantra corpus with the largest available French terminology (union), ordering the detected terms by their frequency in the corpus, and selecting the incorrect terms from the 2,500 top-ranked terms.

Second, for any term-SG-CUI combination and SG-CUI combination that was found by Peregrine and had also been annotated in the training data, we computed precision scores: *true positives/(true positives + false positives)*. For a given term, only term-SG-CUI combinations with a precision above a certain threshold value were kept. If multiple combinations qualified, only the two with the highest precision scores were selected. If for a given term none of the found term-SG-CUI combinations had been annotated in the training data, but precision scores were available for the SG-CUI combinations, a term-SG-CUI combination was still kept if the precision of the SG-CUI combination was higher than the threshold. If multiple combinations qualified, the two with the highest precision were kept if they had the same SG; otherwise, only the combination with the highest precision was kept. If none of the SG-CUI combinations had been annotated, a single term-SG-CUI combination was selected, taking into account whether the term was the preferred term for a CUI, and the CUI number (lowest first). For example, the term "accident de la route" (road accident) was recognized as a synonym of "traffic accident on public road (CUI C0221706, semantic group Disorders) and "vehicle accident" (C0683911, Phenomena). Since "accident de la route" was the preferred term of the latter concept, this was selected. As another example, the term "acide" was recognized as a synonym of "acids" (C0001128, Chemicals and drugs) and "lysergic acid diethylamide measurement" (C0202406, Procedures). Since "acide" was not a preferred term for either concept, the concept with the lowest CUI number (C0001128) was selected.

2.5   Normalization Based on Gold-Standard Entity Recognition

For entity normalization given the gold-standard terms and SGs, we developed the following processing pipeline. First, we computed precision scores for all term-SG-CUI combinations in the training set. If a given term-SG combination in the test set was also present in the training set, we selected the CUI of the term-SG-CUI combination with the highest precision score. If the second largest precision score was larger than 0.3, the CUI of the corresponding term-SG-CUI combination was also selected.

Second, if a term-SG combination in the test set had not been seen in the training set, we searched the terminology for terms that had a Levenshtein edit distance of maximum one. If one such term was found, the corresponding CUI was selected. If multiple terms were found, for each term the corresponding SG-CUI combination was sought in the training data. If present, precision scores were computed and the CUI of the SG-CUI combination with the largest precision was selected. If the SG-CUI combination did not exist in the training data, it was checked if the term was the preferred term for any of the CUIs. If this was the case for just one CUI, it was selected. Otherwise, a single CUI was selected, taking into account whether the CUI had been annotated in the training set, and the CUI number (lowest first).

3   Results

3.1   Performance on the Quaero Training Set

We used the Quaero training data to optimize the performance of the indexing and post-processing steps for entity recognition and normalization. Table 3 shows the results for the five French terminologies that we generated: Baseline (UMLS French), GT, MT, Union, and Intersection. The results have been generated with the task 1b evaluation script, using exact matching for both entity recognition and normalization.

Table 3. Performance of five French terminologies on the Quaero training set

Corpus	Terminology	Entity recognition			Entity normalization		
		Precision	Recall	F-score	Precision	Recall	F-score
EMEA	Baseline	0.724	0.399	0.515	0.588	0.359	0.446
	GT	0.368	0.763	0.496	0.220	0.670	0.332
	MT	0.345	0.791	0.481	0.208	0.687	0.316
	Union	0.298	0.807	0.435	0.172	0.702	0.274
	Intersection	0.454	0.756	0.567	0.273	0.669	0.388
Medline	Baseline	0.716	0.433	0.540	0.591	0.376	0.460
	GT	0.392	0.658	0.491	0.236	0.572	0.335
	MT	0.370	0.664	0.475	0.229	0.579	0.328
	Union	0.343	0.705	0.461	0.199	0.612	0.300
	Intersection	0.447	0.628	0.523	0.274	0.550	0.366

The terminologies based on automatic term translations (GT and MT) substantially increase recall as compared to the UMLS baseline terminology, but at the expense of a large decrease in precision. GT performs slightly better than MT in terms of F-score. The union of both terminologies results in a small further increase of the recall. The intersection improves precision considerably at the expense of some loss of recall. The performance of the terminologies with translated terms is better on the EMEA documents than on the Medline titles, primarily because the recall is higher. Interestingly, the reverse is true for the baseline terminology, which performs slightly better on the Medline titles. As expected, the performance for entity normalization is lower than for entity recognition, mainly because of a lower precision. This is largely caused by the ambiguity of many terms. At this stage, our indexing system did not try to disambiguate when multiple CUIs for the same term were found, and thus many of the CUIs were scored as false positives.

In our further experiments we decided to focus on the Union and Intersection terminologies. First, we tested the effect of expanding our terminologies with terms from concepts in the training data that were missed by our indexing system (false negatives). In order not to optimistically bias our performance results, we split the Quaero training data in an equally-sized training set and test set. Table 4 shows the performance results on the test set.

Table 4. Performance after expanding the terminologies with false negatives from half of the Quaero training set and testing on the other half

Corpus	Terminology	Entity recognition			Entity normalization		
		Precision	Recall	F-score	Precision	Recall	F-score
EMEA	Union	0.301	0.869	0.447	0.182	0.794	0.297
	Intersection	0.433	0.861	0.576	0.264	0.793	0.396
Medline	Union	0.401	0.708	0.512	0.246	0.638	0.355
	Intersection	0.513	0.668	0.580	0.326	0.607	0.424

Addition of the false negatives results in a clear improvement of the recall, with only a small decrease in precision.

Based on the expanded terminologies, we tested the effect of our post-processing steps, aimed at removing incorrectly indexed terms (false positives). An important parameter in this process is the precision threshold (see post-processing description above). Using half of the Quaero training data, we varied this threshold between 0.1 and 0.5 with steps of 0.1, and tested on the other half of the training data. The best F-score was obtained for a threshold of 0.3. Table 5 shows the results of the post-processing steps using this threshold.

Table 5. Performance of the expanded terminologies with post-processing steps on half of the Quaero training set

Corpus	Terminology	Entity recognition			Entity normalization		
		Precision	Recall	F-score	Precision	Recall	F-score
EMEA	Union	0.452	0.786	0.574	0.407	0.727	0.521
	Intersection	0.679	0.784	0.728	0.619	0.736	0.672
Medline	Union	0.579	0.605	0.592	0.477	0.508	0.492
	Intersection	0.747	0.581	0.654	0.634	0.500	0.559

The post-processing steps reduce recall but strongly increase precision, as well as the F-scores.

3.2   Performance on the Quaero Test Data

We submitted two runs for both the entity recognition and normalization tasks, one run using the Union terminology, the other using the Intersection terminology. Both terminologies were expanded with all false negatives of the Quaero training set. Table 6 shows our performance results on the final test set for exact match. (Note: we swapped the test run precision and recall values that the task organizers provided to us, since we could deduce from the FP and FN counts that they had been reversed.)

Table 6. Entity recognition and normalization performance on the Quaero test set

Corpus	Terminology	Entity recognition			Entity normalization		
		Precision	Recall	F-score	Precision	Recall	F-score
EMEA	Union	0.710	0.776	0.741	0.653	0.705	0.678
	Intersection	0.751	0.761	0.756	0.707	0.714	0.711
Medline	Union	0.683	0.642	0.662	0.599	0.552	0.575
	Intersection	0.711	0.625	0.665	0.634	0.547	0.587

Our results on the test set were better than on the training set, mainly because of higher precision values. Overall, the system using the Intersection terminology performed best. These results are well above the average and median of the scores from all runs of the challenge participants [17].

We also submitted two runs for the normalization using the gold-standard entity recognition results. The difference between the two runs was that the first run did not include the final disambiguation step (selection of CUIs if they had been annotated in the training set and based on CUI number). Table 7 gives the performance results.

Table 7. Normalization performance on the test set given the entity recognition, with and without the final disambiguation step

Corpus	Disambiguation	Precision	Recall	F-score
EMEA	No	1.000	0.767	0.868
	Yes	1.000	0.774	0.872
Medline	No	0.817	0.573	0.674
	Yes	0.805	0.575	0.671

As was to be expected, use of the gold-standard entity recognition improved the normalization results. In particular precision was boosted, with a remarkable precision of 1 for the EMEA corpus. The final disambiguation hardly affected the performance results.

4   Discussion

We developed a dictionary-based concept recognition system for French biomedical text. Our evaluation results show that expanding the coverage of the French UMLS baseline terminology with the use of an automated term translator is a viable way to improve the recall for entity recognition and normalization, but also reduces precision considerably. Taking the intersection of the term translations increases precision again, while only slightly reducing recall. The various post-processing steps further improve precision. The union of the term translations did hardly further improve the recall, indicating that the annotated corpus contained few terms that were uniquely provided by one of the translators. Although the precision of the Union terminology on the Quaero training set was substantially less than the precision of the Intersection, the difference on the test set was much smaller.

Our system generally performed better on the EMEA subcorpus than on the Medline subcorpus, mainly because of a higher recall. This may partly be explained by the fact that the Medline corpus consisted of hundreds of different abstract titles, whereas the EMEA corpus consisted of only six documents. While the total number of annotated terms in both corpora was similar, the number of unique terms and concepts in Medline was much higher than in EMEA (cf. Table 1). Therefore, term annotations in EMEA were more redundant than in Medline, and may have involved more common terms that were more likely to be correctly translated. Note that for the French baseline terminology, recall for EMEA was slightly lower than for Medline.

For all three challenge subtasks, our dictionary-based system performed best amongst the systems that participated in the challenge [17]. Most other approaches heavily relied on machine-learning classifiers (conditional random fields or support vector machines) for entity recognition, using rich feature sets of lexical, part-of-speech, orthographic, and lexicon-based features. Only one other team used a dictionary-based approach [26], combining seven French dictionaries partly derived from the UMLS, but their performance was low. Two teams used machine translation (Google Translate or Microsoft Translator), but contrary to what we did, they translated from French to English [27,28]. One team translated all the words in the training corpus into English and then applied MetaMap [29] to generate semantic types as features for training their tagger [27]. The other team translated the terms found by their entity recognizer and used MetaMap to map the terms to CUIs [28].

To gauge automatic systems against human annotators, system performances should be compared with inter-annotator agreement (IAA) scores. Unfortunately, IAA was not assessed for the Quaero corpus. However, IAA scores, taken as the F-score between two annotators, were provided for the multilingual Mantra GSC corpus [14], which is similar to the Quaero corpus. For French, the median IAA in the Mantra GSC was 0.80 for entity normalization. Our F-scores of 0.59 (for Medline) and 0.71 (for EMEA) indicate that there is still room for improvement of our system. Possible ways to achieve this are the use of better curated terminologies, improved disambiguation (e.g., by employing part-of-speech information), and recognition of discontinuous terms.

Acknowledgments. This work was supported by a grant provided by AstraZeneca to S.A.A.

References

1. Ohno-Machado, L.: NIH's big data to knowledge initiative and the advancement of biomedical informatics. J. Am. Med. Inform. Assoc. **21**, 193 (2014)
2. Harpaz, R., Callahan, A., Tamang, S., et al.: Text mining for adverse drug events: the promise, challenges, and state of the art. Drug Saf. **37**, 777–790 (2014)
3. Hurle, M.R., Yang, L., Xie, Q., et al.: Computational drug repositioning: from data to therapeutics. Clin. Pharmacol. Ther. **93**, 335–341 (2013)
4. Preiss, J., Stevenson, M., Gaizauskas, R.: Exploring relation types for literature-based discovery. J. Am. Med. Inform. Assoc. **22**, 987–992 (2015)
5. Andronis, C., Sharma, A., Virvilis, V., et al.: Literature mining, ontologies and information visualization for drug repurposing. Brief. Bioinform. **12**, 357–368 (2011)
6. Krauthammer, M., Nenadic, G.: Term identification in the biomedical literature. J. Biomed. Inf. **37**, 512–526 (2004)
7. Bodenreider, O.: The unified medical language system (UMLS): integrating biomedical terminology. Nucleic Acids Res. **32**, D267–D270 (2004)
8. Névéol, A., Grosjean, J., Darmoni, S.J., Zweigenbaum, P.: Language resources for French in the biomedical domain. In: Language and Resource Evaluation Conference (LREC) 2014, pp. 2146–2151 (2014)
9. Leaman, R., Miller, C., Gonzalez, G.: Enabling recognition of diseases in biomedical text with machine learning: corpus and benchmark. In: Proceedings of the 3rd International Symposium on Languages in Biology and Medicine (LBM), Jeju Island, South Korea, pp. 82–89 (2009)
10. Lu, Z., Kao, H.Y., Wei, C.H., et al.: The gene normalization task in BioCreative III. BMC Bioinform. **12**(Suppl. 8), S2 (2011)
11. Bada, M., Eckert, M., Evans, D., et al.: Concept annotation in the CRAFT corpus. BMC Bioinform. **13**, 161 (2012)
12. Gurulingappa, H., Rajput, A.M., Roberts, A., et al.: Development of a benchmark corpus to support the automatic extraction of drug-related adverse effects from medical case reports. J. Biomed. Inform. **45**, 885–892 (2012)
13. Pradhan, S., Elhadad, N., South, B.R., et al.: Evaluating the state of the art in disorder recognition and normalization of the clinical narrative. J. Am. Med. Inform. Assoc. **22**, 143–154 (2015)
14. Kors, J.A., Clematide, S., Akhondi, S.A., van Mulligen, E.M., Rebholz-Schuhmann, D.: A multilingual gold-standard corpus for biomedical concept recognition: the Mantra GSC. J. Am. Med. Inform. Assoc. **22**, 948–956 (2015)
15. Névéol, A., Grouin, C., Leixa, J., Rosset, S., Zweigenbaum, P.: The QUAERO French medical corpus: a ressource for medical entity recognition and normalization. In: Fourth Workshop on Building and Evaluating Resources for Health and Biomedical Text Processing (BioTxtM), pp. 24–30 (2014)

16. Goeuriot, L., Kelly, L., Suominen, H., Hanlen, L., Névéol, A., Grouin, C., Palotti, J., Zuccon, G.: Overview of the CLEF eHealth evaluation lab 2015. In: Mothe, J., Savoy, J., Kamps, J., Pinel-Sauvagnat, K., Jones, G., San Juan, E., Capellato, L., Ferro, N. (eds.) CLEF 2015. LNCS, vol. 9283, pp. 429–443. Springer, Heidelberg (2015). doi:10.1007/978-3-319-24027-5_44

17. Névéol, A., Grouin, C., Tannier, X., Hamon, T., Kelly, L., Goeuriot, L., Zweigenbaum, P.: CLEF eHealth evaluation lab 2015 task 1b: clinical named entity recognition. CLEF 2015 Online Working Notes. CEUR-WS (2015)

18. Mantra project website. http://www.mantra-project.eu

19. Bodenreider, O., McCray, A.T.: Exploring semantic groups through visual approaches. J. Biomed. Inform. **36**, 414–432 (2003)

20. Google Translate. https://translate.google.com

21. Microsoft Translator. http://www.bing.com/translator

22. Schuemie, M.J., Jelier, R., Kors, J.A.: Peregrine: lightweight gene name normalization by dictionary lookup. In: Proceedings of the BioCreAtIvE II Workshop, Madrid, Spain, pp. 131–133 (2007)

23. Hettne, K.M., van Mulligen, E.M., Schuemie, M.J., Schijvenaars, B.J.A., Kors, J.A.: Rewriting and suppressing UMLS terms for improved biomedical term identification. J. Biomed. Semantics **1**, 5 (2010)

24. Divita, G., Browne, A.C., Rindflesch, T.C.: Evaluating lexical variant generation to improve information retrieval. In: Proceedings of the American Medical Informatics Association Symposium, pp. 775–779 (1998)

25. Peregrine indexer. https://trac.nbic.nl/data-mining

26. Soualmia, L.F., Cabot, C., Dahamna, B., Darmoni, S.J.: SIBM at CLEF e-Health evaluation lab 2015. CLEF 2015 Online Working Notes. CEUR-WS (2015)

27. Jain, D.: Supervised named entity recognition for clinical data. CLEF 2015 Online Working Notes. CEUR-WS (2015)

28. Jiang, J., Guan, Y., Zhao, C.: WI-ENRE in CLEF eHealth evaluation lab 2015: clinical named entity recognition based on CRF. CLEF 2015 Online Working Notes. CEUR-WS (2015)

29. Aronson, A.R.: Effective mapping of biomedical text to the UMLS metathesaurus: the MetaMap program. In: Proceedings of the American Medical Informatics Association Symposium, pp. 17–21 (2001)

A Product Feature-Based User-Centric Ranking Model for E-Commerce Search

Lamjed Ben Jabeur[1]([envelope]), Laure Soulier[2], Lynda Tamine[1], and Paul Mousset[1]

[1] IRIT, Université de Toulouse, CNRS, UPS, 118 Route Narbonne, Toulouse, France
{jabeur,tamine,mousset}@irit.fr
[2] Sorbonne Universités, UPMC Univ Paris 06, LIP6 UMR 7606, 75005 Paris, France
laure.soulier@lip6.fr

Abstract. During the online shopping process, users search for interesting products in order to quickly access those that fit with their needs among a long tail of similar or closely related products. Our contribution addresses *head* queries that are frequently submitted on e-commerce Web sites. Head queries usually target featured products with several variations, accessories, and complementary products. We present in this paper a product feature-based user-centric model for product search involving, in addition to product characteristics, the user engagement toward the product. This model has been evaluated through the product search track of the LL4IR lab at CLEF 2015 in order to highlight the effectiveness of our model as well as the impact of the user engagement factor.

Keywords: Information retrieval · Living labs · LL4IR · e-commerce · Product search · Ranking · User engagement · User preferences

1 Introduction

In the last few years, online retailers and marketplaces have shown a steady growth in terms of popularity as well as benefits. Amazon claims more than 240 million products available for sale on US store amazon.com[1]. The marketplace leader claims also more than 2 billion items sold worldwide by the end of 2014[2]. As the result of this huge quantity of available products, users are facing difficulty to make choice. The diversity of products in terms of functionalities and features makes their shopping experience more difficult.

To tackle this problem, online retailers enhance their Web sites with product search tools. In fact, product search is becoming more important [18], leading to propose adapted retrieval tools in order to help customers to find their products of interest [5]. One example of product search tools is proposed by Google Shopping for which customers have found the utility with around 100 billions of submitted queries by month[3].

---

[1] http://www.ecommercebytes.com/cab/abn/y14/m07/i15/s04.
[2] http://www.businesswire.com/news/home/20150105005186/en/
Amazon-Sellers-Sold-Record-Setting-2-Billion-Items.
[3] http://www.godatafeed.com/resources/google-shopping-campaigns.

© Springer International Publishing Switzerland 2016
N. Fuhr et al. (Eds.): CLEF 2016, LNCS 9822, pp. 174–186, 2016.
DOI: 10.1007/978-3-319-44564-9_14

In the literature, product search has been addressed as an information retrieval (IR) task bridging e-commerce data and customer's information need formulated during the online shopping process. Previous works have proposed to integrate several features which might be split into two categories. On one hand, the proposed approaches focus mainly on the product fields, namely its category and its description [4,18]. On the other hand, users' preferences and search intent are emphasized leading to a user-centered search process [9].

In this paper, we propose a feature-based user-centric ranking model for product search that addresses the problem of head queries on e-commerce Web sites. Head queries represent the set of most frequent queries on featured products [1,17], such as dolls, miniatures, puzzles, cards. The latter may be characterized by several variations, accessories, and/or complementary products. Combining both approaches (product features [4,18] and user-centered [9]), our model ranks products with respect to their descriptive fields and category as well as their popularity highlighting the user engagement toward the product [14]. We evaluate our model while participating to the product search track of the Living Labs for IR (LL4IR) [17] of CLEF 2015 [11] and present also some analysis aiming at understanding the user engagement factor. More particularly, the contribution of our paper is twofold:

- A new product search model including both product characteristics and user engagement. This model is evaluated through the living lab paradigm.
- A statistical analysis highlighting how could be characterized the user engagement in terms of product search.

In the remainder of the paper, Sect. 2 synthesizes the state of the art surrounding product search. Section 3 introduces our product search model and describes its experimental evaluation. We present in Sect. 4 a statistical analysis on the effect of the user engagement on product search. Finally, Sect. 5 concludes the paper and presents perspectives.

2   Related Work

Similarly to the information access perspective, the literature review outlines several dimensions underlying the product search field. Some work focused on the understanding of the product search process according to the users' modeling perspective. First, Detlor et al. [8] compared the exploration and the search processes on e-commerce sites and outlined that the main difference relies on the type of users' intent with respect to the product specificity. More particularly, product search requires basic information (such as the price, the product description, or the information about the seller) as well as more complex specifications of a product. Second, other authors focused on interactions issued from film recommendation systems [2,3]. Although the tracked products (films) are different than the ones tracked by head queries of the LL4IR Labs, the authors highlighted that the diversity of recommended products is an important criterion in terms of users' satisfaction [2] and that it should be personalized to each user with respect to their past actions [2]. Moreover, the integration of the temporal diversity enables to avoid recommending redundant products retrieved over time [13] as well as to enable distinguishing short- and long-term preferences [19].

Other work, more close to our contribution, addressed the product search issue as an information retrieval challenge aiming at leveraging e-commerce data in order to answer customers' information needs.

The first line of work in this category includes retrieval models mainly based on product characteristics (e.g., the category and the description). Chen et al. [4] proposed to diversify product results and to return, among the large collection of similar products, only those significantly different from each others. Product categories and attribute values are used to diversify the list of products. Vandic et al. [18] addressed the issues underlying different hierarchical classifications in online stores and the multiple vocabulary terms used to describe the same product. Based on semantic ontologies, they proposed to match similar products and classify them into a universal product category taxonomy.

In the second line of work in the same category, the focus is oriented towards the user with an attempt to bridge the gap between the vocabulary used to describe the product and the customers' vocabulary used to formulate their search queries. For instance, the query *"cheap PC gamer"* might be difficult to solve by only comparing the query text with the product description since it requires reasoning over the search intent towards a particular product feature, namely the price. To tackle this challenge, Duan et al. [9] propose to represent both products and users through an entity-based representation in which each entity is formalized as a pair of key-value. The product retrieval is then performed through a probabilistic model which estimates the relevance at the level of attribute preferences. Other work leveraged users' search history in order to capture users' interests [16]. This type of model could be enhanced by product characteristics as done by Ghirmatsion and Balog [10] which proposed a model aiming at first identifying relevant products and then re-ranking products using relevance judgments of the search history. This approach has been enhanced by filtering techniques applied on product availability or reduction rate criteria.

In our contribution, we propose to combine both product and user point of view by *(1)* including product characteristics as previously done by [4,18] and *(2)* a metric highlighting the user engagement [14]. In contrast to [9,10,16] which focused on the interest of a particular user, our proposed user engagement metric leverages from the crowd.

3   Product Feature-Based User-Centric Ranking Model

In this section, we present our first contribution consisting in proposing and evaluating a product search model relying on a product feature-based user-centric approach. In the remaining section, we first present the model and then detail the experimental evaluation which has been carried out through the LL4IR lab.

3.1   The Model

Our model aims at leveraging product characteristics and user engagement towards the product. To do so, we estimate the relevance of product p with respect to query q as a combination of two indicators expressing the relevance probability $P(p|q)$ of product p based on its characteristic and a user engagement metric $UE(p)$. The relevance $RSV(p,q)$ of product p given query q is computed as:

$$RSV(p,q) = P(p|q) * UE(p) \tag{1}$$

The Product Feature-Based Probability. Products are commonly described in e-commerce Web site with multiple fields[4]. These fields enable to identify the product (i.e., sku, gtin13, ISBN), describe its purpose (i.e., name, brand, description), list elementary and technical features (i.e., model, speed, weight, color) as well as organize the product collection into a structured hierarchy (i.e., category). With this in mind and inspired by work of Craswell et al. [6] and Dakka et al. [7], we propose to depict product p in two sets of elements consisting in (a) its set of textual descriptive fields d_p that describe the product, and (b) its category that organizes products by categories.

Accordingly, the relevance $P(p|q)$ of product p with respect to query q could be rewritten as $P(c_p, d_p|q)$ (Eq. 2). According to Bayes probability rules (Eq. 3) and assuming that the product category and description are independent (Eq. 4), product relevance is estimated by the following model:

$$P(p|q) = P(c_p, d_p|q) \tag{2}$$
$$= P(c_p|q) \cdot P(d_p|c_p, q) \tag{3}$$
$$\propto P(c_p|q) \cdot P(d_p|q) \tag{4}$$

where $P(c_p|q)$ and $P(d_p|q)$ express respectively the relevance of category c_p of product p and the topical relevance of product description d_p with respect to query q. We detail these probabilities below.

- Topical relevance of product description d_p. The topical relevance focuses on the product descriptive field set d_p. Except for the category field, all remaining fields are part of the product description d_p. We consider *(1)* the title which is usually size limited and includes concise information about the product and *(2)* the description field including broader information.

We propose to use the $BM25F$ scoring schema [6,20] to estimate likelihood $p(d_p|q)$ of descriptive fields d_p given query q. The $BM25F$ computes the similarity with query q while attributing different weights to each field.

We first calculate normalized term frequency $\overline{tf}_{t,f,p}$ for each field:

$$\overline{tf}_{t,f,p} = \frac{tf_{t,f,p}}{1 + b_f(\frac{l_{f,p}}{l_f} - 1)} \tag{5}$$

---

[4] http://schema.org.

where $tf_{t,f,p}$ represents the frequency of term t in field f belonging to description d_p of product p. $l_{f,p}$ is the length of field f in product description d_p and l_f is the average length of field f, b_f is a field-dependant parameter similar to b parameter in $BM25$. The term frequencies estimated over all the field set are combined linearly using weight w_f of field f as follows:

$$\overline{tf}_{t,p} = \sum_{f \in d_p} w_f * \overline{tf}_{t,f,p} \qquad (6)$$

The term frequency $\overline{tf}_{t,p}$ is integrated in the usual $BM25$ saturating function modeling the non-linear relevance distribution of term frequencies. The probability $p(d_p|q)$ is approximated by the $BM25F$ function [6,20]:

$$p(d_p|q) \approx BM25F(q|d_p) = \sum_{t \in q \cap d_p} \frac{\overline{tf}_{t,p}}{k_1 + \overline{tf}_{t,p}} idf(t) \qquad (7)$$

where k_1 and $idf(t)$ express respectively the BM25 parameter and the inverse document frequency of term t.

- *The relevance of category.* The relevance of category c_p with respect to query q aims at identifying to what extent the category is relevant to the product collection. The underlying idea is to decide which eminent category likely matches the query since different categories may respond to the query.

Let S be the set of non-negative topical scores obtained by product description d_p of all products $p \in D(c_p)$, where $D(c_p)$ corresponds to the set of product characterized by category c_p. More formally, S is defined as follows:

$$S = \{p(d_p|q)|p \in D(c_p) \wedge p(d_p|q) \geq 0\} \qquad (8)$$

where $p(d_p|q)$ is approximated by $BM25F(q,d)$ as done in Eq. 7. We propose to estimate the relevance likelihood $p(c_p|q)$ of product category c_p towards query q with similarity $sim(q, c_p)$ of product category c_p given query q. This similarity is estimated as the product of the log scale cardinality of set S and an aggregation function $A(S)$ of topical scores over respective products:

$$p(c_p|q) \approx sim(q, c_p) = log(1 + |S|) * A(S) \qquad (9)$$

where $A(S)$ can be computed as the maximum, the mean and the median scores over the topical distribution of all products $D(c_p)$. We propose to use the 95th percentile as aggregate function $A(S)$. In contrast of mean and maximum, the 95th percentile is resistant to outliers. Similarly to the median, 95th percentile allows measuring the global tendency of topical scores.

As the category includes more relevant products with respect to the query, the category might be relevant to the query. This is reflected by the first part of Eq. 9, noted $log(1 + |S|)|$. The log scale value enables to lower high cardinality and thus smooths the importance of overpopulated categories.

The User Engagement Metric. The integration of the user engagement component is driven by the main aim of e-commerce application which consists in increasing the user conversion rate. Although the user engagement should be derived in accordance with the application goal, such metric emphasizes the positive aspect of the interaction [14]. In the setting of a Web application, the user's engagement is often associated with his/her interactions including visits, clicks, comments, recommendations, etc. In accordance with the search scenario of this model, we propose to consider users' interactions willing to be noticed after a product search. For instance, post-task evidence sources of interaction could be result clicks, product ratings, favorites, or users' actions. The latter aim at bookmarking wishlist, adding to basket, and/or pushing the product. Unfortunately, these data are not available for this edition of LL4IR track. Thus, we estimate the user engagement by the number of social interactions, namely "Like" and "Share" actions, generated on the Facebook[5] social media platform.

In order to get the social engagement toward a product, we first identify significant Web resources that represent a product, typically Web pages with technical description. In this aim, we used the product name as a query for exact search on a Web search engine. We assume that the set of top k resources significantly represent the product and their underlying users' interactions may be associated with the product. With this in mind, let $R_p = \{r_1, r_1 \cdots r_k\}$ be the set of resources that mention product p. $likes(r_i)$, respectively $shares(r_i)$, expresses the number of Facebook likes, respectively Facebook shares, obtained by a particular resource r_i. Please, note that likes and shares are obtained by sending the URL of resource r_i to the Facebook API.

The user engagement of resource r_i identified through is computed is follows:

$$e(r_i) = \frac{\log(1 + \min(s, likes(r_i) + shares(r_i)))}{\log(1 + s)} \qquad (10)$$

with s defines an upper bound on social interactions of resource r_i.

In the end, the user engagement of product p corresponds to the maximal user engagement obtained by the associated resources:

$$\text{UE}(p) = \text{argmax}_{r_i \in R_p} e(r_i) \qquad (11)$$

3.2 Experimental Evaluation

In order to evaluate the effectiveness of the proposed model, we relied on the "Living Labs for Information Retrieval" (LL4IR) campaign [17] aiming at evaluating IR models in real utilization's cases: users submit their queries on a website and interact in real time with retrieved results of participants. The evaluation campaign proposes several evaluation periods (also called "rounds") in which the main search task consists in a product search task on the online commerce site of REGIO JTK[6], Hungarian leader in the sale of toy for children. In this section,

---

[5] http://facebook.com.
[6] http://www.regiojatek.hu/.

we first describe the experimental context implemented during the LL4IR campaign, by introducing the protocol design and the obtained results.

Protocol Design. *Experimental data:* The LL4IR campaign provides a set of experimental data:

- 100 oriented product queries extracted from most frequent queries submitted on the system in the past. To allow comparability between rounds, queries are the same over all rounds. We note that half of the queries are used for training.
- A product collection including both available products and those labeled as unavailable which would be available later. The average number of products associated with each query is around 60 products. Each product is represented by a set of structural and semantic meta-data, like the characters associated with the product (e.g. Spiderman, Hello Kitty), it brand (e.g. Beados, LEGO), or the recommended age/gender.
- The user feedback updated every 5 min throughout a specific round. Each user feedback is represented by a binary value, depending on whether the product presented was clicked by the user.

Evaluation protocol. The aim of the LL4IR campaign is to leverage users' clicks in order to compare the effectiveness of the systems proposed by the participants with respect to the one of the production system. To do so, product ranking of each participating system is interleaved with the product ranking of the production system. The latter corresponds to the default product ranking system provided by Web site owners. For each submitted query belonging to the preselected head query set, the user gets a set of results for which the half comes from website production system and the other half from a random participating system. The same process has been carried out over a baseline model proposed by the organizers of the campaign [17] and other participants [10,16].

Metrics. Five metrics, estimated over all submitted head queries, are proposed by Living Labs organizers in order to evaluate a participating system:

- The number of wins, noted $\#Wins$, which expresses the number of times the test system received respectively more clicks than the product system.
- The number of losses, noted $\#Losses$, which expresses the number of times the test system received respectively fewer clicks than the product systems.
- The number of ties, noted $\#Ties$, which expresses the number of times the test system received respectively as many clicks as the product systems.
- The number of Impressions, noted $\#Impressions$, which expresses the number of times the test system is mixed with production one with $\#Impressions = \#Wins + \#Losses + \#Ties$
- The outcome, noted *Outcome*, is defined as the ratio of wins over the sum of wins and losses (Eq. 12). A ratio higher than 0.5 highlights the system ability

to provide more relevant products than irrelevant ones, assuming that clicks are indicators of product relevance [12].

$$Outcome = \frac{\#Wins}{\#Wins + \#Losses} \qquad (12)$$

Results. In order to evaluate both components of our model, we tested our model differently over rounds (Round 2 and 3 - since we did not participate to round 1): for round 2, we only rank products according to the characteristic-based indicator using Eq. 4 while for round 3 we introduced the user engagement-based indicator as explained in Eq. 1. We outline that, since the LL4IR campaign allows participants to submit only one run for each testing period, we fixed the descriptor and parameter weights according to previous work, respectively [20] for descriptor and [6,20] for the BM25F parameters.

Table 1 presents results obtained by the baseline, the best concurrent participant and our model for these two rounds. We could see that for round 2 we obtained the lowest outcome measure with respect to the baseline and the participant. Results obtained for round 3 highlight that the user engagement allows enhancing the effectiveness of our model. Please note that this statement is limited since the evaluation metric might be impacted by the set of users involved in the evaluation process which is variable over the different rounds. We outline that the ranking model of the system, the queries and the interleaved method are stable over the different rounds.

Table 1. Effectiveness comparison of our model during round 2 and 3 of the LL4IR

	Round 2		Round 3	
	Outcome	% Chg	Outcome	% Chg
Baseline	0.5284	-24.48 %	0.4430	+10.38 %
Best participant	0.4795	-16.78 %	0.4507	+8.49 %
Our model	0.3990		0.4890	

However, the comparison with the baseline as well as the best participant highlights that our model obtains the highest outcome value (0.489) with improvements higher than +8.49 %. This reinforces our intuition that the user engagement should be integrated into IR models [14]. Moreover, our model obtains an outcome value for round 3 closed to 0.5, suggesting that its effectiveness is relatively similar to the one of the product search model of the e-commerce website. The outcome values obtained by the participants are generally even more lower than 0.5. Taken in a whole, this results show the difficulty of formalizing retrieval models for product search, which is a quite young research domain.

In order to compare the effectiveness at the query level, we plot in Fig. 1 results of our model at the query level for round 2 and 3, highlighting the impact

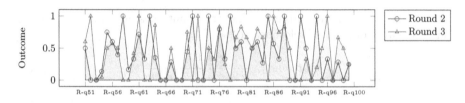

Fig. 1. Effectiveness comparison of our model between round 2 and 3 - Impact of the user engagement metric.

of the user engagement. A descriptive analysis shows that the user engagement indicator enables to improve the effectiveness of 23 queries over the 50 ones, with an average difference equals to 0.391 for those 23 queries (against 0.083 for all queries). Accordingly, we hypothesize that it exists two types of head queries depending on whether they benefit from user engagement factor or not in terms of retrieval effectiveness. In the remaining paper, we call "socially-motivated queries" those leveraging user engagement. A quick overview of query text emphasizes that "socially-motivated queries" seem to be those expressing non-targeted and specific products (e.g., "puzzle", "doll house" or "ball"). In contrast, the "non-socially-motivated queries" (with null or negative improvements) more particularly refer to focused products, generally addressed by a brand (e.g., "Playmobil", "Cars", "Scrabble" or "Angry birds"). This results lead us to analyze more in-depth the user engagement factor.

4   Understanding the Effect of the User Engagement Factor in Product Search

In this section, we address the second contribution of our paper aiming at understanding the user engagement factor. In this aim, we propose to deepen our analysis with a twofold objective: *(1)* identifying "socially-motivated queries" characteristics and *(2)* highlighting the characteristics of product rankings associated to "socially-motivated queries"/"non-socially-motivated queries".

First, we consider two classes of queries (namely "socially-motivated queries" and "non-socially-motivated queries"). We performed a logistic regression aiming at explaining the social responsiveness of queries according to the query characteristics. The latter are those provided by the LL4IR platform (namely, the number of users' clicks, the number of products, the absence/presence of concepts - noted *has.concept*, the absence/presence of brand, the absence/presence of famous character - noted *has.character*) as well as estimated features, namely, the query length. In addition to these characteristics extracted through the textual analysis of the query, we propose to extract new ones based on search result clusters. In particular, we propose to use an unsupervised clustering algorithm called "Lingo" [15]. The latter applies phrases analysis and latent semantic techniques with the aim of clustering search results into meaningful groups. For each query, we then obtained the following features: the number of associated clusters

Table 2. Descriptive model of user preferences for product search on e-commerce sites

Characteristics	Regression estimate	p-value
NbrClusters	0.015	0.0139 *
AvgClusterSize	-0.574	0.0225 *
MinClusterSize	0.681	0.0106 *
has.concept	0.451	0.0222 *
is.character	-0.379	0.0500 *

Table 3. Descriptive model of user preferences for product search on e-commerce sites

Query class	Characteristics	Reg. estimate	p-value
"Socially-motivated queries"	Price	0.002	$\leq$ 2e-16 ***
	Gender (Male)	0.0044770	8.65e-02
	Gender (Female)	0.0165339	1.29e-04 ***
"Non-socially-motivated queries"	Number of pictures	0.008	9.81e-08 ***
	Discount rate	-0.009	6.74e-03 **
	Bonus	0.0329	2.59e-03 **

(*NbrClusters*), the size of the largest cluster (*MaxClusterSize*), the average size of clusters (*AvgClusterSize*), and the minimal size of clusters (*MinClusterSize*).

At each iteration of the backward method, we removed the product characteristic with the highest p-value until all characteristics involved within the model impact significantly on the class ($p-value \leq 0.5$). A positive and significant regression estimate of a particular feature expresses the fact that the higher the value of the feature, the more the query is "socially-motivated". The final statistical model with significant features is presented in Table 2. Results suggest that "socially-motivated queries" are generally queries not referring to famous characters but rather expressing a concept typically related to main themes of products (e.g. "guitar", "kitchen", etc.). Also, those queries generally lead to diversified products. This is shown through the positive correlation with small clusters since the obtained clusters contain few products.

Second, we propose to analyze users' product preferences for both types of queries. We believe that such analysis would help the community to build more effective models for this particular application domain once they have identified "(non-)socially-motivated queries". In this aim, for each query, we consider as evidence source the whole set of products provided by the LL4IR campaign. Instead of using history of click rates that are highly correlated to time ("product trend") and the product availability, we infer the users' preferences from a metric provided by the LL4IR organizers expressing the probability of a product to be clicked by a user. This probability is estimated for a round by the ratio of clicks received by a product and the number of times the product was presented to the user. Accordingly, we build the statistical model for each query class aiming at identifying users' preferences with respect to product characteristics. We used a generalized model and, as done earlier, at each iteration, we removed the product characteristic with the highest p-value until all characteristics impact significantly on the click-based measure ($p - value \leq 0.5$). The higher the value of the feature, the higher the product probability being clicked is. The results are presented in Table 3.

One can see that different features characterize the two query classes, but the price of the product seems to be an important decision-making factor. Indeed, users submitting "socially-motivated queries" are generally interested in products with a higher price than those submitting "non-socially-motivated queries". In addition, the latter users appreciate products with a discount rate (*Bonus*) although low (negative regression estimate of *Discount rate*). Coupled with the query characteristics analysis, this suggests that users expressing "socially-motivated queries"(which mainly address non-targeted information need in terms of brands and characters) considers the price as a product quality indicator. The latter should allow users distinguishing similar products (e.g., among the different types of baby dolls). In contrast, users addressing" non-socially-motivated queries" are looking for particular products with specific characteristics of brands and characters and accordingly appreciate less expensive products.

The gender seems to be an important factor for "socially-motivated queries", orienting the product search model towards products for female. However, it is difficult to infer strong statements from this feature since we do not know the population of users submitting those queries.

Last, the descriptive model reveals that "non-socially-motivated queries" require a picture while this factor is not discriminant for "socially-motivated queries". This suggests that users expressing non-targeted information needs remain general in their decision-making and express small requirements, excepting the price. However, users formulating product need towards specific brands, concepts and characters stay focused on the product design, and the picture is a way to capture the specificity and the credibility of the product. In this case, the presence of pictures is a triggering purchase factor, which is already well-known as a marketing strategy highlighted by some studies. The latter reveals that 67 % of consumers considers product pictures as extremely important[7].

5   Discussion and Conclusion

We presented a product feature-based user-centric model for product search involving in addition to product characteristics the user engagement toward the product. The experimental evaluation has been carried out through the LL4IR framework and suggests that the user engagement is an interesting factor in

---

[7] http://blog.lemonstand.com/7-ways-optimize-product-page-conversions/.

product search. To better understand this factor, we performed statistical analysis highlighting characteristics of queries. With respect to a query classification based on the user engagement responsiveness, we also identify users' preferences in terms of products. These results are not without limitations since analysis are dependent of the experimental framework biases. However, we believe that the naturalness of the experimental evaluation allows considering these results as reasonable. Moreover, our estimation of the user engagement relies on the product popularity [14], but should be refined according to users' interactions.

From this analysis, we pointed out interested users' behaviors and preferences in terms of product search that could be useful for the design of retrieval models in this application domain. One particular statement revealed that some queries are sensible to the user engagement, impacting the features of the product ranking algorithms. For instance, the price is a pivotal feature in product search which should be used differently according to the users' need (users expressing "socially-motivated queries" seems to be willing to buy more expensive products than those expressing "non-socially-motivated queries"). In the future, we plan to enhance our product search model to take into consideration the findings of this paper by proposing a query-adapted product search models which *(1)* detects the query type by taking into account their categories or whether it implies concepts or famous characters, and *(2)* rank products using features that particularly attract users.

References

1. Balog, K., Kelly, L., Schuth, A.: Head first: living labs for ad-hoc search evaluation. In: CIKM 2014, pp. 1815–1818. ACM (2014)
2. Castagnos, S., Jones, N., Pu, P.: Eye-tracking product recommenders' usage. In: RecSys 2010. ACM (2010)
3. Chen, L.: Social influence of product popularity on consumer decisions:usability study of flickr camera finder. In: IUI 2010, pp. 297–300 (2010)
4. Chen, X., Wang, H., Sun, X., Pan, J., Yu, Y.: Diversifying product search results. In: SIGIR 2011, pp. 1093–1094. ACM (2011)
5. Corbitt, B.J., Thanasankit, T., Yi, H.: Trust and e-commerce: a study of consumer perceptions. Electron. Commer. Res. Appl. **2**(3), 203–215 (2003)
6. Craswell, N., Zaragoza, H., Robertson, S.: Microsoft cambridge at TREC 14: enterprise track. In: TREC 2005 (2005)
7. Dakka, W., Gravano, L., Ipeirotis, P.G.: Answering general time-sensitive queries. IEEE ToKDE **24**, 220–235 (2012)
8. Detlor, B., Sproule, S., Gupta, C.: Pre-purchase online information seeking: search versus browse. J. Electron. Commer. Res. **4**(2), 72–84 (2003)
9. Duan, H., Zhai, C.X., Cheng, J., Gattani, A.: Supporting keyword search in product database: a probabilistic approach. Proc. VLDB Endow. **6**(14), 1786–1797 (2013)
10. Ghirmatsion, A.B., Balog, K.: Probabilistic field mapping for product search. In: CLEF 2015 Workshop (2015)
11. Mothe, J., Savoy, J., Kamps, J., Pinel-Sauvagnat, K., Jones, G., San Juan, E., Capellato, L., Ferro, N. (eds.): CLEF 2015. LNCS, vol. 9283. Springer, Heidelberg (2015)

12. Joachims, T.: Optimizing search engines using clickthrough data. In: KDD 2002, pp. 133–142 (2002)
13. Lathia, N., Hailes, S., Capra, L., Amatriain, X.: Temporal diversity in recommender systems. In: SIGIR 2010, pp. 210–217. ACM (2010)
14. Lehmann, J., Lalmas, M., Yom-Tov, E., Dupret, G.: Models of user engagement. In: Masthoff, J., Mobasher, B., Desmarais, M.C., Nkambou, R. (eds.) UMAP 2012. LNCS, vol. 7379, pp. 164–175. Springer, Heidelberg (2012)
15. Osiński, S., Weiss, D.: A concept-driven algorithm for clustering search results. IEEE Intell. Syst. **20**(3), 48–54 (2005)
16. Schaer, P., Tavakolpoursaleh, N.: Historical clicks for product search: Gesis at clef ll4ir 2015. In: CLEF 2015 Workshop (2015)
17. Schuth, A., Balog, K., Kelly, L.: Overview of the living labs for information retrieval evaluation (LL4IR) CLEF lab 2015. In: Mothe, J., Savoy, J., Kamps, J., Pinel-Sauvagnat, K., Jones, G., San Juan, E., Capellato, L., Ferro, N. (eds.) CLEF 2015. LNCS, vol. 9283, pp. 484–496. Springer, Heidelberg (2015). doi:10.1007/978-3-319-24027-5_47
18. Vandic, D., van Dam, J.-W., Frasincar, F.: Faceted product search powered by the semantic web. Dec. Supp. Systems **53**(3), 425–437 (2012)
19. Xiang, L., Yuan, Q., Zhao, S., Chen, L., Zhang, X., Yang, Q., Sun, J.: Temporal recommendation on graphs via long- and short-term preferencefusion. In: KDD 2010, pp. 723–732. ACM(2010)
20. Zaragoza, H., Craswell, N., Taylor, M.J., Saria, S., Robertson, S.E.: Microsoft cambridge at TREC 13: web and hard tracks. In: TREC 2004 (2004)

Random Performance Differences Between Online Recommender System Algorithms

Gebrekirstos G. Gebremeskel[1(✉)] and Arjen P. de Vries[2]

[1] CWI, Amsterdam, The Netherlands
g.g.gebremeskel@cwi.nl
[2] Radboud University, Nijmegen, The Netherlands
arjen@acm.org

Abstract. In the evaluation of recommender systems, the quality of recommendations made by a newly proposed algorithm is compared to the state-of-the-art, using a given quality measure and dataset. Validity of the evaluation depends on the assumption that the evaluation does not exhibit artefacts resulting from the process of collecting the dataset. The main difference between online and offline evaluation is that in the online setting, the user's response to a recommendation is only observed once. We used the NewsREEL challenge to gain a deeper understanding of the implications of this difference for making comparisons between different recommender systems. The experiments aim to quantify the expected degree of variation in performance that cannot be attributed to differences between systems. We classify and discuss the non-algorithmic causes of performance differences observed.

1 Introduction

The literature on recommender systems shows that offline and online recommender system evaluations may not concur with each other [1,3,6]. This is to say that recommender systems may behave differently in offline and online evaluations, both in terms of absolute and relative performance. This has a serious implication for recommender system research, because the whole point of offline evaluation is the assumption that at least the relative performance of recommender systems is indicative of their relative online performance and thus an important step for selecting algorithms that can be deployed in a live recommendation setting.

Prior literature has pointed out a variety of explanations for the performance discrepancy between online and offline evaluations [6,7]. First, offline evaluations can only measure accuracy in a static manner, leaving out the differences between resulting from actual user behaviour. Naturally, offline datasets provide only an incomplete and imprecise model of the real world. The abstraction from user behaviour and context by taking a snapshot of recommendations and user responses may deviate too much from reality to allow for a valid comparison between different recommender systems.

© Springer International Publishing Switzerland 2016
N. Fuhr et al. (Eds.): CLEF 2016, LNCS 9822, pp. 187–198, 2016.
DOI: 10.1007/978-3-319-44564-9_15

The online evaluation of recommender systems overcomes some of these limitations, because we can observe the actual user's responses to recommendations originating from a specific system. A drawback of this setup, however, is the additional "randomness" in the evaluation process that will have to be accounted for. As, each recommendation can only be presented to a single user in his or her real context. The research presented here attempts to improve our understanding of how to accommodate for this element of chance, and still make the right inferences from the evaluation data obtained in CLEF NewsREEL. To identify factors that may explain observed performance differences in online recommender system evaluation, we conduct experiments using several algorithms, *two of which are distinct instances of the exact same algorithm*. We use the experimental results obtained to quantify the effect of randomness in online evaluation on the measured performance.

The paper is organized as follows. In Sect. 2, we discuss our approach, followed by experiments in Sect. 3. In Sects. 4 and 5, we discuss the evaluation results, and identify explanations for the performance differences observed. Section 6 summarizes the lessons learned.

2 Approach

In 2015, we participated in the Living Lab setting of the CLEF News Recommendations Evaluation Lab (NewsREEL) [4]. CLEF NewsREEL is a campaign-like online recommender system evaluation, where participants in need of testing their algorithms are connected with real-life online information portals in need of recommendation services.

In order to investigate the effect of the online setting on the performance measurement of recommendation algorithms, we devised several simple but effective algorithms. Among our algorithms, we included two instances of the same algorithm, with the objective to measure the differences in performance that would have to be attributed to randomness - differences between distinct instances of the exact same algorithm, deployed in the same online recommendation scenario, during the exact same period of operation. A direct comparison of the results that should be identical provides us with the opportunity to consider one instance as the baseline, and obtain a quantitative measure of the performance difference that can only originate from non-algorithmic factors. By also logging the recommendation requests, responses, and clicks, we can recreate the recommendation scenario of one algorithm and compare its results to those that would have been given by the other algorithms. Mixing online and offline evaluation methods provides a more controlled way of measuring differences between different recommender systems, that we can use to estimate the part of the difference in performance that should be attributed to chance.

3 Experiments

We experimented with five algorithms, all of them modifications of a straightforward approach to recommendation based on *recency*. The Recency algorithm takes into account recency and popularity of an item, and it has been shown to be a strong baseline in previous online evaluations. The algorithmic variations that we experimented with are listed below.

Recency: This algorithm keeps the 100 most recently viewed items for each publisher in consideration for being recommended to the user. The most recently read items are returned in response to a recommendation request. We run two instances of this algorithm to get a sense of the randomness involved in the selection of algorithms by the Plista framework [2] and/or clicks on recommendations by users.

RecencyRandom: Instead of recommending the five or six most recently viewed items, this approach returns a random selection from the top 100 most recently viewed items.

GeoRec: The geographical recommender takes the geographical region (states to be specific) of users and the local category of news items into account when generating recommendations. We generate two sets of recommendations, one by the recency recommender and one by a purely geographical recommender. For the purely geographical recommender, we take the 100 most recently viewed items and sort them according to their geographic conditional likelihood scores generated by Eq. 1:

$$r_{u_a, i_k} = P(c_{i_k} | g_{u_a}) \tag{1}$$

where c_{i_k} is a binary corresponding to the local category of item i_k and g_{u_a} is the state-level geographical information of the user u_a, that is, the state the user belongs to. We combine geographical recommendations with recency recommendations as follows. First, we intersect twice the number of recommendations requested from the geographic recommender with the requested number of recommendations from the recency recommender. If the resulting set is smaller than the number of recommendations requested, we append *half − 1* items from the geographic recommender and another *half + 1* from the recency recommender.

GeoRecHistory: This modification of the GeoRec recommender excludes items that the user has already visited from recommendation.

We have run recommendation systems that implement these algorithms over a period of 86 days, between April 12th and July 6th, with one exception; the RecencyRandom algorithm was started 12 days later, on April 24th.

4   Results and Analysis

We present two types of performance scores: cumulative and daily click-through rates (CTR). The cumulative CTR is presented in Table 1. We see that the performance differences are small. If we would rank the algorithms based on their performance, however, we see that the GeoRec recommender leads, followed by Recency and GeoRecHistory. Figure 1 shows the performance measurements by day, for the first 53 days. Figure 2 shows cumulative CTR as a function of the number of days, for the same period.

Table 1. Live performance of the five algorithms

Algorithms	Requests	Clicks	CTR(%)
Recency	56,350	478	0.85
Recency2	53,863	420	0.78
GeoRec	54,338	470	0.86
GeoRecHistory	47,001	395	0.84
RecencyRandom	39,616	283	0.71

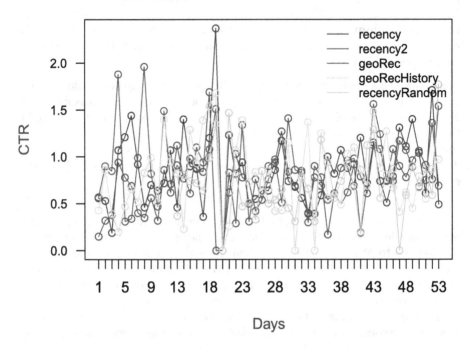

Fig. 1. The daily CTR performances of the five algorithms

From the daily (Fig. 1) and cumulative (Fig. 2) plots, we see that the performance measurements vary considerably. In the cumulative plot, we see that the results for Recency and Recency2 differ considerably during a large part of the evaluation period, although, eventually, converging to a stable situation. If one were to continuously monitor the measured performance of the two algorithms, one might easily conclude (wrongly) that the Recency algorithm is a better approach to recommendation than Recency2.

When observed for a period that is too short, we need appropriate tools to help differentiate the identical recommender systems from their competitors. Imagine for example an experimenter peeking at the experiments every day, to make a decision to choose the best among the competing algorithms. How many times would the experimenter declare statistically significant differences

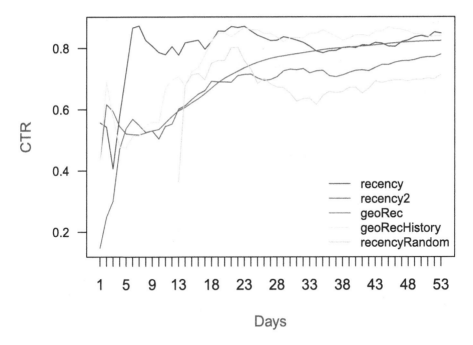

Fig. 2. The cumulative CTR performances of the five algorithms as they progress on a daily basis

between the different algorithms? To compute statistical significance, we used Thumbtack's Abba, a test for binomial experiments [5]. We examined this by using two baselines: the random recommender (RecencyRandom) and Recency2. The results when using the RecencyRandom recommender as a baseline are given in Table 2. Similarly, the results for the baseline of Recency2 are given in Table 3. We see that, when RecencyRandom is used as the baseline, Recency, GeoRec and GeoRecHistory achieve significantly different performance for a majority of the days tested. With Recency2 as the baseline, we see that these percentages are lower; the difference with Recency is considered significant according to the test on two days (perhaps surprising, but a percentage that is in line with the p-value chosen).

The two instances of the same algorithm show large enough differences in performance that there is a chance of concluding one is better than itself. This observation raises questions regarding interpreting the results of the evaluation; it is not so easy to conclude that one algorithm is better than another one based on just an observed difference in performance, even if a statistical test supports that decision. Given the dynamic nature of user-item interactions and the resulting differences in the particular settings that the algorithms operate in, we should be careful when interpreting a small but seemingly significant performance difference. Recommendation evaluations that involve user-item interactions must

Table 2. Statistical significance over the baseline of RecencyRandom. Bracket results are obtained by a recent run.

Algorithm	Days of significance	Percentage (%)
Recency	20	27.4
GeoRec	41	56.2
GeoRecHistory	42	57.5

Table 3. Statistical significance over the baseline of Recency2.

Algorithm	Days of significance	Percentage (%)
Recency	2	2.7
GeoRec	25	34.3
GeoRecHistory	26	35.6

account for some level of randomness, and perhaps a more strict level of statistical significance should be considered than the commonly used 5 %.

5   Causes of Performance Differences

We have seen above that the two instances of the same algorithm can achieve statistically significant difference in performance in an online setting. This is indicative of the extent of performance difference that can arise due to non-algorithmic factors. The two instances of the same algorithm receive different user-item interactions from the evaluation framework. Although they operate in the same recommendation setting, the users and items that they deal with create a unique setting for each instance. We distinguish three types of non-algorithmic factors that may cause the differences in performance: (1) operational differences in the evaluation framework, (2) differences in user-item pairs for which recommendations have been observed, and (3) remaining differences that we consider randomness.

5.1   Operation Causes

By non-algorithmic operational causes, we refer to decisions in the evaluation framework that could affect the observed performance of the recommender systems evaluated. Recommendation systems under evaluation are served requests by a system that distributes the incoming requests in a supposedly "fair" manner. From the perspective of the CLEF NewsREEL participant, fairness of this process is a matter of faith, and difficult to assess. We know that some publishers are more likely to trigger clicks on recommendations than others, such that biases in the distribution of recommendation requests can easily result in performance differences between the algorithms under evaluation. The approach of assigning recommendation requests to participant systems may exhibit an (implicit) bias with respect to pairing some teams and/or systems with a subset of publishers, or assigning specific users (e.g., those logged-in) to some teams or algorithms, or serving a skewed subset of items from specific categories (e.g., political), or a combination of such factors.

5.2   User-Item Causes

Another source of differences in performance that are not algorithmic could arise due to differences in the sets of items and users that are assigned to the two algorithms. Every algorithm under evaluation receives a different subset of all recommendation requests, resulting in inherent differences in performance if, by chance, certain user-item interactions are incomparable (which would also render the measured results incomparable). In the evaluation of information retrieval systems, for example, it is well known that results obtained on different test collections cannot be compared directly; here, to some extent, we could consider the different performance measurements to result from different test collections, and direct comparison may suffer from the same problems as in the information retrieval evaluation case.

5.3   Random Causes

We refer to all remaining factors that might cause performance differences as random causes, including factors like the user's mood as well as causes that result from idiosyncrasies of the particular datasets (settings, in the online case). Imagine an offline setting with two algorithm (algorithm one and algorithm two) and two datasets (dataset one and dataset two). If on dataset one, algorithm one performs better than algorithm two, but on dataset two the situation is vice versa, the difference between the performance measurements cannot be attributed to the difference in users and items.

One of the advantages of running four algorithms at the same time is that we have datasets that have one big advantage over disparate datasets used for research and that is that we have their online behavior and performance. These logs are, therefore, very important to the performance difference that arises as a result of the random causes in an online setting, as discussed below.

5.4   Overlap in Performance

How can we find out that the random causes (idiosyncrasies of the particular settings) are having an impact on the performance differences of algorithms? To measure the effect of artifacts in evaluation data on performance estimates in an offline setting, we could evaluate two different algorithms on two datasets, and measure the performance differences between the algorithms on each individual dataset. The absolute difference between these two differences can be considered an estimate of the "dataset artifact" on performance. For, if there is no difference, then the measurements are accurate, and both datasets lead to the same conclusions. However, if a difference is observed, then we would seek the cause for these variations in the differences between the evaluation data. In an online setting, it is not possible to follow this exact procedure, but it is possible to quantify a part of this dataset (setting) artifact using a similar method.

Imagine an ideal world where you can run two algorithms simultaneously in an exactly the same environment for the two algorithms. Users, items, and time are exactly the same. The only things that differ in this ideal world are the recommendations responses by the algorithms. Table 4 shows how different (similar) the recommendation by other algorithms on the different settings would be. The scores are the percentages of shared recommendation over the total number of recommendations. The Table gives two scores for each pair, the first being the exact similarity per recommendation response both in order and content (the number given in each table cell), and the other being the set similarity per recommendation response (order can vary, given between brackets). Each cell corresponds to the similarity measured when the algorithm listed in the column is applied to a dataset constructed from the log obtained when using the algorithm listed in the row. GeoRec-Recency and GeoRec-Recency2 show large similarities, which is not surprising since the GeoRec recommender is only a minor modification of the recency recommender that diversifies its results; which apparently does not diversify the results very much in practice.

Table 4. Shared recommendations. The score in each cell is the percentage of the lists that the two recommendations shared, and the second number, between brackets, is a percentage of the sets of recommendations that the algorithms shared. GeoRec-Recency2 and GeoRec-Recency show the highest similarities.

Algorithms	Recency	GeoRec	RecencyRandom
Recency	100	**85.82(97.96)**	0.0(74.11)
Recency2	100	85.79(97.97)	0.0(73.84)
GeoRec	50.99(91.64)	100	0.0(76.18)
RecencyRandom	0.01(73.28)	0.01(73.40)	100

The idealized system described above would enable us to determine, in the true sense, the algorithm that is the better one; at least, in the evaluation framework in which the algorithms in question are being tested. In practice, such a test would be an approximation, since it does not account to the many factors that can cause performance differences. Obviously such an idealized system is hard to create, but we can create one aspect of that idealized system. That aspect is the overlap in performance that two algorithms would have if they were to be run in the idealized system. The overlap in performance is defined in Eq. 2.

$$Setting_A Overlap_{AB} = \frac{Clicks_{AB}}{Recommendations_{AB}} \qquad (2)$$

In Eq. 2, $Setting_A$ is the log generated by running algorithm A, and $Setting_A Overlap_{AB}$ is the overlap in performance of algorithms A and B in dataset $Setting_A$. $Clicks_{AB}$ and $Recommendation_{AB}$ are counted from intersection of recommended items and the intersections of recommended-and-clicked items respectively of algorithms A and B, when they would be run in an exact online setting that would generate $Setting_A$. The overlap in performance is the ratio of the intersection of recommended-and-clicked items and the intersection of recommended items that two online-deployed algorithms would share if they were to be run in the idealized system. We use this overlap in performance to quantify a part of the performance difference as a result of the random causes by comparing the overlap in performance of two algorithms in two datasets.

To explain how we would obtain the overlap in performance, consider the two algorithms which we used in the NewsREEL challenge. For each algorithm, we have logged the recommendation request, recommendation response, and clicks. If we rerun the other algorithm on the logs of the first algorithm, everything remains the same except the recommendation responses. By determining to what extent the recommendations are the same for the two algorithms, and the ratio of the clicks received by the online-deployed algorithm could also have been obtained by the competing algorithm running on the logs, we obtain the overlap in performance. To obtain the overlap in performance of two algorithms in the idealized system we described, one does not need to run both algorithms online. Running one algorithm online to obtain logs that form a dataset for evaluation, and subsequently running the other algorithm on these logs, is sufficient; for, it is only the overlap of the two algorithms that we are interested, and not the overall performances of the algorithms.

Difference in Overlap. If we have two online-deployed algorithms and record both of their logs, we can determine a measure of overlap between the two algorithms on each of these logs. We call the difference between the two measures of overlap the **difference in overlap**, its definition given by Eq. 3. Note that to compute this difference in overlap, we need to deploy both algorithms and collect their respective logs. If there are no differences in behavior of these algorithms on the same logs, this difference would be zero. The difference in overlap therefore gives us then a measure that quantifies the overall difference in performance that should be attributed to non-algorithmic causes.

$$DiffinOverlap_{Setting_A Setting_B} = |Setting_A Overlap_{AB} - Setting_B Overlap_{AB}| \tag{3}$$

Since we have four algorithms that ran during the complete evaluation campaign (excluding GeoRecHistory), we can quantify differences in overlap between several pairs of algorithms, and, together, these differences in overlap will give us a clue of the extent to which performance differences between algorithms should be attributed to chance. In other words, even though the full difference in overlap cannot be measured, as we can not create the idealized system where two different algorithms would receive the exact same recommendation requests for the exact same user and item combinations, by zooming in on the performance

Table 5. Difference in overlap of our algorithms. Each entry is obtained by subtracting overlap in performance in one dataset of two algorithms from their overlap in performance in another dataset. GeoRec-Recency2 and GeoRec-RecencyRandom show the highest overlap difference

Algorithms	Recency	Recency2	GeoRec	RecencyRandom
Recency	0	0	0.001	0.006
Recency2		0	**0.026**	0.004
GeoRec				**0.026**

overlap we can still obtain an estimate of the level of non-algorithmic differences in the evaluation.

To calculate the difference in overlap, we make one assumption, and that is that we do not take into account the order of the recommended items. If two algorithms have recommended two lists of the same items, but in different order and a click happened on the online deployment, we consider a click happened on the latter too, regardless of the order. Also, the CTR scores were expressed as percentages before any calculations. We take the absolute value as we are interested in the magnitude only. The results are presented in Table 5. To help interpret the Table, the score listed in the cell Recency2-GeoRec corresponds to the difference in overlap between Recency2 and GeoRec obtained as the difference between the overlaps in performances of Recency2 and GeoRec when they ran in two identical online settings (which are represented by the logs of Recency2 and the logs of GeoRec).

The highest differences in overlap observed are between Recency2 and Geo-Rec and between GeoRec and RecencyRandom, each equal to **0.026**. Given that GeoRec and Recency are closely related algorithms, and Recency and Recency2 are identical, one would expect that the differences in overlaps of GeoRec-Recency, and GeoRec-Recency2 should have been the same, and smaller than the difference in overlap of Georec-RecencyRandom. In an ideal evaluation environment, we would expect the difference in overlap to equal 0, because we would assume that the two settings under which the two algorithms run should affect the two algorithms in similar ways. Why do the two settings then affect the two algorithms in different ways? The positive scores of differences in overlap, we argue, are a results of the idiosyncrasies of the particular settings.

6   Conclusion

We set out to investigate the performance differences in online algorithms. We employed several algorithms among which were two instances of the same algorithm. We demonstrated that two instances of the same algorithms may diverge, and occasionally even to the extent of showing statistically significant differences in performance. The difference in performance seems to indicate that care must be taken to take into account some degree of randomness in recommender systems evaluation that involve users in a live setting, in addition to statistical significance tests using commonly used statistical significance levels.

We classified and discussed the possible causes of performances differences between online-deployed algorithms and argued that even in the absence of obvious causes of performance differences such as operational biases and the selection of users and items observed in the experiment, performances can vary due to other artifacts in the data collected. These artifacts will also exist in offline datasets, but in the online setting, the researcher is much more susceptible to being mislead by such artifacts, as it involves users and items and their dynamic interactions. We cannot claim that these artifacts are the sole reason for observed significant performance differences between two instances of the same algorithm; and forming an important confounding factor when comparing any two algorithms in general. We may however conclude that we have to take into account these random biases that can only be smoothed out over a sufficiently long evaluation period.

Our results suggest that we should be reluctant in adopting small (statistically significant) improvements as indicative of real performance differences when the evaluation involves real world settings, users and items. We have proposed a new method to quantify the effect of randomness in the evaluation by zooming in on the differences in overlap of the results obtained from two competing algorithms, that are tested on two settings simultaneously. In future work, we plan to develop this approach further to help understand the level of randomness that we should take into account when we compare the performance measurements obtained in an online experiment, to help improve inferences about the quality of different recommender systems.

Acknowledgements. This research was partially supported by COMMIT project Infiniti.

References

1. Beel, J., Genzmehr, M., Langer, S., Nürnberger, A., Gipp, B.: A comparative analysis of offline and online evaluations and discussion of research paper recommender system evaluation. In: Proceedings of the International Workshop on Reproducibility and Replication in Recommender Systems Evaluation, pp. 7–14. ACM (2013)
2. Brodt, T., Hopfgartner, F.: Shedding light on a living lab: the clef newsreel open recommendation platform. In: Proceedings of the 5th Information Interaction in Context Symposium, pp. 223–226. ACM (2014)
3. Garcin, F., Faltings, B., Donatsch, O., Alazzawi, A., Bruttin, C., Huber, A.: Offline and online evaluation of news recommender systems at swissinfo. In: Proceedings of the 8th ACM Conference on Recommender Systems, pp. 169–176. ACM (2014)
4. Hopfgartner, F., Kille, B., Lommatzsch, A., Plumbaum, T., Brodt, T., Heintz, T.: Benchmarking news recommendations in a living lab. In: Kanoulas, E., Lupu, M., Clough, P., Sanderson, M., Hall, M., Hanbury, A., Toms, E. (eds.) CLEF 2014. LNCS, vol. 8685, pp. 250–267. Springer, Heidelberg (2014)
5. Howard, S.: Abba: Frequently asked questions. https://www.thumbtack.com/labs/abba/. Accessed 18 July 2016

6. Kirshenbaum, E., Forman, G., Dugan, M.: A live comparison of methods for personalized article recommendation at forbes.com. In: Flach, P.A., De Bie, T., Cristianini, N. (eds.) ECML PKDD 2012, Part II. LNCS, vol. 7524, pp. 51–66. Springer, Heidelberg (2012)
7. McNee, S.M., Kapoor, N., Konstan, J.A.: Don't look stupid: avoiding pitfalls when recommending research papers. In: Proceedings of the 2006 20th Anniversary Conference on Computer Supported Cooperative Work, pp. 171–180. ACM (2006)

Short Papers and Posters

SS4MCT: A Statistical Stemmer
for Morphologically Complex Texts

Javid Dadashkarimi, Hossein Nasr Esfahani, Heshaam Faili,
and Azadeh Shakery$^{(\boxtimes)}$

School of Electrical and Computer Engineering, College of Engineering,
University of Tehran, Tehran, Iran
{dadashkarimi,h_nasr,hfaili,shakery}@ut.ac.ir

Abstract. There have been multiple attempts to resolve various inflection matching problems in information retrieval. Stemming is a common approach to this end. Among many techniques for stemming, statistical stemming has been shown to be effective in a number of languages, particularly highly inflected languages. In this paper we propose a method for finding affixes in different positions of a word. Common statistical techniques heavily rely on string similarity in terms of prefix and suffix matching. Since infixes are common in irregular/informal inflections in morphologically complex texts, it is required to find infixes for stemming. In this paper we propose a method whose aim is to find statistical inflectional rules based on minimum edit distance table of word pairs and the likelihoods of the rules in a language. These rules are used to statistically stem words and can be used in different text mining tasks. Experimental results on CLEF 2008 and CLEF 2009 English-Persian CLIR tasks indicate that the proposed method significantly outperforms all the baselines in terms of MAP.

Keywords: Stemming · Infix recognition · Inflectional/derivation formation matching · Dictionary-based cross-language information retrieval

1 Introduction

Uniforming different inflections of words is a required task in a wide range of text mining algorithms, including, but not limited to text classification, text clustering, document retrieval, and language modeling [1]. Stemming has been considered as a common approach for this goal in several studies [1,2]. Stemmers usually remove affixes from the words to present them in the form of their morphological roots. Conventional rule-based stemmers tailor the linguistic knowledge of experts. On the other hand, statistical stemmers provide language-independent approaches which generally group related words based on various string-similarity measures. Such approaches often involve n-grams; equivalence classes can be formed from words that share the same properties: word-initial letter n-grams, common n-grams throughout the word, or by refining these classes

© Springer International Publishing Switzerland 2016
N. Fuhr et al. (Eds.): CLEF 2016, LNCS 9822, pp. 201–207, 2016.
DOI: 10.1007/978-3-319-44564-9_16

with clustering techniques. This kind of statistical stemming has been shown to be effective for many languages, including English, Turkish, and Malay. For example, Bhat introduced a method for Kannada where the similarity of two words is determined by three distance measures based on prefix and suffix matching and the first mismatch point in the words [3].

Defining precise rules for morphologically complex texts, especially for the purpose of infix removal is sometimes impossible [4]. Informal/irregular forms usually do not obey the conventional rules in the languages. For instance, '$k\hat{h}unh$' (home) is a frequent form for '$k\hat{h}anh$' in Persian conversations or '$goood$' and '$good$' are used interchangeably in English tweets.

In this paper, we propose a statistical technique for finding inflectional and derivation formations of words. To this end, we introduce an unsupervised method to cluster all morphological variants of a word. The proposed algorithm learns linguistic patterns to match a word and its morphological variants based on a given large collection of documents, which is readily available on the Web. A linguistic pattern captures a transformation rule between a word and its morphological variant. The extracted rules indicate which letters in which positions of a word should be modified. Affix characters, positions of the characters, operations on the characters based on the minimum edit distance (MED) algorithm (i.e., *insertion* or *deletion*) [5], and part-of-speech (POS) tag of the input word are the attributes of a rule. Our algorithm assigns a score to each rule, indicating its confidence. The higher the frequency of a rule in the input collection, the higher the confidence value of that rule. Finally, a small subset of the obtained rules are selected based on their scores and a learned threshold as valid rules. We demonstrate that using this subset for query expansion can significantly improve English-Persian CLIR performance compared to comprehensive baselines.

In Sect. 2 we elaborate on the subject, in Sect. 3 we assess its quality in an IR task, and in Sect. 4 we conclude the paper.

2   SS4MCT: A Statistical Stemmer for Morphologically Complex Texts

In this section we propose an unsupervised method for finding inflections in a language. To this end, we first introduce a transformation rule which is an edit path transforming the word w into w' based on a number of actions. Our goal is to estimate the probability of each transformation rule $P(R)$ and compute the likelihood of generating inflections for a given term (i.e., $p(w'|w)$). In Sects. 2.1 and 2.2 we introduce the proposed method in more details and in Sect. 2.3 we propose an evaluation framework for the method.

2.1   Transformation Rules

Each transformation rule contains a number of actions transforming a word into an inflection. If two terms are k points distant from each other, the rule that

Table 1. Examples of transformation rules

w	$\bar{w}$	Transformation Rule						
		o_1	p_1	c_1	o_2	p_2	c_2	POS
jhangrd (tourist)	*jhangrdi* (tourism)	i	e	i	-	-	-	N_SING
jhangrd	*jhangrdan* (tourists)	i	e	n	i	e	a	N_SING
jhangrd	*jhangir* (proper noun)	d	m	i	i	e	d	N_SING
ksart (damage)	*ksarat* (damages)	i	m	a	-	-	-	N_SING
shabe (friend)	*ashab* (friends)	i	b	a	d	e	e	N_SING
jzirh (island)	*jzair* (islands)	i	m	a	d	e	e	N_SING

transforms the input term to the output term contains k actions and the maximum likelihood POS tag of the input word. Each action consists of the following attributes: **c**, the character in difference, **p**, the position of that character (*begin*, *middle*, and *end*), and **o**, the corresponding operation on the character in the MED algorithm (*deletion* or *insertion*). Intuitively we define a few general positions for affixes to prevent sparsity of the rules. A *substitution* operation can be replaced by a couple of *insertion/deletion* operations; therefore we ignore the *substitution* operation. Table 1 shows a number of examples for the rules.

2.2 Probability of the Rules

To compute the probability of generating an inflection for a given term (i.e., $p(w'|w)$) we can compute the transformation rule (R) between w and w' and estimate $p(w'|w)$ by $p(R)$. To compute the probability of each rule we use a large collection of words extracted from a document collection. For each pair of words in the collection (w and w'), we compute the rule for transforming w into w' and count the number of times this rule has happened in the collection. The higher the occurrences of a rule, the more likely it is to be a valid one. Finally we estimate the rules probability with maximum likelihood estimator.

2.3 How to Evaluate the Algorithm

In this section we provide a framework for the stemming algorithm to evaluate its effectiveness. We use dictionary-based cross-lingual information retrieval (CLIR) to this end. In highly inflected languages, bilingual dictionaries contain only original forms of the words. Therefore, in dictionary-based CLIR, retrieval systems are obliged either to stem documents and queries, or to leave them intact [6–8], or expand the query with inflections. We opted the query expansion approach which is a widely used approach to compensate the shortage of inflections [2,4,9]. We used the following probabilistic framework to this end [4]:

$$p(c_{i,j}|q_i) = \sum_{i' \neq i} \left(\sum_{j'=1}^{|\mathbf{c}_{i'}|} p(c_{i,j}, c_{i',j'}) + \sum_{j'=1}^{|\mathbf{c}'_{i'}|} p(c_{i,j}, c'_{i',j'}) \right),$$

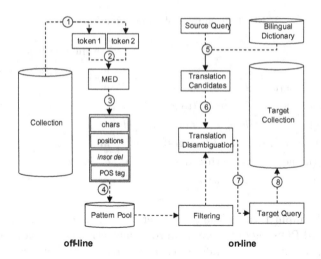

Fig. 1. Outline the proposed SS4MCT and its evaluation framework.

$$p(c'_{i,j}|q_i) = \sum_{i'\neq i} \sum_{j'=1}^{|\mathbf{c}_{i'}|} p(c'_{i,j}, c_{i',j'}). \tag{1}$$

where q_i is a query term and $\mathbf{c}_i$ is the set of translation candidates provided in a bilingual dictionary for q_i. $\mathbf{c}'_i$ is the set of the most probable inflections of the words appeared in $\mathbf{c}_i$ selected by a tuned threshold. Then, we compute the translation probability of $c_{i,j}$ or $c'_{i,j}$ for the given q_i. To avoid adding noisy terms, we only compute the joint probabilities between either a pair of translation candidates from the dictionary ($c_{i,j}$ and $c_{i',j'}$) or a pair of a candidate from the dictionary and an inflection from the collection ($c_{i,j}$ and $c'_{i',j'}$) [4].

Our goal is to find $\bar{\mathbf{c}}_i$ using the proposed SS4MCT (i.e. set of top-ranked $\bar{c}_{i',j'}$ according to $p_t(\bar{c}_{i',j'}|c_{i,j})$) and then evaluate its impact on the performance of the CLIR task. Figure 1 shows the whole process of extracting rules (off-line part) and the evaluation framework (on-line part).

3   Experiments

3.1   Experimental Setup

The statistics of the collection used for both rule extraction and evaluation is provided in Table 2. We employed the statistical language modeling framework with Kullback-Leibler similarity measure of Lemur toolkit for our retrieval task. Dirichlet Prior is selected as our document smoothing strategy. Top 30 documents are used for the mixture pseudo-relevance feedback algorithm. Queries are expanded by the top 50 terms generated by the feedback model [10, 11]. We removed Persian stop words from the queries and documents [4,7].

Table 2. Collections characteristics

ID	Lang.	Collection	Queries (title only)	#docs	#qrels
FA	Persian	Hamshahri 1996–2002	CLEF 2008–09, topics 551–650	166,774	9,625

We used STeP1 [12] in our stemming process in Persian. We also stem the source English queries in all experiments with the Porter stemmer. We use *Google* English-Persian dictionary[1] as the translation resource. Dadashkarimi et al., demonstrated that *Google* has better coverage compared to other English-Persian dictionaries [4]. We have exploited 40 Persian POS tags in our experiments.[2] The retrieval results are mainly evaluated by Mean Average Precision (MAP) over top 1000 retrieved documents. Significance tests are computed using two-tailed paired t-test with 95 % confidence. Precision at top 5 documents (P@5) and top 10 documents (P@10) are also reported.

3.2 Comparing Different Morphological Processing Methods

In this section we aim at evaluating the proposed SS4MCT method. To this end we compare the proposed SS4MCT with a number of dictionary-based CLIR methods; the 5-gram truncation method (SPLIT) proposed in [13], rule-based query expansion (RBQE) based on inflectional/derivation rules from Farazzin machine translator[3], and the STeP1 stemmer [12] are the morphological processing approaches for the retrieval system. On the other hand, we run another set of experiments without applying any morphological processing method similar to the Persian state-of-the-art CLIR methods. Iterative translation disambiguation (ITD) [13], joint cross-lingual topical relevance model (JCLTRLM) [14], top-ranked translation (TOP-1), and the bi-gram coherence translation method (BiCTM), introduced in [4] (assume $|\bar{c}_i| = 0$), are the baselines without any morphological processing units. As shown in Table 3 BiCTM outperforms all the baselines when there is no morphological processing unit. Although the improvement compared to JCLTRLM is not statistically significant, for simplicity we assume this model as a base of comparisons in the next set of experiments. In other words, we study the effect of the morphological processing units on the performance of BiCTM. As shown in Table 3 the performance of the CLIR task degraded when we use the SPLIT approach. It is due to expanding the query with irrelevant tokens (e.g., *normal/abnormal*). RBQE suffers from a similar problem to some extent; for example *jat* is a valid suffix for *sabzi* (=vegetable) in Persian whereas it is an invalid suffix for *ketab* (=book). The results demonstrate that SS4MCT outperforms all the baselines in terms of MAP. This is due to a couple of reasons; first the ability of SS4MCT at finding infixes along with other affixes, particularly in irregular inflections and second its ability at deriving the likelihood/relevance of the rules in the collection/query.

---

[1] https://translate.google.com/#en/fa/.
[2] http://ece.ut.ac.ir/dbrg/bijankhan/.
[3] http://www.faraazin.ir.

Table 3. Comparing different methods in dictionary-based CLIR. Superscripts show that the MAP improvements over baselines are statistically significant.

Without morphological processing					With morphological processing				
id		MAP	%M	P@5	P@10	id		MAP	%M	P@5	P@10
	Mono	0.383		0.640	0.605		Mono	0.384		0.640	0.605
1	TOP 1	0.213	55.6	0.348	0.346	5	SPLIT	0.223	58.2	0.362	0.363
2	ITD	0.238^1	62.0	0.404	0.38	6	STEM	0.247	65.0	0.412	0.401
3	JCLTRLM	0.2523	65.70	0.4000	0.3910	7	RBQE	0.245	63.8	0.380	0.389
4	BiCTM	$\mathbf{0.257^{12}}$	67.0	0.406	0.406	8	SS4MCT	$\mathbf{0.268^{4567}}$	69.8	0.412	0.411

4   Conclusion and Future Works

In this paper we proposed a new method for statistical stemming in morphologically complex texts. SS4MCT extracts a number of morphological rules based on edit distances of a large number of word pairs from a collection. Evaluating SS4MCT on a dictionary-based English-Persian CLIR task demonstrates its effectiveness. Considering adjacency of the characters in the rules and evaluating the method on informal text mining remained as future works.

Acknowledgement. The author would like to thank Razieh Rahimi and the anonymous reviewers for their helpful comments and feedback.

References

1. Aggarwal, C.C., Zhai, C.: Mining Text Data. Springer, New York (2012)
2. Krovetz, R.: Viewing morphology as an inference process. In: Proceedings SIGIR 1993, pp. 191–202. SIGIR (1993)
3. Bhat, S.: Statistical stemming for kannada. In: WSSANLP 2013 (2013)
4. Dadashkarimi, J., Shakery, A., Faili, H.: A probabilistic translation method for dictionary-based cross-lingual information retrieval in agglutinative languages. In: CCL 2014, Tehran, Iran (2014)
5. Levenshtein, V.I.: Binary codes capable of correcting deletions, insertions and reversals. Sov. Phys. Dokl. **10**(8), 707–710 (1966)
6. Hashemi, H.B., Shakery, A.: Mining a Persian-English comparable corpus for cross-language information retrieval. Inf. Process. Manage. **50**(2), 384–398 (2014)
7. Dadashkarimi, J., Shahshahani, M.S., Tebbifakhr, A., Faili, H., Shakery, A.: Dimension projection among languages based on pseudo-relevant documents for query translation. arXiv preprint (2016). arXiv:1605.07844
8. Rahimi, R., Shakery, A., Dadashkarimi, J., Aryannejad, M., Dehghani, M., Esfahani, H.N.: Building a multi-domain comparable corpus using a learning to rank method. Nat. Lang. Eng. **22**(Special Issue 04), 627–653 (2016)
9. Cao, G., Robertson, S., Nie, J.Y.: Selecting query term alternations for web search by exploiting query contexts. In: Proceedings of ACL 2008: HLT, Columbus, Ohio, pp. 148–155. Association for Computational Linguistics, June 2008
10. Zhai, C., Lafferty, J.: Model-based feedback in the language modeling approach to information retrieval. In: CIKM, Atlanta, Georgia, USA, pp. 403–410 (2001)

11. Esfahani, H.N., Dadashkarimi, J., Shakery, A.: Profile-based translation in multilingual expertise retrieval. In: Proceedings of MultilingMine@ECIR (2016)
12. Shamsfard, M., Jafari, H.S., Ilbeygi, M.: Step-1: a set of fundamental tools for persian text processing. In: LREC (2010)
13. Monz, C., Dorr, B.J.: Iterative translation disambiguation for cross-language information retrieval. In: SIGIR, Salvador, Brazil, pp. 520–527 (2005)
14. Ganguly, D., Leveling, J., Jones, G.: Cross-lingual topical relevance models. In: COLING 2012, Mumbai, India, pp. 927–942 (2012)

Index-Based Semantic Tagging for Efficient Query Interpretation

José Devezas[(⊠)] and Sérgio Nunes

INESC TEC and DEI, Faculdade de Engenharia, Universidade do Porto,
Rua Dr. Roberto Frias, s/n, 4200-465 Porto, Portugal
{jld,ssn}@fe.up.pt

Abstract. Modern search engines are evolving beyond ad hoc document retrieval. Nowadays, the information needs of the users can be directly satisfied through entity-oriented search, by ranking the entities or attributes that better relate to the query, as opposed to the documents that contain the best matching terms. One of the challenges in entity-oriented search is efficient query interpretation. In particular, the task of semantic tagging, for the identification of entity types in query parts, is central to understanding user intent. We compare two approaches for semantic tagging, within a single domain, one based on a Sesame triple store and another one based on a Lucene index. This provides a segmentation and annotation of the query based on the most probable entity types, leading to query classification and its subsequent interpretation. We evaluate the run time performance for the two strategies and find that there is a statistically significant speedup, of at least four times, for the index-based strategy over the triple store strategy.

Keywords: Entity-oriented search · Query segmentation · Semantic annotation · Query interpretation

1 Introduction

In the last few years, search engines have been evolving from full-text document search into a richer, more entity-oriented search. Entity-oriented or semantic search [2] is a step towards a more direct answer to the user's information needs; it differs from regular full-text search, as results are expected to be entities or attributes, as opposed to full-text search, where results are expected to be documents. Several new problems emerged from the need for entity retrieval. Full-text indexing techniques proved inadequate or insufficient, ranking strategies posed new challenges, as an expanding world of linked data could now contribute to determine the relevance of entities, and the traditional keyword query as a set of terms became unsuitable to support entity-oriented search. When we are looking for entities, we can't necessarily find them through their content, like we do with documents, but rather through their features (e.g., attributes, types, relations). Thus, there is a need to somehow capture and use this information during the search process.

© Springer International Publishing Switzerland 2016
N. Fuhr et al. (Eds.): CLEF 2016, LNCS 9822, pp. 208–213, 2016.
DOI: 10.1007/978-3-319-44564-9_17

The search process begins with the query, making query analysis essential to extract additional information, such as the parts of the query that represent entities, as well as their types or attributes, and the parts of the query that represent traditional keywords. Identifying entities in a query through segmentation, as well as matching them to a particular category is frequently called semantic tagging [5]. In our system, query interpretation is fully supported by the information obtained from semantic tagging. This enables the subsequent construction of knowledge base queries to retrieve entities, types or attributes matching the text and identified category of each query part. The resulting ranked set of candidates can then be used to support the interpretation of the query, helping in the final query answering process.

In this paper, we evaluate the efficiency of the candidate retrieval subtask, based on a Sesame triple store, using SPARQL queries, as well as on a Lucene index, optimized for this task, using keyword queries.

2   Reference Work

Pound et al. [6] have provided a relevant contribution to entity-oriented search by structuring the queries for ad hoc object retrieval into five categories: *entity* query (directly find a specific entity), *type* query (find entities of a given type), *attribute* query (find values of an attribute of an entity or type), *relation* query (discover how two or more entities or types are connected) and *keyword* query (for any traditional full-text query that doesn't fit the other categories).

Guo et al. [4] proposed a new application of named entity recognition in the context of search queries, based on a Weakly Supervised Latent Dirichlet Allocation (WS-LDA) algorithm that used partially labeled entities as seeds. The idea was to use a query log, discovering queries that contained a given entity and class, to obtain an associated context (remaining terms). Based on a context "document" and a class "topic", they generated training data that could be used to learn a topic model and reiterate with new seeds to improve the overall model.

Blanco et al. [3] presented an extremely effective and efficient algorithm for entity linking in queries (Fast Entity Linking, or FEL) that took advantage of context (using word2vec), based on query logs and Wikipedia articles on the entity (as determined by the anchor text linking to the Wikipedia article). While the methodology we present here does not seem to outperform FEL (the mean run time for our whole search process is 49 ms for a different dataset), our technique might have a lower implementation cost, as it easily builds on top of existing information retrieval frameworks like Lucene.

Aggarwal and Buitelaar [1] focused on the interpretation of natural language queries to facilitate querying over linked data, with languages like SPARQL. Their pipeline included: entity annotation (supported on two indexes, one for labels and URIs of all DBpedia instances and another one for all DBpedia classes), deep linguistic analysis (at this stage, a central entity, as well as the dependencies between all entities, were identified), and semantic similarity/relatedness (similarity was defined on the basis of *is-a* relations of concepts, while relatedness covered other types of relations).

3 Data Characterization

The work we present here aimed at improving search within the University of Porto. We implemented an entity-oriented search system capable of answering queries by taking advantage of the untapped underlying linked data present in the current information system. We considered search tasks like the discovery of the department for a given staff member or the finding of students enrolled in two given courses. We first tackled this problem at a faculty level and then extended our support to the fourteen schools of the University of Porto.

The main performance issues that led us to explore an alternative to directly using the triple store for query analysis were identified when we scaled from faculty-centric entities to university-centric entities. Growing from a dataset restricted to the students at the Faculty of Engineering to a dataset including the students for all the schools at the University of Porto meant growing our triple store from $546,760$ to $2,594,511$ statements. Including the students for the whole university had a tremendous impact in the growth of our dataset, translating into $139,640$ more students, associated with $193,650$ additional enrollments, $1,166$ more courses, 14 more academic years and 10 more faculties.

4 Semantic Tagging in Queries

Semantic tagging in queries is the act of annotating queries with entity types, for query understanding. We followed this approach by segmenting the query and annotating groups of sequential terms (*n*-grams) with the most probable category (*entity*, *attribute*, *type* or *keyword*), based on a set of matching candidate labels from the knowledge base. In this work, we focused on the efficiency of two alternative methodologies for candidate retrieval, one based on a Sesame triple store and SPARQL querying, and another one based on a Lucene index and keyword querying. The techniques we describe here can easily be used to also identify entity types or to establish entity links.

The first step for query analysis was to build a collection of all n-grams for $n \in [1, n]$. We used $n = 6$ as the maximum n-gram size, given it provided a coverage of 94.28% for the labels of our entities, resulting in a good compromise between performance and accuracy (a higher number of n-grams would result in additional candidate retrieval queries). The second step was to retrieve matching candidates for each n-gram. We did this either by using the Sesame triple store or the specialized Lucene index. We also computed the number of candidates per class using either technology. This enabled us to calculate the probability of associating a given candidate to an n-gram: $1 - |C_t^x| \ / \ |C_t|$, where C_t^x is the set of candidates for n-gram x and type t, and C_t is the set of candidates for type t. The probability is higher when the fraction of candidates is smaller, which means that rarer labels will have priority over common labels, resulting in better precision. Finally, in the last step, we selected the n-gram with the highest probability, keeping only the longest n-gram in case of term overlap between selected n-grams. Each candidate could be directly categorized into *entity*, *attribute* or *type*. This information was used to classify the query based on templates for these three categories.

Our first attempt at retrieving matching candidates was directly based on the Sesame triple store. This contained our knowledge graph and was the obvious choice for an initial approach. As described in Sect. 3, we first experimented with a knowledge base containing $546,760$ statements or facts. While this approach did not allow for sub-second query times, it resulted in a reasonable query time of under 5 s. The SPARQL query we built returned four columns associated with candidate entities: Label, URI, Class and Category. This was obtained from the union of three sub-queries for *entity*, *attribute* and *type* individuals, associating the value of the property `rdfs:label`, or equivalent, to the Label column. These results were filtered using a case insensitive regular expression that matched the n-grams generated from the search query.

As an alternative for better performance, we built a Lucene index based on the triple store data, combining documents for *entities*, *attributes* and *types*. Each document contained four fields: Label, URI, Class and Category. We iterated through the same items returned by the SPARQL query described above, dropping, however, the regular expression filter. This enabled us to create an index of query parts, as supported by our knowledge base. We then queried this index in order to return the results for each n-gram generated from the search query. We used proximity search within $n = 6$ terms of distance (the same as the n-gram size) and ensured that the query was parsed in order. For each query to the index, we only returned the top-$\mathcal{N}$ results. Specifically we used $\mathcal{N} = 10$, which is a low value that results in high performance.

5   Evaluation

We compared the performance of both candidate retrieval strategies by measuring overall search time over a set of synthetic test queries. We synthetically built a query test set by combining terms from randomly selected individuals of the ontology with terms from a Portuguese dictionary with over $400,000$ words. Our generation method required five parameters: the number of queries to generate, the minimum and maximum number of terms associated with ontology individuals, and the minimum and maximum number of keyword terms. For this evaluation process, we generated $1,000$ queries with the number of terms associated with ontology individuals ranging from 3 to 8, and with a number of keyword terms ranging from 0 to 2, resulting in queries with a minimum of 3 terms and a maximum of 10 terms overall.

5.1 Comparing Query Analysis Time for the Retrieval Strategies

We did several runs based on the same set of synthetic queries. In particular, we did one run based on the Sesame triple store strategy, that we directly compared with a run based the Lucene index strategy for the top-$\mathcal{N}$ results. We picked $\mathcal{N} = 10$ since it provided a near-optimal speedup, also having a positive impact on the quality of the results for a small set of manually tested queries.

Table 1. Statistics for the query analysis time of the Sesame triple store and the Lucene index strategies, using $\mathcal{N} = 10$ for the Lucene index.

	Sesame triple store	Lucene index
Avg.	7.435765 s	0.048580 s
Std.	±3.206806 s	±0.019115 s
Speedup	153.062268 ($\sim$ 153× faster)	
Mann-Whitney U Test	p-value $\approx 0 \ll 0.01$	

In Table 1, we show the mean query analysis time (Avg.) along with the standard deviation (Std.), in seconds, for the 1,000 synthetically generated test queries. These tests were ran on a laptop with a dual core Intel® Core™ i7-5600U, 16 GB of RAM and a 256 GB solid-state drive. We calculated the speedup of the Lucene index strategy over the Sesame triple store strategy, concluding that it was about 153 times faster, for $\mathcal{N} = 10$. Increasing the parameter $\mathcal{N}$ resulted in lower, but still positive, speedup values, as will be shown in Sect. 5.2.

5.2 Influence of $\mathcal{N}$ over the Speedup

Figure 1a shows a run time comparison between the Sesame strategy (all matching results) and various $\mathcal{N}$ values of the Lucene strategy (top-$\mathcal{N}$ results).

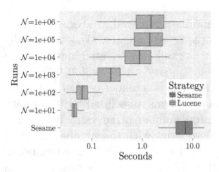
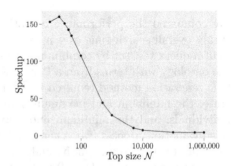

(a) Run times for the Sesame and Lucene strategies (log scale for the x-axis).

(b) Speedup for different values of $\mathcal{N}$ (log scale for the x-axis).

Fig. 1. Efficiency evaluation of the overall search process. The same 1,000 synthetic queries were used in each run.

As we can see, the index-based strategy outperforms the triple store strategy even when retrieving the top $\mathcal{N} = 1$ million matching candidates. Figure 1b illustrates the evolution of the speedup for growing values of $\mathcal{N}$. Higher values for the parameter $\mathcal{N}$ were expected to result in a lower speedup. However, by analyzing the progression of $\mathcal{N}$, from 10 to 1 million, we found that the speedup actually increased, from $\mathcal{N} = 10$ to $\mathcal{N} = 20$. This can be explained by the fact that our testing routine continuously read from the same location in disk, to load the index before running each set of queries, which resulted in better read performance through system caching. However, as expected, for $\mathcal{N} > 20$, the speedup consistently decreased, nearly stabilizing at 4× faster.

6   Conclusions

We approached the problem of efficient query interpretation and understanding for entity-oriented search. Based on our practical implementation of a semantic search engine, we proposed a probabilistic methodology for segmenting and annotating query parts with categories, in order to facilitate subsequent interpretation.

We proposed two different strategies for the efficient retrieval of matching candidates from a knowledge base, one of them directly supported on a SPARQL query over a Sesame triple store, and another one supported on a Lucene index directly created from the statements in the knowledge base and built for the specific task of finding candidates that matched different query parts. We evaluated both strategies regarding run time and showed that the index-based strategy outperformed the direct querying of the triple store by a minimum speedup of 4, when retrieving the top 1 million results, and a maximum speedup of over 100, when retrieving a smaller number of results. Based on a synthetic test set of variable length queries, we have shown, with a confidence of over 99 %, that the difference in run times between the two strategies was statistically significant.

References

1. Aggarwal, N., Buitelaar, P.: A system description of natural language query over DBpedia. In: CEUR Workshop Proceedings, vol. 913(Ild), pp. 96–99 (2012)
2. Bautin, M.: Entity Oriented Search. Technical report. State University of New York at Stony Brook (2007)
3. Blanco, R., Ottaviano, G., Meij, E.: Fast and space-efficient entity linking for queries. In: Proceedings of the Eighth ACM International Conference on Web Search and Data Mining - WSDM 2015, pp. 179–188 (2015)
4. Guo, J., Xu, G., Cheng, X., Li, H.: Named entity recognition in query. In: Proceedings of the 32nd International ACM SIGIR Conference on Research and Development in Information Retrieval (SIGIR 2009), pp. 267–274 (2009)
5. Liu, J., Pasupat, P., Wang, Y., Cyphers, S., Glass, J.: Query understanding enhanced by hierarchical parsing structures. In: IEEE Workshop on Automatic Speech Recognition and Understanding (ASRU 2013), pp. 72–77 (2013)
6. Pound, J., Mika, P., Zaragoza, H.: Ad-hoc object retrieval in the web of data. In: Proceedings of the 19th International Conference on World Wide Web, WWW 2010, p. 771 (2010)

A Gamified Approach to Relevance Judgement

Debasis Ganguly$^{(\boxtimes)}$ and Gareth J.F. Jones

ADAPT Centre, School of Computing, Dublin City University, Dublin, Ireland
{dganguly,gjones}@computing.dcu.ie

Abstract. In contrast to standard procedures for pooled relevance judgments which require considerable manual effort, we take a radically different approach to obtaining relevance assessments as the by-product of a game designed with a purpose (GWAP). The objective is to harness human processing skills via fun and entertainment. *DocMiner* is a document guessing game where a human player (H) needs to correctly guess a document chosen by the computer (C). To start the game, C chooses an information need and a document that is relevant to it. C then shares the information need, expressed as a query string, with H. H wins the round if he correctly guesses the document that C has chosen, and is either rewarded with bonus points or penalized by deducting points on submission of relevant and non-relevant documents respectively. The human player, as a part of his game playing strategy, thus needs to find relevant documents with the help of a search engine. Experiments on the TREC-8 ad-hoc task with the objective of reproducing the existing relevance assessments demonstrate that gamified assessments, when used to evaluate the official submissions to TREC-8, show fair correlation (Pearson's correlation coefficient of up to 0.84) with the official assessments (depth-100 pooling).

Keywords: Gamification · Relevance assessments

1 Introduction

Manual relevance assessments play a pivotal role in automatic laboratory-based evaluation of information retrieval (IR) systems. This relevance data enables multiple repeatable experimental runs to be carried out with different IR systems and avoids the need to involve users in the evaluation of each experimental run. Construction of the set of relevance assessments for a topic set in an IR test collection is itself an intensive process requiring careful reading of the content from each document from a *pool* of documents, constructed by a process known as *pooling*. The pool of documents judged by an human relevance assessor is constructed by taking the union of the set of top k ranked documents (called depth-k pooling) from a number of retrieval systems with varying parameters [1]. For instance, in the TREC ad-hoc collections, the relevance assessments were obtained with depth-100 pooling [2]. The average number of documents judged with depth-100 pooling for a search query is typically of the order of thousands.

© Springer International Publishing Switzerland 2016
N. Fuhr et al. (Eds.): CLEF 2016, LNCS 9822, pp. 214–220, 2016.
DOI: 10.1007/978-3-319-44564-9_18

For example, the average number of documents judged for a query (the average being computed over the set of 50 queries) in the TREC-8 test collection was $1,712$ [1]. This implies that the process of manual relevance assessment is not only time consuming but a mentally strenuous exercise as well.

We take a radically different approach to obtaining relevance assessments. Our approach is motivated from designing games with a purpose (GWAP) [3] to harness human processing skills with motivational game-like interfaces. Rather than asking users to solve a problem instance, a GWAP creates a *situation* within a game where the *action* taken by a user in response to the situation can be considered as a reasonable approximation to the solution of the problem instance. In the context of our work, we are interested in investigating whether the process of manual relevance assessment, which is otherwise a strenuous and time consuming activity, can be transformed into an entertaining game, the outcome of which can then be used to evaluate IR systems.

We emphasize that our proposed gamification method is not necessarily meant to compete against the standard pooling technique for obtaining the relevance judgements. Rather, the intention is to investigate whether a gamification technique can be applied to *reproduce* pooled relevance judgements with a satisfactory level of accuracy. It is reasonable to assume that for an effective gamification strategy that outputs relevant documents with satisfactory effectiveness, it is possible to apply a manual post editing step to further *refine* the set of relevant documents obtained after the game playing. Since the number of documents to post-edit would be much lower than the average pool depth of the standard technique of relevance judgements, the manual effort involved in the post editing step would be lower in comparison to pool based relevance assessments.

2 DocMiner: Gamified Relevance Assessment

Our gamified relevance assessment approach is based on *DocMiner* a single player game where a human player (H) plays against the computer (C). The objective in DocMiner is for H to correctly guess a document that C chooses from amongst a set of documents.

Initiating the Game. To start a new game, C chooses a query Q. C also picks a document D that is relevant to the query Q. For the time being, we assume that there exists (hence known to C) a given set of queries and a set of relevant documents associated with each query. H's objective is to correctly guess D. After fixing the query Q and a document relevant to it, namely D, C then shares Q with H. The only information which H has at the start of the game is the query Q. To guess D, H can make use of a search system that retrieves a ranked list of documents in response to a query. At the start of the game, without the presence of any information other than Q, all H can do is to use human intelligence to understand the intention behind the query Q. H can then execute Q, or a variant of it (say with more words added to Q to make the query

more specific [4] if H is able to understand the real intention behind Q) on the
search system to obtain a ranked list of documents.

Events on Submitting a Document. Since H knows that he/she should submit a document that is relevant to Q, as a part of the game playing strategy,
he/she may look into a few top ranked documents in the retrieved list of documents and choose one that *appears* relevant (note that H does not know the
exact relevance criterion, as expressed in the narrative of a TREC style query).
Three cases can arise after H submits D' to C. If $D' = D$, i.e. on guessing the
correct document, H improves his score by 20 points and wins the game. Otherwise, if D' is indeed relevant to Q then 10 points are added to H's score. If
on the other hand, D' is not relevant to the query then 2 points are deducted
from H's score. The game continues until H finds D, or H's score reaches zero
(a way in which this may happen is if H consecutively submits 5 non-relevant
documents each causing 2 points to be deducted from his initial score of 10).

Game Continuation. After every incorrect guess, C firstly lets H know whether
D' is relevant to Q or not. Secondly, C shares two more words of D with H as
clues. In each iteration, two words with the topmost tf-idf values that have not
been already shared are returned to H. From this available information, H can
firstly attempt to guess the true intent of the query. A better understanding of
the relevance criteria may help H to find more relevant documents and improve
his score. Secondly, H can selectively make use of the additional terms of D by
making his queries more specific to the topical content of D. The additional
terms, if used intelligently in combination with the original query terms, can
help retrieve D within the top ranks, e.g., the first search engine result page
(SERP). Note that skilled searchers, who are likely to formulate effective search
queries to retrieve D within the first SERP, similar to the *PageHunt* game skills
[3], are likely to score more points and eventually win the game.

2.1   Game Properties

Since the documents relevant to an information need tend to form clusters [5],
the game makes use of the hypothesis in assuming that H will eventually find
documents that are similar to D and hence likely to be relevant to Q. Although H
is not explicitly told to judge the relevance of a document against a query with
the help of a given TREC style narrative, yet according to his game playing
strategy, H needs to find relevant documents. The hypothesis is that the process
becomes easier and the quality of the judgements become more reliable if the
document that H needs to guess is relevant to the information need shared with
H. Since the game penalizes a player on submitting each non-relevant document,
it is likely that such a non-competent player is likely to lose the game quickly.
In fact, this ensures a 'survival of the fittest' type of environment, in which
a competent player (one who guesses relevant documents correctly) gets more
chance of finding such documents, whereas on the other hand, a non-competent
player is prevented from submitting more guesses if he/she has already submitted
too many non-relevant documents. Next, we discuss two scenarios of the game,

the first in which the set of relevance assessments is known and the second in which this information is (partially) absent.

Deterministic Mode of Game Play. This mode of game playing is only available when a set of relevance judgements already exists. We call this the *deterministic mode* of the DocMiner game because C has prior knowledge of the relevance assessments. The intention in this case is to see how accurately one can reproduce the known set of relevance judgements obtained with the pooling mechanism. With a set of existing relevance assessments, C simply performs a table lookup to see if the document D' submitted by H as a guess is relevant or not. It then takes actions according to the rules of the game, i.e. deducts or adds points to H's score.

Non-deterministic Game Play Mode. According to the assumption that relevant documents are more likely to be present at top ranks, C can choose a document at random from the top ranked documents retrieved in response to the initial query. Further, during game playing, when H submits a document D', C needs to decide whether D' is relevant to the query. This decision is taken with the help of a random variable, the value of which is proportional to the similarity score of D'. These relevance decisions do not need to be perfect for the game to continue. Moreover, these decisions are also not considered as the relevance assessment outputs obtained from the game. This probabilistic process simply ensures that the game can continue in a non-deterministic scenario. Note that as by-products of the game, played in this non-deterministic scenario, we still collect the documents submitted by H (having some level of manual relevance judgements as a part of his game playing strategy) as relevant documents.

3   User Study Evaluation

In order to investigate how well the gamification based approach produces relevance judgements, we need to have a ground truth of known relevance judgements obtained with pooling. For our study to investigate this, we make use of the TREC-8 ad-hoc test collection, comprised of volumes 4 and 5 of the TREC disks, 50 topics, and the relevance judgements created by NIST assessors with depth-100 pooling on this set of topics. We would like to emphasize that the purpose of our proposed method is not just to *reproduce* pre-existing relevance

Table 1. DocMiner game statistics.

Game statistics	Game mode	
	D	ND
#Wins/Games	31/196	24/123
Avg. #submitted/Total #rel Docs	8.67/110	5.86/39
Avg. #Rel docs/Precision per game	3.82/0.41	1.82/0.21

assessments. Rather, our intention is to evaluate the effectiveness of our proposed method against a known set of relevance assessments so that its application can be justified for the collection of relevance assessments for new datasets. To implement the search engine for the DocMiner game interface, we used Lucene. Each action that a player takes during playing the game was logged for analyzing game statistics. For our experiments, the game mode was kept hidden from the players, i.e., while playing, a user did not know if he/she was playing a deterministic game or an non-deterministic one. This was done so as to ensure that the players would not be able to adapt their decisions according to the game mode, i.e. true or random. In total, 10 users registered and played the game in anonymous mode.

Game Statistics. Table 1 shows the overall game statistics collected from the game logs for two different modes of playing as described in Sect. 2.1. Table 2 shows the confusion matrix, where R denotes true relevance and R' denotes predicted relevance. Firstly, it can be seen that the accuracy of the random process, which makes use of the standard assumption that top ranked documents are more likely to be relevant and thus draws from a uniform distribution having a length given by the normalized RSV value, is moderately high (0.73). This means that the game can be played successfully and reasonably accurate judgements be collected even without the presence of existing relevance assessments. It can also be seen that the non-deterministic game incorrectly outputs a manually judged relevant document as non-relevant less often than it does the other way round. This suggests that the game playing can reasonably continue as per user expectations of perceived relevance, which is also one of the reasons why the average number of game iterations for the non-deterministic mode is not very different from the deterministic one. This also ensures reasonable fairness in C's game playing, in the sense that it does not frequently penalize H for submitting a truly relevant document.

Gamified Assessments Quality. Table 1 presents some statistics about the relevant documents discovered during game playing. The primary observation from Table 1 is that both the game playing modes (D and ND denoting deterministic and non-deterministic modes respectively) can identify a fair number of relevant documents. Although the average number of relevant documents discovered is much lower than that obtained with explicitly judged pools, we would like to emphasize that the initial results obtained from this small scale user study conducted with a small number of users indicate promising results, and with more game playing activity it is likely to accumulate a higher number of

Table 2. Confusion matrix for the non-deterministic game mode.

	$R' = 0$	$R' = 1$
$R = 0$	54	27
$R = 1$	5	34

relevant documents. Another important observation is that the total number of submitted documents that are truly relevant is much higher when the game is played in the deterministic mode as compared to its counterpart. This is intuitive because the deterministic mode of game playing conforms more to user expectation of relevance by making use of the available pooled judgements. Results show that even with the probabilistic mode of game playing, it is possible to discover relevant documents, which verifies the hypothesis that pre-existing relevance assessments are not mandatory for a meaningful operation of the game. However, without the presence of true relevance judgements, the game results in a lower number of average relevant documents found per game (compare 1.82 with 3.82 in Table 1), the average being computed over games with at least one relevant document found. Furthermore, the non-deterministic game model results in lower precision of the submitted documents in terms of relevance (compare 0.21 with 0.41 in Table 1).

Evaluation with Gamified Assessments. To measure the correlation between the measured MAP values of the official runs computed with the gamified and the pooled assessments, we compute the well known measures, namely Pearson's σ, Spearman's ρ and Kendall's τ, the latter two being correlation measures for system rankings. Table 3 shows the overall correlation results of the 129 IR runs computed by the gamified and the pooled assessments. Table 3 shows that even with only a small set of judged documents (more game playing in the course of time will help to accumulate more) and presence of non-relevant documents, there exists a fair degree of correlation between the MAP values of the IR runs. However, the presence of non-relevant documents in the gamified judgements leads to a lower correlation between the rankings of the runs.

Table 3. Correlation between gamified assessments and TREC-8 official assessments.

Game mode		Correlation measures		
	#Queries	σ	ρ	τ
Deterministic	23	0.8425	0.6554	0.4884
Non-deterministic	20	0.6835	0.5146	0.3909

4   Conclusions and Future Work

In this paper, we report our initial work in a new direction of applying gamification techniques for obtaining relevance assessments as a substitute for the standard depth pooling process. In order to test the new approach, we conducted a pilot user study. The results are encouraging because of the following key observations: (a) a considerable number of relevant documents are found by collecting the game output indicating that with more game play we could collect more useful data in due course of time; and (b) evaluation of the official submissions of TREC-8 with the gamified assessments shows fair correlation with the official assessments (depth-100 pooling).

Since the initial trends with the gamification pilot study experiments are promising, there are various ways in which our work could be extended. Firstly, the game could be made more interesting and entertaining for the players by adding features such as time constraints, leader boards etc. Secondly, the *DocMiner* game could be extended to a two player version, where two human players would play against each other instead of a single human playing against the computer. The relevance decisions, instead of being probabilistic, can then be based on a mutual consensus, similar to the approach in [6].

Acknowledgements. This research is supported by Science Foundation Ireland (SFI) as a part of the ADAPT centre (Grant No. 13/RC/2106) in DCU.

References

1. Yilmaz, E., Aslam, J.A.: Estimating average precision when judgments are incomplete. Knowl. Inf. Syst. **16**(2), 173–211 (2008)
2. Voorhees, E.M., Harman, D.: Overview of the eighth text retrieval conference (TREC-8). In: Proceedings of TREC 1999 (1999)
3. von Ahn, L., Dabbish, L.: Labeling images with a computer game. In: Proceedings of CHI 2004, pp. 319–326 (2004)
4. Kanoulas, E., Hall, M.M., Clough, P.D., Carterette, B., Sanderson, M.: Overview of the TREC 2011 session track. In: Proceedings of TREC 2011 (2011)
5. Xu, J., Croft, W.B.: Query expansion using local and global document analysis. In: Proceedings of SIGIR 1996, pp. 4–11. ACM (1996)
6. Megorskaya, O., Kukushkin, V., Serdyukov, P.: On the relation between assessor's agreement and accuracy in gamified relevance assessment. In: Proceedings of SIGIR 2015, pp. 605–614 (2015)

Evaluating Categorisation in Real Life – An Argument Against Simple but Impractical Metrics

Vide Karlsson[1,2], Pawel Herman[2], and Jussi Karlgren[1,2(✉)]

[1] Gavagai, Stockholm, Sweden
[2] KTH, Stockholm, Sweden
jussi@kth.se

Abstract. Text categorisation in commercial application poses several limiting constraints on the technology solutions to be employed. This paper describes how a method with some potential improvements is evaluated for practical purposes and argues for a richer and more expressive evaluation procedure. In this paper one such method is exemplified by a precision-recall matrix which sacrifices convenience for expressiveness.

1 The Use Case: Practical Cold Start Text Categorisation

Text categorisation in commercial application often involves texts of very various quality and genre, in large quantities, with categories of differing size and urgency, and which sometimes overlap. Text categorisation is used primarily to lessen the human effort involved in keeping track of and reading text streams, and thus will typically proceed without continuous human oversight and intervention, frequently with the results of the categorisation filed and archived for potential future reference, never to be examined by human readers: the end result of the effort are more typically statistics or summaries of the processed material.

In this present study, which is a pre-study for a practical text categorisation methodology with minimal start-up time, the stakeholder party wishes to offer its customers a service which can categorise texts without recourse to manually labelled training data, using only the category labels for categorisation and with the following minimal technology requirements:

Requirement 1: The system cannot rely on a previously manually labeled training set. Providing manually labeled training data requires too much work and is too data-intensive: a human takes about 1 minute per abstract to categorise 100 abstracts. [5,8] Instead categories will be defined by a small set of manually chosen *seed labels*.

Requirement 2: The coverage and precision for the categories to be targeted should assessable automatically. The quality of the system output must be monitored and the customer will want to know how it performs on their categories.

© Springer International Publishing Switzerland 2016
N. Fuhr et al. (Eds.): CLEF 2016, LNCS 9822, pp. 221–226, 2016.
DOI: 10.1007/978-3-319-44564-9_19

Requirement 3: The baseline system uses simple string search for the category label. A marketed system must perform better than the baseline.

Requirement 4: The algorithm should be language independent. The stakeholder's customers operate in many of the languages of the world and not all of them have online terminologies or ontologies available.

Requirement 5: The system should be able to handle any topical category on any level of abstraction, as long as there are the category seed label is found in the data.

Requirement 6: The system should not require the topics to be structured hierarchically or to be disjoint in the data.

Requirement 7: The system should accommodate new categories being entered into the palette with little or no burn-in period and little cost.

2   Keyword-Based Categorisation

To meet the requirements of the use case, keyword-based categorisation was identified as a low-footprint technology, possibly enhanced by human intervention. Keyword-based categorisation schemes start from the original category label and then enrich it from knowledge of human language in general or from inspection of material from the data set under consideration. Many such approaches have been suggested. [1–4,6] Besides conforming to the above requirements by providing a natural starting point with the category label as a seed term, a keyword-based approach has the additional advantage of the representation being handily inspectable and editable by a human editor without special training, and without reliance on hidden variables which even a human knowledge engineer would not be able to inspect, improve, and maintain.

  This appears to be quite promising for the purpose of commercially viable application to customer tasks, but on closer inspection, reveals that the most of the methods under consideration rely on some hand-edited resource such as Wikipedia or Wordnet, which render them unsuitable with respect to the stakeholder requirements given above. Many of the methods take purchase in assumption of disjoint categories, using term distribution over categories as a criterion for selection. This does not conform to the expectations of the stakeholder and any such method will have to be left aside.

  The test conditions in our first set of experiments were

grep Simple string matching to original one-word category label;
dice Category label enriched with terms selected and ranked by their Dice score, a simplified pointwise mutual information metric, calculated by collocation statistics of each term to other terms in the categorised gold standard [4]:

$$Dice(w_a, w_b) = \frac{D(w_a, w_b)}{D(w_a) + D(w_b)} \tag{1}$$

where $D(w_i, w_j)$ is the number of documents that contain both terms w_i and w_j and where $D(w_i)$ is the number of documents that contain w_i.

rich category label enriched with *manually selected* terms from the list of terms with highest Dice scores and subsequent addition of *manually approved* (1) terms given by consulting an online lexicon with synonymous terms, [7] and (2) morphological variants of each term in the representation.

The evaluation challenge is to determine whether the additional effort in the **dice** and **rich** conditions would improve results enough over the **grep** condition to warrant the investment in implementation, execution, and human editorial effort for practical projects.

Established public data sets for evaluating categorisation mostly share the qualities of being balanced in size, disjoint and non-overlapping, and – frequently – homogenous with respect to genre and style. The need for more realistic and messy data sets has been established and to a large extent redressed with the data set provided by Liebeskind et al. [4], which consists of 2 000 user-generated movie reviews, manually categorised, but copied into a collection of 400 000 reviews from IMDB. For these experiments, we selected only categories with more than five manually assessed documents in the gold standard set, leaving 44 categories to be considered for our experimental evaluation.

The data set, the categories it is split up into, and their initial labels are input parameters for the evaluation of the categorisation method.

1. If the data set is unrealistic in any important respect this will affect the results. Examples, would be how an unrealistically balanced, cleaned, and homogenous data set is used to evaluate methods intended to be deployed on new text.
2. If the initial label of the category is misleading, too specific, or too general this will affect the results.
3. If the categories in the experimental set are impractical or unrealistic, or if there are complex dependencies or overlaps between categories this will affect the results.

In these experiments, the data set is designed by Liebeskind to be realistic. The experiment we performed (based on Liebeskind's method) is designed to meet the challenge of enriching original category labels. In terms of the category palette, we use the set given in the data set.

2.1   The F-Score Evaluation Metric

Typically categorisation methods are optimised for performance by collapsing their recall and precision performance into one scalar by their harmonic mean, the F-score. This representation of the comparative performance of the methods shows us that the additional effort put into enriching the category labels indeed translates into higher evaluation scores. However, we have very little sense of what this means for practical purposes. Does this mean that the enriched labels give us better recall? Does this mean that the manual addition of items improve precision? In practice, the F-scores need to be immediately decomposed into their component recall and precision scores to be useful.

2.2   The R@P Curve

For the above and related reasons Liebeskind et al. use the *R@P curve* as their main evaluation tool. It illustrates the level of recall a classifier gives at a given level of precision. This is conformant with transparent and predictable performance. Curves for the present experimental conditions are given in Fig. 1 These curves show us that the improvements are at the low-recall high-precision end. This is useful information, and will help the client make a decision if the improvements to the baseline method are useful or not. We still cannot address the third evaluation question given above, however: we do not know what the difference across categories is.

2.3   P & R Matrix — A More Expressive Representation

We propose the following rather more expressive (but correspondingly rather less handy) representation of evaluation results. For each level of precision and recall we note how many of the test categories achieve that performance or better and arrange the results in a precision-recall matrix, recording in each cell the number of categories on a given performance level. This means that the quality requirements from a client can be mapped to a cell in the matrix, and the corresponding performance of the categorisation method can be read out immediately.

The P & R-matrix is a much more challenging representation to digest and process at first glance. It is less useful for the immediate purpose of ranking systems with respect to each other, where a scalar metric is preferred for the convenience of the human evaluator. However, this, by contrast to the obfuscatory F-score, allows the evaluator in e.g. a procurement process to assess the number of categories which actually are of practical use in a live system.

The evaluation results for the three experimental conditions are given in Table 1. The cells in the bottom rows of the matrices hold all the 44 categories: every experimental category can — unsurprisingly — achieve 0.0 precision or better at any level of recall.

If we raise our expectations to require a 0.6 precision or better we find that less than half of categories can be brought to 0.6 precision or better, even at very low recall rates, and that the **dice** and **rich** methods increase the recall noticeably for that precision level. We also find that the manual enhancement reduces the number of categories with full precision at low recall levels. Further, we find that, conversely, only one category can give full recall at the reasonable precision level of 0.5 and that no experimental condition succeeds in improving this result. This means that the improvements to the baseline model mainly appear to improve recall at low precision levels. This is a clear result with effects on how a system based on the methods investigated can be expected to be

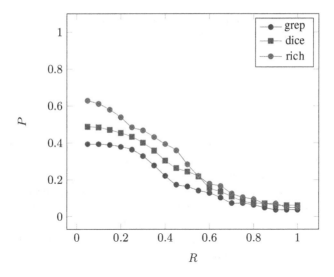

Fig. 1. R@P curves for the three experimental conditions

marketed and deployed in real industrial use cases. That information would neither have been obtainable from F-score comparisons nor from R@P curves.

We also see, more discouragingly for our experimental results, that most categories cannot be brought up to this level. This, again, will be a very valuable result in practical application scenario. If a customer requests a system test for a number of categories of interest to them, that test should demonstrate (as given by the requirements above) how well the system can be expected to perform for the categories of interest, not averaged over them, but identified per category, identifying categories such as those which never are able rise above 0.2 recall

Table 1. P & R evaluation matrices for the three experimental conditions

						F_1 **scores (micro averaged)**																									
			Method **grep**										Method **dice**											Method **rich**							
			0.313										0.354											0.399							
											P & R Matrices																				
			Method **grep**										Method **dice**											Method **rich**							
													recall																			
p	0.1	0.2	0.3	0.4	0.5	0.6	0.7	0.8	0.9	1.0	0.1	0.2	0.3	0.4	0.5	0.6	0.7	0.8	0.9	1.0	0.1	0.2	0.3	0.4	0.5	0.6	0.7	0.8	0.9	1.0
1.0	6	4	2	2	1	0	0	0	0	0	12	4	2	1	1	0	0	0	0	0	9	5	3	2	1	1	1	0	0	0
0.9	6	4	2	2	1	0	0	0	0	0	12	4	2	1	1	0	0	0	0	0	10	6	3	2	1	1	1	0	0	0
0.8	8	7	3	2	1	0	0	0	0	0	13	4	2	1	1	1	0	0	0	0	11	7	5	4	2	2	2	0	0	0
0.7	10	7	4	2	1	1	1	1	0	0	15	8	5	2	2	2	1	0	0	0	14	10	7	5	4	3	2	0	0	0
0.6	17	9	7	7	1	1	1	1	0	0	18	11	6	4	3	2	2	2	0	0	20	13	10	9	6	5	3	3	0	0
0.5	21	13	9	8	5	3	2	2	1	1	26	19	13	10	7	4	3	2	1	1	32	21	14	14	7	7	5	3	1	1
0.4	23	14	12	8	7	6	3	2	1	1	29	21	17	13	11	7	6	4	1	1	36	27	21	19	13	10	6	4	2	2
0.3	26	17	15	14	11	9	4	2	1	1	32	23	21	17	14	11	8	6	3	2	38	31	26	23	19	14	10	5	3	2
0.2	32	21	20	16	14	12	6	6	2	1	36	26	22	19	15	12	12	8	4	3	38	36	29	25	23	17	12	9	5	3
0.1	33	22	20	17	14	12	8	7	2	1	36	27	23	19	17	15	15	12	5	3	40	38	35	32	28	25	20	16	7	3
0.0	44	44	44	44	44	44	44	44	44	44	44	44	44	44	44	44	44	44	44	44	44	44	44	44	44	44	44	44	44	44

and 0.1 precision in the example, irrespective of method. That sort of informed feedback to (potential) customers is necessary if they are to trust the technology solutions they are interested in procuring for their business or other activities.

3   Conclusions

Keyword-based categorisation is motivated as a low-effort method for text categorisation. However, most methods rely heavily on precompiled resources, and are impracticable for the practical industrial use cases.

The evaluated methods show great volatility over topic categories. For more than 10 % of the categories, it proved impossible to reach precision over 0.1 and for only a small portion of the categories a precision of more than 0.6 was attained. We note that not only – as has been discussed and shown in previous work, and to a great extent remedied by more realistic data sets – is the collection a parameter in an evaluation, but the category palette itself influences the result of the evaluation.

To determine the difference between the approaches chosen we need a more fine-grained evaluation method than the standard ones. The P & R evaluation matrix presented here is one such method which gives a more fine-grained result for evaluating and demonstrating the utility of a categorisation approach. A simpler evaluation method is a lossy compression of the information which is necessary to meet the requirements of a practicioner.

References

1. Barak, L., Dagan, I., Shnarch, E.: Text categorization from category name via lexical reference. In: Proceedings of Human Language Technologies: Annual Conference of the North American Chapter of the Association for Computational Linguistics, pp. 33–36. Association for Computational Linguistics (2009)
2. Gliozzo, A., Strapparava, C., Dagan, I.: Improving text categorization bootstrapping via unsupervised learning. ACM Trans. Speech Lang. Process. (TSLP) **6**(1), 1 (2009)
3. Ko, Y., Seo, J.: Text classification from unlabeled documents with bootstrapping and feature projection techniques. Inf. Process. Manage. **45**(1), 70–83 (2009)
4. Liebeskind, C., Kotlerman, L., Dagan, I.: Text categorization from category name in an industry-motivated scenario. Lang. Resour. Eval. **49**(2), 227–261 (2015)
5. McCallum, A., Nigam, K., Rennie, J., Seymore, K.: A machine learning approach to building domain-specific search engines. In: IJCAI, vol. 99, pp. 662–667. Citeseer (1999)
6. Qiu, Q., Zhang, Y., Zhu, J., Qu, W.: Building a text classifier by a keyword and wikipedia knowledge. In: Huang, R., Yang, Q., Pei, J., Gama, J., Meng, X., Li, X. (eds.) ADMA 2009. LNCS, vol. 5678, pp. 277–287. Springer, Heidelberg (2009)
7. Sahlgren, M., Gyllensten, A.C., Espinoza, F., Hamfors, O., Holst, A., Karlgren, J., Olsson, F., Persson, P., Viswanathan, A.: The Gavagai living lexicon. In: 10th Language Resources and Evaluation Conference, Portoroz (2016)
8. Schohn, G., Cohn, D.: Less is more: active learning with support vector machines. In: ICML, pp. 839–846. Citeseer (2000)

How Relevant is the Long Tail?

A Relevance Assessment Study on Million Short

Philipp Schaer[1]([✉]), Philipp Mayr[2], Sebastian Sünkler[3], and Dirk Lewandowski[3]

[1] Cologne University of Applied Sciences, Cologne, Germany
philipp.schaer@th-koeln.de
[2] GESIS – Leibniz Institute for the Social Sciences, Cologne, Germany
philipp.mayr@gesis.org
[3] Hamburg University of Applied Sciences, Hamburg, Germany
{sebastian.suenkler,dirk.lewandowski}@haw-hamburg.de

Abstract. Users of web search engines are known to mostly focus on the top ranked results of the search engine result page. While many studies support this well known information seeking pattern only few studies concentrate on the question what users are missing by neglecting lower ranked results. To learn more about the relevance distributions in the so-called long tail we conducted a relevance assessment study with the Million Short long-tail web search engine. While we see a clear difference in the content between the head and the tail of the search engine result list we see no statistical significant differences in the binary relevance judgments and weak significant differences when using graded relevance. The tail contains different but still valuable results. We argue that the long tail can be a rich source for the diversification of web search engine result lists but it needs more evaluation to clearly describe the differences.

1 Introduction

The ranking algorithms of web search engines try to predict the relevance of web pages to a given search query by a user. By incorporating hundreds of "signals" modern search engines do a great job in bringing a usable order to the vast amounts of web data available. Users are used to rely mostly on the first few results presented in search engine result pages (SERP). Search engines like Google or Bing are constantly optimizing their ranking algorithms to improve the top results on their SERP. While earlier studies on the retrieval effectiveness of web search engines mainly focused on comparing the top results from different search engines, we would like to focus on the comparison of different sections from the same result list. How does the head of a result list compare to it's tail?

In contrast to commercial search engines, so-called long-tail search engines try to support more unfamiliar usage pattern by deliberately redirecting users away from the head of result lists. Prominent examples of such long-tail search engines are bananaslug.com and Million Short. Both search engines incorporate different ideas to access the long tail: While bananaslug.com randomly expands queries with an additional keyword to bring in unexpected results, Million Short

© Springer International Publishing Switzerland 2016
N. Fuhr et al. (Eds.): CLEF 2016, LNCS 9822, pp. 227–233, 2016.
DOI: 10.1007/978-3-319-44564-9_20

removes the most popular websites from the result list. Both search engines point out that these alternative approaches are not meant for everyday use. Their primary goal is to "offer an interesting view on what usually is hidden from the user" by the ranking algorithms of search engines, the long tail.

Therefore in this study we try to learn more about the long tail of web search engines' result lists. The motivation behind this observation is that web search engine result lists are more diverse than the first one to three hits might suggest [1]. Intuition tells us that the web pages listed on the second, third or even deeper result page might also contain valuable information, but most of the time we don't see them due to the fixation on the top results. By incorporating and reorganising results from the long tail the serendipity effect might be supported. Another motivation might be the wish to explicitly see different results like unpopular, old or controversial web pages that would never be included in the head results due to weak page ranks or other negative ranking factors.

Research Question. Does the long tail as presented by a special long-tail web search engine contain valuable information for users? Can we quantify this using relevance scores gained from an online relevance assessment? In other words: Are the filtered results of a long-tail web search engine better, same or worse compared to a standard result list. What else can we learn about the composition of the long-tail results?

Approach. We conducted a relevance assessment study to learn about the relevance distributions in the head and the tail of typical search engine's result lists. We used everyday and domain-specific topics to undertake a relevance assessment study with 33 undergraduate students of a Library and Information Sciences (LIS) course. Each participant judged on up to 30 documents that came from different depths of the long tail of the Million Short web search engine.

Related Work. Only few studies focus on the analysis of the long tail of web search engines. In 2010 Zaragoza et al. reviewed the top five results of 1000 queries sampled from the query log of a major search engine. They report that more than 90 % of these queries are served excellent by all major search engines [6]. Most consequently as reported by Sterling only 8 % of the users are willing to inspect more than three result pages [5]. Hariri [1] conducted a study on 34 real search sessions and compared the relevance assessments on the first four result pages (i.e. the first 40 results). While 47.06 % of the first results were judged relevant an even higher percentage of relevant documents (50 %) were found at the 5th SERP position. Even on the 4th results page there were three documents that were judged most relevant by the users in more than 40 % of the searches. In summary Hariri did not find significant differences between the precision of the first four result pages.

Contributions. While we see a clear difference between the head and the tail of the search engine's result list (measured using Kendall's τ and intersecting percentages), we see no statistical significant differences in the binary relevance judgments. This means that the tail contains different but still relevant and therefore valuable results for the users. When using graded relevance values we see a slight decrease but still no truly significant difference. Therefore we argue that the long tail contains valuable information and is a rich source for the diversification of web search engine result lists.

2   Materials and Methods

In this paper we focus on Million Short, an experimental web search engine that filters the top million (or top 100k, 10k, 1k, 100) sites from the result list. To identify these top sites Million Short is using a combination of its own crawl data and the Alexa Internet traffic statistics. To implement the actual retrieval process Million Short is using the Bing API that is augmented with some own crawl data. The Million Short website describes the main motivation as: "We thought it might be somewhat interesting to see what we'd find if we just removed an entire slice of the web"[1]. This slice usually consists of the most popular sites of the web (like Wikipedia, Facebook or Ebay). By removing these sites Million Short pushes results that are in the long tail of the result list (due to low popularity scores, poor search engine optimizations, small marketing budget, non-competitive keywords or simple non-linkage) to the top of it's own results. In this paper we will regard the results presented by Million Short as being part of the long tail, although other definitions or implementations are possible.

The relevance assessments were conducted using a tool called RAT. The Relevance Assessment Tool (RAT) is a self-developed web-based software that provides an integrated framework for conducting retrieval effectiveness tests on web search engines [3]. It has been developed to support researchers to design complex system-orientated search engine retrieval effectiveness studies, and to significantly reduce the effort to conduct such tests, as well. By its architecture, it allows us to collect judgements from a multitude of assessors using a crowd-sourcing approach. The assessment tool can be used to design a test, to automatically fetch results from multiple search engines through screen scraping, and to collect relevancy judgments. The toolkit consists of four different modules: (1) test design and project administration, (2) search engine results scraping, (3) assessor interface to the collecting of judgments, and (4) export of assessment results.

The relevance assessments were gathered in a Library and Information Science course called "Semantics Part II" at Hochschule Darmstadt, Germany in the winter semester of 2012/2013. The task of the assessment exercise was to assess topical relevance (graded relevance) of web pages concerning a given topic. The students of this course were in the second semester and had experiences in evaluating relevance in previous lessons and exercises. In a self assessment they rated their web search experience with an average experience of 7.3 years. The group of assessors consisted of 23 male and 10 female students with an average age of 23.8 years. The users were given an written exercise description with a short oral introduction and a description of the general task and the relevance scale that ranged from 0 (non-relevant) to 4 (fully relevant). The topic descriptions were a mixture of specific and broad topics. They covert topics from day-to-day

---

[1] https://millionshort.com/about.html.

life, celebrities and politics and could be considered as mostly informational and only few navigational or transactional topics. Each topic had a title and a short description that was two to three sentences long. Since we let each assessor evaluate the top 10 results from three different systems for 25 different topics each system delivered 250 results.

As soon as the assessors logged into the assessment toolkit one of the 25 topics was assigned to them using a round robin approach. After all topics were assigned the following assessors were given a random topic. This resulted in six topics that were rated by more than one assessor. Theoretically each assessor had to evaluate 30 single web pages, 10 top results for three different systems. The three systems are named 0k, 10k, and 1000k. 0k is the Million Short result list without any filtered sites, 10k is the result list with the top 10,000 sites removed and 1000k with the top million sites removed, respectively. In practice due to the pooling process the actual numbers of assessments per topic ranged from 10 to 26. In total we gathered 990 single relevance assessment from 33 different assessors, 30 assessments per assessor. From the total number of 990 assessments we had 459 unique relevance assessments on the websites that formed our pool and were the basis for a clean Qrels file. The relevance assessment from different assessors on the same topic were combined using a majority vote approach as described by Hosseini et al. [2]. Given a five-point scale we measured inter-rater agreement using Krippendorf's α and found low agreement rates with α values around 0.36. Although the agreement values were generally low and should be handled with care they were in the same range compared to previous studies with non-professional assessors [4]. We encouraged the assessors to comment on their relevance assessments and gathered 60 free text comments that were manually classified into eight different groups of comments (see Table 3).

3   Results

Differences Between 0k, 10k and 1000k and the Pooling Process. We see the different impact the filtering of popular website has on the corresponding result lists per topic. When we compare the set-wise intersection between the three systems 0k, 10k and 1000k we see that 0k and 10k share 161 common results while the intersection between 0k and 1000k was only 85 websites. Therefore more than 1/3 of the results from 0k are replaced by long tail results to form 10k and more than 2/3 are replaced to form 1000k (see Table 1). Taking a ranked list-wise and not set-wise look on the results using Kendall's τ we see no similarities between the different results lists' ranking of 0k, 10k and 1000k. Table 1 shows the result of the analysis on Kendall's τ to check on the consistency between the different systems' rankings. Since all systems values are around 0.1 in average it is clear to say that the three different systems return weak intersecting result sets and non-comparable result lists.

Retrieval Performance. We use two binary (MAP@n and P@n) and one graded (NDCG@n) relevance measure to evaluate the retrieval performance of

Table 1. Kendall's τ (left) and intersection values (right) for all rankings from the three systems 0k, 10k and 1000k.

	0k	10k	1000k
0k	1	0.0984	0.0904
10k		1	0.1160
1000k			1

	0k	10k	1000k
0k	250	161	85
10k		250	130
1000k			250

0k, 10k, and 1000k. All measures were calculated for n = 5 and n = 10. The relevance scores are generally very high with a top P@5 value of 0.8 for 0k.

Although the three systems return different results (in regard to intersections and rankings) the binary performance measures are more or less the same. In fact the differences are so low that we have to compare four decimal places to see an actual difference (i.e. MAP@10 0k: 0.4637 and 1000k: 0.4635). Of course these differences are marginal and therefore not statistical different when applying a Student's t-test. A slightly different situation arises when we interpret the graded relevance levels instead of binary judgements. Here we see a slight drop in NDCG@5 or NDCG@10 that is weakly statistical significant ($\alpha \leq 0.1$) (Table 2).

Table 2. Retrieval results on the three different depths in the long tail. We see no significant differences using a two-tailed t-test with $\alpha \leq 0.05$ but weak significance when using $\alpha \leq 0.1$ (marked with *)

	MAP@5	MAP@10	P@5	P@10	NDCG@5	NDCG@10
0k	0.2498	0.4637	0.8000	0.7720	0.5845	0.6469
10k	0.2460	0.4647	0.7920	0.7800	0.5625	0.6413
1000k	0.2399	0.4635	0.7760	0.7880	0.5413*	0.6079*

Table 3. Analysis of assessors' comments that could be categorized into eight different groups of comments and their distribution in total and on the three systems.

Comment type	Total	0k	10k	1000k
Reliability	5	0	3	2
Technical error	6	2	2	2
Language	21	8	5	8
Misleading title	4	2	1	1
Missing content	14	5	4	5
Paid content	2	1	1	0
Too specific/too broad	3	0	0	3
Wrong content type	20	7	7	6

Analysis of Assessors' Comments. From the 60 free text comments that were in the data set we extracted eight different types of comments. Each free text was mapped to one or two comment group, depending on the exhaustiveness of the comment (see Table 3). Two comment types have to be highlighted because they only were mentioned for the two long-tail systems 10k and 1000k: reliability and broadness/specificity of the results. The assessors never commented on these two comment types for results from 0k. Given the fact that all other comment types were uniformly distributed between head and tail these two stood out.

4   Discussion and Conclusion

We were not able to find significant differences in the retrieval performance of the head and the tail of the Million Short result list for 25 different topics when using MAP@n and P@n. The use of graded relevance introduced a slightly different view on the results. We see some weak hints that the retrieval performance of the long tail search engine is not 1:1 comparable to the head. We got some additional hints on differences in the details of the assessors' comments. Analyzing the free text comments we see two types of issues that were only mentioned for the long tail results: reliability and broadness/specificity of the results. To further interpret these results and also other complaints like i.e. language concerns we need more (meta-)data about the actual retrieval sessions. It would be useful to gather these additional data during the scraping process or to allow the integration of additional tools like page classification or language detection systems. Otherwise these data might not be available at a later point.

We should see the results in the light of the ongoing discussion about the evaluation criterion for IR systems that make a strong argument for having a look at the actual usefulness of the results. Having an evaluation criterion like usefulness might help to better differentiate between the actual characteristics and performance of the long tail compared to the head. This can be seen in the context that we only let our assessors rate on topical relevance while Bing incorporates hundreds of other relevance signals. A clear limitation of this study is the fact that Million Short is based on Bing which is a black box. Nevertheless we see strong hints that our general claim regarding new evaluation methods and (meta-)data for online assessment tools is valid and should be further investigated.

References

1. Hariri, N.: Relevance ranking on Google: are top ranked results really considered more relevant by the users? Online Inf. Rev. **35**(4), 598–610 (2011)
2. Hosseini, M., Cox, I.J., Milić-Frayling, N., Kazai, G., Vinay, V.: On aggregating labels from multiple crowd workers to infer relevance of documents. In: Baeza-Yates, R., Vries, A.P., Zaragoza, H., Cambazoglu, B.B., Murdock, V., Lempel, R., Silvestri, F. (eds.) ECIR 2012. LNCS, vol. 7224, pp. 182–194. Springer, Heidelberg (2012)
3. Lewandowski, D., Sünkler, S.: Designing search engine retrieval effectiveness tests with RAT. Inf. Serv. Use **33**(1), 53–59 (2013)

4. Schaer, P.: Better than their reputation? On the reliability of relevance assessments with students. In: Catarci, T., Forner, P., Hiemstra, D., Peñas, A., Santucci, G. (eds.) CLEF 2012. LNCS, vol. 7488, pp. 124–135. Springer, Heidelberg (2012)
5. Sterling, G.: iProspect: blended search resulting in more clicks on news, images, and video (2008). http://searchengineland.com/iprospect-blended-search-resulting-in-more-clicks-on-news-images-and-video-13708
6. Zaragoza, H., Cambazoglu, B.B., Baeza-Yates, R.: Web search solved?: all result rankings the same? In: Proceedings of the 19th ACM International Conference on Information and Knowledge Management, CIKM 2010, pp. 529–538. ACM, New York (2010)

Towards an Understanding of Transactional Tasks

Natalia Shepeleva and Krisztian Balog[(✉)]

University of Stavanger, Stavanger, Norway
{natalia.shepeleva,krisztian.balog}@uis.no

Abstract. Understanding search behavior in the context of the larger work task is of key importance in order to build search systems that can assist users in achieving work task completion. This study explores a particular type of task, transactional, that has not received due attention in the literature so far. A total of 38 users were observed in a laboratory experiment where they completed tasks at different complexity and difficulty levels. We perform both qualitative and quantitative analysis of users' perception of task difficulty and search engine support. Further, we identify two main search strategies that people employ when completing transactional tasks.

1 Introduction

Search engines are one of the main instruments people use when seeking information to accomplish some task, e.g., planning a travel or a writing a report for a school assignment. For a long time, information retrieval (IR) research has focused on the identification of relevant items [12]. However, the work task that motivated the use of a search engine in the first place generally involves more than just search; it requires a particular outcome (e.g., a report, an email response, or a decision). For example, it has been shown for decision-making tasks that people spend two-thirds of their time on task completion even after a sufficient set of relevant documents has been found [12]. Understanding how search systems perform on the work task level has gained increasing attention over the past years. There exists a large body of work on examining search tasks through query and click logs, see, e.g., [1,3,8,11]. Some particular problems have been investigated extensively, e.g., identifying cross-session search tasks within a user's search activity [1,8,11] and providing task-aware query recommendations [4]. Importantly, search logs reveal only a portion of the actual user activity that is spent on completing a given work task. The process itself, as well as various other tools that may be involved, cannot be understood unless the user's entire task-related activity is observed; this is exactly what we are aiming to study in this work.

Exploring the relationship between work task and interactive search behavior is a topic that lies in the intersection of information seeking and interactive IR research [7,10]. A broad range of tasks have been analyzed in the past,

© Springer International Publishing Switzerland 2016
N. Fuhr et al. (Eds.): CLEF 2016, LNCS 9822, pp. 234–240, 2016.
DOI: 10.1007/978-3-319-44564-9_21

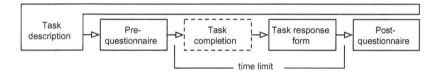

Fig. 1. Experimental workflow. The dashed box represents the step where participants were working on the task. The task description was visible throughout all stages.

including factual [7,9], navigational [5], interpretive [7], exploratory [7,9], and decision-making [10,12]. One task type that has not received due attention in the literature is *transactional tasks*, which we define as follows: tasks motivated by the intent of conducting a specific transaction, typically involving a monetary consideration or exchange. Common examples include purchasing an item, making travel arrangements, or planning an event.

The completion of a transactional task involves (i) the process of searching for information, (ii) decision making (which might give rise to additional information needs, i.e., going back to (i)), and (iii) the actual completion of the transaction. One distinctive element of transactional tasks, as opposed to some of the other task types (e.g., exploratory or informational) is that there is a clear and definite point that marks its accomplishment: typically, when the payment (or booking) is made.

We study, in a laboratory setting, how people go about completing such tasks. The goals of this research are threefold. First, we aim to gain an understanding of the perceived difficulty of such tasks. Second, we aim to determine what level of support users expect from the web search engine and what is the functionality that they lack. Third, we aim to identify general behavioral patters (in particular, strategies w.r.t. search engine usage) that people exhibit when completing transactional tasks.

2 Experimental Setup

To understand how people search for information when working on transactional tasks, we set up a laboratory experiment.

2.1 Setup and Design

For the purpose of this experiment a specific website was designed. Both the presentation of instructions and the delivery of results was done through this website. Each participant was given two tasks to complete, sequentially, one from each complexity level. The difficulty (familiarity) of the task was chosen randomly. For each task a certain time limit was given (10 or 20 mins). Participants were instructed to submit the task outcomes via a web form; the form was to be submitted even if they did not manage to complete the task entirely. We shall refer to these submissions as the *task response forms*. Additionally, before and after each task, participants were asked to fill in *pre- and post-questionnaires*, which included the following questions: (i) difficulty of the task (on a scale from 1 to 10); (ii) search engine support (on a scale from 1 to 10); (iii) if they will be able (pre) or were able (post) to complete the task (yes/no); (iv) what is it that they find difficult about the task (free text); (v) reasons for being/not being able to complete the task (free text); (vi) recommendations on how to improve the search experience/service (free text, post-questionnaire only).

All participants were from the same age group, computer science bachelor students, with both genders represented. Each person was provided with a personal computer and a screen capture program. Before the experiment, they were given instructions on how to use screen recording software. The video recordings were collected after the experiment. Participants were not given any instructions or hints on how to go about the tasks and were free to use any (online/offline) tool of their choosing. All responses and video recordings were collected anonymously. Figure 1 illustrates the experimental workflow.

2.2   Tasks

We study two transactional tasks that are frequently performed on the web [6]: purchasing a product (PRC) and travel planning (TRV). The two tasks differ in their complexity: finding a single item to purchase is a relatively simple task, while travel planning involves a series of interdependent (transactional) subtasks. Each task is studied on two difficulty levels: in familiar (A) and unfamiliar (B) task domains. Since all participants are from the same population (in terms of age, location, and profession), familiarity is established based on their assumed background. The tasks are considered complete when the target items are identified (i.e., no actual purchases were made).

Purchasing a product. The task is to find a product to be purchased that matches a set of requirements. Participants were given a max. of 10 min to complete the task. Then, the webpage of the selected product was to be submitted; they were also given a free text input field to provide any additional comments they might have. The two difficulty levels are as follows:

- **(PRCA)** Find a laptop with given a set of min. requirements (processor, memory, etc.), with constraints on price and delivery date.
- **(PRCB)** Find a motor boat with a given min. specification (length, facilities, etc.), with constraints on price and delivery date.

Since our participants are computer science students, their level of familiarity with laptop configurations is high. On the other hand, most of them probably have little awareness of boat specifications.

Travel planning. The task is to plan a travel, with time and budget constraints. Participants were given (max) 20 min to find (i) means of transportation, (ii) accommodation, (iii) place(s) to eat at, (iv) places to visit, and (v) a budget

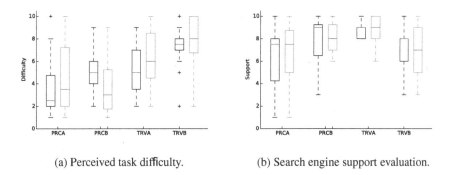

(a) Perceived task difficulty.   (b) Search engine support evaluation.

Fig. 2. For each task, pre-survey results are on the left, in black, and post-survey results are on the right, in grey. Whiskers correspond to 25 and 75 percentiles.

breakdown for each category of expense. A free text field was given for each of (i)–(v) on the response form, along with an optional comments field. The two flavors of the task are as follows:

- **(TRVA)** Plan a conference travel to a neighboring country, given the travel dates and budget. Find flight, accommodation, a place to eat at, and five places to visit.
- **(TRVB)** Plan a holiday trip to a country, on another continent, that involves visiting two different cities. Find means of transportation, accommodation (for both cities), places to eat at (one per city), and five places to visit.

It is likely that participants have knowledge about the neighboring country, and have even been there already for a visit, rather than about a country on another continent. The budget constraints were set in both cases such that fitting within them is non-trivial.

3   Results and Analysis

We collected a total of 60 complete submissions (including pre- and post-questionnaires as well as the task response forms), from 38 users. These are roughly evenly distributed among the four tasks: 14 for PRCA, 15 for PRCB, 15 for TRVA, and 16 for TRVB.

3.1   Perceived Difficulty

Users were asked to rate the perceived difficulty of the assigned task and to indicate whether they will be able/were able to complete it. Figure 2a shows the level of difficulty for each task, as indicated before (left, in black) and after (right, in grey) completing the task. We observe that the travel planning tasks are considered more difficult than the purchase tasks, which is expected. Also not surprisingly, the unfamiliar flavors of the tasks are always regarded more difficult than the familiar ones. With the exception of PRCB, users tend to underestimate task difficulty.

To gain a better understanding of what makes these tasks difficult, we analyzed the comments left behind in the free text fields. We developed a coding scheme based on a first pass over the responses. Once the various aspects were identified, all responses were labeled using this coding scheme in a second pass over the data. The annotations were done by two authors of the paper. Due to space constraints we summarize our main findings without presenting quantitative results. For the purchase task, the low pre-task difficulty can be attributed to users' confidence in search tools and domain knowledge; the requirements are clear, thus the task is generally considered easy. The most difficult aspects identified after completion include fitting within (all the) requirements and finding specific information. As for travel planning, the prime reason that makes the task appear easy is the availability of search tools and services, coupled with prior experience. On the other hand, finding specific entities, preparing and meeting the budget, and lack of time make the task hard. In the end, these are indeed the top 3 reasons that made the task difficult. However, the lack of time turned out to be a more severe problem than the budget. In summary, we find that users can identify the most difficult aspects of these tasks, even though they tend to underestimate the degree of those difficulties.

3.2   Search Engine Support

How well search engines support the completion of these particular tasks? What kind of support do users lack? Fig. 2b shows the *expected* (pre-task) and *actual* (post-task) level of search engine support. It is clear from the figure that for the familiar tasks (PRCA and TRVA) users have realistic expectations towards search engine support; their initial evaluations do not change after completing the task. For unfamiliar tasks (PRCB and TRVB), on the other hand, people tend to expect more than what they can actually get from search engines; support levels drop by 1 point on average.

We find that for PRCA the support level remains the same, while for PRCB, the initially very high values drop. The most common feedback response was that users would prefer to have more categories for filtering results (e.g., searching for boats that have kitchen). For both purchase tasks, some users commented in the post-survey that they would like to have the possibility of putting in specific requirements in the (Google) search box (requirements that specialized sites provide, e.g., as filtering options).

The familiar travel task (TRVA) did not yield any surprises. One particular information need that lacked proper support, based on the comments, was finding "cheap restaurants." Users apparently were prepared to have only limited support for that the unfamiliar travel task (TRVB), but the actual support was even lower than what they expected. For both travel tasks, users expressed a wish for "a tool that plans the trip."

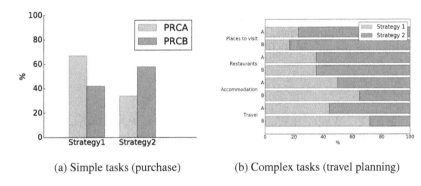

(a) Simple tasks (purchase)   (b) Complex tasks (travel planning)

Fig. 3. Strategy usage for simple and complex tasks.

3.3 Task Completion Patterns

Are there general behavioral patterns or search strategies that we can observe?
To answer this question, we manually annotated the recorded screen captures
with the actions users performed. We can observe two general strategies for
simple (purchase) tasks:

- **Strategy 1** Users use the search engine merely to find a known site. Then,
  they navigate there and use the site's internal search and filter functionality
  to find the item that is subject of the transaction.
- **Strategy 2** The search engine is used for locating the specific items of interest
  directly. Further details are then obtained from the website of the item (and
  that is also where they conclude the transaction).

From Fig. 3a it is clear that for the familiar flavor of the purchase task (PRCA),
more users tend to follow Strategy 1, while for the unfamiliar version Strategy 2
is preferred. Interestingly, for complex tasks, we find that users first break them
down to a sequence of simple tasks, and then employ either Strategy 1 or 2 for
each sub-task. Figure 3b shows how the two main strategies are used for the
various sub-tasks of travel planning.

4 Conclusions

In this paper we have studied how users behave when completing transactional
tasks, in a laboratory experiment, and have reported on our initial findings.
Transactional queries are generally considered very hard as "most external factors important for users (e.g., price of goods, speed of service, quality of pictures, etc.) are usually unavailable to generic search engines" [2]. Indeed, we
have observed that users generally perceive transactional tasks as difficult. We
have also found that users have a tendency of overestimating the level of support
they can get from the search engine when facing unfamiliar tasks. Based on users'
feedback, we could identify aspects where search engines could improve current

services: finding specific entities (e.g., products, hotels, restaurants), properties of entities (e.g., shipping date, prices, menu), and offering additional filtering and sorting options on the SERP (similar to what specific verticals provide).

References

1. Agichtein, E., White, R.W., Dumais, S.T., Bennet, P.N.: Search, interrupted: understanding and predicting search task continuation. In: Proceedings of SIGIR (2012)
2. Broder, A.: A taxonomy of web search. SIGIR Forum **36**, 3–10 (2002)
3. Donato, D., Bonchi, F., Chi, T., Maarek, Y.: Do you want to take notes? identifying research missions in Yahoo! search pad. In: Proceedings of WWW (2010)
4. Feild, H., Allan, J.: Task-aware query recommendation. In: Proceedings of SIGIR (2013)
5. Gwizdka, J., Spence, I.: What can searching behavior tell us about the difficulty of information tasks? a study of web navigation. J. Am. Soc. Inf. Sci. Technol. **43**(1), 1–22 (2006)
6. Jansen, B.J., Spink, A., Pedersen, J.: A temporal comparison of altavista web searching: research articles. J. Am. Soc. Inf. Sci. Technol. **56**(6), 559–570 (2005)
7. Jiang, J., He, D., Allan, J.: Searching, browsing, and clicking in a search session: changes in user behavior by task and over time. In: Proceedings of SIGIR (2014)
8. Jones, R., Klinkner, K.L.: Beyond the session timeout: automatic hierarchical segmentation of search topics in query logs. In: Proceedings of CIKM (2008)
9. Kim, J.Y., Cramer, M., Teevan, J., Lagun, D.: Understanding how people interact with web search results that change in real-time using implicit feedback. In: Proceedings of CIKM (2013)
10. Li, Y., Belkin, N.J.: An exploration of the relationships between work task and interactive information search behavior. J. Am. Soc. Inf. Sci. Technol. **61**(9), 1771–1789 (2010)
11. Lucchese, C., Orlando, S., Perego, R., Silvestri, F., Tolomei, G.: Discovering tasks from search engine query logs. ACM Trans. Inf. Syst. **31**(3), 14:1–14:43 (2013)
12. Toms, E.G., Villa, R., McCay-Peet, L.: How is a search system used in work task completion? J. Inf. Sci. **39**(1), 15–25 (2013)

Health Suggestions: A Chrome Extension to Help Laypersons Search for Health Information

Carla Teixeira Lopes[1,2]([✉]) and Tiago Almeida Fernandes[1]

[1] Department of Informatics Engineering, Faculty of Engineering,
University of Porto, Porto, Portugal
{ctl,ei11054}@fe.up.pt
[2] INESC TEC, Porto, Portugal

Abstract. To help laypeople surpass the common difficulties they face when searching for health information on the Web, we built Health Suggestions, an extension for Google Chrome to assist users obtaining high-quality search results in the health domain. This is achieved by providing users with suggestions of queries formulated in different terminologies and languages. Translations of health expressions might not be obvious and queries in languages with a strong presence on the Web facilitate the access to high-quality health contents. On the other hand, the use of lay terminology might contribute to increase users' comprehension and medico-scientific terminology to obtain more detailed and technical contents. Results show a good acceptance of the suggestions, confirm the utility of a multilingual and multi-terminology approach and show its usefulness to more successful searches.

Keywords: Query suggestion · Health · Interactive IR · Multilingual

1 Introduction

Nowadays it is common to check the Internet for health-related information before consulting the doctor, 72 % of Internet users say they looked online for health information within the past year [1]. However, lack of scientific vocabulary or searching in languages with less information (e.g.: Portuguese compared to English) might limit users' access to health information on the Web. In the health domain, obtaining non-accurate contents might result in serious consequences. Since few users assess the quality of health-related web contents and a minority (41 %) checks their diagnosis with medical professionals [1], it is urgent to remove or reduce barriers in health information access.

Expectations on search results may differ depending on the user's knowledge. Although searching with medico-scientific terminology leads to more detailed contents, these may not be understandable for users with less health literacy. On the other hand, users with more expertise in a subject might prefer more scientific contents [3].

© Springer International Publishing Switzerland 2016
N. Fuhr et al. (Eds.): CLEF 2016, LNCS 9822, pp. 241–246, 2016.
DOI: 10.1007/978-3-319-44564-9_22

Health Suggestions assists laypeople searching for medical information, providing suggestions using lay and medico-scientific terminology related with user's original query. For now, we provide suggestions both in Portuguese and English despite Portuguese being only shown if it is the original query language. The assistance is made in search engines, the starting point for health information seeking for 77 % of people [1]. We are supporting: Google, Bing and Yahoo, having together a share of 89.9 % worldwide in 2016 [5]. We aim to provide laypeople with a mechanism for reaching higher-quality health contents fitted to users' health expertise.

2   Related Work

The impact of queries terminology on health information retrieval has already been studied. A study addressing the impact of lay and medico-scientific terminology in users with different levels of health literacy and topic familiarity [3], concluded that medico-scientific queries achieve higher precision. However, documents retrieved with these queries are less readable and less understood by users. Authors conclude that a medico-scientific query should be suggested whenever a person has the capacity to digest scientific documents. If the person has not enough health literacy, a lay query is preferred.

A different study evaluated the impact of translating a health query to English in users with different English proficiencies [2]. Authors concluded that non-English' speaking users having at least elementary English proficiency can benefit from this type of query translation.

3   Health Suggestions

We decided to implement Health Suggestions as a Google Chrome extension for two main reasons. First, since our focus is web information retrieval, we wanted to extend browser's functionality and reach all the main search engines. Second, we picked Chrome due to its current dominance as users' preferred browser. On May, 2016 it had a share of 71.4 % [8]. The extension is available on the Web[1].

Health Suggestions presents itself as a panel in Chrome's bottom right corner (Fig. 1) where several actions can be triggered, including: search for suggested queries; switch search engines; minimise/maximise the panel and close the panel. For example, if a suggestion is clicked a new search is performed for that suggestion, or if Bing's icon is clicked then the same search is performed in Bing.

To provide an easy access to all the above actions, the panel follows the user across the entire health-related search session. The panel is only visible when Health Suggestions finds a match for the query in our data structures. This way, the panel won't disturb the user in other types of searches. The extension has an options page (Fig. 2) which can be accessed by clicking the extension icon (blue heart) in the navigation bar. In this page the user can: turn the extension on/off;

---

[1] http://irlab.fe.up.pt/p/healthsuggestions.

Fig. 1. Suggestions' panel   **Fig. 2.** Options page

(dis)allow logging; opt for a local or remote database; specify queries' language or ask the extension to automatically detect it.

The system is divided in two distinct modules: suggestion engine and logging engine. The suggestion engine is responsible for generating the suggestions. It uses an English and Portuguese version of the Consumer Health Vocabulary (CHV), a vocabulary that links everyday words about health to technical terms used by health care professionals [6]. The Portuguese version was translated using the Google Translator API with an estimated accuracy of 84.2 %, notwithstanding we are continuously working to improve it [7]. The extension is standalone as the user can decide to use a local database instead of the remote one.

The architecture of the suggestion system is similar to the one used in a previous work [4] where more information is provided. In sum we created two inverted indices, one in each language, with the CHV. In the inverted index each stemmed term is associated with an inverse string frequency (isf) and a postings list, that is, the list of CHV strings where it appears. To determine the vocabulary of terms, CHV's strings were tokenized and stop words were removed. In the remaining terms, letters were reduced to lower case, the diacritics were removed and terms were also stemmed.

The steps to obtain suggestions are presented in Fig. 3. Steps in blue are performed in the extension while steps in red can be either performed in the extension or in the server. It can be either a function call, if in standalone mode, or a call to a REST API in the server. The majority of the work is accomplished on the extension in order to achieve a faster response time.

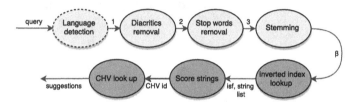

Fig. 3. Suggestion engine architecture

The extension was generated using a boilerplate[2] following the best practices for Google Chrome extensions development. The technologies involved are the ones used for front-end development: HTML, CSS and JavaScript. For the databases, we used WebSQL for storing the inverted indices and the CHV, we picked it because in the server this data is already stored in a SQL database. Local database updates are subject to extension updates. We have used the following third party libraries: Snowball.js[3]; franc.js[4]; sha1.js[5]; TimeMe.js[6]. The server provides a REST API. We have decided to use Django-Rest-Framework (Python) due to its ease of use and the possibility to obtain a working API vary fast. We chose PostgreSQL as our database management system.

In order to understand users' search process and to improve Health Suggestions we developed a logging system that tracks most of users' actions while performing health-related searches. The logs are anonymous and the user can disable them through the options page. Logging is focused on: query, search engine, search results, search engine's related queries and the suggestions provided by the Health Suggestions; time spent on SERP and Health Suggestions' panel; visited web pages: time on page and number of scroll events; clicks: on the extension's panel, search results or any page hyperlink; copy/cut events; find events. The logging engine is divided in two modules: the extension and the server. In the client we decided to use IndexedDB for its capacity to save JavaScript objects and its transaction support. In the server, logs are saved permanently in a PostgreSQL database.

4   Experiment

An user experiment was conducted to evaluate Health Suggestions. Four major research questions drove the experiment: (1) How are suggestions used? (2) Why are suggestions used? (3) How do users assess the utility of the suggestions provided by the system? (4) Do the suggestions lead to a more successful search?. For the fourth question, we considered the number of relevant documents saved by the users and their feeling of success with the task.

For the study, 36 students (30 female and 6 male) were recruited. Their average age is 21,9 (standard deviation 5,9). The majority of the participants search the web for 8 to 13 years (78 %). The search frequency for 19 % is daily and for 81 % it is more frequent than daily. In a scale from 1 to 5 about how often participants find what they are looking for, 4 participants (11 %) classified it as 3, 26 participants (72 %) as a 4 and 6 participants (17 %) as a 5.

---

[2] http://extensionizr.com.
[3] https://github.com/fortnightlabs/snowball-js.
[4] https://github.com/wooorm/franc.
[5] https://github.com/sytelus/CryptoJS.
[6] https://github.com/jasonzissman/TimeMe.js.

4.1   Setup

For the study we used two systems, one including Health Suggestions and the other one without it. Participants were divided in two groups. Half of them, the assisted group, used the system with the extension and the other group, the unassisted one, didn't have access to the suggestions. None of the participants was involved in the definition of the task. Participants were unaware of the fact that some received assistance and that some did not. No significant difference in average search experience was found between the groups, neither regarding the number of years searching the Web (10.9 years vs. 9.7 years, p-value = 0.2), neither regarding users' self assessment of success in web searching (both groups with a mode and median of 4).

Each participant was assigned 4 simulated work task situations. To define the simulated situations, we asked 20 persons with no medical expertise and spanning a wide range of ages and education levels to state the health topic for which they had most recently searched on the Web. Then, we randomly selected topics and created a scenario for each. The information situations were described to the users in Portuguese. The order of the tasks was rotated.

Users had to freely formulate 3 queries for each task and save the relevant documents from the top 10 results for each query. In the end of each search task, the users of the assisted group had to explain if and how they used the suggestions (clicked on them, used terms from one of the suggestions, used terms from several suggestions), why they were considered useful and were also asked to assess their utility.

4.2   Results

How are suggestions used? To answer this research question we analysed the behaviour of users in the assisted group. Suggestions were presented in 71 % of the issued queries. In 27 % of these cases users clicked on them, in 15 % have used one suggestion to extract terms that were then used in the following query and in 4 % of the cases have extracted terms from more than one suggestions.

Why are suggestions used? Users presented 5 main reasons for using suggestions. In 35 % of the cases, users simply said they used them because they presented synonymous. However, the most popular reason is presenting alternatives in medico-scientific terminology (37 %). English suggestions are also very valued (24 %). Although in a smaller scale, lay (3 %) terminology and the Portuguese language (1 %) were also reasons for using the suggestions.

How do users assess the utility of the suggestions provided by the system? We asked users to assess the utility of the provided suggestions in a scale of 1 (not useful) to 3 (useful). From the set of presented suggestions, 38 % were considered useful and 33 % partially useful. The remaining proportion (29 %) was considered not useful.

Do the suggestions lead to a more successful search? The average number of relevant documents saved by the users was significantly higher in the assisted group (16.3 versus 14.1, p-value = 0.017). Regarding users' assessment of task success, in a scale of 1–5, we found that the unassisted group had a larger median (5) than the assisted group (4). However, this is not a significant difference.

5   Conclusions and Future Work

By providing both lay and medico-scientific suggestions, Health Suggestions support laypersons reaching information accordingly to their knowledge. Although preliminary, results show a good acceptance of the suggestions, confirm the rationale that is behind the development of this extension, that is, the utility of a multilingual and multi-terminology approach and show their usefulness in the retrieval of a larger number of relevant documents.

Our next step is to use the data logged in this user study, to deeply understand people interactions with the search panel and the given suggestions. We are also planning to analyse if the extension contributes to improve the knowledge users acquire during the health searching.

Acknowledgments. This work was partially funded by project "NanoSTIMA: Macro-to-Nano Human Sensing: Towards Integrated Multimodal Health Monitoring and Analytics/NORTE-01-0145-FEDER-000016", financed by the North Portugal Regional Operational Programme (NORTE 2020), under the PORTUGAL 2020 Partnership Agreement, and through the European Regional Development Fund (ERDF).

References

1. Fox, S., Duggan, M.: Health online 2013. Technical report, Pew Research Center's Internet & American Life Project, Washington, D.C., January 2013
2. Lopes, C.T., Ribeiro, C.: Measuring the value of health query translation: an analysis by user language proficiency. J. Am. Soc. Inform. Sci. Technol. **64**(5), 951–963 (2013). http://dx.doi.org/10.1002/asi.22812
3. Lopes, C.T., Ribeiro, C.: Effects of terminology on health queries: an analysis by user's health literacy and topic familiarity, vol. 39, Chap. 10, pp. 145–184. Emerald Group Publishing Limited (2015). http://www.emeraldinsight.com/doi/abs/10.1108/S0065-283020150000039013
4. Lopes, C.T., Ribeiro, C.: Effects of language and terminology on the usage of health query suggestions. In: Conference and Labs of the Evaluation Forum (2016)
5. NetMarketShare: Search Engine Market Share (2016). https://www.netmarketshare.com/search-engine-market-share.aspx?qprid=4&qpcustomd=0&qpsp=2016&qpnp=1&qptimeframe=Y. Accessed 17 June 2016
6. NLM: 2012AA Consumer Health Vocabulary Source Information (2012). http://www.nlm.nih.gov/research/umls/sourcereleasedocs/current/CHV/index.html
7. Silva, A.C., Lopes, C.T.: Health translations: a crowdsourced, gamified approach to translate large vocabulary databases. In: CISTI 2016 - 11th Iberian Conference on Information Systems and Technologies (2016)
8. w3schools.com: Browser Statistics (2016). http://www.w3schools.com/browsers/browsers_stats.asp. Accessed 17 June 2016

Brazilian Social Mood: The Political Dimension of Emotion

Leila Weitzel[1(✉)], Flávia Bernardini[1], Paulo Quaresma[2], Claudio André Alves[1], Wladek Zacharski[1], and Luis G. de Figueiredo[1]

[1] Computer Science Department, Universidade Federal Fluminense, Rio de Janeiro, Brazil
{leila_weitzel,fcbernardini}@id.uff.br, claudiondr@gmail.com,
wladek29@gmail.com, gugabfigueiredo@gmail.com
[2] Universidade de Évora, Évora, Portugal
pq@uevora.pt

Abstract. Brazil faces a major economic and political crisis. Millions of people joined anti-government protests across the country. Social media sites are a way for some people to vent their emotions without feeling self-conscious. Thus, emotion mining on social media can be viewed as effective tool to conduct Presidential approval rating. This research aims to automatically recognize emotion in texts extracted from social media in Brazilian Portuguese (PT-BR). The ultimate goal is knowing how emotions influence a writer of a text in choosing certain words and/or other linguistic elements. In this research, we perform keyword-based approaches using affect lexicon and a Support Vector Machine and Naïve Bayes algorithms.

Keywords: Emotion mining · Categorical model · Dimensional model · Arousal-valence approach

1 Introduction

Brazil faces a major economic and political crisis in 2016. Millions joined anti-government protests across the country. Dilma Roussef's popularity is at near-record lows. Presidential approval rating is usually conducted through questionnaires, electronic or paper, in order to measure the president's job performance. The most widely used version of questioning is "Do you approve or disapprove of the way [president's name] is handling his/her job as president?", while other question wordings are still employed, such as the one using a four-point scale (excellent, good, fair, or poor). Even in a democratic country, a person may feel uncomfortable to answer this question face-to-face to the questioner, and he/she can feel forced to answer "Yes, I approve" [1].

On the other hand, one has the right to express his or her personal opinion through social media; this is the real "freedom of expression". Social media sites are a way for some people to vent anger, fear, happiness, hate, hope, love and sadness without feeling self-conscious, nervous, or upset. Everyone has the right to say what they think and can express their opinions or feelings about practically everything very spontaneously and without "censorship". For example, retweets, liking, or even posting your own status can be as effective as screaming at a political protest. Thus, emotion mining on social

© Springer International Publishing Switzerland 2016
N. Fuhr et al. (Eds.): CLEF 2016, LNCS 9822, pp. 247–252, 2016.
DOI: 10.1007/978-3-319-44564-9_23

media can be viewed as effective tool to conduct approval rating. Computational models of emotion can be categorized according to the emotional theories [1, 2].

Sentiment and emotion mining may be very useful in this context, trying to capture the nation sentiment. Yet, there is a demand for new tools in sentiment analysis, which attracted the researcher's attention. Based on the context described above, this research aims to automatically recognize emotion in texts extracted from social media in Brazilian Portuguese (PT-BR) using affect lexicon and machine learning algorithms. Here we focus on emotion recognition and restrict our attention to situations where emotions are expressed in (and can be extracted from) social media, more precisely, from Dilma Roussef's official Facebook page. We opted Dilma Roussef´s official pages mainly because we want to uncover emotions related to President Dilma or actions of Brazilian Federal Government.

2   Related Work

New methods for sentiment and emotion analysis have been presented in literature. In [3] the authors explore social affective text mining, aiming at discovering and modeling the connections between online documents and user-generated social emotions. According to [4, 5], the two most prominent means of emotion characterization have relied on either a discrete lexicon of emotional words (categorical model) or a dimensional scale (dimensional model) for estimating levels of affect. In the categorical model, emotions are labelled with a small number of basic emotions (e.g., "happy", "sad", "angry", "disgust", "surprise" and "fear") or complex emotions (a combination of two or more basic emotions experienced by a person at an instance). Roussel's model [6] hypothesizes that each basic emotion represents a bipolar entity being a part of the same emotional continuum. The first polarity is Valence of an experienced emotion (the degree to which it is strongly positive or negative); the second polarity is level of Arousal (the amount of energy perceived). Identifying Valence and Arousal linked to a particular word is likely to be easier and more reliable than other types of emotion detection. Kim [4] observes that, while categorical and dimensional approaches are promising for identifying emotions or sentiments, there are challenges to overcome, because affective expressivity of text rests on the basis of more complex linguistic features, which are specific for each language.

3   The Proposed Approach

There are two main approaches to the problem of emotion mining: lexical approach and machine learning approach. In both approaches, we employed two different models for representing emotions, the categorical and dimensional models. It is worth highlighting that, this research represents the first systematic evaluation of a technique, which combine these two emotion models under consistent conditions and evaluation methodologies using Portuguese Language. The *categorical model* is keyword-based approach, based on NRC – Emotion Lexicon (or EmoLex) [7]. It contains about 14,183 individual terms and their associations to each of the eight Plutchik [8] basic emotions (anger, anticipation, disgust, fear, joy, sadness, surprise, trust) and two sentiments (negative and positive). It works on multilingual sentiment resource mapping into others twenty languages. NRC has mainly addressed mapping emotion and sentiment resources from English into Portuguese by Google translator. The *dimensional models* is based on circular configuration called Circumplex of Affect proposed by Russel [9]. The author argues that, emotional states are not independent of each other. This model is based on the hypothesis that each basic emotion represents a bipolar entity being a part of the same emotional continuum. The proposed polarities are Arousal (high or low) and Valence (positive or negative). Arousal-High and Valence-Negative (*AHVN*) = [anger, fear, disgust, etc.]; Arousal-High and Valence-Positive (*ARVP*) = [surprise, joy, etc.]; Arousal-Low and Valence-Negative (*ALVN*) = [Sadness, bored, etc.]; Arousal-Low and Valence-Positive (*ALVP*) = [anticipation, calm, optimism, etc.]. In the machine learning approach, we intend to explore different classification methodologies considering the domain complexity. We performed a classic Support Vector Machine (*SVM*) and Naïve Bayes (*NB*) algorithms from Weka. It is worth to mention that we tried other classifiers too, but the results were poorer. We created a corpus from Roussef's Official Facebook page. We collected all user's comments from 2014–2015 – about 220 thousand. The following preprocessing phases were performed (not necessarily in the following order): (i) Withdraw of comments lower than three words or with only hashtags, emoticons or link; (ii) Tokenization of the comments; (iii) Vectorization of the comments using TF-IDF transformation; and (iv) Spelling correction. For vectorization, Bag-of-word (BoW), Uni-Gram, Bi-gram and Tri-gram approaches were used. Stemming was not employed because it might hide important differences as in between "*advers*(ário)" (opponent) and "*advers*(idade)" (adversity), for instance. Manual Annotation is an effective method for labeling data for supervised machine learning. It is not a trivial task and it takes many hours of work. Due to the fact that this research is in its early stages, therefore from the 220 thousand comments, we annotated 1640 comments. **Manual Annotation Method (MAM)**: Each comment was tagged depending on its relative subjectivity/objectivity, as well as the polarity expressed on a 3-value scale (positive +1, neutral - 0, negative -1, as Valence Dimension). The data was labeled according to each polar entity and emotion classes: AHVN = [anger, fear, disgust, tense]; ARVP = [surprise, joy]; ALVN = [Sadness]; ALVP = [hope, relaxed, optimism, antic-ipation]. Each annotator (a total of five) mark up a comment with one or more emotional label, in accordance with emotion intensity as [1 – low, 2 –medium, 3 –high]. We considered only intensity of three. For example, if a comment was labelled as hope +1 and optimism +3, thus the final evaluation is that the comment is strongly optimistic. Positive emotion has a positive sign (+), and negative emotions has a negative sign (-). Sentences with ambiguous labels will be judged by another independent annotator in order to decide the final label. The agreement between annotators is calculated by finding observed and expected agreement. We use kappa coefficient, such that, if the annotators are in complete agreement then kappa = 1. If there is no agreement among the annotator then kappa = 0.0 (for complete instructions on how to calculate kappa, see [10]). **Auto-matic Annotation Method (AAM)**: To find the emotion associations from each source word, the approach first searches for that word in the NRC lexicon, if found then it generates a vector of size three, one value for categorical model, one value for dimensional model and one for the Valence.

4   Evaluation and Results

The kappa values achieved was about 0.524, it is considered moderate agreement. Most of agreement was over negative emotion such as, anger, disgust, etc. *MAM results from Categorical Model*: The frequency of top emotion was "hope", with a percentage of 36 %, followed by anger = 28 %, disgust = 24 %, happy = 5 %, optimism = 4 %, tense = 2 % and fear = 1 %. There was a balance between Valence positive (45 %) and negative (55 %). *MAM results from Dimensional Model*: AHVN = 55 %, AHVP = 5 %, ALVP = 40 %. *AAM results from Categorical Model:* The frequency of top emotion was anger 13 %, followed by disgust = 10 %, happy = 9 %, sadness = 7 %, hope = 5 % and fear = 1 %. It is important to notice that, some comments were not classified since there was no corresponding tokens (words) in the NRC lexicon (total of 47 %) and 8 % of data has only Valence (positive or negative), i.e., it has no emotion. The outcomes shows that, in spite of NRC has about 14 thousand words, this was not enough to categorize emotions from text in Portuguese language. *AAM results from Dimensional Model*: AHVN = 52 %, AHVP = 21 %, ALVP = 12 % AHVP = 21 %. We noticed that there is many divergences between *MAM* and *AAM*, mostly because NRC was not robust enough. For instance, some words are clearly classified as anger, but they are not specified as such in NRC, for example, "Who elected this plague was the electronic ballot box of the devil?" – Quem elegeu esta praga foi a urna do capeta? The word "capeta" is a slang of demon (or devil). Others are regular expressions, regional dialect, "name calling" or Figurative Language such as sarcasm, irony and metaphor undermined the performance. **Categorical model classification results:** Table 1 shows the supervised learning results. The meaning of abbreviations are: SVML: SVM linear Kernel; NB: Naïve Bayes; w-stpwrd: no stopword (and stpwrd otherwise); All-Label means that all 10 label were considered; and Valence: only positive and negative classes. The Table 1 gives guidelines for interpretation of the outcomes. Overall, results of all-label are quite poor, when compared to Valence results. Therefore, the results of all-label indicates that, Uni-Gram was a little better than others for All-Label class, where Precision = 54 % and Recall = 53 %. The Valence classification was the one who showed the best results, the accuracy was about 84 % to SVML, Bi-Gram and w-stpwrd (the linear kernel yielded the best results), the Precision and Recall were equal to 82 %. This means that, the algorithm was able to recognize the polarity of emotion but not the exact emotion. In order to understand the low performance achieved by All-Label class, we also perform a new approach, we create a data sample of "3-Label". Only the three major label (disgust, hope and anger) was considered mostly because the data sample was not balanced. The best result (67 %) was achieved by SVML, Bi-Gram and stpwrd. Precision was equal to 68 % and Recall = 67 % (Table 2).

Table 1. The average results for dataset using accuracy, the best results are in bolt and highlighted.

Accuracy	Uni-Gram				Bi-Gram				Three-Gram			
	stpwrd		w-stpwrd		stpwrd		w-stpwrd		stpwrd		w-stpwrd	
	NB	SVML	NB	SVML	NB	SVML	NB	SVML	NB	SVML	NB	SVML
all-label	**55%**	51%	52%	52%	53%	51%	52%	52%	47%	47%	49%	41%
Valence	77%	77%	79%	75%	80%	82%	82%	**84%**	82%	82%	76%	70%

Table 2. The average results for dataset using accuracy, the best results are in bolt and highlighted

Accuracy	Uni-Gram				Bi-Gram			
	stpwrd		w-stpwrd		stpwrd		w-stpwrd	
	NB	SVML	NB	SVML	NB	SVML	NB	SVML
3-label	59%	60%	55%	53%	58%	**67%**	59%	56%

Dimensional Model Result. The Table 3 shows the best results of dimensional model. The SVML achieved the best score of accuracy for both stpwrd and w-stpwrd. There is a small deviation between precision and recall for both NB and SVML. The dimension *ALVP* achieves Precision equal to 83 % and Recall = 71 %, and dimension *AHVN* reaches Precision = 79 % and Recall = 94 %. Barrett [11] suggested that the applicability of one of two models might differ individually based on valence focus and arousal focus. A categorical model is appropriate for capturing the affective states in the negative valence and higher arousal focus (ALVP). By contrast, a dimensional model is better when emotions are positive in valence focus and low in arousal focus (AHVN). In our study, the Barrett [10] assumption was not corroborated by the results. The dimensional model was better for capturing both, ALVP (precision = 83 %, recall = 71 %) and AHVN (precision = 79 %, recall = 94 %) on the contrary, the precision and recall of AHVP were equal to zero. The categorical model was better to identify the positive emotion, e.g., hope with precision = 65 % and recall = 73 %. Negative emotion fear and tense achieve the lowest value of precision and recall (equal to zero or very close to it).

Table 3. The average results, the best results are in bolt and highlighted

metrics	Bi-Gram			
	stpwrd		w-stpwrd	
	NB	SVML	NB	SVML
accuracy	71%	**80%**	78%	**80%**
precision	68%	77%	75%	76%
recall	71%	80%	78%	80%

5   Conclusions and Future Works

In this paper, we conducted several experiments exploring two broad approaches: lexical approach and machine learning approach. In both approaches, we employed two different models for representing emotions, the categorical and dimensional models on a small set of basic emotions. The results and conclusions of the experiments raise remarks and new questions. A first remark to be made is that using emotion keywords is a straightforward way to detect associated emotions, nevertheless the meanings of keywords could be multiple and vague, especially when it comes to more structured languages such as Brazilian Portuguese. For instance, except those words standing for emotion labels themselves, most words could change their meanings according to different usages and contexts. We noticed that Bi-grams are helpful in emotion classification too. We also noticed that, removing the style features (features based on hashtags, exclamations, stopword) does not result in a large drop (or increase) in performance. The second remark was that the predominant emotion is *hope* followed by *anger* and they are located in opposite Russell's Circumplex quadrant. We found a balance between negative and positive emotion. The last, but not least, we need to focus on the automatic collection of word (or regular expressions) in order to enrich the NRC lexicon, mostly because Brazilian Portuguese language is highly rich and complex. Moreover, Brazil has large cultural diversity and, consequently, has many regions, each with their own idiomatic expressions and different ways of communication, such as the people from Rio Grande do Sul state, in contrast to the people from Bahia state. Cultural and life style differences between Brazilian and English speakers lead to different sentiment associations of the English word and its translation.

References

1. Contractor, D., Chawda, B., Mehta, S., Subramaniam, L.V., Faruquie, T.A.: Tracking political elections on social media: applications and experience. In: Proceedings of the 24th International Conference on Artificial Intelligence, pp. 2320–2326. AAAI Press, Buenos Aires (2015)
2. O'Connor, B., Balasubramanyan, R., Routledge, B.R., Smith, N.A.: From Tweets to Polls: Linking Text Sentiment to Public Opinion Time Series (2010)
3. Dhawan, S., Singh, K., Sehrawat, D.: Emotion mining techniques in social networking sites. Int. J. Inf. Comput. Technol. **4**, 1145–1153 (2014)
4. Kim, S.M.: Recognising Emotions and Sentiments in Text. School of Electrical and Information Engineering. Master of Philosophy, p. 128. University of Sydney, Sidney- AU (2011)
5. Dhawan, S., Singh, K., Khanchi, V.: A framework for polarity classification and emotion mining from text International. J. Eng. Comput. Sci. **3**, 7431–7436 (2014)
6. Russell, J.: Affective space is bipolar. J. Pers. Soc. Psychol. **37**, 345–356 (1979)
7. Mohammad, S., Turney, P.D.: Crowdsourcing a word-emotion association lexicon. Comput. Intell. **8**, 436–465 (2013)
8. Plutchik, R.: The nature of emotions. Am. Sci. **89**, 344–350 (2001)
9. Russel, J.A.: A circumplex model of affect. J. Pers. Soc. Psychol. **39**, 1161–1178 (1980)
10. Siegel, S., Castellan, N.J.: Nonparametric Statistics for the Behavioral Sciences. McGraw-Hill, New York (1988)
11. Barrett, L.F.: Discrete emotions or dimensions? the role of valence focus and arousal focus. Cogn. Emot. **12**, 579–599 (1998)

CLEF 2016 Labs Overviews

Overview of the CLEF eHealth Evaluation Lab 2016

Liadh Kelly[1]([⊠]), Lorraine Goeuriot[2], Hanna Suominen[3,4], Aurélie Névéol[5], João Palotti[6], and Guido Zuccon[7]

[1] ADAPT Centre, Trinity College, Dublin, Ireland
Liadh.Kelly@tcd.ie
[2] LIG, Université Grenoble Alpes, Grenoble, France
Lorraine.Goeuriot@imag.fr
[3] Data61, The Australian National University, University of Canberra,
Canberra, ACT, Australia
hanna.suominen@data61.csiro.au
[4] University of Turku, Turku, Finland
[5] LIMSI CNRS UPR 3251 Universitté Paris-Saclay, 91405 Orsay, France
Aurelie.Neveol@limsi.fr
[6] Vienna University of Technology, Vienna, Austria
palotti@ifs.tuwien.ac.at
[7] Queensland University of Technology, Brisbane, Australia
g.zuccon@qut.edu.au

Abstract. In this paper we provide an overview of the fourth edition of the CLEF eHealth evaluation lab. CLEF eHealth 2016 continues our evaluation resource building efforts around the easing and support of patients, their next-of-kins and clinical staff in understanding, accessing and authoring eHealth information in a multilingual setting. This year's lab offered three tasks: Task 1 on handover information extraction related to Australian nursing shift changes, Task 2 on information extraction in French corpora, and Task 3 on multilingual patient-centred information retrieval considering query variations. In total 20 teams took part in these tasks (3 in Task 1, 7 in Task 2 and 10 in Task 3). Herein, we describe the resources created for these tasks, evaluation methodology adopted and provide a brief summary of participants to this year's challenges and some results obtained. As in previous years, the organizers have made data and tools associated with the lab tasks available for future research and development.

Keywords: Evaluation · Entity linking · Information retrieval · Information extraction · Medical informatics · Nursing records · Patient handoff/handover · Speech recognition · Test-set generation · Text classification · Text segmentation · Self-diagnosis

---

In alphabetical order, LK & LG co-chaired the lab. HS led Task 1. AN led Task 2. JP & GZ led Task 3.

N. Fuhr et al. (Eds.): CLEF 2016, LNCS 9822, pp. 255–266, 2016.
DOI: 10.1007/978-3-319-44564-9_24

1   Introduction

This paper presents an overview of the CLEFeHealth 2016 evaluation lab, organized within the Conference and Labs of the Evaluation Forum (CLEF) to support the development of approaches for helping patients, their next-of-kins, and clinical staff in understanding, accessing and authoring health information. This fourth year of the evaluation lab aimed to build upon the resource development and evaluation approaches offered in the previous three years of the lab [1–3], which focused on patients and their next-of-kins' ease in understanding and accessing health information.

Task 1 addressed *handover information extraction* (IE) related to Australian nursing shift changes. This extended the 2015 Task 1a of converting verbal nursing handovers to written free-text records by using *automated speech recognition* (ASR) [4]; in 2016, we challenged participants to maximise the correctness in structuring these written free-text records by pre-filling a handover form by automatically identifying relevant text-snippets for each slot of the form. That is, the tasks were parts of a following processing cascade whose empirical clinical justification has been provided in our previous paper [5] and references therein:

1. Verbal handover audio is recorded and ASR transcribes these voice recordings into computer-readable free-form text (i.e., CLEF eHealth 2015 Task1a).
2. IE is used to pre-fill a handover form by automatically identifying relevant text-snippets for each slot of the form (i.e., CLEF eHealth 2016 Task 1).
3. An information visualisation system[1] associates the pre-filled form with the original context of the extracted information in the speech-recognised, free form text by highlighting text for a clinician to proof, edit, and sign off.

Task 2 addressed *information extraction* from French biomedical narratives. Part of the task continued the 2015 task 1b of named entity recognition and normalization (or "entity linking") from the QUAERO French medical corpus [6], which comprises titles of scientific articles and drug inserts [7]. In 2016, we challenged participants with unseen data from the QUAERO corpus. In addition, we also introduced a new corpus of French Death Certificates, the CépiDC corpus. The task associated with the new corpus was to assign one or more codes from the International Classification of Diseases, tenth revison (ICD10) to each document line. As ICD10 is one of the vocabularies included in the UMLS metathesaurus used for normalizing entities in the QUAERO corpus, systems already developed for the QUAERO corpus could be applied in this new task. Furthermore, the task is geared towards a concrete public health application as it encourages the development of systems that could assist CépiDC curators with the coding of death certificates. We also emphasised the need for robust systems by giving participants the opportunity to submit their systems to a *replication track*, in which organizers attempted to replicate the runs submitted by participants.

---

[1] See our live demostration at http://nicta-stct.s3-website-ap-southeast-2.amazonaws .com, last accessed on 25 May 2016.

Task 3, the IR Task, aimed at evaluating the effectiveness of information retrieval systems when searching for health content on the web, with the objective to foster research and development of search engines tailored to health information seeking. This year's IR task continued the growth path identified in 2014 and 2015's CLEF eHealth information retrieval challenges [8,9]. Compared to 2015's task, we used a larger corpus (ClueWeb12B), which is more representative of the current state of health information online. Also, we explored health web forums to create queries, mining real user cases. We generated query variations based on the fact that there are multiple ways to express a single information need (in this case, multiple queries were created from a single post in a web health forum). Last, we kept the multilingual search task, in which we provided query translation into several languages for the English queries. Participants had to translate the queries back to English and use the English translation to search the collection.

This paper is structured as follows: in Sect. 2 we will detail the tasks, evaluation and datasets created; in Sect. 3 we will describe the submission and results for each task; and in Sect. 4 we will give a conclusion.

2   Materials and Methods

2.1   Text Documents

The *NICTA Synthetic Nursing Handover Data* [10,11] was used in Task 1 as training data. This set of 301 synthetic patient cases (i.e., 101, 100, and 100 for training, validation, and testing, respectively) was developed for ASR and IE related to nursing shift-change handover in 2012–2016. The dataset was authored by a registered nurse (RN) with over twelve years' experience in clinical nursing. The text was thus very similar to real documents in Australian English (which cannot be made available). Each case consisted of a patient profile; a written, free-form text paragraph (i.e., the written handover document); and for ASR purposes, its spoken (i.e., the verbal handover document) and speech-recognized counterparts. The written handover documents were used in Task 1 with the training, validation, and test set having $8,487$; $7,730$; and $6,540$ words in total. In the CLEF eHealth 2015 Task 1a on clinical ASR [4], the 100 training and 100 validation cases were used for training and testing; for this year's Task 1 the dataset was supplemented with another independent test set of 100 cases. The data releases were approved at NICTA and the RN provided written consent. The spoken, free-form text documents were licensed under Creative Commons—Attribution Alone—Non-commercial—No Derivative Works (CC-BY-NC-ND) and the remaining documents under CC-BY.

Task 2 ran two separate challenges, which used two distinct data sets. The first data set, QUAERO FrenchMedical Corpus [6], was used in CLEF eHealth 2015 [7]. The data released in 2015 was used as a training and development set in 2016 (two sets of 833 annotated MEDLINE titles and 3 EMEA documents) and a new unseen test set was released for CLEF eHealth 2016 (833 annotated MEDLINE titles and 4 EMEA documents). It comprises annotations for 10 types of clinical entities with normalization to the Unified Medical Language System (UMLS) and covers scientific articles titles and drug inserts. The second data set is called the CépiDC Causes of Death Corpus. It comprises free-text descriptions of causes of death as reported by physicians in the standardized causes of death forms. Each document (65,843 death certificates in total) was manually coded by experts with ICD-10, as per international WHO standards.

The information retrieval challenge, Task 3, used a new web corpus this year, ClueWeb12 B13[2], which is a large snapshot of the Web, crawled between February and May 2012. Unlike the Khresmoi dataset [12] used in the previous years of the IR task [8,9,13], ClueWeb12 does not contain only Health On the Net certified pages and pages from a selected list of known health domains, making the dataset more in line with the material current web search engines index and retrieve. ClueWeb12 B13 contains approximately 52.3 million web pages, for a total of 1.95 TB of data, once uncompressed. For participants who did not have access to the ClueWeb dataset, Carnegie Mellon University granted the organisers permission to make the dataset available through cloud computing instances provided by Microsoft Azure[3]. The Azure instances that were made available to participants for the IR challenge included (1) the Clueweb12 B13 dataset, (2) standard indexes built with the Terrier [14] and the Indri [15] toolkits, (3) additional resources such as a spam list [16], Page Rank scores, anchor texts [17], urls, etc. made available through the ClueWeb12 website.

2.2 Human Annotations, Queries, and Relevance Assessments

In Task 1, the written handover documents were annotated, by the aforementioned RN using the *Protégé 3.1.1 Knowtator 1.9 beta*, with respect to a form with 49 headings (aka classes) to fill out. Aphabetically, the following 35 of these classes were present in the training set:

1. Appointment/Procedure_City,
2. Appointment/Procedure_ClinicianGivenNames/Initials,
3. Appointment/Procedure_ClinicianLastname,
4. Appointment/Procedure_Day,
5. Appointment/Procedure_Description,
6. Appointment/Procedure_Status,
7. Appointment/Procedure_Time,
8. Appointment/Procedure_Ward,
9. Future_Alert/Warning/AbnormalResult,
10. Future_Discharge/TransferPlan,
11. Future_Goal/TaskToBeCompleted/ExpectedOutcome,

---

[2] http://lemurproject.org/clueweb12/index.php.

[3] The organisers are thankful to Carnegie Mellon University, and in particular to Jamie Callan and Christina Melucci, for their support in obtaining the permission to redistribute ClueWeb 12. The organisers are also thankful to Microsoft Azure who provided the Azure cloud computing infrastructure that was made available to participants through the Microsoft Azure for Research Award CRM:0518649.

12. Medication_Dosage,
13. Medication_Medicine,
14. Medication_Status,
15. MyShift_ActivitiesOfDailyLiving,
16. MyShift_Contraption,
17. MyShift_Input/Diet,
18. MyShift_OtherObservation,
19. MyShift_Output/Diuresis/BowelMovement,
20. MyShift_RiskManagement,
21. MyShift_Status,
22. MyShift_Wounds/Skin,
23. PatientIntroduction_AdmissionReason/Diagnosis,
24. PatientIntroduction_Ageinyears,
25. PatientIntroduction_Allergy,
26. PatientIntroduction_CarePlan,
27. PatientIntroduction_ChronicCondition,
28. PatientIntroduction_CurrentBed,
29. PatientIntroduction_CurrentRoom,
30. PatientIntroduction_Disease/ProblemHistory,
31. PatientIntroduction_Gender,
32. PatientIntroduction_GivenNames/Initials,
33. PatientIntroduction_Lastname,
34. PatientIntroduction_UnderDr_GivenNames/Initials, and
35. PatientIntroduction_UnderDr_Lastname.

Irrelevant text was to be classified as 36. *NA* and the annotation task was seen as multi-class classification, that is, each word could belong to precisely one class. To improve the annotation consistency in including/excluding articles or titles and in marking gender information in each document if it was available, some light proofing was performed semi-automatically before releasing the classification *gold standard* (GS) under the CC-BY license.

For Task 2's QUAERO challenge, the annotations covered ten types of entities of clinical interest, defined by Semantic Groups in the Unified Medical Language System (UMLS) [18]: *Anatomy, Chemicals & Drugs, Devices, Disorders, Geographic Areas, Living Beings, Objects, Phenomena, Physiology, Procedures.* The annotations marked each relevant entity mention in the documents, and assigned the corresponding semantic type(s) and Concept Unique Identifier(s) or CUIs. Each document was annotated by one professional annotator (two annotators participated in total) according to detailed guidelines [6]. The annotations were then validated and revised by a senior annotator to ensure annotation consistency and correctness throughout the corpus. The CLEF eHealth Task 1b annotated corpus was used as training data supplied to the participants at the beginning of the lab, and an equally sized unseen test set was supplied later to evaluate participants' systems.

For Task 2's CépiDC challenge, the ICD10 codes were extracted from the raw lines of death certificate text by professional curators at INSERM over the period of 2006–2013. During this time, curators also manually built dictionaries of terms associated with ICD10 codes. Several versions of these lexical resources were supplied to participants in addition to the training data.

For the IR task, Task 3, this year's queries extended upon the focus of the 2015 task (self-diagnosis) by considering real health information need expressed by the general public through posts published in public health web forums. Forum posts were extracted from the 'askDocs' section of Reddit[4], and presented to query creators. Query creators were asked to formulate queries based on what they read in the initial user post. Six query creators with different medical expertise were used for this task. Previous research has shown that different users tend to issue different queries for the same observation need and that the use of query variations for evaluation of IR systems leads to as much variability as system variations [9,19,20]. This was the case also for this year's task. Note that we explored query variations also in the 2015 IR task [9]–and there we also found that for the same image, different query creators issued very different queries: these differed not only in terms of the keywords contained in them, but also with respect to their retrieval effectiveness. When appropriate, we fixed misspellings found in the queries by the Linux program 'aspell'. However, we did not remove punctuation marks from the queries. For the query variations element of the task (subtask 2 of the IR Task), participants were told which queries relate to the same information need, to allow them to produce one set of results to be used as answer for all query variations of an information need. For the multilingual element of the challenge, (subtask 3 of the IR Task), Czech, French, Hungarian, German, Polish and Swedish translations of the queries were provided. Queries were translated by medical experts hired though a professional translation company.

Relevance assessments were collected by pooling participants' submitted runs as well as baseline runs. Assessment was performed by paid medical students who had access to the queries, to the documents, and to the relevance criteria drafted by a junior medical doctor that guided assessors in the judgement of document relevance. The relevance criteria were drafted considering the entirety of the forum posts used to create the queries; a link to the forum posts was also provided to the assessors. Along with relevance assessments, readability/understandability and reliability/trustworthiness judgements were also collected for the assessment pool; these were used to evaluate systems across different dimensions of relevance [21,22].

2.3 Evaluation Methods

Task 1. *Precision* (Prec), *Recall* (Rec), and their harmonic mean

$$F1 = \frac{2 \text{ Prec Rec}}{\text{Prec} + \text{Rec}}$$

were measured. Performance was evaluated first separately in every heading and NA. That is, if TP_c, FP_c, and FN_c refer to the *numbers of true positives, false*

---

[4] https://www.reddit.com/r/AskDocs/.

positives, and *false negatives* for a class $c \in \{1, 2, 3, \ldots, 36 = \mathrm{NA}\}$, respectively, and the class-specific measures were defined as

$$\mathrm{Prec}_c = \frac{TP_c}{TP_c + FP_c}, \mathrm{Rec}_c = \frac{TP_c}{TP_c + FN_c}, \text{ and}$$

$\mathrm{F1}_c$ as their harmonic mean. Then, we documented the performance in the dominant class of $36 = \mathrm{NA}$ and averaged over the form headings $c \in \{1, 2, 3, \ldots, 35\}$ by using *macro-averaging* (MaA), because our desire was to perform well in all classes, and not only in the majority classes, with

$$\mathrm{Prec}_{\mathrm{MaA}} = \frac{\sum_{c=1}^{35} \mathrm{Prec}_c}{35}, \mathrm{Rec}_{\mathrm{MaA}} = \frac{\sum_{c=1}^{35} \mathrm{Rec}_c}{35}, \text{ and}$$

$\mathrm{F1}_{\mathrm{MaA}}$ their harmonic mean. This macro-averaged F1 was used to rank methods and the p value from the *R 3.2.4* implementation of the *Wilcoxon signed-rank test* [23] with the significance level of 0.05 was used to determine if the median performance of the higher-ranked method was significantly better than this value for the lower-ranked method. The ranking was based on $\mathrm{F1}_{\mathrm{MaA}}$ on the entire test set, p was computed for the paired comparisons from the best and second-best method to the second-worst and worst method. The 14 validation words and 27 test words annotated with a class not present in the training set were excluded from the evaluation.

This year we were aiming to lower the entry barrier and encourage novelty in Task 1 by providing participants with not only an evaluation script (i.e., the *CoNLL 2000 Shared Task on Chunking*[5]) but also processing code for IE, together with all its intermediate and final outputs from our previous paper [10]. This organizers' method called *NICTA* served as one of the four *baseline methods*. The other three baselines were *Random* (i.e., classifying each word by selecting one out of the 36 classes randomly[6]), *NA* (i.e., classifying each word as belonging to the dominant training class of NA), and *Majority* (i.e., classifying each word as belonging to the majority training class of Future_Goal/TaskToBeCompleted/ExpectedOutcome).

Task 2. Teams could submit up to two runs for each of the four tasks. For the QUAERO corpus, a separate evaluation was carried out for each type of text supplied (MEDLINE and EMEA): 1/for plain entity recognition, raw text was supplied to participants who had to submit entity annotations comprising entity offsets and entity types. 2/for normalized entity recognition, raw text was supplied to participants who had to submit entity annotations comprising entity offsets, entity types, and entity normalization (UMLS CUIs). 3/for entity normalization, raw text and plain entity annotations were supplied to participants who had to submit entity normalization (UMLS CUIs). 4/for ICD10 coding, raw text and 9 types of metadata (including patient age, patient gender, location of

---

[5] See http://www.cnts.ua.ac.be/conll2000/chunking/, last accessed on 25 May 2016.
[6] using https://www.random.org/, last accessed on 25 May 2016.

death...) were supplied to participants who had to submit a list of ICD10 codes associated to each line of text. For each of the subtasks, the system output on the unseen test set was compared to the gold standard annotations and precision recall and F-measure was computed.

After submitting their result files for the IE challenges, participating teams had one extra week to submit the system used to produce them, or a remote access to the system, along with instructions on how to install and operate the system. The organizers are carrying out the attempts to replicate the participants runs at the time of writing this paper.

Task 3. Teams could submit up to three runs for the ad-hoc search on the English queries, an additional three runs for the query variations challenge on the English queries, and an additional three runs for each of the multilingual query languages. Teams were required to number runs such as that run 1 was a baseline run for the team; other runs were numbered from 2 to 3, with lower number indicating higher priority for selection of documents to contribute to the assessment pool (i.e., run 2 was considered of higher priority than run 3). The organisers also generated baseline runs and a set of benchmark systems using popular retrieval models implemented in Terrier and Indri. See the IR Task overview paper [24] for details.

System evaluation was conducted using precision at 10 (p@10) and nor-malised discounted cumulative gain [25] at 10 (nDCG@10) as the primary and secondary measures, respectively. Precision was computed using the binary rel-evance assessments; nDCG was computed using the graded relevance assess-ments. A separate evaluation was conducted using the multidimensional rele-vance assessments (topical relevance, understandability and trustworthtiveness) following the methods in [22]. For all runs, Rank biased precision (RBP)[7] was computed along with the multidimensional modifications of RBP, namely uRBP (using binary understandability assessments), uRBPgr (using graded under-standability assessments), u+tRBP (using binary understandability and trust-worthtiveness assessments). More details on this multidimensional evaluation are provided in the Task overview paper [24].

Precision and nDCG were computed using `trec_eval`; while the multidimen-sional evaluation (comprising RBP) was performed using `ubire`[8].

3   Results

The number of people who registered their interest in CLEF eHealth tasks was 25, 33 and 58 respectively (and a total of 67 teams). In total, 20 teams with unique affiliations submitted to the shared tasks.

The number of teams who registered their interest in Task 1 was 25, and regardless of the difficulty of 36-class classification with only about 16, 200 train-ing and validation instances in total, 3 teams were successful in submitting 2

---

[7] The persistence parameter p in RBP was set to 0.8.
[8] https://github.com/ielab/ubire, [22].

methods (referred to as using the suffixes A and B) each by 1 May 2016. The training and validation instances were released by 30 October 2015 and the test instances on 15 April 2016. The team *TUC-MI* originated from Germany, *LQRZ* from the Netherlands, and *ECNU_ICA* from China.

The organizers' were excited to learn that all participant methods outperformed all baselines in Task 1. The top-2 methods had the $F1_{MaA}$ percentages of 38.2 (TUC-MI-B with $F1_{NA}$ of 80.7 %) and 37.4 (ECNU_ICA-A with $F1_{NA}$ of 80.2 % for NA), respectively. Their difference was not statistically significant but they were significantly better than the 34.5 % performance of the third-best method (LQRZ-B with $F1_{NA}$ of 81.3 %). In comparison, the NICTA baseline with its $F1_{MaA}$ percentage of 24.6 (and $F1_{NA}$ of 74.9 %) was significantly worse than the participant methods but significantly better than the Random, Majority, and NA baselines with the respective $F1_{MaA}$ percentages of 1.9, 0.1, and 0.0.

Task 2 received considerable interest with 33 registered participants. However, only 7 teams submitted runs, including four teams from France (ECSTRA-INSERM, LIMSI, LITL and SIBM), one team from the Netherlands (Erasmus), one team from Spain (UPF) and one team from Switzerland (BITEM). Three teams also submitted systems. The training datasets were released by mid February 2016 and the test datasets by early May 2016. For the plain entity recognition task, five teams submitted a total of 9 runs for each of the corpora, EMEA and MEDLINE (18 runs in total). For the normalized entity recognition task, three teams submitted a total of 5 runs for each of the corpora (10 runs in total). For the normalization task, two teams submitted a total of 3 runs for each of the corpora (6 runs in total). For the coding task, five teams submitted a total of 7 runs. The best performance was achieved with an F-measure of 0.702 on the EMEA corpus and 0.651 on the MEDLINE corpus for plain entity recognition, an F-measure of 0.529 on the EMEA corpus and 0.474 on the MEDLINE corpus for normalized entity recognition, an F-measure of 0.524 on the EMEA corpus and 0.552 on the MEDLINE corpus for normalization and an F-measure of 0.848 on the CépiDC corpus for the coding task. Of note, the technical problems experienced by many teams last year seem resolved this year, and results are representative of the methods developed by the participants. Interestingly, not all teams working with the QUAERO and CépiDC corpus used the same system for both datasets.

A total of 58 teams registered to the IR Task (Task 3) and 10 submitted runs; details of run submissions for the participating teams are provided in Table 1.

Relevance assessment for the IR Task (Task 3) is still ongoing at the time of writing this overview paper. Unlike previous years, in fact, this year we aimed to assess a larger set of documents (approximately 25,000 documents) to improve the robustness of our evaluation and the reusability of the collection. As expected, we found that query variations introduced variability across the assessment pool, also thus enlarging the size of candidate documents to be considered for assessment.

Table 1. Number of runs submitted to the IR task (Task 3) by the 10 participating groups. * Team CUNI submitted runs for the languages CS, DE, ES (created by the team and not distributed within the task), FR, HU, PL, SV; they also submitted 3 additional runs for each language in the multilingual task considering dependencies among query variations. ** Team ECNU submitted 2 runs for each of the following languages only: CS, FR, PL, SV.

	# Runs Submitted		
Team	Task 1	Task 2	Task 3
CUNI	2	2	3*
ECNU	3	3	2**
GUIR	3	3	-
InfoLab	3	3	-
KDEIR	3	2	-
KISTI	3	-	-
MayoNLPTeam	3	-	-
MRIM	3	-	-
ub_botswana	3	-	-
WHUIRGroup	3	3	-
# Runs Submitted	29	16	5

4   Conclusions

In this paper we provided an overview of the CLEF eHealth 2016 evaluation lab. This fourth edition of CLEF eHealth offered three tasks. Task 1 was a new challenge on handover information extraction related to Australian nursing shift changes, which extended the 2015 task of converting verbal nursing handover to written free-text records. Task 2 continued 2015's French information extraction challenge, this year offering a new clinical text dataset and a new challenge on causes of death extraction from French death reports. Task 3 offered another multilingual patient-centred information retrieval challenge, using a new web crawl (ClueWeb12 B13), new query generation approach through online forums and new evaluation criteria considering query variation. Once again this year, the lab attracted much interest with 20 teams submitting runs to the shared tasks. Given the significance of the tasks, all test collections and resources associated with the lab have been made available to the wider research community through our CLEF eHealth website[9].

Acknowledgements. The CLEF eHealth 2016 evaluation lab has been supported in part by (in alphabetical order) the ANR, the French National Research Agency, under grant CABeRneT ANR-13-JS02-0009-01; CLEF Initiative; ESF ELIAS network program Horizon 2020 program (H2020-ICT-2014-1) under grant agreement 644753

---

[9] https://sites.google.com/site/clefehealth/.

(KCONNECT); Microsoft Azure for Research Award CRM:0518649; NICTA, funded by the Australian Government through the Department of Communications and the Australian Research Council through the Information and Communications Technology (ICT) Centre of Excellence Program; and PhysioNetWorks Workspaces.

We express our gratitude to Maricel Angel, Registered Nurse at NICTA, for helping us to create the Task 1 dataset, using the Protégé resource, which is supported by grant GM10331601 from the National Institute of General Medical Sciences of the United States National Institutes of Health. We are also thankful to the people involved in the query creation and relevance assessment exercise. Last but not least, we gratefully acknowledge the participating teams' hard work. We thank them for their submissions and interest in the lab.

References

1. Suominen, H., et al.: Overview of the ShARe/CLEF eHealth evaluation lab 2013. In: Forner, P., Müller, H., Paredes, R., Rosso, P., Stein, B. (eds.) CLEF 2013. LNCS, vol. 8138, pp. 212–231. Springer, Heidelberg (2013)
2. Kelly, L., et al.: Overview of the ShARe/CLEF eHealth evaluation lab 2014. In: Kanoulas, E., Lupu, M., Clough, P., Sanderson, M., Hall, M., Hanbury, A., Toms, E. (eds.) CLEF 2014. LNCS, vol. 8685, pp. 172–191. Springer, Heidelberg (2014)
3. Goeuriot, L., Kelly, L., Suominen, H., Hanlen, L., Névéol, A., Grouin, C., Palotti, J., Zuccon, G.: Overview of the CLEF eHealth evaluation lab 2015. In: Mothe, J., Savoy, J., Kamps, J., Pinel-Sauvagnat, K., Jones, G.J.F., SanJuan, E., Cappellato, L., Ferro, N. (eds.) CLEF 2015. LNCS, vol. 9283, pp. 429–443. Springer, Heidelberg (2015)
4. Suominen, H., Hanlen, L., Goeuriot, L., Kelly, L., Jones, G.J.: Task 1a of the CLEF eHealth evaluation lab 2015: Clinical speech recognition. In: CLEF 2015 Online Working Notes, CEUR-WS (2015)
5. Suominen, H., Johnson, M., Zhou, L., Sanchez, P., Sirel, R., Basilakis, J., Hanlen, L., Estival, D., Dawson, L., Kelly, B.: Capturing patient information at nursing shift changes: methodological evaluation of speech recognition and information extraction. J. Am. Med. Inform. Assoc. (JAMIA) **22**(e1), e48–e66 (2015)
6. Névéol, A., Grouin, C., Leixa, J., Rosset, S., Zweigenbaum, P.: The QUAERO French medical corpus: a resource for medical entity recognition and normalization. In: Proceeding of BioTextMining Work, pp. 24–30 (2014)
7. Névéol, A., Grouin, C., Tannier, X., Hamon, T., Kelly, L., Goeuriot, L., Zweigenbaum, P.: CLEF eHealth evaluation lab 2015 task 1b: clinical named entity recognition. In: CLEF 2015 Online Working Notes, CEUR-WS (2015)
8. Goeuriot, L., Kelly, L., Li, W., Palotti, J., Pecina, P., Zuccon, G., Hanbury, A., Jones, G.J., Mueller, H.: ShARe/CLEF eHealth Evaluation Lab 2014, Task 3: user-centred health information retrieval. In: CLEF 2014 Evaluation Labs and Workshop: Online Working Notes, Sheffield (2014)
9. Palotti, J., Zuccon, G., Goeuriot, L., Kelly, L., Hanburyn, A., Jones, G.J., Lupu, M., Pecina, P.: CLEF eHealth evaluation lab 2015, task 2: Retrieving information about medical symptoms. In: CLEF 2015 Online Working Notes, CEUR-WS (2015)
10. Suominen, H., Zhou, L., Hanlen, L., Ferraro, G.: Benchmarking clinical speech recognition and information extraction: new data, methods and evaluations. JMIR Med. Informatics **3**, e19 (2015)

11. Suominen, H., Zhou, L., Goeuriot, L., Kelly, L.: Task 1 of the CLEF eHealth evaluation lab 2016: Handover information extraction. In: CLEF 2016 Evaluation Labs and Workshop: Online Working Notes, CEUR-WS (2016)

12. Hanbury, A., Müller, H.: Khresmoi - multimodal multilingual medical information search. In: MIE village of the future (2012)

13. Goeuriot, L., Jones, G.J., Kelly, L., Leveling, J., Hanbury, A., Müller, H., Salantera, S., Suominen, H., Zuccon, G.: Share, CLEF eHealth evaluation lab 2013, task 3: Information retrieval to address patients' questions when reading clinical reports. CLEF: Online Working Notes **8138** (2013)

14. Macdonald, C., McCreadie, R., Santos, R.L., Ounis, I.: From puppy to maturity: experiences in developing terrier. In: Proceding of OSIR at SIGIR, pp. 60–63 (2012)

15. Strohman, T., Metzler, D., Turtle, H., Croft, W.B.: Indri: a language model-based search engine for complex queries. In: Proceedings of the International Conference on Intelligent Analysis. vol. 2, pp. 2–6, Citeseer (2005)

16. Cormack, G.V., Smucker, M.D., Clarke, C.L.: Efficient and effective spam filtering and re-ranking for large web datasets. Inform. Retrieval **14**, 441–465 (2011)

17. Hiemstra, D., Hauff, C.: Mirex: Mapreduce information retrieval experiments. arXiv preprint arXiv:1004.4489 (2010)

18. Bodenreider, O., McCray, A.T.: Exploring semantic groups through visual approaches. J. Biomed. Inform. **36**, 414–432 (2003)

19. Bailey, P., Moffat, A., Scholer, F., Thomas, P.: User Variability and IR System Evaluation. In: Proceeding of SIGIR (2015)

20. Azzopardi, L.: Query side evaluation: an empirical analysis of effectiveness and effort. In: Proceeding of SIGIR (2009)

21. Zuccon, G., Koopman, B.: Integrating understandability in the evaluation of consumer health search engines. In: Medical Information Retrieval Workshop at SIGIR 2014, p. 32 (2014)

22. Zuccon, G.: Understandability biased evaluation for information retrieval. In: Advances in Information Retrieval, pp. 280–292 (2016)

23. Wilcoxon, F.: Individual comparisons by ranking methods. Biometrics Bull. **1**, 80–83 (1945)

24. Zuccon, G., Palotti, J., Goeuriot, L., Kelly, L., Lupu, M., Pecina, P., Mueller, H., Budaher, J., Deacon, A.: The IR Task at the CLEF eHealth evaluation lab 2016: user-centred health information retrieval. In: CLEF 2016 Evaluation Labs and Workshop: Online Working Notes, CEUR-WS (2016)

25. Järvelin, K., Kekäläinen, J.: Cumulated gain-based evaluation of IR techniques. ACM Trans. Inform. Syst. **20**, 422–446 (2002)

General Overview of ImageCLEF at the CLEF 2016 Labs

Mauricio Villegas[1]([✉]), Henning Müller[2], Alba García Seco de Herrera[3],
Roger Schaer[2], Stefano Bromuri[4], Andrew Gilbert[5], Luca Piras[6],
Josiah Wang[7], Fei Yan[5], Arnau Ramisa[8], Emmanuel Dellandrea[9],
Robert Gaizauskas[7], Krystian Mikolajczyk[10], Joan Puigcerver[1],
Alejandro H. Toselli[1], Joan-Andreu Sánchez[1], and Enrique Vidal[1]

[1] Universitat Politècnica de València, Valencia, Spain
mauvilsa@prhlt.upv.es
[2] University of Applied Sciences Western Switzerland (HES-SO),
Sierre, Switzerland
[3] National Library of Medicine, Bethesda, USA
[4] Open University of the Netherlands, Heerlen, The Netherlands
[5] University of Surrey, Guildford, UK
[6] University of Cagliari, Cagliari, Italy
[7] University of Sheffield, Sheffield, UK
[8] Institut de Robòtica i Informàtica Industrial (UPC-CSIC), Barcelona, Spain
[9] École Centrale de Lyon, Écully, France
[10] Imperial College London, London, UK

Abstract. This paper presents an overview of the ImageCLEF 2016 evaluation campaign, an event that was organized as part of the CLEF (Conference and Labs of the Evaluation Forum) labs 2016. ImageCLEF is an ongoing initiative that promotes the evaluation of technologies for annotation, indexing and retrieval for providing information access to collections of images in various usage scenarios and domains. In 2016, the 14th edition of ImageCLEF, three main tasks were proposed: (1) identification, multi-label classification and separation of compound figures from biomedical literature; (2) automatic annotation of general web images; and (3) retrieval from collections of scanned handwritten documents. The handwritten retrieval task was the only completely novel task this year, although the other two tasks introduced several modifications to keep the proposed tasks challenging.

1 Introduction

With the ongoing proliferation of increasingly cheaper devices to capture, amongst others, visual information by means of digital cameras, developing technologies for the storage of this ever growing body of information and providing means to access these huge databases has been and will be an important requirement. As part of this development, it is important to organise campaigns for evaluating the emerging problems and for comparing the proposed techniques for solving the problems based on the exact same scenario in a reproducible way.

© Springer International Publishing Switzerland 2016
N. Fuhr et al. (Eds.): CLEF 2016, LNCS 9822, pp. 267–285, 2016.
DOI: 10.1007/978-3-319-44564-9_25

Motivated by this, ImageCLEF has for many years been an ongoing initiative that aims at evaluating multilingual or language independent annotation and retrieval of images [20]. The main goal of ImageCLEF is to support the advancement of the field of visual media analysis, classification, annotation, indexing and retrieval, by proposing novel challenges and developing the necessary infrastructure for the evaluation of visual systems operating in different contexts and providing reusable resources for benchmarking. Many research groups have participated over the years in its evaluation campaigns and even more have acquired its datasets for experimentation. The impact of ImageCLEF can also be seen by its significant scholarly impact indicated by the substantial numbers of its publications and their received citations [30].

There are other evaluation initiatives that have had a close relation with ImageCLEF. LifeCLEF [16] was formerly an ImageCLEF task. However, due to the need to assess technologies for automated identification and understanding of living organisms using data not only restricted to images, but also videos and sound, it was decided to be organised independently from ImageCLEF. Other CLEF labs linked to ImageCLEF, in particular the medical task, are: CLEFeHealth [11] that deals with processing methods and resources to enrich difficult-to-understand eHealth text and the BioASQ [2] tasks from the Question Answering lab that targets biomedical semantic indexing and question answering. Due to their medical topic, the organisation is coordinated in close collaboration with ImageCLEF. In fact, at CLEF 2015 there was a joint session on the "Challenges and synergies in the evaluation of health IR/IE".

This paper presents a general overview of the ImageCLEF 2016 evaluation campaign[1], which as usual was an event organised as part of the CLEF labs[2]. Section 2 presents a general description of the 2016 edition of ImageCLEF, commenting about the overall organisation and participation in the lab. Followed by this are sections dedicated to the three main tasks that were organised this year, Sect. 3 for the medical task that deals mainly with compound figures from biomedical literature and how to make their visual content accessible, Sect. 4 for the image annotation task, and Sect. 5 for the new task introduced this year targeted at the retrieval from scanned handwritten document collections. These sections are only short summaries of the tasks. For the full details and complete results, the readers should refer to the the corresponding task overview papers [9,15,36]. The final section of this paper concludes by giving an overall discussion, and pointing towards the challenges ahead and possible new directions for future research.

2   Overview of Tasks and Participation

The 2016 edition of ImageCLEF consisted of three main tasks that covered challenges in diverse fields and usage scenarios. In 2015 [31] all the tasks addressed

---

[1] http://imageclef.org/2016/.

[2] http://clef2016.clef-initiative.eu/.

topics related to processing the images in order to automatically assign meta-data to them, not directly evaluating retrieval, but techniques that produce valuable annotations that can be used for subsequent image database indexing, mining or analysis. This year there was also a new task that evaluated retrieval of small segments from images containing handwritten text. The three tasks organised were the following:

- **Medical Classification:** addresses the identification, multi-label classification, caption prediction and separation of compound figures commonly found in the biomedical literature.
- **Image Annotation:** aims at developing systems for automatic annotation of concepts, their localization within the image, and generation of sentences describing the image content in a natural language. A pilot task on text illustration is also introduced in this edition.
- **Handwritten Scanned Document Retrieval:** targets the challenge of retrieval of page segments in scanned handwritten documents for multi-word textual queries.

The medical and annotation tasks were continuations from previous years, however, both introduced changes. In comparison to 2015, the medical task provided a larger amount of data with more training data and also introduced a new subtask of which the objective was the prediction of figure captions given the image, so providing 5 subtasks. The photo annotation task was also changed, having 4 subtasks this year, two of which were continued from last year and two new ones: selection of concepts for inclusion in generated image descriptions, and finding the best image to illustrate a given text snippet.

In order to participate in the evaluation campaign, the groups first had to register either on the CLEF website or from the ImageCLEF website. To actually get access to the datasets, the participants were required to submit a signed End User Agreement (EUA) by email. Table 1 presents a table that summarize the participation in ImageCLEF 2016, including the number of registrations and number of signed EUAs, indicated both per task and for the overall lab. The table also shows the number of groups that submitted results (a.k.a. runs) and the ones that submitted a working notes paper describing the techniques used.

The number of registrations could be interpreted as the initial interest that the community has for the evaluation. However, it is a bit misleading because several people from the same institution might register, even though in the end they count as a single group participation. The EUA explicitly requires all groups that get access to the data to participate. Unfortunately, the percentage of groups that submit results is often relatively small. Nevertheless, as observed in studies of scholarly impact [30], in subsequent years the datasets and challenges provided by ImageCLEF do get used quite often, which in part is due to the researchers that for some reason were unable to participate in the original event.

Although for the 2015 edition of ImageCLEF the participation increased considerably with respect to previous years, this was no longer the case for the current 2016 edition. This could be in part due to a CLEF restriction that required to reduce the number of tasks from four to three. However, the number

Table 1. Key figures of participation in ImageCLEF 2016.

Task	Online registrations	Signed EUA	Groups that subm. results	Submitted working notes
Medical classification	46	24	8	5
Image annotation	53	28	7	7
Handwritten retrieval	48	24	4	3
Overall[a]	98	54	19	15

[a]Unique groups. None of the groups participated in multiple tasks.

of registrations and signed EUAs for the continuing tasks also decreased. The new handwritten retrieval task had quite a large number or registrations and EUAs, comparable to the other tasks. In fact, 13 groups signed the EUA only for this task, giving the impression that there is a considerable interest in this area.

The following three sections are dedicated to each of the tasks. Only a short overview is reported, including general objectives, description of the tasks and datasets and a short summary of the results.

3 The Medical Task

An estimated over 40 % of the figures in the medical literature in PubMed Central are compound figures (images consisting of several subfigures) [13] like the images in Fig. 1. The compound figures in the articles are made available in a single block and are not separated into subfigures. The figures contain diverse information and often subfigures of various image types or modalities. Therefore, being able to separate and/or label each of the figures can help image retrieval systems to focus search and deliver focused results. For more details on this task please refer to the task overview paper [15].

3.1 Past Editions

Since 2004, ImageCLEF has run the medical task, ImageCLEFmed, to promote research on biomedical image classification and retrieval [17]. ImageCLEFmed has evolved strongly to adapt to the current challenges in the domain. The objective of ImageCLEFmed 2015 [14] and 2016 has been to work in large part on compound figures of the biomedical literature and to separate them if possible and/or attach to the subparts labels about the content. In 2013 a compound figure separation subtask was already introduced as a pilot task. A totally new subtask to predict image captions was introduced in 2016. The objective is also to create manually labelled resources on the many images in PubMed Central.

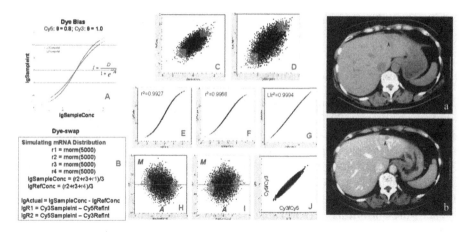

Fig. 1. Examples of compound figures in the biomedical literature.

3.2   Objectives and Subtasks for the 2016 Edition

The novelties introduced in the tasks for 2016 are the distribution of a larger number of compound figures compared to the previous years and the introduction of the caption prediction subtask. Thus, there were five types of subtasks in 2016:

- **Compound figure detection:** This subtask was first introduced in 2015. Compound figure identification is a required first step to separate compound figures from images with a single content. Therefore, the goal of this subtask is to identify whether a figure is a compound figure or not. The subtask makes training data available containing compound and non compound figures from the biomedical literature.
- **Multi-label classification:** This subtask was first introduced in 2015. Characterization of the content in compound figures is difficult, as they may contain subfigures from various imaging modalities or image types. This subtask aims to label each compound figure with each of the image types (of the 30 classes of a defined hierarchy [21]) of the subfigures contained without knowing where the separation lines are.
- **Figure separation:** This subtask was first introduced in 2013. The subtask makes available training data with separation labels of the figures and then a test data set where the labels are made available after the submission of the results for the evaluation. Evaluation is not based on strict placement of separation lines but on proximity to separation lines.
- **Subfigure classification:** This subtask was first introduced in 2015 but similar to the modality classification subtask organized in 2011–2013. This subtask aims to classify images into the 30 classes of the image type hierarchy. The images are the subfigures extracted from the compound figures distributed for the multi-label subtask.
- **Caption prediction:** This is a new subtask that was introduced in 2016. The subtask aims to evaluate algorithms that can predict captions for the diagnostic

images provided as training and test set. The performance is measured based on word similarity between predictions and real captions.

3.3 Participation and Results

Table 1 shows the participation in this task. In 2016, there were slightly fewer registrations than in 2015, however the same number of groups submitted runs and the total number of submitted runs increased to 69.

Three groups participated in the compound figure detection subtask. The DUTIR group obtained the best results achieving a 92.7% of accuracy (see Table 2). Multi-label classification had two participants BMET and MLKD. BMET has achieved the best combined result of an Hamming loss of 1.35% and an f-measure of 32% (see Table 3). Only one participant, UDEL CIS [26], submitted 10 runs to the figure separation subtask with an accuracy of 84.43% (see Table 4). The subfigure classification subtask was the most popular with 42 runs submitted. BCSG [18] achieved the best results with an accuracy of 88.43%, a good increase compared to past years (Table 5). Unfortunately, there were no participants in the caption prediction task, however the data are made available and will hopefully be used in the future. A more detailed analysis of the medical classification tasks including tables with results of all runs is presented in the task overview paper of the working notes [15].

Table 2. Results of the best runs of the compound figure detection task.

Group	Run	Run type	Accuracy
DUTIR	CFD_DUTIR_Mixed_AVG	Mixed	92.70
CIS UDEL	CFDRun10	Mixed	90.74
MLKD	CFD2	Textual	88.13
DUTIR	CFD_DUTIR_Visual_CNNs	Visual	92.01

Table 3. Best runs for the multi-label classification task.

Group	Run	Hamming loss	F-measure
BMET	1462019299651__MLC-BMET-multiclass-test-max-all	0.0131	0.295
BMET	1462019365690__MLC-BMET-multiclass-test-prob-max-all	0.0135	0.32
MLKD	1462024417416__MLC2	0.0294	0.32

Table 4. Best runs of the figure separation task.

Run	Group	Run type	Accuracy
CIS UDEL	FS.run9	Visual	84.43

Table 5. Results of the best runs of the subfigure classification task.

Run	Group	Run type	Accuracy
BCSG	SC_BCSG_run10_Ensemble_Vote	Mixed	88.43
BCSG	SC_BCSG_run2_Textual	Textual	72.22
MLKD	SC2	Textual	58.37
BCSG	SC_BCSG_run8_DeCAF_ResNet-152_PseudoInverse	Visual	85.38
BCSG	SC_BCSG_run1_Visual	Visual	84.46
IPL	SC_enriched_GBOC_1x1_256_RGB_Phow_Default_1500_EarlyFusion	Visual	84.01
BMET	SC-BMET-subfig-test-prob-sum	Visual	77.55
CIS UDEL	SCRun1	Visual	72.46
NWPU	sc.run2	Visual	71.41
NOVASearch	SC_NOVASearch_cnn_10_dropout_vgglike.run	Visual	65.31

4   The Image Annotation Task

Since 2010, ImageCLEF has run a scalable concept image annotation task to promote research into the annotation of images using large-scale, noisy web page data in a weakly-supervised fashion. The main motivation for the task comes from the large number of mixed-modality data (e.g. web page text and images) which can be gathered cheaply from the Internet. Such data can potentially be exploited for image annotation. Thus, the main goal of the challenge is to encourage creative ideas of using such noisy web page data to improve various image annotation tasks: localizing different concepts depicted in images, generating descriptions of the scenes, and text-to-image retrieval.

4.1   Past Editions

The Scalable Concept Image Annotation task is a continuation of the general image annotation and retrieval task that has been held every year at ImageCLEF since its very first edition in 2003. In the first editions the focus was on retrieving images relevant to given (multilingual) queries from a web collection, while from 2006 onwards annotation tasks were also held, initially aimed at object detection, but more recently also covering semantic concepts. In its current form, the 2016 Scalable Concept Image Annotation task [9] is its fifth edition, having been organized in 2012 [32], 2013 [34], 2014 [33], and 2015 [8]. In the 2015 edition [8], the image annotation task was expanded to concept localization and also natural language sentential description of images. In the 2016 edition, we further introduced a text illustration 'teaser' task[3], to evaluate systems that analyze a text document and select the best illustration for the text from a large collection of images provided. As there is an increased interest in recent years in research combining text and vision, the new tasks introduced in both the 2015 and 2016 editions aim at further stimulating and encouraging multimodal research that use both text and visual data for image annotation and retrieval.

4.2   Objective and Task for the 2016 Edition

Image annotation has generally relied on training data that are manually, and thus reliably annotated. Annotating training data is an expensive and laborious endeavour that cannot easily scale, particularly as the number of concepts grow. However, images for any topic can be cheaply gathered from the Web along with associated text from the web pages that contain the images. The degree of relationship between these web images and the surrounding text varies greatly, i.e., the data are very noisy but overall these data contain useful information that can be exploited to develop annotation systems. Figure 2 shows examples of typical images found by querying search engines. As can be seen, the data obtained are useful and furthermore a wider variety of images is expected, not only photographs, but also drawings and computer generated graphics. Likewise there are other resources available that can help to determine the relationships between text and semantic concepts, such as dictionaries or ontologies.

The goal of this task is to evaluate different strategies to deal with the noisy data so that it can be reliably used for annotating, localizing, generating natural sentences and retrieving images from practically any topic. As in the 2015 task, external training data such as ImageNet ILSVRC2015 and MSCOCO are allowed and encouraged. However, in contrast to previous years, in this edition participants are expected to produce two sets of related results:

1. One approach using only externally trained data;
2. The second approach using both external data and the noisy web data of 510,123 web pages.

The motivation for this is to encourage participants to utilize the provided 510,123 web pages to improve the performance of systems trained using external data. This also distinguishes the ImageCLEF image annotation task from other similar image annotation challenges. This year's challenge comprises four subtasks:

---

[3] A second teaser task was actually also introduced, aimed at evaluating systems that identify the GPS coordinates of a text documents topic based on its text and image data. However, we had no participants for this task, and thus will not discuss the second teaser task in this paper.

(a) Images from a search query of "rainbow".

(b) Images from a search query of "sun".

Fig. 2. Examples of images retrieved by a commercial image search engine.

1. **Subtask 1: Image Annotation and Localization.** This subtask required participants to develop a system that receives as input an image and produces as output a prediction of which concepts are present in that image, selected from a predefined list of concepts, and where they are located within the image. Participants were requested to annotate and localize concepts in all 510,123 images.
2. **Subtask 2: Natural Language Caption Generation.** This subtask required the participants to develop a system that receives as input an image and produces as annotation a sentential, textual description of the visual content depicted in the image. Again, the test set is all 510,123 images.
3. **Subtask 3: Content Selection.** This subtask is related to Subtask 2, but is aimed primarily at those interested only in the natural language generation aspects of the task. It concentrates on the content selection phase of image description generation, i.e. which concepts should be selected to be mentioned in the corresponding description? Gold standard input (bounding boxes labelled with concepts) is provided for each of the 450 test images, and participants are expected to develop systems that predict the bounding box instances most likely to be mentioned in the corresponding image descriptions. Unlike the 2015 edition, participants were not required to generate complete sentences, but were only requested to provide a list of bounding box instances per image.
4. **Teaser task: Text Illustration.** The teaser task is designed to evaluate the performance of methods for text-to-image matching. Participants were asked to develop a system to analyse a given text document and find the best illustration for it from a set of all available images. The 510,123 dataset was split into 310,123 and 200,000 documents for training and testing respectively. At test time, participants were provided as input 180,000 text documents

extracted from a subset of the test documents as queries, and the goal is to select the best illustration for each text from the 200,000 test images.

The concepts this year (for the main subtasks) were retained from the 2015 edition. They were chosen to be visual objects that are localizable and that are useful for generating textual descriptions of visual content of images, including animated objects (person, dogs), inanimated objects (houses, cars) and scenes (city, mountains).

The noisy dataset used in this task was based on the 2015 edition with 500,000 documents. In the 2016 edition, the dataset was augmented with approximately 10,123 new image-document pairs from a subset of the BreakingNews dataset [24] which we developed, bringing the total number of documents to approximately 510,123. However, the subset of the data used for evaluating the three main subtasks remains the same, thus making the evaluation process comparable to the 2015 edition.

4.3   Participation and Results

In 2016, 7 groups participated in the task, submitting over 50 runs across the subtasks, and all 7 also produced working notes.

Four teams submitted results in Subtask 1 to produce localized predictions of image concepts on images. The subtask was evaluated using the PASCAL VOC style metric of intersection over union (IoU), the area of intersection between the foreground in the output segmentation and the foreground in the ground-truth segmentation, divided by the area of their union. The final results are presented in Table 6 in terms of mean average precision (MAP) over all images of all concepts, with both 0 % overlap (i.e. no localization) and 50 % overlap. The method of computing the performance was adjusted from the previous year, it now includes recall at a concept level, penalising approaches that only detect a few concepts (for example face parts) by averaging the precision overall concepts. This has reduced the overall scores, however if the approaches are analysed using last years evaluation method, the approach by CEA, has increased by around 8 %, indicating progress is continuing in this area. All approaches use a deep learning framework, including a number using the Deep Residual Convolutional Neural Network (ResNet) [12]. This explains and verifies much of the improvement over previous years. Face detection was fused into a number of approaches, however, in general, it was not found to provide much improvement in comparison to the improved neural network. A shortcoming of the challenge, however, is still present and with increasing performance is being a larger problem. There is a difficulty in ensuring that the ground truth has 100 % of the concepts labelled, thus allowing a recall measure to be used. The current crowdsourcing-based hand labelling of the ground truth is found to not achieve this and so a recall measure is not evaluated.

Two teams participated in Subtask 2 to generate natural language image descriptions. The subtask was evaluated using the Meteor evaluation metric [4]. Table 7 shows the Meteor scores for the best run for each participant. ICTisia

Table 6. Results for subtask 1: image annotation and localization.

Group	0 % overlap	50 % overlap
CEA	0.54	0.37
MRIM	0.25	0.14
CNRS	0.20	0.11
UAIC	0.003	0.002

achieved the better Meteor score of 0.1837 by fine-tuning on the state-of-the-art joint CNN-LSTM image captioning system. UAIC who also participated last year improved their score with 0.0934 compared to their performance from last year (0.0813), using a template-based approach to the problem.

Table 7. Results for subtask 2: natural language caption generation.

Team	Meteor
ICTisia	0.1837 ± 0.0847
UAIC	0.0934 ± 0.0249

Subtask 3 on content selection was also represented by two teams. The subtask was evaluated using the fine-grained metric proposed for last year's challenge [8,37]. Table 8 shows the F-score, Precision and Recall across 450 test images for each participant. DUTh achieved a higher F-score compared to the best performer from last year (0.5459 vs. 0.5310), by training SVM classifiers given various image descriptors. While UAIC did not significantly improve their F-score from last year, their recall score shows improvement.

Table 8. Results for subtask 3: content selection.

Team	Content selection score		
	Mean F	Mean P	Mean R
DUTh	0.5459 ± 0.1533	0.4451 ± 0.1695	0.7914 ± 0.1960
UAIC	0.4982 ± 0.1782	0.4597 ± 0.1553	0.5951 ± 0.2592

Table 9 shows the result of the pilot teaser task of text illustration. This task yielded interesting results. Bearing in mind the difficulty of the task (selecting one correct image from 200,000 images), CEA yielded a respectable score that is much better than chance performance, by mapping visual and textual modalities onto a common space and combining this with a semantic signature. INAOE on the other hand produced superior results with a bag-of-words approach. Both

Table 9. Results for teaser task: Text Illustration. The Recall@K are shown for each participant's best run, for a selected subset of the test set (10 K) and the full test set (180 K).

Team	Test set	Recall (%)					
		R@1	R@5	R@10	R@25	R@50	R@100
Random chance	-	0.00	0.00	0.01	0.01	0.03	0.05
CEA	10 K	0.02	0.05	0.11	0.26	0.46	0.80
	180 K	0.18	0.63	1.05	1.97	3.00	4.51
INAOE	10 K	37.05	73.12	78.06	79.55	79.74	79.77
	180 K	28.75	63.50	75.48	84.39	86.79	87.59

teams performed better on the larger 180 K test set than the more restricted 10 K test set (news domain), although INAOE performed better on the 10 K test set at smaller ranks (1–10).

For a more detailed analysis and discussion of the results, please refer to the task overview paper [9].

5   The Handwritten Retrieval Task

In recent years there has been an increasing interest in digitising the vast amounts of pre-digital age books and documents that exist throughout the world. Many of the emerging digitisation initiatives are for huge collections of handwritten documents, for which automatic recognition is not yet as mature as for printed text Optical Character Recognition (OCR). Thus, there is a need to develop reliable and scalable indexing techniques for manuscripts, targeting its particular challenges. Users for this technology could be libraries with fragile historical books, which for preservation are being scanned to make them available to the public without the risk of further deterioration. Apart from making the scanned pages available, there is also great interest in providing search facilities so that the people consulting these collections have information access tools that they are already accustomed to. The archaic solution is to manually transcribe and then use standard text retrieval technologies. However, this becomes too expensive for large collections. Alternatively, handwritten text recognition (HTR) techniques can be used for automatic indexing, which requires to transcribe only a small part of the document for training the models, or reuse models obtained from similar manuscripts, thus requiring the least human effort.

5.1   Previous Work

Traditionally the task of searching in handwritten documents has been known as *Keyword Spotting* (KWS), which actually can be seen as a particular case of image retrieval. The goal of KWS is to find all instances of a query in a given document. Among the noteworthy KWS paradigms aiming to fulfil this goal, two main kinds are distinguished: *Query by Example* (QbE) [1,7,10,38] and *Query by String* (QbS) [5,6,25,29]. While in QbE a query is specified by providing a text image to be searched for, in QbS, queries are directly specified as character strings. Likewise other distinctions considered are: training-based/free [5,38]; i.e., whether the KWS system needs or not to be trained on appropriate (annotated) images, and segmentation-based/free [7,38]; i.e., whether KWS is applied to full document (page) images or just to images of individual words (previously segmented from the original full images).

In the last years, several KWS contests on handwritten documents have been organised, mainly within the frame of conferences like ICFHR and ICDAR. These focused first on benchmarking QbE approaches [22][4,5], although lately, QbS approaches have also been considered in the ICDAR'15 [23][6] ICFHR'16[7].

Regarding literature about how to deal with hyphenated words, it is worth mentioning the approaches described in [19,27,28].

5.2   Objective and Task for the 2016 Edition

The task targeted the scenario of free text search in a set of handwritten document images, in which the user wants to find sections of the document for a given multiple word textual query. The result of the search is not pages, but smaller regions (such as a paragraph), which can even include the end of a page and start of the next. The system should also be able to handle words broken between lines and words that were not seen in the data used for training the recognition models. Figure 3 shows an example search result that illustrates the intended scenario.

Since the detection of paragraphs is in itself difficult, to simplify the problem somewhat the segments to retrieve were defined to be a concatenation of 6 consecutive lines (from top to bottom and left to right if there page had columns), ignoring the type of line it may be (e.g. title, inserted word, etc.). More precisely, the segments are defined by a sliding window that moves one line at a time (thus neighbouring segments overlap by 5 lines) traversing all the pages in the document, so there are segments that include lines at the end of a page and at the beginning of the next.

The queries were one or more words that had to be searched for in the collection, and a segment is considered relevant if all the query words appear in the given order. The participants were expected to submit for each query, only for the segments considered relevant, a relevance score and the bounding boxes of all appearances of the query words within the segment irrespectively if it was or not an instance of the word that made the segment relevant. The queries were selected such that key challenges were included: words broken between lines,

---

[4] http://users.iit.demokritos.gr/~bgat/H-WSCO2013
[5] http://vc.ee.duth.gr/H-KWS2014
[6] http://transcriptorium.eu/~icdar15kws
[7] https://www.prhlt.upv.es/contests/icfhr2016-kws

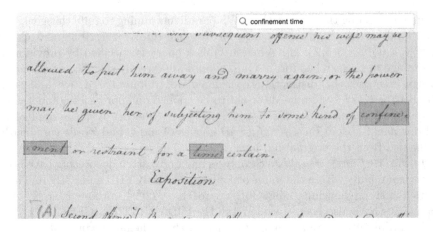

Fig. 3. Example of a page segment search result in a handwritten document.

queries with words not seen in the training data, queries with repeated words, and queries with zero relevant results.

The dataset used in the task was a subset of pages from unpublished manuscripts written by the philosopher and reformer, Jeremy Bentham, that were digitised and transcribed under the Transcribe Bentham project [3]. All of the provided data for the task and scripts for computing the evaluation measures and the baseline system are publicly available and citable [35].

These kinds of evaluations related to handwriting recognition are normally organised in conjunction with more specialised conferences such as ICDAR and ICFHR. The reason for organising it at CLEF was that most of the research done up to now in this area does not address all challenges from the perspective of information retrieval. So the objective was to disseminate these problems to experts from the information retrieval community so that they get more involved. Thus, the task was designed to allow easy participation from different research communities by providing prepared data for each, with the aim of having synergies between these communities, and providing different ideas and solutions to the problems being addressed. The original page images were provided, so that the all parts of the task could be addressed, including extraction of lines, preprocessing of the images, training of recognition models, decoding, indexing and retrieval. Also recognition results for a baseline system were provided in plain text so that groups working on text retrieval could participate without worrying about images. Finally the training set included bounding boxes automatically obtained for all of the words, so that groups working on query-by-example keyword spotting could participate, although with the twist that the example images could be incorrectly segmented, so a technique to select the among the available example words would be required.

For further details on the task, results and data please refer to the overview paper [36] and/or the dataset repository [35].

5.3   Participation and Results

There was considerable interest in the task. Over twenty groups signed the EUA, and based on the data server logs, the test queries (only useful if there was an intention of submitting results) were downloaded from 9 countries: Germany, India, Israel, Japan, Mexico, Morocco, Tunisia, Turkey and USA. In the end, only four groups submitted results and three of them submitted a working notes paper describing their system.

Table 10 presents for each group that participated, the best result both for the development and test sets, and including only the segment based performance measures, i.e., does not consider the predicted word bounding boxes. The assessment uses the Average Precision (AP) and Normalized Discounted Cumulative Gain (NDCG), measured both globally or as the mean (preceded by a lower-case m) for all evaluated queries.

Each group followed quite a different approaches. The IIIT team participated as query by example, thus their results are not directly comparable with any of the others. Two teams, MayoBMI and UAEMex, based their work on the provided recognition results, although considered only the 1-best, thus being limited in comparison to the baseline system. Furthermore, the test set was considerably more difficult than the development and the baseline system performed poorly, so their results were also affected by this. Two groups, CITlab and MayoBMI, dealt with the broken words, though both based it on the detection of hyphenation symbols, even thought there could be broken words without any hyphenation. The MayoBMI did not finally submit results with hyphenation detection since they considered the performance insufficient. Only the CITlab group tackled the complete problem, training recognition models and retrieving broken words and words unseen in training. They also used Recurrent Neural Networks, which is the current state of the art in handwriting recognition, which clearly reflects in the obtained results.

For the complete results, including specific analysis of the words unseen in training and the broken words, the reader is invited to read the task specific overview paper [36].

Table 10. Summary of results (in %) for the handwritten retrieval task.

Group	AP		mAP		NDCG		mNDCG	
	Dev.	Test	Dev.	Test	Dev.	Test	Dev.	Test
CITlab	95.0	47.1	89.8	39.9	96.8	62.7	90.9	41.7
IIIT	41.5	3.4	22.5	3.4	49.4	8.8	26.1	3.9
MayoBMI	25.8	2.5	23.4	2.9	33.1	7.0	26.6	3.6
UAEMex	61.1	0.3	38.5	0.4	69.1	1.2	41.7	0.4
Baseline	74.2	14.4	49.9	8.1	80.1	27.5	51.7	9.4

6   Conclusions

This paper presents a general overview of the activities and outcomes of the 2016 edition of the ImageCLEF evaluation campaign. Three main tasks were organised covering challenges in: identification, multi-label classification, caption prediction and separation of compound figures from biomedical literature; automatic concept annotation, localization, sentence description generation and retrieval of web images; and retrieval of page segments in handwritten documents.

The participation was similar to the 2013 and 2014 editions, although it decreased with respect to the 2015 edition, in which the participation was outstandingly high. Nineteen groups submitted results and fifteen of them provided a working notes paper describing their work. Even though the participation was not as good as hoped, the obtained results are interesting and useful.

Several new challenges in the medical tasks were provided focusing on the challenges dealing with compound figures. Many groups now employed deep learning algorithms or mixed handcrafted approaches with deep learning. Results obtained were very good in several of the tasks showing a general increase in the quality of the algorithms.

The image annotation challenges indicate the mainstream acceptance of deep neural networks, with much of the improvement in subtask 1 being provided by improved neural networks. Several groups used a face detection to improve results, however the text analysis for image annotation has in general been dropped at the moment, due to the neural network improvements. In subtask 2, one team also utilised the state-of-the-art neural network based image captioning system, while the others used a conventional template-based approach. Subtask 3 on the other hand relied on conventional techniques such as SVMs, due to the smaller development set. Interesting, a simple bag-of-words approach yielded significantly better results in the large-scale text illustration teaser task compared to neural network based techniques.

In the new task related to handwritten retrieval, very good results were obtained by one of the participants, in particular handling moderately well the novel challenge of retrieving words broken between lines. The other groups did not obtain optimal results, but tried interesting ideas for working with the automatic recognition of the images in order to index them. The produced dataset and proposed challenges surely will serve as basis for future works and evaluations.

ImageCLEF brought again a together an interesting mix of tasks and approaches and we are looking forward to the discussions at the workshop.

Acknowledgements. The general coordination and the handwritten retrieval task have been supported by the European Union (EU) Horizon 2020 grant READ (Recognition and Enrichment of Archival Documents) (Ref: 674943), EU project HIMANIS (JPICH programme, Spanish grant Ref: PCIN-2015-068) and MINECO/FEDER, UE under project TIN2015-70924-C2-1-R. The image annotation task is co-organized by the VisualSense (ViSen) consortium under the ERA-NET CHIST-ERA D2K 2011 Programme, jointly supported by UK EPSRC Grants EP/K01904X/1 and EP/K019082/1, French ANR Grant ANR-12-CHRI-0002-04 and Spanish MINECO Grant PCIN-2013-047. This research was supported in part by the Intramural Research Program of the National Institutes of Health (NIH), National Library of Medicine (NLM), and Lister Hill National Center for Biomedical Communications (LHNCBC).

References

1. Aldavert, D., Rusinol, M., Toledo, R., Llados, J.: Integrating visual and textual cues for query-by-string word spotting. In: 2013 12th International Conference on Document Analysis and Recognition (ICDAR), pp. 511–515, August 2013
2. Balikas, G., Kosmopoulos, A., Krithara, A., Paliouras, G., Kakadiaris, I.A.: Results of the bioasq tasks of the question answering lab at CLEF 2015. In: Working Notes of CLEF 2015 - Conference and Labs of the Evaluation forum, Toulouse, France, 8–11 September 2015 (2015)
3. Causer, T., Wallace, V.: Building a volunteer community: results and findings from transcribe Bentham. Digit. Humanit. Q. **6**(2) (2012). http://www.digitalhumanities.org/dhq/vol/6/2/000125/000125.html
4. Denkowski, M., Lavie, A.: Meteor universal: language specific translation evaluation for any target language. In: Proceedings of the EACL 2014 Workshop on Statistical Machine Translation (2014)
5. Fischer, A., Keller, A., Frinken, V., Bunke, H.: Lexicon-free handwritten word spotting using character HMMs. Pattern Recognit. Lett. **33**(7), 934–942 (2012). Special Issue on Awards from (ICPR)
6. Frinken, V., Fischer, A., Bunke, H.: A novel word spotting algorithm using bidirectional long short-term memory neural networks. In: Schwenker, F., El Gayar, N. (eds.) Artificial Neural Networks in Pattern Recognition. LNCS, vol. 5998, pp. 185–196. Springer, Heidelberg (2010)
7. Gatos, B., Pratikakis, I.: Segmentation-free word spotting in historical printed documents. In: 10th International Conference on Document Analysis and Recognition (ICDAR 2009), pp. 271–275, July 2009
8. Gilbert, A., Piras, L., Wang, J., Yan, F., Dellandrea, E., Gaizauskas, R., Villegas, M., Mikolajczyk, K.: Overview of the ImageCLEF 2015 scalable image annotation, localization and sentence generation task. In: CLEF2015 Working Notes, CEUR Workshop Proceedings, CEUR-WS.org, Toulouse, France, 8–11 September 2015 (2015)
9. Gilbert, A., Piras, L., Wang, J., Yan, F., Ramisa, A., Dellandrea, E., Gaizauskas, R., Villegas, M., Mikolajczyk, K.: Overview of the ImageCLEF 2016 scalable concept image annotation task. In: CLEF2016 Working Notes, CEUR Workshop Proceedings, CEUR-WS.org, Évora, Portugal, 5–8 September 2016 (2016)
10. Giotis, A., Gerogiannis, D., Nikou, C.: Word spotting in handwritten text using contour-based models. In: 2014 14th International Conference on Frontiers in Handwriting Recognition (ICFHR), pp. 399–404, September 2014
11. Goeuriot, L., Kelly, L., Suominen, H., Hanlen, L., Névéol, A., Grouin, C., Palotti, J.R.M., Zuccon, G.: Overview of the CLEF ehealth evaluation lab 2015. In: Experimental IR Meets Multilinguality, Multimodality, and Interaction - 6th International Conference of the CLEF Association, CLEF 2015, Toulouse, France, 8–11 September 2015, Proceedings, pp. 429–443 (2015). doi:10.1007/978-3-319-24027-5_44
12. He, K., Zhang, X., Ren, S., Sun, J.: Delving deep into rectifiers: surpassing human-level performance on imagenet classification. In: The IEEE International Conference on Computer Vision (ICCV), December 2015

13. García Seco de Herrera, A., Kalpathy-Cramer, J., Demner Fushman, D., Antani, S., Müller, H.: Overview of the ImageCLEF 2013 medical tasks. In: Working Notes of CLEF 2013 (Cross Language Evaluation Forum) (2013). http://ceur-ws.org/Vol-1179/CLEF2013wn-ImageCLEF-SecoDeHerreraEt2013b.pdf

14. García Seco de Herrera, A., Müller, H., Bromuri, S.: Overview of the Image-CLEF 2015 medical classification task. In: Working Notes of CLEF 2015 (Cross Language Evaluation Forum), CEUR Workshop Proceedings, CEUR-WS.org, September 2015

15. García Seco de Herrera, A., Schaer, R., Bromuri, S., Müller, H.: Overview of the ImageCLEF 2016 medical task. In: CLEF2016 Working Notes, CEUR Workshop Proceedings, CEUR-WS.org, Évora, Portugal, 5–8 September 2016 (2016)

16. Joly, A., Goëau, H., Glotin, H., Spampinato, C., Bonnet, P., Vellinga, W., Planquè, R., Rauber, A., Palazzo, S., Fisher, B., Müller, H.: LifeCLEF 2015: multimedia life species identification challenges. In: Experimental IR Meets Multilinguality, Multimodality, and Interaction - 6th International Conference of the CLEF Association, CLEF 2015, Toulouse, France, 8–11 September 2015, Proceedings, pp. 462–483 (2015). doi:10.1007/978-3-319-24027-5_46

17. Kalpathy-Cramer, J., García Seco de Herrera, A., Demner-Fushman, D., Antani, S., Bedrick, S., Müller, H.: Evaluating performance of biomedical image retrieval systems an overview of the medical image retrieval task at ImageCLEF 2004–2014. Comput. Med. Imaging Graph. **39**, 55–61 (2015). doi:10.1016/j.compmedimag.2014.03.004

18. Koitka, S., Friedrich, C.M.: Traditional feature engineering and deep learning approaches at medical classification task of ImageCLEF 2016. In: CLEF2016 Working Notes, CEUR Workshop Proceedings, CEUR-WS.org, Évora, Portugal, 5–8 September 2016 (2016)

19. Lavrenko, V., Rath, T.M., Manmatha, R.: Holistic word recognition for handwritten historical documents. In: First International Workshop on Document Image Analysis for Libraries, Proceedings, pp. 278–287 (2004)

20. Müller, H., Clough, P., Deselaers, T., Caputo, B. (eds.): ImageCLEF: Experimental Evaluation in Visual Information Retrieval. The Information Retrieval Series, vol. 32. Springer, Heidelberg (2010). doi:10.1007/978-3-642-15181-1

21. Müller, H., Kalpathy-Cramer, J., Demner-Fushman, D., Antani, S.: Creating a classification of image types in the medical literature for visual categorization. In: SPIE Medical Imaging (2012)

22. Pratikakis, I., Zagoris, K., Gatos, B., Louloudis, G., Stamatopoulos, N.: ICFHR 2014 competition on handwritten keyword spotting (H-KWS 2014). In: 2014 14th International Conference on Frontiers in Handwriting Recognition (ICFHR), pp. 814–819, September 2014

23. Puigcerver, J., Toselli, A.H., Vidal, E.: ICDAR 2015 competition on keyword spotting for handwritten documents. In: 2015 13th International Conference on Document Analysis and Recognition (ICDAR), pp. 1176–1180, August 2015

24. Ramisa, A., Yan, F., Moreno-Noguer, F., Mikolajczyk, K.: Breakingnews: article annotation by image and text processing. CoRR abs/1603.07141 (2016). http://arxiv.org/abs/1603.07141

25. Rodríguez-Serrano, J.A., Perronnin, F.: Handwritten word-spotting using hidden Markov models and universal vocabularies. Pattern Recognit. **42**, 2106–2116 (2009)

26. Sorensen, S., Li, P., Kolagunda, A., Jiang, X., Wang, X., Shatkay, H., Kambhamettu, C.: UDEL CIS working notes in ImageCLEF 2016. In: CLEF2016 Working Notes, CEUR Workshop Proceedings, CEUR-WS.org, Évora, Portugal, 5–8 September 2016 (2016)

27. Snchez, J.A., Romero, V., Toselli, A.H., Vidal, E.: ICFHR 2014 competition on handwritten text recognition on transcriptorium datasets (HTRTS). In: 2014 14th International Conference on Frontiers in Handwriting Recognition (ICFHR), pp. 785–790, September 2014

28. Sánchez, J.A., Toselli, A.H., Romero, V., Vidal, E.: ICDAR 2015 competition HTRtS: Handwritten text recognition on the transcriptorium dataset. In: 2015 13th International Conference on Document Analysis and Recognition (ICDAR), pp. 1166–1170, August 2015

29. Toselli, A.H., Puigcerver, J., Vidal, E.: Context-aware lattice based filler approach for key word spotting in handwritten documents. In: 2015 13th International Conference on Document Analysis and Recognition (ICDAR), pp. 736–740, August 2015

30. Tsikrika, T., de Herrera, A.G.S., Müller, H.: Assessing the scholarly impact of ImageCLEF. In: Forner, P., Gonzalo, J., Kekäläinen, J., Lalmas, M., Rijke, M. (eds.) CLEF 2011. LNCS, vol. 6941, pp. 95–106. Springer, Heidelberg (2011). doi:10.1007/978-3-642-23708-9_12

31. Villegas, M., et al.: General overview of ImageCLEF at the CLEF 2015 labs. In: Mothe, J., et al. (eds.) CLEF 2015. LNCS, vol. 9283, pp. 441–461. Springer, Heidelberg (2015). doi:10.1007/978-3-319-24027-5_45

32. Villegas, M., Paredes, R.: Overview of the ImageCLEF 2012 scalable web image annotation task. In: Forner, P., Karlgren, J., Womser-Hacker, C. (eds.) CLEF 2012 Evaluation Labs and Workshop, Online Working Notes, Rome, Italy, 17–20 September 2012 (2012). http://ceur-ws.org/Vol-1178/CLEF2012wn-ImageCLEF-VillegasEt2012.pdf

33. Villegas, M., Paredes, R.: Overview of the ImageCLEF 2014 scalable concept image annotation task. In: CLEF2014 Working Notes, CEUR Workshop Proceedings, vol. 1180, pp. 308–328, CEUR-WS.org, Sheffield, UK, 15–18 September 2014 (2014). http://ceur-ws.org/Vol-1180/CLEF2014wn-Image-VillegasEt2014.pdf

34. Villegas, M., Paredes, R., Thomee, B.: Overview of the ImageCLEF 2013 scalable concept image annotation subtask. In: CLEF 2013 Evaluation Labs and Workshop, Online Working Notes, Valencia, Spain, 23–26 September 2013 (2013). http://ceur-ws.org/Vol-1179/CLEF2013wn-ImageCLEF-VillegasEt2013.pdf

35. Villegas, M., Puigcerver, J., Toselli, A.H.: ImageCLEF 2016 Bentham handwritten retrieval dataset (2016). doi:10.5281/zenodo.52994

36. Villegas, M., Puigcerver, J., Toselli, A.H., Sánchez, J.A., Vidal, E.: Overview of the ImageCLEF 2016 handwritten scanned document retrieval task. In: CLEF2016 Working Notes, CEUR Workshop Proceedings, CEUR-WS.org, Evora, Portugal, 5–8 September 2016 (2016)

37. Wang, J., Gaizauskas, R.: Generating image descriptions with gold standard visual inputs: motivation, evaluation and baselines. In: Proceedings of the 15th European Workshop on Natural Language Generation (ENLG), pp. 117–126. Association for Computational Linguistics, Brighton, UK (2015). http://www.aclweb.org/anthology/W15-4722

38. Zagoris, K., Ergina, K., Papamarkos, N.: Image retrieval systems based on compact shape descriptor and relevance feedback information. J. Vis. Commun. Image Represent. **22**(5), 378–390 (2011)

LifeCLEF 2016: Multimedia Life Species Identification Challenges

Alexis Joly[1]([✉]), Hervé Goëau[2], Hervé Glotin[3], Concetto Spampinato[4],
Pierre Bonnet[5], Willem-Pier Vellinga[6], Julien Champ[1], Robert Planqué[6],
Simone Palazzo[4], and Henning Müller[7]

[1] Inria, LIRMM, Montpellier, France
alexis.joly@inria.fr
[2] IRD, UMR AMAP, Montpellier, France
[3] AMU, CNRS LSIS, ENSAM, Univ. Toulon, IUF, Toulon, France
[4] University of Catania, Catania, Italy
[5] CIRAD, UMR AMAP, Montpellier, France
[6] Xeno-canto Foundation, Breskens, The Netherlands
[7] HES-SO, Sierre, Switzerland

Abstract. Using multimedia identification tools is considered as one of
the most promising solutions to help bridge the taxonomic gap and build
accurate knowledge of the identity, the geographic distribution and the
evolution of living species. Large and structured communities of nature
observers (e.g., iSpot, Xeno-canto, Tela Botanica, etc.) as well as big
monitoring equipment have actually started to produce outstanding collections of multimedia records. Unfortunately, the performance of the
state-of-the-art analysis techniques on such data is still not well understood and is far from reaching real world requirements. The LifeCLEF
lab proposes to evaluate these challenges around 3 tasks related to multimedia information retrieval and fine-grained classification problems in
3 domains. Each task is based on large volumes of real-world data and
the measured challenges are defined in collaboration with biologists and
environmental stakeholders to reflect realistic usage scenarios. For each
task, we report the methodology, the data sets as well as the results and
the main outcomes.

1 LifeCLEF Lab Overview

Identifying organisms is a key for accessing information related to the ecology
of species. This is an essential step in recording any specimen on earth to be
used in ecological studies. But unfortunately, this is difficult to achieve due to
the level of expertise necessary to correctly record and identify living organisms
(for instance plants are one of the most difficult group to identify with more
than 300.000 species). This *taxonomic gap* has been recognized since the Rio
Conference of 1992, as one of the major obstacles to the global implementation
of the Convention on Biological Diversity. Among the diversity of methods used
for species identification, Gaston and O'Neill [21] discussed in 2004 the potential

© Springer International Publishing Switzerland 2016
N. Fuhr et al. (Eds.): CLEF 2016, LNCS 9822, pp. 286–310, 2016.
DOI: 10.1007/978-3-319-44564-9_26

of automated approaches typically based on machine learning and multimedia data analysis methods. They suggested that, if the scientific community is able to (i) overcome the production of large training datasets, (ii) more precisely identify and evaluate the error rates, (iii) scale up automated approaches, and (iv) detect novel species, it will then be possible to initiate the development of a generic automated species identification system that could open up vistas of new opportunities for pure and applied work in biological and related fields.

Since the question raised in [21], "automated species identification: why not?", a lot of work has been done on the topic [1,9,17,20,38,46,62,68,69] and it is still attracting much research today, in particular on deep learning techniques. In parallel to the emergence of automated identification tools, large social networks dedicated to the production, sharing and identification of multimedia biodiversity records have increased in recent years. Some of the most active ones like iNaturalist[1], iSpot [58], Xeno-Canto[2] or Tela Botanica[3] (respectively initiated in the US for the two first and in Europe for the two last), federate tens of thousands of active members, producing hundreds of thousands of observations each year. Noticeably, the Pl@ntNet initiative was the first one attempting to combine the force of social networks with that of automated identification tools [38] through the release of a mobile application and collaborative validation tools. As a proof of their increasing reliability, most of these networks have started to contribute to global initiatives on biodiversity, such as the Global Biodiversity Information Facility (GBIF[4]) which is the largest and most recognized one. Nevertheless, this explicitly shared and validated data is only the tip of the iceberg. The real potential lies in the automatic analysis of the millions of raw observations collected every year through a growing number of devices but for which there is no human validation at all.

The performance of state-of-the-art multimedia analysis and machine learning techniques on such raw data (e.g., mobile search logs, soundscape audio recordings, wild life webcams, etc.) is still not well understood and is far from reaching the requirements of an accurate generic biodiversity monitoring system. Most existing research before LifeCLEF has actually considered only a few douzen or up to hundreds of species, often acquired in well-controlled environments [28,43,50]. On the other hand, the total number of living species on earth is estimated to be around 10 K for birds, 30 K for fish, 300 K for flowering plants (cf. ThePlantlist[5]) and more than 1.2M for invertebrates [3]. To bridge this gap, it is required to boost research on large-scale datasets and real-world scenarios.

In order to evaluate the performance of automated identification technologies in a sustainable and repeatable way, the LifeCLEF[6] research platform was created in 2014 as a continuation of the plant identification task [39] that was run

---

[1] http://www.inaturalist.org/.

[2] http://www.xeno-canto.org/.

[3] http://www.tela-botanica.org/.

[4] http://www.gbif.org/.

[5] http://www.theplantlist.org/.

[6] http://www.lifeclef.org/.

within the ImageCLEF lab[7] the three years before [27–29]. LifeCLEF enlarged the evaluated challenge by considering birds and fishes in addition to plants, and audio and video contents in addition to images. In this way, it aims at pushing the boundaries of the state-of-the-art in several research directions at the frontier of information retrieval, machine learning and knowledge engineering including (i) large scale classification, (ii) scene understanding, (iii) weakly-supervised and open-set classification, (iv) transfer learning and fine-grained classification and (v), humanly-assisted or crowdsourcing-based classification. More concretely, the lab is organized around three tasks, each based:

PlantCLEF: An image-based plant identification task making use of Pl@ntNet collaborative data

BirdCLEF: An audio recordings-based bird identification task making use of Xeno-canto collaborative data

SeaCLEF: A video and image-based identification task dedicated to sea organisms (making use of submarine videos and aerial pictures).

As described in more detail in the following sections, each task is based on big and real-world data and the measured challenges are defined in collaboration with biologists and environmental stakeholders so as to reflect realistic usage scenarios. The main novelties of the 2016th edition of LifeCLEF compared to the previous years are the following:

1. **Introduction of new contents types**: Both the plant and the bird tasks introduced new types of contents in their respective test sets so as to focus on more automated biodiversity monitoring scenarios. The test set of the plant task was composed of the raw image search logs of the Pl@ntNet mobile application (whereas previous editions were based on explicitly shared and collaboratively validated citizen sciences data). For the bird task, the novelty was the inclusion of *soundscape recordings*, i.e. continuous recordings of a specific environment over a long period.
2. **Identification of the individual level**: Previous editions of LifeCLEF were only concerned with species identification, i.e. retrieving the taxonomic name of an observed living plant or animal. The sea task conducted in 2016, however, included an identification challenge at the individual level. For some groups, notably whales, it is actually preferable to monitor the organisms at the individual level rather than at the species level. This problem is much less studied than species recognition and, to the best of our knowledge, Whale-CLEF is the first system-oriented evaluation dedicated to this challenge in the literature.

Overall, more than 130 research groups from around the world registered to at least one task of the lab. Fourteen of them finally crossed the finish line by participating in the collaborative evaluation and by writing technical reports describing in details their evaluated system.

---

[7] http://www.imageclef.org/.

2   Task1: PlantCLEF

Image-based plant identification is the most promising solution towards bridging the botanical taxonomic gap, as illustrated by the proliferation of research work on the topic [2, 10, 33, 35, 41] as well as the emergence of dedicated mobile applications such as LeafSnap [43] or Pl@ntNet [38]. As promising as these applications are, their performance is still far from the requirements of a real-world's ecological surveillance scenario. Allowing the mass of citizens to produce accurate plant observations requires to equip them with much more effective identification tools. As an illustration, in 2015, 2,328,502 millions queries have been submitted by the users of the Pl@ntNet mobile apps but only less than 1% of them were finally shared and collaboratively validated. Allowing the exploitation of the unvalidated observations could scale up the world-wide collection of plant records by several orders of magnitude. Measuring and boosting the performance of automated identification tools is therefore crucial. As a first step towards evaluating the feasibility of such an automated biodiversity monitoring paradigm, we created a new testbed entirely composed of image search logs of the Pl@ntNet mobile application (contrary to the previous editions of the PlantCLEF benchmark that were only based on explicitly shared and validated observations).

As a concrete scenario, we focused on the monitoring of invasive exotic plant species. These species represent today a major economic cost to our society (estimated at nearly 12 billion euros a year in Europe) and one of the main threats to biodiversity conservation [71]. This cost can even be more important at the country level, such as in China where it is evaluated to be about 15 billion US dollars annually [72], and more than 34 billion US dollars in the US [52]. The early detection of the appearance of these species, as well as the monitoring of changes in their distribution and phenology, are key elements to manage them, and reduce the cost of their management. The analysis of Pl@ntNet search logs can provide a highly valuable response to this problem because the presence of these species is highly correlated with that of humans (and thus to the density of data occurrences produced through the mobile application).

2.1   Dataset and Evaluation Protocol

For the training set, we provided the PlantCLEF 2015 dataset enriched with the ground truth annotations of the test images (that were kept secret during the 2015 campaign). In total, this data set contains 113,205 pictures of herb, tree and fern specimens belonging to 1,000 species (living in France and neighboring countries). Each image is associated with an XML file containing the taxonomic ground truth (species, genus, family), as well as other meta-data such as the type (fruit, flower, entire plant, etc.), the quality rating (social-based), the author name, the observation Id, the date and the geo-loc (for some of the observations).

For the test set, we created a new annotated dataset based on the image queries that were submitted by authenticated users of the Pl@ntNet mobile application in 2015 (unauthenticated queries had to be removed for copyright issues). A fraction of that queries were already associated to a valid species name because they were explicitly shared by their authors and collaboratively revised. We included in the test set the 4633 ones that were associated to a species belonging to the 1000 species of the training set (populating the known classes). Remaining pictures were distributed to a pool of botanists in charge of manually annotating them either with a valid species name or with newly created tags of their choice (and shared between them). In the period of time devoted to this process, they were able to manually annotate 1821 pictures that were included in the test set. Therefore, 144 new tags were created to qualify the unknown classes such as for instance *non-plant objects, legs* or *hands, UVO* (Unidentified Vegetal Object), *artificial plants, cactaceae, mushrooms, animals, food, vegetables* or more precise names of horticultural plants such as roses, geraniums, ficus, etc. For privacy reasons, we had to remove all images tagged as *people* (about 1.1 % of the tagged queries). Finally, to complete the number of test images belonging to unknown classes, we randomly selected a set of 1546 image queries that were associated to a valid species name that do not belong to the France flora (and thus, that do not belong to the 1000 species of the training set or to potentially highly similar species). In the end, the test set was composed of 8,000 pictures, 4633 labeled with one of the 1000 known classes of the training set, and 3367 labeled as new unknown classes. Among the 4633 images of known species, 366 were tagged as *invasive* according to a selected list of 26 potentially invasive species. This list was defined by aggregating several sources (such as the National Botanical conservatory, and the Global Invasive Species Programme) and by computing the intersection with the 1000 species of the training set. Based on the previously described testbed, we conducted a system-oriented evaluation involving different research groups who downloaded the data and ran their system. To avoid participants tuning their algorithms on the invasive species scenario and keep our evaluation generalizable to other ones, we did not provide the list of species to be detected. Participants only knew that the targeted species were included in a larger set of 1000 species for which we provided the training set. Participants were also aware that (i) most of the test data does not belong to the targeted list of species (ii) a large fraction of them does not belong to the training set of the 1000 species, and (iii) a fraction of them might not even be plants. In essence, the task to be addressed is related to what is sometimes called *open-set* or *open-world* recognition problems [5,56], i.e., problems in which the recognition system has to be robust to unknown and never seen categories. Beyond the brute-force classification across the known classes of the training set, a big challenge is thus to automatically reject the false positive classification hits that are caused by the unknown classes i.e., by the distractors). To measure this ability of the evaluated systems, each prediction had to be associated with a confidence score in $p \in [0,1]$ quantifying the probability that this prediction is true (independently from the other predictions).

The metric used to evaluate the performance of the systems is the classification Mean Average Precision (MAP-open), considering each class c_i of the training set as a query. More concretely, for each class c_i, we extract from the run file all predictions with $PredictedClassId = c_i$, rank them by decreasing probability $p \in [0,1]$ and compute the average precision for that class. The mean is then computed across all classes. Distractors associated to high probability values (i.e., false alarms) are likely to highly degrade the MAP, it is thus crucial to try rejecting them. To evaluate more specifically the targeted usage scenario (i.e., invasive species), a secondary MAP was computed by considering as queries only a subset of the species that belong to a black list of invasive species.

2.2 Participants and Results

94 research groups registered to LifeCLEF plant challenge 2016 and downloaded the dataset. Among this large raw audience, 8 research groups succeeded in submitting *runs*, i.e., files containing the predictions of the system(s) their ran. Details of the methods and systems used in the runs are synthesised in the overview working note of the task [26] and further developed in the individual working notes of the participants (Bluefield [34], Sabanci [22], CMP [64], LIIR, Floristic [30], UM [47], QUT [48], BME [4]). We give hereafter a few more details of the 3 systems that performed the best:

Bluefield system: A VGGNet [59] based system with the addition of Spatial Pyramid Pooling, Parametric ReLU and unknown class rejection based on the minimal prediction score of training data (Run 1). Run 2 is the same as run 1 but with a slightly different rejection making use of a validation set. Run 3 and 4 are respectively the same as Run 1 and 2 but the scores of the images belonging to the same observation were summed and normalised.

Sabanci system: Also a CNN-based system with 2 main configurations. Run 1: An ensemble of GoogleLeNet [66] and VGGNet [59] fine-tuned on both Life-CLEF 2015 data (for recognizing the targeted species) and on 70 K images of the ILSCVR dataset (for rejecting unknown classes). Run 2 is the same than Run 1 but without rejection.

CMP system: A ResNet [36] based system with the use of bagging in Run 1 (3 networks) and without bagging (in Run 2).

We report in Fig. 1 the scores achieved by the 29 collected runs for the two official evaluation metrics (MAP-open and MAP-open-invasive). To better assess the impact of the distractors i.e., the images in the test set belonging to unknown classes), we also report the MAP obtained when removing them (and denoted as MAP-closed). As a first noticeable remark, the top-26 runs which performed the best were based on Convolutional Neural Networks (CNN). This definitely confirms the supremacy of deep learning approaches over previous methods, in particular the one bases on hand-crafted features (such as BME TMIT Run 2). The different CNN-based systems mainly differed in (i) the architecture of the used CNN, (ii) the way in which the rejection of the unknown classes was managed and (iii), various system design improvements such as classifier ensembles, bagging or observation-level pooling. An impressive MAP of 0.718 (for the targeted invasive species monitoring scenario) was achieved by the best system configuration of Bluefield (run 3). The gain achieved by this run is however more related to the use of the observation-level pooling (looking at Bluefield run 1 for comparison) than to a good rejection of the distractors. Comparing the metric MAP-open with MAP-closed, the figure actually shows that the presence of the unknown classes degrades the performance of all systems in a roughly similar way. This difficulty of rejecting the unknown classes is confirmed by the very low difference between the runs of the participants who experimented their system with or without rejection (e.g., Sabanci Run 1 vs. Run 2 or FlorisTic Run 1 vs. Run 2). On the other side, it is noticeable that all systems are quite robust to the presence of unknown classes since the drop in performance is not too high. Actually, as the CNNs were pre-trained on a large generalist data set beforehand, it is likely that they have learned a diverse enough set of visual patterns to avoid underfitting. Now it is important to notice that the proportion of unknown classes in the test set was still reasonable (actually only 42%) because of the procedure used to create it. In further work, we will attempt to build a test set closer to the true statistics of the queries. This is however a hard problem. Even experts are actually doubtful of the true label of many images that do not contain enough visual evidences. Thus, they tend to annotate only the contents they are sure of i.e., the less confused ones. To build a more complete ground truth, it is required to take into account this doubt, during the annotation process, but also when measuring the accuracy of the evaluated systems.

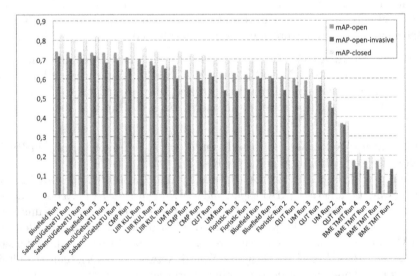

Fig. 1. Scores achieved by all systems evaluated within the plant identification task of LifeCLEF 2016, **MAP-open**: mean Average Precision on the 1000 species of the training set and distractors in the test set, **MAP-open-invasive**: mean Average Precision with distractors but restricted to 26 invasive species only, **MAP-closed**: mean Average Precision on the 1000 species but without distractors in the test set

3 Task2: BirdCLEF

The general public as well as professionals like park rangers, ecological consultants and of course the ornithologists themselves are potential users of an automated bird identifying system, typically in the context of wider initiatives related to ecological surveillance or biodiversity conservation. Using audio records rather than bird pictures is justified by current practices [8,9,68,69]. Birds are actually not easy to photograph as they are most of the time hidden, perched high in a tree or frightened by human presence, and they can fly very quickly, whereas audio calls and songs have proved to be easier to collect and very discriminant.

Before LifeCLEF started in 2014, three previous initiatives on the evaluation of acoustic bird species identification took place, including two from the SABIOD[8] group [7,24,25]. In collaboration with the organizers of these previous challenges, BirdCLEF 2014, 2015 and 2016 challenges went one step further by (i) significantly increasing the species number by an order of magnitude, (ii) working on real-world social data built from thousands of recordists, and (iii) moving to a more usage-driven and system-oriented benchmark by allowing the use of meta-data and defining information retrieval oriented metrics. Overall, the task is much more difficult than previous benchmarks because of the higher confusion risk between the classes, the higher background noise and the higher diversity in the acquisition conditions (different recording devices, contexts diversity, etc.). It therefore produces substantially lower scores and offers a better progression margin towards building real-world general identification tools.

The main novelty of the 2016 edition of the task with respect to the two previous years was the inclusion of *soundscape recordings* in addition to the usual xeno-canto recordings that focus on a single foreground species (usually thanks to mono-directional recording devices). Soundscapes, on the other hand, are generally based on omnidirectional recording devices that continuously monitor a specific environment over a long period. This new kind of recording fits better to the (possibly crowdsourced) passive acoustic monitoring scenario that could augment the number of collected records by several orders of magnitude.

3.1 Data and Task Description

The training and test data of the challenge consists of audio recordings collected by Xeno-canto (XC)[9]. Xeno-canto is a web-based community of bird sound recordists worldwide with about 3,000 active contributors that have already collected more than 300,000 recordings of about 9550 species (numbers for June 2016). Nearly 1000 (in fact 999) species were used in the BirdCLEF dataset, representing the 999 species with the highest number of recordings in October 2014 (14 or more) from the combined area of Brazil, French Guiana, Suriname,

---

[8] Scaled Acoustic Biodiversity http://sabiod.univ-tln.fr.
[9] http://www.xeno-canto.org/.

Guyana, Venezuela and Colombia, totalling 33,203 recordings produced by thousands of users. This dataset includes the entire dataset from the 2015 BirdCLEF challenge [32], which contained about 33,000 recordings.

The newly introduced test data in 2016 contains 925 soundscapes provided by 7 recordists, sometimes working in pairs. Most of the soundscapes have a length of (more or less) 10 min, each coming often from a set of 10–12 successive recordings collected from one location. The total duration of new testing data to process and analyse is thus equivalent to approximately 6 days of continuous sound recording. The number of known species (i.e. belonging to the 999 species in the training dataset) varies from 1 to 25 species, with an average of 10.1 species per soundscape.

To avoid any bias in the evaluation related to the used audio devices, each audio file has been normalized to a constant bandwidth of 44.1 kHz and coded in 16 bits in wav mono format (the right channel was selected by default). The conversion from the original Xeno-canto data set was done using ffmpeg, sox and matlab scripts. The optimized 16 Mel Filter Cepstrum Coefficients for bird identification (according to an extended benchmark [15]) were computed, together with their first and second temporal derivatives on the whole set. They were used in the best systems run in ICML4B and NIPS4B challenges. However, due to technical limitations, the soundscapes were not normalized and directly provided to the participants in mp3 format (shared on the xeno-canto website, the original raw files being not available).

All audio records are associated with various meta-data including the species of the most active singing bird, the species of the other birds audible in the background, the type of sound (call, song, alarm, flight, etc.), the date and location of the observations (from which rich statistics on species distribution can be derived), some text comments of the authors, multilingual common names and collaborative quality ratings. All of them were produced collaboratively by the Xeno-canto community.

Participants were asked to determine all the active singing birds species in each query file. It was forbidden to correlate the test set of the challenge with the original annotated Xeno-canto data base (or with any external content as many of them are circulating on the web). The whole data was split in two parts, one for training (and/or indexing) and one for testing. The test set was composed of (i) all the newly introduced soundscape recordings and (ii), the entire test set used in 2015 (equal to about 1/3 of the observations in the whole 2015 dataset). The training set was exactly the same as the one used in 2015 (i.e., the remaining 2/3 of the observations). Note that recordings of the same species done by the same person on the same day are considered as being part of the same observation and cannot be split across the test and training set. The XML files containing the meta-data of the *query* recordings were purged so as to erase the taxon name (the ground truth), the vernacular name (common name of the bird) and the collaborative quality ratings (that would not be available at query stage in a real-world mobile application). Meta-data of the recordings in the training set were kept unaltered.

The groups participating in the task were asked to produce up to 4 runs containing a ranked list of the most probable species for each query record of the test set. Each species was associated with a normalized score in the range $[0, 1]$ reflecting the likelihood that this species is singing in the sample. The primary metric used was the Mean Average Precision averaged across all queries.

3.2   Participants and Results

84 research groups registered for the bird challenge and downloaded the data and 6 of them finally submitted runs. Details of the systems and the methods used in the runs are synthesised in the overview working note of the task [31] and further developed in the individual working notes of the participants [18,45,51,54,67]. We give hereafter more details of the 3 systems that performed the best.

Cube system was based on a CNN architecture of 5 convolutional layers combined with the use of a rectify activation function followed by a max-pooling layer. Based on spectrogram analysis and some morphological operations, silent and noisy parts were first detected and separated from the birds song (or call) parts. Spectrograms were then split into chunks of 3 seconds that were used as inputs of the CNN after several data augmentation techniques. Each chunk identified as a bird song was first concatenated with 3 randomly selected chunks of background noise. Time shift, pitch shift and randomized mixes of audio files from the same species were then used as complementary data augmentation techniques. All the predictions of the distinct chunks are finally averaged to get the prediction of the entire test record. Run 1 was an intermediate result obtained after only one day of training. Run 2 differs from run 3 by using 50 % smaller spectrograms in (pixel) size for doubling the batch size and thus allowing to have more iterations for the same training time (4 days). Run 4 is the average of predictions from run 2 and 3 and reaches the best performance, showing the benefit of bagging (as for the plant identification task).

TSA system: As in 2014 and 2015, this participant used two hand-crafted parametric acoustic features and probabilities of species-specific spectrogram segments in a template matching approach. Long segments extracted during BirdCLEF2015 were re-segmented with a more sensitive algorithm. The segments were then used to extract Segment-Probabilities for each file by calculating the maxima of the normalized cross-correlation between all segments and the target spectrogram image via template matching. Due to the very large amount of audio data, not all files were used as a source for segmentation (i.e., only good quality files without background species were used). The classification problem was then formulated as a multi-label regression task solved by training ensembles of randomized decision trees with probabilistic outputs. The training was performed in 2 passes, one selecting a small subset of the most discriminant features by optimizing the internal MAP score on the training set, and one training the final classifiers on the selected features. Run 1 used one single model on a small but highly optimized selection of segment-probabilities. A bagging approach was used consisting in calculating further segment-probabilities from additional segments and to combine them either by blending (24 models in Run 3). Run 4 also used blending to aggregate model predictions, but the predictions were included that after blending resulted in the highest possible MAP score calculated on the entire training set (13 models including the best model from 2015).

WUT system: like the Cube team, they used a CNN-based learning framework. Starting from denoised spectrograms, silent parts were removed with percentile thresholding, giving thus around 86.000 training segments varying in length and associated each with a single main species. As a data augmentation technique and for fitting the 5 seconds fixed input size of the CNN, segments were adjusted by either trimming or padding. The 3 first successive runs are produced by deeper and deeper or/and wider and wider filters. Run 4 is as an ensemble of neural networks averaging the predictions of the 3 first runs.

Figure 2 reports the performance measured for the 18 submitted runs. For each run (i.e., each evaluated system), we report the overall mean Average Precision (official metric) as well as the MAP for the two categories of queries: the soundscapes recordings (newly introduced) and the common observations (the same as the one used in 2015). To measure the progress over last year, we also plot on the graph the performance of last year's best system [44] (orange dotted line). The first noticeable conclusion is that, after two years of resistance of bird song identification systems based on engineering features, convolutional neural networks finally managed to outperform them (as in many other domains). The best run based on CNN (Cube Run 4) actually reached an impressive MAP of 0.69 on the 2015 testbed to be compared to respectively 0.45 and 0.58 for the best systems based on hand-crafted features evaluated in 2015 and 2016. To our knowledge, BirdCLEF is the first comparative study reporting such an important performance gap in bio-acoustic large-scale classification. A second important remark is that this performance of CNNs was achieved without any fine-tuning contrary to most computer vision challenges in which the CNN is generally pre-trained on a large training data such as ImageNet. Thus, we can hope for even better performance, e.g., by transferring knowledge from other bio-acoustic contexts or other domains. It is important to notice that the second system based on CNN (WUT) did not perform as well as the Cube system and did not outperform the system of TSA based on hand-crafted features. Looking at the detailed description of the two CNN architectures and their learning framework, it appears that the way in which audio segments extraction and data augmentation is performed does play a crucial role. The Cube system does notably include a randomized background noise addition phase which makes it much more robust to the diversity of noise encountered in the test data.

If we now look at the scores achieved by the evaluated systems on the soundscape recordings only (yellow plot), we can draw very different conclusions. First of all, we can observe that the performance on the soundscapes is much lower than on the classical queries, whatever the system. Although the classical recordings also include multiple species singing in the background, the soundscapes appear to be much more challenging. Several tens of species and even much more individual birds can actually be singing simultaneously. Separating all these sources seem to be beyond the scope of state-of-the-art audio representation learning methods. Interestingly, the best system on the soundscape queries was the one of TSA based on the extraction of very short species-specific spectrogram segments and a template matching approach. This very fine-grained approach allows the extracted audio patterns to be more robust to the species overlap problem. On the contrary, the CNN of Cube and WUT systems were optimized for the mono-species segments classification problem. The data augmentation method of the Cube system was in particular only designed for the single species case. It addressed the problem of several individual birds of the same species singing together (by mixing different segments of the same class) but it did not address the multi-label issue (i.e., several species singing simultaneously [16]), and is getting close to the simple reference MFCC model provided for comparison to the baseline [54].

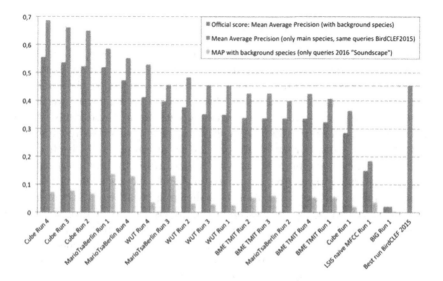

Fig. 2. Scores of the LifeCLEF 2016 bird identification task

4   Task3: SeaCLEF

The SeaCLEF 2016 task originates from the previous editions of the fish identification task (in 2014 and 2015), i.e., video-based coral fish species identification for ecological surveillance and biodiversity monitoring. SeaCLEF 2016 extends the previous ones in that it does not only consider fish species, but sea organisms in general. The need of automated methods for sea-related visual data is driven by the advances in imaging systems (in particular underwater) and their employment for marine ecosystem analysis and biodiversity monitoring. Indeed in recent years we have assisted an exponential growth of sea-related visual data, in the forms of images and videos, for disparate reasoning ranging from fish bio-diversity monitoring to marine resource managements to fishery to educational purposes. However, the analysis of such data is particularly expensive for human operators, thus limiting greatly the impact of that the technology may have in understanding and sustainably exploiting the sea.

The task aims at evaluating two kinds of automated identification scenar-ios: species recognition and individuals recognition. Whereas species recognition is the most common practice, it is preferable for some groups to monitor the organisms at the individual level rather than at the species level. This is notably the case of big animals, such as whales and elephants, whose population might be scarce and travelling for long distances. Monitoring individual animals allows gathering valuable information about population sizes, migration, health, sexual maturity and behavior patterns.

4.1   Coral Reef Species Identification in Underwater Videos

The goal of the task was to automatically detect and recognize coral reef species in underwater videos. The typical usage scenario of automated underwater video analysis tools is to support marine biologists in studying thoroughly the marine ecosystem and fish biodiversity. Also, scuba divers, marine stakeholders and other marine practitioners may benefit greatly from these kinds of tools. Recently, underwater video and imaging systems have been employed since they do not affect fish behavior and may provide large amounts of visual data at the same time. However, manual analysis as performed by human operators is largely impractical, and requires automated methods. Nevertheless, the develop-ment of automatic video analysis tools is challenging because of the complexities of underwater video recordings in terms of the variability of scenarios and factors that may degrade the video quality such as water clarity and/or depth.

Despite some preliminary work, mainly carried out in controlled environ-ments (e.g., labs, cages, etc.) [19,49], the most important step in the auto-mated visual analysis has been done in the EU-funded Fish4Knowledge (F4K)[10] project, where computer vision methods were developed to extract informa-tion about fish density and richness from videos taken by underwater cam-eras installed at coral reefs in Taiwan [6,61–63]. Since the F4K project, many researchers have directed their attention towards underwater video analysis [53,55], including some recent initiatives by the National Oceanographic and Atmospheric Administration (NOAA) [57] and the fish identification task at LifeCLEF 2014 and 2015 [12,13,60]. Although there are recent advances in the underwater computer vision field, the problem is still open and needs several (joint) efforts to devise robust methods able to provide reliable measures on fish populations.

Data. The training dataset consists of 20 videos manually annotated, a list of fish species (15) and for each species, a set of sample images to support the learn-ing of fish appearance models. Each video is manually labelled and agreed by two

---

[10] http://www.fish4knowledge.eu/.

expert annotators and the ground truth consists of a set of bounding boxes (one for each instance of the given fish species list) together with the fish species. In total the training dataset contains more than 9,000 annotations (bounding boxes + species) and more than 20000 sample images. However, it is not a statistical significant estimation of the test dataset rather its purpose is as a familiarization pack for designing the identification methods. The training dataset is unbalanced in the number of instances of fish species: for instance it contains 3165 instances of "Dascyllus Reticulates" and only 72 instances of "Zebrasoma Scopas". This was done not to favour nonparametric methods against model-based methods. For each considered fish species, its *fishbase.org* link is also given so as to give access to more detailed information about fish species including complementary high quality images. In order to evaluate the identification process independently from the tracking process, temporal information was not be exploited. This means that the annotators only labelled fish for which the species was clearly identifiable regardless from previous identifications. Each video is accompanied by an XML file containing instances of the provided list species. For each video, information on the location and the camera recording the video is also given.

The test dataset consists of 73 underwater videos. The list of considered fish species is the same than the one released with the training dataset (i.e., 15 coral reef fish species). The number of occurrences per fish species is provided in Table 1. It is noticeable, that for three fish species there were no occurrences in the test set, and also that in some video segments there were no fish at all. This was done to evaluate the method's capability to reject false positives.

Task Description. The main goal of the video-based fish identification task is to automatically count fish per species in video segments (e.g., video X contains $N1$ instances of fish of species 1, ..., N_n instances of fish species N). However, participants were also asked to identify fish bounding boxes. The ground truth for each video (provided as an XML file) contains information on fish species and location. The participants were asked to provide up to three runs. Each run had to contain all the videos included in the set and for each video the frame where the fish was detected together with the bounding box, and species name (only the most confident species) for each detected fish.

Metrics. As metrics, we used the "**Counting Score (CS)**" and the "**Normalized Counting Score (NCS)**", defined as:

$$CS = e^{-\frac{d}{N_{gt}}} \tag{1}$$

with d being the difference between the number of occurrences in the run (per species) and, N_{gt}, the number of occurrences in the ground truth. The Normalised Counting S instead depends on precision Pr:

$$NCS = CS \times Pr = CS \times \frac{TP}{TP + FP} \tag{2}$$

Table 1. Fish species occurrences in the test set.

Fish Species Name	Occurrences	Fish Species Name	Occurrences
Abudefduf vaigiensis	93	Acanthurus nigrofuscus	129
Amphirion clarkii	517	Chaetodon lunulatus	1876
Chaetodo speculum	0	Chaetodon trifascialis	1317
Chromis chrysura	24	Dacyllus aruanus	1985
Dascyllus reticulatus	5016	Hemigymnus melapterus	0
Myripristis kuntee	118	Neoglyphidodon nigroris	1531
Pempheris vanicolensis	0	Plectrogly-phidodon dickii	700
Zebrasoma scopas	187		

with TP and FP being the True Positive and the False Positive. As detection was considered a true positive if the intersection over union score of its bounding box and the ground truth was over 0.5 and the species was correctly identified.

Participants and Results. Figure 3 shows, respectively, the average (per video and species) normalized counting score, precision and counting score obtained by the two participating teams (CVG [37] and BMETMIT [14]) who submitted one run each.

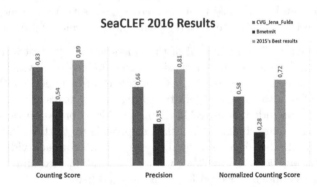

Fig. 3. SeaCLEF 2016 Results.

Figure 4 gives the detailed normalized counting scores per fish species. In addition to the results obtained in 2016, the graphs also show the best performance achieved on the same dataset in 2015. This comparison shows that, unfortunately, none of the 2016 approaches outperformed the one by SNUMED INFO, which performed the best in 2015 (described in details in [11]). This system was based on the GoogLeNet [65] Convolutional Neural Network (CNN). Potential fish instances were previously segmented from the video through a stationary foreground detection using background subtraction and a selective search strategy [70]. Producing the final output counts was finally achieved by grouping the temporally connected video segments classified by the CNN. The system used in 2016 by CVG [37] was inspired by a region-based convolutional neural network (R-CNN [23]), with the difference that it employed background subtraction instead of selective search for bounding box proposal generation. More specifically, CVG's method used off-the-shelf AxelNet CNN [42] for feature extraction (7th hidden layer relu7), and then trained a multiclass support vector machine (MSVMs) for species classification. Its achieved performance, in terms of counting score of 0.83, over the 15 considered fish species was fairly good. Its lower value with respect to SNUMED INFO's one (0.89) can be explained with the fact that CVG did not apply any domain-specific fine tuning of CNN. In the case of normalised counting score, the gap between CVG and SNUMED INFO was higher, and this is due to the fact that CVG employed background subtraction for proposal generation, which is known to be prone to false positives, instead of the more effective selective search used by SNUMED INFO. For a similar reason BMETMIT achieved the lowest normalised counting score, while its lower counting score can be ascribed to the used shallow classifier operating on SURF features, while the other two methods (CVG and SNUMED INFO) resorted on deep-learning methods.

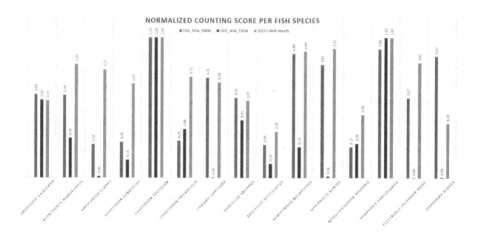

Fig. 4. Normalised Counting Score detailed by fish species.

4.2   Individual Humpback Whale Identification

Using natural markings to identify individual animals over time is usually known as *photo-identification*. This research technique is used on many species of marine mammals. Initially, scientists used artificial tags to identify individual whales, but with limited success (most tagged whales were actually lost or died). In the 1970s, scientists discovered that individuals of many species could be recognized by their natural markings. These scientists began taking photographs

of individual animals and comparing these photos against each other to identify individual animal's movements and behavior over time. Since its development, photo-identification has proven to be a useful tool for learning about
many marine mammal species including humpbacks, right whales, finbacks, killer
whales, sperm whales, bottlenose dolphins and other species to a lesser degree.
Nowadays, this process is still mostly done manually making it impossible to get
an accurate count of all the individuals in a given large collection of observations.
Researchers usually survey a portion of the population, and then use statistical
formulae to determine population estimates. To limit the variance and bias of
such an estimator, it is however required to use large-enough samples which still
makes it a very time-consuming process. Automating the *photo-identification*
process could drastically scale-up such surveys and open brave new research
opportunities for the future.

Data and related challenges. The dataset used for the evaluation consisted
of 2005 images of humpback whales caudals collected by the CetaMada NGO
between 2009 and 2014 in the Madagascar area. Each photograph was manually
cropped so as to focus only on the caudal fin that is the most discriminant pattern
for distinguishing an individual whale from another. Figure 5 displays six of such
cropped images, each line corresponding to two images of the same individual. As
one can see, the individual whales can be distinguished thanks to their natural
markings and/or the scars that appear along the years. Automatically finding
such matches in the whole dataset and rejecting the false alarms is difficult for
three main reasons. The first reason is that the number of individuals in the
dataset is high, around 1, 200, so that the proportion of true matches is actually
very low (around 0.05% of the total number of potential matches).

The second difficulty is that distinct individuals can be very similar at a
first glance as illustrated by the false positive examples displayed in Fig. 6. To
discriminate the true matches from such false positives, it is required to detect
very small and fine-grained visual variations such as in a spot-the-difference
game. The third difficulty is that all images have a similar water background of
which the texture generates quantities of local mismatches.

Task Description. The task was simply to detect as many true matches
as possible from the whole dataset, in a fully unsupervised way. Each evaluated system had to return a *run file* (i.e., a raw text file) containing as much
lines as the number of discovered matches, each match being a triplet of the
form *imageX.jpg;imageY.jpg;score* where *score* is a confidence score in $[0, 1]$
(1 for highly confident matches). The retrieved matches had to be sorted by
decreasing confidence score. A run should not contain any duplicate match (e.g.,
image1.jpg;image2.jpg;score and *image2.jpg;image1.jpg;score* should not appear
in the same run). The metric used to evaluate each run is the Average Precision:

$$AveP = \frac{\sum_{k=1}^{K} P(k) \times rel(k)}{M}$$

where M is the total number of true matches in the groundtruth, k is the rank in
the sequence of returned matches, K is the number of retrieved matches, $P(k)$ is

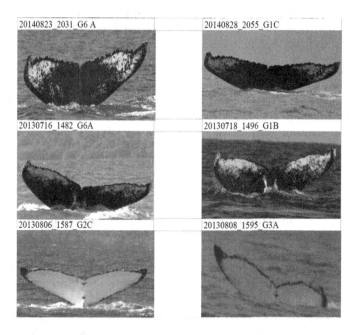

Fig. 5. 3 good matches (each line corresponds to 2 images of the same individual whale)

Fig. 6. 3 false positives (each line corresponds to 2 distinct individual whales)

the precision at cut-off k in the list, and $rel(k)$ is an indicator function equaling 1 if the match at rank k is a relevant match, 0 otherwise. The average is over all true matches and the true matches not retrieved get a precision score of 0.

Participants and Results. Two research groups participated to the evaluation and submitted a total of 6 run files. Table 2 provides the scores achieved by the six runs. Details of the systems and methods used can be found in the individual working notes of the participants (INRIA [40], BME-MIT [14]). We give hereafter a synthetic description of the evaluated systems/configurations:

INRIA system. This group used a large-scale matching system based on local visual features, approximate k-nn search of each individual local feature via multi-probe hashing, and a RANSAC-like spatial consistency refinement step used to reject false positives (based on a rotation-and-scale transformation model). The run named *ZenithINRIA_SiftGeo* used affine SIFT features whereas the one named *ZenithINRIA_GoogleNet_3layers_borda* used off-the-shelf local features extracted at three different layers of GoogLeNet [65] (layer *conv2-3x3*: 3136 local features per image, layer *inception_3b_output*: 784 local features par image, layer *inception_4c_output*: 196 local features per image). The matches found using the 3 distinct layers were merged through a late-fusion approach based on Borda. Finally, the last run *ZenithINRIA_SiftGeo_QueryExpansion* differs from *ZenithINRIA_SiftGeo* in that a query expansion strategy was used to re-issue the regions matched with a sufficient degree of confidence as new queries.

BME-MIT system. This group used aggregation-based image representations based on SIFT features (extracted either on a dense grid or around Laplace-Harris points), a GMM-based visual codebook learning (256 visual words), and Fisher Vectors (FVs) for the global image representation. A RBF kernel was used to measure the similarity between image pairs. Runs *bmetmit_whalerun_2* and *bmetmit_whalerun_3* differ from *bmetmit_whalerun_1* in that segmentation propagation was used beforehand so as to separate the background (the water) from the whale's caudal fin. In *bmetmit_whalerun_3* the segmentation mask was applied only for filtering the features during the codebook learning phase. In run 2 the mask was also used to when computing the FVs of each image.

Table 2. Individual whale identification results: AP of the 6 evaluated systems

Run name	AP
ZenithInria SiftGeo	0.49
ZenithInria SiftGeo QueryExpansion	0.43
ZenithInria GoogleNet 3layers borda	0.33
bmetmit whalerun 1	0.25
bmetmit whalerun 3	0.10
bmetmit whalerun 2	0.03

The main conclusion we can draw from the results of the evaluation (cf. Table 2) is that spatial consistency of the local features is crucial for rejecting the false positives (as proved by the much higher performance of INRIA system). As powerful as aggregation-based methods such as Fisher Vectors are for fine-grained classification, they do not capture the spatial arrangement of the local features which is a precious information for rejecting the mismatches without supervision. Another reason explaining the good performance of the best run *ZenithINRIA_SiftGeo* is that it is based on affine invariant local features contrary to *ZenithINRIA_GoogleNet_3layers_borda* and **BME-MIT** runs that use grid-based local features. Such features are more sensitive to small shifts and local affine deformations even when learned through a powerful CNN. Finally, neither segmentation nor query expansion succeeded in improving the results. Segmentation is always risky because of the risk of over segmentation which might remove the useful information from the image. Query expansion is also a risky solution in that it is highly sensitive to the decision threshold used for selecting the re-issued matched regions. It can be considerably increase recall when the decision threshold is well estimated but at the opposite, it can also boost the false positives when the threshold is too low.

5   Conclusions and Perspectives

With more than 130 research groups who downloaded LifeCLEF 2016 datasets and 14 of them who submitted runs, the third edition of the LifeCLEF evaluation did confirm a high interest in the evaluated challenges. The main outcome of this collaborative effort is a snapshot of the performance of state-of-the-art computer vision, bio-acoustic and machine learning techniques towards building real-world biodiversity monitoring systems. The results did show that very high identification success rates can be reached by the evaluated systems, even on large number of species (up to 1000 species). The most noticeable progress came from the deployment of deep Convolutional Neural Networks for the bird songs identification challenge. We observed a similar performance gap to the one observed in many domains beforehand (in particular the LifeCLEF plant identification task two years ago). Interestingly, this was achieved without any fine-tuning which means that the xeno-canto dataset is sufficiently rich to allow the CNN learning relevant audio features. This opens the door to transfer learning opportunities in other bio-acoustic domains for which training data are sparser. Regarding the plant task, the main conclusion was that CNNs appeared to be quite robust to the presence of unknown classes in the test set. The proportion of novelty was however still moderate, near 50 % and might be increased in further evaluations so as to better fit reality. Finally, the two newly introduced scenarios, i.e., soundscape-based monitoring of birds and unsupervised identification of individual whales appeared to be quite challenging. Bird soundscapes, in particular, seem to be out of reach for current audio representation learning methods because of the very large number of overlapping sound sources in single recordings. The identification of individual whales was more effective (thanks to the use of spatial verification) but there is still room for improvement before fully automating the *Photo-identification* process used by biologists.

Acknowledgements. The organization of the PlantCLEF task is supported by the French project Floris'Tic (Tela Botanica, INRIA, CIRAD, INRA, IRD) funded in the context of the national investment program PIA. The organization of the BirdCLEF task is supported by the Xeno-Canto foundation for nature sounds as well as the French CNRS project SABIOD.ORG and Floris'Tic. The organization of the SeaCLEF task is supported by the Ceta-mada NGO and the French project Floris'Tic.

References

1. MAED 2012: Proceedings of the 1st ACM International Workshop on Multimedia Analysis for Ecological Data. NY, USA, 433127. ACM, New York (2012)
2. Aptoula, E., Yanikoglu, B.: Morphological features for leaf based plant recognition. In: Proceedings IEEE International Conference Image Process. Melbourne, Australia (2013)
3. Baillie, J.E.M., H.T.C., Stuart, S.: 2004 iucn red list of threatened species. a global species assessment. IUCN, Gland, Switzerland and Cambridge, UK (2004)
4. Tóth, B.P., Márton Tóth, D.P., Szúcs, G.: Deep learning and svm classification for plant recognition in content-based large scale image retrieval. In: Working notes of CLEF 2016 Conference (2016)
5. Bendale, A., Boult, T.E.: Towards open world recognition. CoRR (2014)
6. Boom, B.J., He, J., Palazzo, S., Huang, P.X., Beyan, C., Chou, H.M., Lin, F.P., Spampinato, C., Fisher, R.B.: A research tool for long-term and continuous analysis of fish assemblage in coral-reefs using underwater camera footage. Ecol. Inf. **23**, 83–97 (2014)
7. Briggs, F., Huang, Y., Raich, R., Eftaxias, K.Z.L., et al.: The 9th mlsp competition: New methods for acoustic classification of multiple simultaneous bird species in noisy environment. In: IEEE Workshop on Machine Learning for Signal Processing (MLSP), pp. 1–8 (2013)
8. Briggs, F., Lakshminarayanan, B., Neal, L., Fern, X.Z., Raich, R., Hadley, S.J., Hadley, A.S., Betts, M.G.: Acoustic classification of multiple simultaneous bird species: A multi-instance multi-label approach. J. Acoust. Soc. Am. **131**, 4640 (2012)
9. Cai, J., Ee, D., Pham, B., Roe, P., Zhang, J.: Sensor network for the monitoring of ecosystem: Bird species recognition. In: 3rd International Conference on Intelligent Sensors, Sensor Networks and Information. ISSNIP 2007 (2007)
10. Cerutti, G., Tougne, L., Vacavant, A., Coquin, D.: A parametric active polygon for leaf segmentation and shape estimation. In: Bebis, G. (ed.) ISVC 2011, Part I. LNCS, vol. 6938, pp. 202–213. Springer, Heidelberg (2011)
11. Choi, S.: Fish identification in underwater video with deep convolutional neural network: Snumedinfo at lifeclef fish task 2015. In: Working Notes of CLEF (2015)
12. Concetto, S., Palazzo, S., Fisher, B., Boom, B.: Lifeclef fish identification task 2014. In: CLEF working Notes 2014 (2014)
13. Concetto, S., Palazzo, S., Fisher, B., Boom, B.: Lifeclef fish identification task 2015. In: CLEF Working Notes 2015 (2015)

14. Dävid Papp, D.L., Szücs, G.: Object detection, classification, tracking and individual recognition for sea images and videos. In: Working Notes of CLEF (2016)

15. Dufour, O., Artieres, T., Glotin, H., Giraudet, P.: Clusterized mfcc and svm for bird song. In: Identification, Soundscape Semiotics, Localization, Categorization (2014)

16. Dufour, O., Glotin, H., Artieres, T., Bas, Y., Giraudet, P.: Multi-instance multilabel acoustic classification of plurality of animals: birds, insects & amphibian. In: 1st Workshop on Neural information Proceedings Scaled for Bioacoustics, pp. 164–174. in conj. with NIPS (2013)

17. Dugan, P., Zollweg, J., Popescu, M., Risch, D., Glotin, H., LeCun, Y., Clark, C.: High performance computer acoustic data accelerator: A new system for exploring marine mammal acoustics for big data applications (2015)

18. Sprengel, E., Martin Jaggi, Y.K., Hofmann, T.: Audio based bird species identification using deep learning techniques. In: Working Notes of CLEF (2016)

19. Evans, F.: Detecting fish in underwater video using the em algorithm. In: Proceedings of the 2003 International Conference on Image Processing, 2003. ICIP 2003. vol. 3, pp. III-1029-32 vol. 2 (2003)

20. Farnsworth, E.J., Chu, M., Kress, W.J., Neill, A.K., Best, J.H., Pickering, J., Stevenson, R.D., Courtney, G.W., VanDyk, J.K., Ellison, A.M.: Next-generation field guides. BioScience **63**(11), 891–899 (2013)

21. Gaston, K.J., O'Neill, M.A.: Automated species identification: why not? 359(1444), 655–667 (2004)

22. Ghazi, M.M., Yanikoglu, B., Aptoula, E.: Open-set plant identification using an ensemble of deep convolutional neural networks. In: Working notes of CLEF (2016)

23. Girshick, R.B., Donahue, J., Darrell, T., Malik, J.: Rich feature hierarchies for accurate object detection and semantic segmentation (2013). CoRR abs/1311.2524

24. Glotin, H., Clark, C., LeCun, Y., Dugan, P., Halkias, X., Sueur, J.: Bioacoustic challenges in icml4b. In: Proceedings of 1st workshop on Machine Learning for Bioacoustics. No. USA, ISSN 979–10-90821-02-6 (2013). http://sabiod.org/ICML4B2013_proceedings.pdf

25. Glotin, H., Dufour, O., Bas, Y.: Overview of the 2nd challenge on acoustic bird classification. In: Glotin, H., LeCun, Y., Artières, T., Mallat, S., Tchernichovski, O., Halkias, X., (eds.) Proceedings of the Neural Information Processing Scaled for Bioacoustics. NIPS International Conference, USA (2013). http://sabiod.univ-tln.fr/nips4b

26. Goëau, H., Bonnet, P., Joly, A.: Plant identification in an open-world (lifeclef 2016). In: CLEF Working Notes 2016 (2016)

27. Goëau, H., Bonnet, P., Joly, A., Bakic, V., Barthélémy, D., Boujemaa, N., Molino, J.F.: The Imageclef 2013 plant identification task. In: CLEF Valencia (2013)

28. Goëau, H., Bonnet, P., Joly, A., Boujemaa, N., Barthélémy, D., Molino, J.F., Birnbaum, P., Mouysset, E., Picard, M.: The imageclef 2011 plant images classification task. In: CLEF 2011 (2011)

29. Goëau, H., Bonnet, P., Joly, A., Yahiaoui, I., Barthélémy, D., Boujemaa, N., Molino, J.F.: Imageclef 2012 plant images identification task. In: CLEF12. Rome

30. Goëau, H., Champ, J., Joly, A.: Floristic participation at lifeclef 2016 plant identification task. In: Working notes of CLEF 2016 Conference (2016)

31. Goëau, H., Glotin, H., Planqué, R., Vellinga, W.P., Joly, A.: Lifeclef bird identification task 2016. In: CLEF working notes 2016 (2016)

32. Goëau, H., Glotin, H., Vellinga, W.P., Planque, R., Rauber, A., Joly, A.: Lifeclef bird identification task 2015. In: CLEF working notes 2015 (2015)

33. Goëau, H., Joly, A., Selmi, S., Bonnet, P., Mouysset, E., Joyeux, L., Molino, J.F., Birnbaum, P., Bathelemy, D., Boujemaa, N.: Visual-based plant species identification from crowdsourced data. In: ACM Conference on Multimedia (2011)

34. Hang, S.T., Tatsuma, A., Aono, M.: Bluefield (kde tut) at lifeclef 2016 plant identification task. In: Working Notes of CLEF 2016 Conference (2016)

35. Hazra, A., Deb, K., Kundu, S., Hazra, P., et al.: Shape oriented feature selection for tomato plant identification. Int. J. Comput. Appl. Technol. Res. 2(4), 449–454 (2013). 449–meta

36. He, K., Zhang, X., Ren, S., Sun, J.: Deep residual learning for image recognition. arXiv preprint (2015). arXiv:1512.03385

37. Jäger, J., Rodner, E., Denzler, J., Wolff, V., Fricke-Neuderth, K.: Seaclef 2016: Object proposal classification for fish detection in underwater videos. In: Working Notes of CLEF 2016 Conference (2016)

38. Joly, A., Goëau, H., Bonnet, P., Bakić, V., Barbe, J., Selmi, S., Yahiaoui, I., Carré, J., Mouysset, E., Molino, J.F., et al.: Interactive plant identification based on social image data. Ecol. Inf. 23, 22–34 (2014)

39. Joly, A., Goëau, H., Bonnet, P., Bakic, V., Molino, J.F., Barthélémy, D., Boujemaa, N.: The imageclef plant identification task 2013. In: International Workshop on Multimedia Analysis for Ecological Data (2013)

40. Joly, A., Lombardo, J.C., Champ, J., Saloma, A.: Unsupervised individual whales identification: spot the difference in the ocean. In: Working Notes of CLEF (2016)

41. Kebapci, H., Yanikoglu, B., Unal, G.: Plant image retrieval using color, shape and texture features. Comput. J. 54(9), 1475–1490 (2011)

42. Krizhevsky, A., Sutskever, I., Hinton, G.E.: Imagenet classification with deep convolutional neural networks. In: Advances in Neural Information Processing Systems, pp. 1097–1105 (2012)

43. Kumar, N., Belhumeur, P.N., Biswas, A., Jacobs, D.W., Kress, W.J., Lopez, I.C., Soares, J.V.B.: Leafsnap: a computer vision system for automatic plant species identification. In: Fitzgibbon, A., Lazebnik, S., Perona, P., Sato, Y., Schmid, C. (eds.) ECCV 2012, Part II. LNCS, vol. 7573, pp. 502–516. Springer, Heidelberg (2012)

44. Lasseck, M.: Improved automatic bird identification through decision tree based feature selection and bagging. In: Working Notes of CLEF 2015 Conference (2015)

45. Lasseck, M.: Improving bird identification using multiresolution template matching and feature selection during training. In: Working Notes of CLEF Conference (2016)

46. Lee, D.J., Schoenberger, R.B., Shiozawa, D., Xu, X., Zhan, P.: Contour matching for a fish recognition and migration-monitoring system. In: Optics East, pp. 37–48. International Society for Optics and Photonics (2004)

47. Lee, S.H., Chang, Y.L., Chan, C.S., Remagnino, P.: Plant identification system based on a convolutional neural network for the lifeclef 2016 plant classification task. In: Working Notes of CLEF 2016 Conference (2016)

48. McCool, C., Ge, Z., Corke, P.: Feature learning via mixtures of dcnns for fine-grained plant classification. In: Working Notes of CLEF 2016 Conference (2016)

49. Morais, E., Campos, M., Padua, F., Carceroni, R.: Particle filter-based predictive tracking for robust fish counting. In: 18th Brazilian Symposium on Computer Graphics and Image Processing, 2005. SIBGRAPI 2005, pp. 367–374 (2005)

50. Nilsback, M.E., Zisserman, A.: Automated flower classification over a large number of classes. In: Proceedings of the Indian Conference on Computer Vision, Graphics and Image Processing, December 2008

51. Piczak, K.: Recognizing bird species in audio recordings using deep convolutional neural networks. In: Working Notes of CLEF 2016 Conference (2016)
52. Pimentel, D., Zuniga, R., Morrison, D.: Update on the environmental and economic costs associated with alien-invasive species in the united states. Ecol. Econ. **52**(3), 273–288 (2005)
53. Ravanbakhsh, M., Shortis, M.R., Shafait, F., Mian, A., Harvey, E.S., Seager, J.W.: Automated fish detection in underwater images using shape-based level sets. Photogram. Rec. **30**(149), 46–62 (2015)
54. Ricard, J., Glotin, H.: Bag of mfcc-based words for bird identification. In: Working notes of CLEF 2016 Conference (2016)
55. Rodriguez, A., Rico-Diaz, A.J., Rabuñal, J.R., Puertas, J., Pena, L.: Fish monitoring and sizing using computer vision. In: Vicente, J.M.F., Álvarez-Sánchez, J.R., López, F.P., Toledo-Moreo, F.J., Adeli, H. (eds.) Bioinspired Computation in Artificial Systems. LNCS, vol. 9108, pp. 419–428. Springer, Heidelberg (2015)
56. Scheirer, W.J., Jain, L.P., Boult, T.E.: Probability models for open set recognition. IEEE Trans. Pattern Anal. Mach. Intell. **36**, 2317–2324 (2014)
57. Sigler, M., DeMaster, D., Boveng, P., Cameron, M., Moreland, E., Williams, K., Towler, R.: Advances in methods for marine mammal and fish stock assessments: Thermal imagery and camtrawl. Marine Technol. Soc. J. **49**(2), 99–106 (2015)
58. Silvertown, J., Harvey, M., Greenwood, R., Dodd, M., Rosewell, J., Rebelo, T., Ansine, J., McConway, K.: Crowdsourcing the identification of organisms: A casestudy of ispot. ZooKeys **480**, 125 (2015)
59. Simonyan, K., Zisserman, A.: Very deep convolutional networks for large-scale image recognition. CoRR abs/1409.1556 (2014)
60. Spampinato, C., Palazzo, S., Joalland, P., Paris, S., Glotin, H., Blanc, K., Lingrand, D., Precioso, F.: Fine-grained object recognition in underwater visual data. Multimedia Tools and Applcations (MTAP-D-14-00618) (2014)
61. Spampinato, C., Beauxis-Aussalet, E., Palazzo, S., Beyan, C., van Ossenbruggen, J., He, J., Boom, B., Huang, X.: A rule-based event detection system for real-life underwater domain. Mach. Vis. Appl. **25**(1), 99–117 (2014)
62. Spampinato, C., Chen-Burger, Y.H., Nadarajan, G., Fisher, R.B.: Detecting, tracking and counting fish in low quality unconstrained underwater videos. VISAPP **2**, 514–519 (2008). Citeseer
63. Spampinato, C., Palazzo, S., Boom, B., van Ossenbruggen, J., Kavasidis, I., Di Salvo, R., Lin, F.P., Giordano, D., Hardman, L., Fisher, R.B.: Understanding fish behavior during typhoon events in real-life underwater environments. Multimedia Tools Appl. **70**(1), 199–236 (2014)
64. Šulc, M., Mishkin, D., Matas, J.: Very deep residual networks with maxout for plant identification. In: Working Notes of CLEF 2016 Conference (2016)
65. Szegedy, C., Liu, W., Jia, Y., Sermanet, P., Reed, S., Anguelov, D., Erhan, D., Vanhoucke, V., Rabinovich, A.: Going deeper with convolutions. CoRR (2014)
66. Szegedy, C., Liu, W., Jia, Y., Sermanet, P., Reed, S., Anguelov, D., Erhan, D., Vanhoucke, V., Rabinovich, A.: Going deeper with convolutions. In: Proceedings of the IEEE Conference on Computer Vision and Pattern Recognition (2015)
67. Tóth, B.P., Czeba, B.: Convolutional neural networks for large-scale bird song classification in noisy environment. In: Working Notes of CLEF Conference (2016)
68. Towsey, M., Planitz, B., Nantes, A., Wimmer, J., Roe, P.: A toolbox for animal call recognition. Bioacoustics **21**(2), 107–125 (2012)
69. Trifa, V.M., Kirschel, A.N., Taylor, C.E., Vallejo, E.E.: Automated species recognition of antbirds in a mexican rainforest using hidden markov models. J. Acoust. Soc. Am. **123**, 2424 (2008)

70. Uijlings, J.R., van de Sande, K.E., Gevers, T., Smeulders, A.W.: Selective search for object recognition. Int. J. Comput. Vis. **104**, 154–171 (2013)
71. Weber, E., Gut, D.: Assessing the risk of potentially invasive plant species in central europe. J. Nat. Conserv. **12**(3), 171–179 (2004)
72. Weber, E., Sun, S.G., Li, B.: Invasive alien plants in china: diversity and ecological insights. Biol. Invasions **10**(8), 1411–1429 (2008)

Overview of NewsREEL'16: Multi-dimensional Evaluation of Real-Time Stream-Recommendation Algorithms

Benjamin Kille[1]([✉]), Andreas Lommatzsch[1], Gebrekirstos G. Gebremeskel[2],
Frank Hopfgartner[3], Martha Larson[4,7], Jonas Seiler[5], Davide Malagoli[6],
András Serény[8], Torben Brodt[5], and Arjen P. de Vries[7]

[1] TU Berlin, Berlin, Germany
{benjamin.kille,andreas.lommatzsch}@dai-labor.de
[2] CWI, Amsterdam, The Netherlands
g.g.gebremeskel@cwi.nl
[3] University of Glasgow, Glasgow, UK
frank.hopfgartner@glasgow.ac.uk
[4] TU Delft, Delft, The Netherlands
m.a.larson@tudelft.nl
[5] Plista GmbH, Berlin, Germany
{jonas.seiler,torben.brodt}@plista.com
[6] ContentWise R&D — Moviri, Milan, Italy
davide.malagoli@moviri.com
[7] Radboud University Nijmegen, Nijmegen, The Netherlands
arjen@acm.org
[8] Gravity Research, Budapest, Hungary
sereny.andras@gravityrd.com

Abstract. Successful news recommendation requires facing the challenges of dynamic item sets, contextual item relevance, and of fulfilling non-functional requirements, such as response time. The CLEF NewsREEL challenge is a campaign-style evaluation lab allowing participants to tackle news recommendation and to optimize and evaluate their recommender algorithms both online and offline. In this paper, we summarize the objectives and challenges of NewsREEL 2016. We cover two contrasting perspectives on the challenge: that of the operator (the business providing recommendations) and that of the challenge participant (the researchers developing recommender algorithms). In the intersection of these perspectives, new insights can be gained on how to effectively evaluate real-time stream recommendation algorithms.

Keywords: Recommender Systems · News · Multi-dimensional Evaluation · Living Lab · Stream-based Recommender

1 Introduction

Comparing the performance of algorithms requires evaluation under controlled conditions. Conventionally, in the recommender system research community,

© Springer International Publishing Switzerland 2016
N. Fuhr et al. (Eds.): CLEF 2016, LNCS 9822, pp. 311–331, 2016.
DOI: 10.1007/978-3-319-44564-9_27

controlled conditions are created by adopting a static data set, and a single evaluation metric. In this paper, we discuss how evaluation of real-time stream recommendation algorithms presents challenges that cannot be so easily controlled for. Our topic is the News Recommendation Evaluation Lab (News-REEL) [12] at CLEF 2016. NewsREEL makes it possible for participants to test news recommendation algorithms online. We focus here on two particular issues that online recommenders face: data variation and non-functional requirements. Our novel focus is a contrast between two perspectives in the online challenge: the perspective of *recommender system operators*, who wish to make a pragmatic choice of the best recommender algorithm for their purposes and the perspective of the *participants* of the challenge, researchers who are trying to understand the extent to which their experiments represent controlled conditions. First, we present the two issues in more depth. The data variation in the ecosystem of a real-time stream-recommendation algorithm is extreme, bringing to mind the adage "the only thing that stays the same is change". User interaction patterns with news items may shift radically, during a high-profile event, or unexpected breaking news. Interaction patterns may differ depending on region, device, or news source. New items are generated constantly, and the shelf life of old items expires. Different user subpopulations interact with content in different ways. Evaluating real-life recommender systems is challenging, since it is no longer possible to carefully control conditions in the face of such variation. Real-life recommender systems must be responsive to these variations, and, at the same time, must also fulfill non-functional requirements. Users request information continuously in stream of interactions. Huge numbers of simultaneously interacting users create peak loads. Recommender systems must remain available, and provide sub-second responses. Both recommender system operators and challenge participants agree that A/B testing is the approach to take in order to assess algorithms for stream recommendation. A/B testing splits users into disjoint groups each of which interacts with a specific system. A decision can then be made on which system is better. Operators and challenge participants contrast in their perspectives on how the comparison is made. We cover the position of each briefly in turn. The goal of the operator is to run a successful service and/or business. The operator is interested in making a practical choice between algorithms. As differences emerge between systems running online, the operator disables inferior systems. The algorithm that survives this "survival of the fittest" process suits the operators' needs. However, the particularities of the performance of the recommender algorithms during the test window are tied to the specific time of the window and the specific user assignments. Repeating the evaluation is infeasible. Businesses deploy sophisticated system architectures which enable them to cope with the requirements of scale and response time. The value of an algorithm is related to its ability to perform within a certain architecture. The goal of the challenge participant is to test algorithms in a real-world system, as well as to understand the differences between algorithms in detail. A participant in CLEF NewsREEL (Task 1) must deploy a recommendation engine that serves different publishers of online news in real-time. Participants are interested in repeatable experiments. In past years, we have noted that participation in NewsREEL requires the investment of a great deal of engineering effort on the part of participants. This year, we go beyond that observation to look at the contrast between the operators' and the participants' point of view. We hope that explicitly examining the differences will lead us to deeper insight on how they can productively complement each other. The operator/participant perspective contrast makes NewsREEL arguably more difficult and less straightforward than other recommender system benchmarks. Researchers who are accustomed to working with static data sets face a steep learning curve when it comes to stream-recommendation. Anyone who starts with the assumption that NewsREEL is just another Netflix-type competition will soon be frustrated. Offline evaluation procedures abstract from functional restrictions. Researchers who are used to offline evaluation tend not to consider such requirements. These skills are not taught in conventional machine learning or data science courses. Further, within NewsREEL, the 'view' of the participant on the data is limited because the associations between items and interactions is not explicit, but rather established via temporal proximity. For this reason, researchers might find that the depth to which they can analyze their results is more limited than they would otherwise expect. Such limitations arise because online systems exist to serve users, and their function as a living lab to evaluate algorithms, although important, remains secondary. The contrast, however, gives rise to a number of advantages. We believe that the interplay between functional and non-functional aspects is not taught in conventional courses, since it is simply very hard to teach without concrete example systems. NewsREEL allows researchers to experience in real-life what it means to have a highly promising algorithm which turns out to struggle when faced with real-world variation in data patterns and volume flow. Further, the contrast inspires us to dig more deeply into what can be done in order to add a certain amount of control to real-time recommender system evaluation. Specifically, NewsREEL releases a dataset (Task 2) that allows researchers to replay a certain period of the recommender system. The remainder of the paper discusses the objectives and challenges of NewsREEL 2016, and presents the contrasting perspectives of operator and participant in more depth. Section 2 sheds light on existing efforts to benchmark recommender systems. Section 3 introduces both tasks defined in the scope of NewsREEL. Section 4 elaborates on benchmarking tools used in NewsREEL. We introduce ORP (Task 1) and Idomaar (Task 2) supporting evaluation. Section 6 presents preliminary findings. Finally, Sect. 7 summarizes objectives of NewsREEL and outlines steps to further enhance benchmarking of news recommender systems.

2   Related Work

Evaluating information access systems challenges academia and industry alike, but conventionally they take different approaches. Academic researchers tend to focus on data-driven evaluation. Industry favors exploring algorithms in form of A/B tests. This section provides an overview of related work on these two approaches.

2.1 Benchmarking in Static Environments

Recommender systems carry out evaluation on standard test collections, similar to those performed in the field of information retrieval. A test collection usually consists of time-aligned ratings on items provided by a larger number of users, and of user attributes. The most popular test collection consists of movie ratings [11]. In order to benchmark recommendation performance, the dataset is usually split based on the time when a rating was provided, resulting in a training and a test dataset. The recommendation task is then to predict the rating that a user provided for an item in the test set. Over the years, various benchmarking campaigns have been organized to promote recommender systems evaluation, e.g., as part of scientific conferences [2,19,21] or as Kaggle[1] competitions (e.g., [18]). Apart from providing static datasets and organizing challenges to benchmark recommendation algorithms using these datasets, the research community has been very active in developing software and open source toolkits for the evaluation of static datasets. For example, Ekstrand et al. [7] introduce the LensKit[2] framework that contains several recommendation algorithms and benchmarking parameters. Similar frameworks have been been developed by Gantner et al. [8] and Said and Bellogín [20]. Such frameworks approach recommender systems evaluation from a static point of view, i.e., given a static dataset, the recommendation task is to predict users' ratings. Although this approach has some merits, it fails to address dynamic aspects that might influence recommendation tasks. Little work has focused on the relation between findings in static environments and online performances. Maksai et al. [17] evaluate how accuracy, diversity, coverage, and serendipity measured offline transfer to online settings. Their results indicate that offline accuracy does not suffice to predict users reactions. An overview of limitations of offline evaluation is provided in the next section.

2.2 Benchmarking in Dynamic Environments

In recent years, an increase has been observed in research efforts focusing on the evaluation of recommender system performance outside of the standard evaluation setting outlined above. For example, Chen et al. [4] performed experiments on recommending microblog posts. Similar work is presented by Diaz-Avilez et al. [6]. Chen et al. [5] studied various algorithms for real-time bidding of online ads. Garcin et al. [9] and Lommatzsch [16] focus on news recommendation. These approaches have in common that they are all evaluated in a live scenario, i.e., recommender algorithms have been benchmarked by performing A/B testing. A/B testing addresses various limitations that arise when using static datasets.

---

[1] http://www.kaggle.com
[2] http://lenskit.org/

In particular, research on static databases does not take external factors into account that might influence users' rating behavior. In the context of news, such external factors could be emerging trends and news stories. In the same context, the freshness of items (i.e., news articles) plays an important role that needs to be considered. At the same time, computational complexity is out of focus in most academic research scenarios. Quick computation is of uttermost importance for commercial recommender systems. Differing from search results provided by an information retrieval system, recommendations are provided proactively without any explicit request. Another challenge is the large number of requests and updates that online systems have to deal with. Offline evaluation using a static dataset conducts an exact comparison between different algorithms and participating teams. However, offline evaluation requires assumptions, such as that past rating or consumption behavior is able to reflect future preferences. The benchmarking community is just starting to make progress in overcoming these limitations. Notable efforts from the Information Retrieval community include the CLEF Living Labs task [1], which uses real-world queries and user clicks for evaluation. Also, the TREC Live Question Answering task[3] involves online evaluation, and requires participants to focus on both response time and answer quality.

3 Problem Description

Publishers let users access news stories on digital news portals. The number of articles available can overwhelm users inducing an information overload problem. To address this problem, publishers deploy recommender systems suggesting interesting articles to their users. CLEF NewsREEL evaluates such systems on the basis of how well users respond to the suggestions provided. NewsREEL divides into two tasks. Task 1 interfaces with an operating news recommender system making it possible to conduct A/B testing. For a detailed description of the evaluation scenario, we refer to [13]. Task 2 uses a dataset [14] to compare recommendation algorithms. For a detailed overview of this task, we refer to [15]. Both settings are subject to a variety of challenges. First, we cannot reliably track users over longer periods of time. Publishers use session cookies to recognize visitors. Those entail multiple issues. Users may share devices creating ambiguous profiles. Users may use multiple devices spreading their activity across multiple identifiers. Finally, users may prohibit cookies. Consequently, systems only receive limited knowledge about their users. Second, we deal with fluctuating collections of items. New stories emerge every day. Simultaneously, older stories become less interesting to the public.

3.1 Task 1: Benchmark News Recommendations in a Living Lab

Task 1 has participants access an operating recommender system — the Open Recommendation Platform (ORP) [3]. Publishers run webportals offering

---

[3] https://sites.google.com/site/trecliveqa2015/

news articles. As users visit these portals, they trigger recommendation requests. ORP receives these requests and distributes them randomly across recommendation engines deployed by participants. Subsequently, the chosen recommendation engine returns a ranked list of news articles which ORP forwards to the publisher. The length of the list depends on the publishers' user interface. ORP keeps track of how recipients respond to recommendations embedded in the publishers' website. Users signal interest when they click on recommendations. Missing clicks represent a somewhat unclear form of feedback. We cannot determine whether the lack of a click means that the user was not interested in the recommendation, or simply did not notice it. An underlying assumption is that disparities between groups of users will even out as participants serve a sufficiently large number of requests. In other words, the chance that an individual participant has a noticeable disadvantage becomes small as the number of requests gets larger. We determine the best contribution in terms of *click-through-rate* (CTR). The CTR represents the proportion of suggestions which recipients click. Later we will see that a key question is at which rate the differences between two streams of recommendation requests even out.

3.2   Task 2: Benchmark News Recommendations in a Simulated Environment

In addition to the online task evaluated based on live feedback, NewsREEL also offers Task 2, which involves offline evaluation based on a large dataset. The dataset has been created by recording the messages in the online evaluation over two months. The dataset consists of $\approx$ 100 million messages (Table 1). Each message contains a timestamp allowing the simulation of the online stream by replaying the dataset in the original order. A detailed description of the nature of the dataset is provided in [14].

Table 1. The key figures of the offline dataset provided for Task 2

Item create/update	User-item	Interactions	Sum of messages
July 2014	618 487	53 323 934	53 942 421
August 2014	354 699	48 126 400	48 481 099
sum of messages	973 186	101 450 334	102 423 520

The offline task focuses on reproducible evaluation of recommender algorithms. Simultaneously, the goal is to stay as close to the online system as possible. The participants should show that their recommender algorithms achieve a high CTR in different contexts (compared to the baseline recommender). In addition, the participants should show that the recommender scales well with the number of messages per minute. Since the offline tasks enables the simulation of different load levels, participants can show how new algorithms handle load peaks and how much time is required for processing the requests (expected response time distribution). NewsREEL Task 2 enables the reproducible evaluation of recommender algorithms. The realistic simulation of the NewsREEL message streams enables the detailed debugging as well as the simulation of different load levels. Since the evaluation is offline, teams can abstract away from network problems and optimize the algorithms on a well-defined dataset. Problems can be debugged and the performance of algorithms can be analyzed with respect to different metrics.

3.3 Summary

In this section, we have presented the two tasks that NewsREEL offers to participants. We have introduced ORP, which lets participants connect to a stream of recommendation requests issued by actual users. We have detailed the dataset released by NewsREEL to allow participants to evaluate recommendation algorithms offline and optimize their algorithms prior to deploy them online. It provides more than 100 million interactions, representing a comprehensive data set. Participants can implement collaborative filtering as well as content-based recommenders as the data set contains both interaction logs and item descriptions.

4   Multi-dimensional Evaluation Online and Offline

CLEF NewsREEL uses two tools supporting participants evaluating their news recommendation algorithms. First, we introduce a platform to access a stream of recommendation requests thus enabling A/B testing. Second, we present a framework that lets participants repeat recorded interaction thus allowing offline evaluation.

4.1   Online Evaluation Methods

NewsREEL lets participants connect with a continuous stream of requests in order to evaluate their recommendation algorithms online. The setting resembles the situation which industrial recommender systems face as they serve suggestions. The Open Recommendation Platform (ORP) lets participants access a request distribution interface. ORP receives recommendation requests by a variety of news publishers. Subsequently, ORP delegates requests randomly to linked recommendation servers. Such requests entail a variety of information. This includes references to the session, the news article currently displayed, browser settings, and keywords. Participants' systems ought to select a subset of permissible articles to return to the user. ORP takes the list and forwards it to the user. Subsequently, ORP monitors users' reactions and keeps track of click events. In this way, we gain insights on how well recommendation algorithms perform over time.

Multi-dimensional Objectives. Businesses determine their success in part by their market share. Market share reduces to the number of visits in the context of online media. Visits signal attention which represents a valuable asset for marketing. Whenever users click on a recommended item, they prolong their session thus adding another visit. Consequently, businesses seek to determine the recommendation strategy yielding best expected chance of clicks. In other words, businesses maximize the *click-through rate* (CTR). Additionally, however, there are other aspects which we have to consider. In particular, we need to assure availability and scalability. Availability concerns the proportion of time during which the system can receive requests. This proportion may be limited by maintenance, model updating, and failures. Scalability concerns how well systems handle large numbers or sudden increases of requests. ORP reports an error rate for each system. This error rate reveals how many requests resulted in error states. Errors arise whenever systems delay their recommendations or return invalid items.

Expected Setting. The contest allowed participants to operate multiple recommendation services simultaneously. ORP delegates requests randomly to responsive recommendation services. Consequently, we expect recommendation services with similar availability and error rate to receive similar numbers of requests. ORP has a fixed set of publishers assigned. This limits the total number of requests. The more algorithms participants deploy, the fewer requests each recommendation service receives. Experiences from previous editions of News-REEL indicate that we can expect 5000 to 10000 requests per day for recommendation services with high availability and low error rate. This corresponds to a mean request frequency of 0.06 Hz to 0.12 Hz. Requests distribute unevenly across the day. As a result, we expect participants to experience considerably higher frequencies of more than 10 Hz at peak times.

4.2 Offline Evaluation Methods

The offline task allows participants to evaluate recommender algorithms in a replicable way. It enables the detailed debugging as well as the analysis of algorithms in predefined load scenarios. Due to the possibility to replicate the experiments exactly, the offline evaluation ensures the comparability of different recommender algorithms and the optimization of parameters.

Replaying Recorded Streams. The sequence of messages in a stream often contains important information. In order to ensure a realistic evaluation, we preserve the message order (recorded in an online setting) also in the offline evaluation. We provide a component that, roughly spoken, replays the stream of messages. We preserve the order of the messages as well as the timestamps keeping the stream as similar as possible to the originally recorded stream. The simulation of the stream ensures realistic simulation of the online stream. At every timeslot the recommender algorithms "knows" only the items the recommender would also "know" in the online evaluation.

Evaluation Method. In the evaluation, we use a window-based approach. We do not use cross-validation, since cross-validation does not preserve order of the messages. Instead of the n-fold splitting used in cross-validation, we use a continuously growing training window. The window begins with the start of the simulated stream and grows continuously over time. The part of the stream consisting of the 5 min right after the training window is used as ground truth window. A recommendation for a user is handled as correct if the user reads the recommended article in the 5 min after the request.

CTR-Related Metrics. In contrast to the online evaluation, there is no direct feedback from users. Thus, we have to define the Click-Through-Rate based on the log data collected in the online challenge. In order to decouple the offline evaluation from the recommender algorithms used while recording the offline dataset, we define the metric based on the impressions. Impressions characterize all events when users access news articles. They arise from search, browsing, and recommendations. Empirically, clicks occur in approximately 1 of 100 impressions. Thus, we expect at most a marginal bias by shifting our focus to impressions. Figure 1 illustrates the procedure.

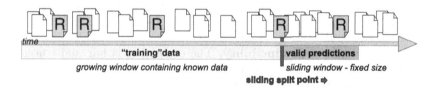

Fig. 1. The figure visualizes the calculation of the offline Click-through-Rate based on a simulated stream.

Metrics Focusing on Technical Aspects. Ensuring short response time as well as the scalability of the recommender algorithms are important requirements in the NewsREEL challenge. Based on the requirements we define metrics allowing us measuring the performance of the analyzed algorithms with respect to technical aspects. We use response time to determine how well algorithms scale to the load of requests.

Response Time. In order to ensure that recommendations can be seamlessly embedded into websites, they must be delivered within a predefined time limit. That is the motivation for analyzing the response time of the recommender algorithms in detail. Typically, the response time varies. We address this observation by calculating the distribution of response time values. The distribution expresses how frequently specific response times are measured. The distribution allows us to determine average and variance of response times. In addition, we compute the average response time and the fraction of requests that are not answered within the predefined time limit.

Offline Evaluation Framework. The exact reproducibility of offline evaluation requires that all steps and all environmental parameters are exactly defined. In order to compare the technical complexity of different algorithms, the computational environment must be defined in a reproducible way. We address this issue by using the evaluation framework *Idomaar*[4]. The framework is a recommender system reference framework developed in the settings of the European Project CrowdRec[5]. It builds reproducible computing environments based on virtual machines having an exactly defined software environment based on PUPPET. The resources and all software components (and versions) available during the evaluation are clearly defined, ensuring that neither old software components nor remainders from earlier evaluation runs may distort the results. All steps of the evaluation are executed based on scripts ensuring that the complete evaluation is reproducible.

- **Architecture independence**. Participants can use their preferred environments. Idomaar provides an evaluation solution that is independent of the programming language and platform. The evaluation framework can be controlled by connecting to two given communication interfaces by which data and control messages are sent by the framework.
- **Effortless integration**. The interfaces required to integrate the custom recommendation algorithms make use of open-source, widely-adopted technologies: Apache Spark and Apache Flume. Consequently, the integration can take advantage of popular, ready-to-use clients existing in almost all languages.
- **Consistency and reproducibility**. The evaluation is fair and consistent among all participants as the full process is controlled by the reference framework, which operates independently from the algorithm implementation.
- **Stream management**. Idomaar is designed to manage, in an effective and scalable way, a stream of data (e.g., users, news, events) and recommendation requests.

Advantages of Idomaar. Idomaar automates the evaluation process. It implements a three-stage workflow: (i) data preparation, (ii) data streaming, and (iii) result evaluation. The Orchestrator controls the environment. This includes setting up virtual machines, regulating communication between components, and measuring aspects such as response times. The configuration of virtual machines is fully specified including hardware resources and installed software packages. Therefore, evaluations will reproduce identical results. In addition, manual mistakes are limited due to automated evaluation protocols.

4.3 Discussion

In this section, we introduced two tools supporting participants evaluating news recommendation algorithms. First, we discussed how ORP enables participants

---

[4] http://rf.crowdrec.eu/
[5] http://www.crowdrec.eu/

to connect to a stream of recommendation requests. This yields a similar experience to A/B testing. Second, we presented Idomaar which is designed to support the efficient, reproducible evaluation of recommender algorithms. Idomaar is a powerful tool allowing users to abstract from concrete hardware or programming languages by setting up virtual machine having exactly defined resources. The evaluation platform allows a high degree of automation for setting up the runtime environment and for initializing the evaluation components. This ensures the easy reproducibility of evaluation runs and the comparability of results obtained with different recommender algorithms. Idomaar supports the set-based as well as the stream-based evaluation of recommender algorithms. In NewsREEL Task 2, the stream-based evaluation mode is used. In contrast to most existing evaluation frameworks Idomaar can be used out of the box and, for evaluation, considers not only the recommendation precision but also the resource demand of the algorithms.

5   The Participant Perspective

In this section, we present an appraisal of CLEF NewsREEL from the participants' perspective. In particular, we discuss opportunities, validity, and fairness. A more detailed discussion of the analysis presented in this section can be found in [10].

5.1   Opportunities

CLEF NewsREEL provides a unique opportunity for researchers working on recommender systems. It enables researchers to test their algorithms in a real-world setting with real users and items. In addition, participants compete with one another. Thus, they get feedback on how their algorithms compare with competitors' algorithms. Further, participants get access to a large number of log files comprising interactions between users and items. They can conduct offline experiments with these data thus optimizing their system prior to deploying them. Researchers hardly have access to such conditions otherwise, making CLEF NewsREEL a unique form of benchmarking.

5.2   Validity and Fairness

Participants seek to compare their algorithms with competing algorithms. They need to know how valid comparisons are in order to estimate how well their systems will perform in the future. Determining validity represents a challenging task. Unlike the operators of recommender systems, participants only perceive parts of the environment. Various effects can potentially bias observed performance. We distinguish operational and random biases, the latter resulting from random effects such as the dynamics in user and item collections. Operational bias refers to the result of operational choices of the evaluation framework, including those that lead to favoring some participants' systems over others, or delegating a disproportional number of requests from specific publishers to a few systems. The latter in particular would skew results, as items originating from specific publishers have been found to receive a stronger user response.

Fairness of the competition is closely related to the validity of findings, especially when considering operational biases. A (limited) level of random bias due to dynamic fluctuations in user and item collections is to be expected, but it would be very useful to be able to quantify its influence. In the absence of biases, we would expect to observe similar performance of identical systems over sufficiently long periods of time. Therefore, we have applied a method of evaluation that is best described as A/A testing; unlike in the usual A/B testing, A/A testing subjects the users to different instances of the exact same algorithm. The instances were run in the same computer and the same environment; just the port numbers they used to interact with ORP were different. With this setup, we do not expect the ORP to treat the two algorithms differently, since their behavior should be identical. Since the exact same algorithm was used to generate the recommendations, we attribute differences in the responses by users to those recommendations to bias, and we analyze those differences to quantify its effect.

Experiment. As participants, we conducted an experiment to estimate operational and random biases in CLEF NewsREEL. We set up two instances of the same recommendation algorithm, implementing an A/A testing procedure. We implemented a recency-driven recommender, which keeps the 100 most recently viewed items and suggests the five or six most recent upon request. Random biases may cause performance variations on a daily level. In the absence of operational biases, we may expect these performance measures to converge in the long-term. Both instances of the recency recommender have run in NewsREEL's editions 2015 and 2016. In 2015, the two instances ran from Sunday 12th April, 2015 to Monday 6th July, 2015, a total of 86 days. In 2016, both instances ran from Monday 22nd February, 2016 to Saturday 21st May, 2016, a total of 70 days. We considered only the recommendation requests and clicks of days on which the two instances of our algorithms ran simultaneously. Table 2 presents requests, clicks, and the CTR for both periods. The observed difference in CTR is small, 0.04% in 2015 and 0.07% in 2016, based on which we conclude that the evaluation does not show evidence of an operational bias. On the other hand, we notice a marginal level of random bias. Figure 2 shows the average CTR as a function of the number of days, for the year 2015 and Fig. 3 for the year 2016. Initially, we observe fairly high levels of variance between both instances in 2015. Over time, the variance levels off and both instances of the algorithm approach a common level of $\approx 0.85\%$. In 2016, we observe the opposite trend in that the algorithms perform more similarly and diverge towards the end.

Log Analysis. We noticed that A/A testing with two instances of the same algorithm results in performance variations, that, in 2015, smoothed out when observed over a sufficiently long period of time, but in 2016 showed divergence

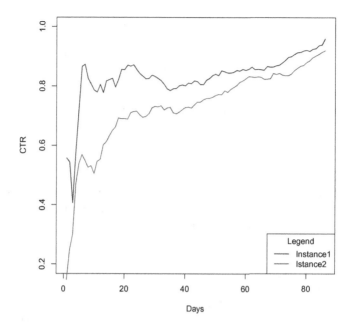

Fig. 2. The cumulative CTR performances of the two instances as they progress on a daily basis in 2015.

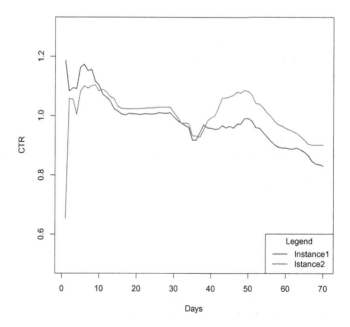

Fig. 3. The cumulative CTR performances of the two instances as they progress on a daily basis in 2015.

Table 2. Data collected by running two instances of the Recency recommender in the 2015 and 2016 editions of NewsREEL.

	2015			2016		
Algorithms	Requests	Clicks	CTR (%)	Requests	Clicks	CTR (%)
Instance1	90 663	870	0.96	450 332	3741	0.83
Instance2	88 063	810	0.92	398 162	3589	0.90

towards the end. We analyzed our log files from 2015 to identify two hypotheses to explain these variations. First, operational bias might induce an unfair setting, in which some algorithms naturally perform better than others. Alternatively, random bias due to the selection of users and items presented to each recommender may explain the performance variation observed.

Analyzing Recommendation Requests by Publisher: We look into the distribution of requests across publishers. In a fair competition, each participant will be subject to a similar distribution across publishers. We aggregated all requests on a publisher-level for both instances. Subsequently, we computed the Jensen-Shannon Divergence (JSD) metric to quantify the differences between both distributions. We obtained a divergence score of approximately 0.003, indicating that both instances received similar distributions of requests. At the level of a publisher, We conclude that we did not find a noticeable bias that would be attributed to operational design choices in the evaluation framework.

Analyzing Recommendation Requests and Responses at Item and User Levels: We investigate the overlap between the sets of users and items processed by both instances, by measuring their Jaccard similarity; high overlap would signal the absence of random biases. Comparison of the sets of items produced a Jaccard similarity of 0.318 whereas the sets of users resulted in a score of 0.220. Given the low overlap between users and items presented to both instances, we conjecture that the chance to observe the same user on both systems is relatively low (which can be explained by the limited number of events in each session). We note that the overlap is impacted by the fact that there are tens of other systems running simultaneously. The observed overlap is not inconsistent with the conclusion that user and item variation arises due to natural dynamics.

5.3   Discussion

In this section, we have discussed the NewsREEL challenge from the participants perspective. Our focus has been understanding the perspective that is accessible to the participants on whether or not the NewsREEL evaluation treats all participating algorithms fairly. We reported on the results of A/A testing conducted to estimate the level of variance in CTR for identical algorithms. We hypothesized that random effects or operational design choices could cause varying performances. We observed varying trends, in 2015 and 2016, in the cumulative performances of the two instances. In 2015, the variance diminished over time, but in 2016 the variance emerged later. We analyzed the logs of our participating systems to determine which kind of effect produced the variance. We found that requests were distributed equally across publishers for both instances. On the basis of this observation we were able to conclude, from the participant perspective, that operational design choices are unlikely to have caused the variance. Instead, we observed that collections of users and items differed between both instances.

From the participants perspective and the current setup, it is possible to conduct partial investigation into possible operational biases, have a reasonable estimate of the impact of those causes on the performance of a participating system. We conclude that participants do have the means to assure themselves of NewsREEL's fairness only using information available form the participants' perspective. We note, however, that an exhaustive investigation of all possible operational biases is either too complicated and/or impossible from the participant's perspective. For instance, operational biases could be implemented at the level of contextual factors, pariing some item categories to some participants or systems, and disvavoring one system on the basis of response and other network factors. The possibility to explore some of the biases is somewhat hampered by the fact that participants do not receive direct information on whether their recommendation are clicked. It is possible to extract a system's recommendation clicks from the logs, but it requires expensive implementation, and is also subject to error. The error is in turn dependent on the way in which the participant chooses to implement the mapping of recommendations to clicks.

6 Evaluation Results

At the time of writing, we have not yet received participants' working notes. This section highlights preliminary results observed for baseline method and some additional systems contributed by the organizers.

6.1 Task 1: Online Competition

Participants are required to provide suggestions maximizing the expected response rate. For this reason, we monitor how often users click recommended articles. Figure 4 shows the relation of clicks to requests for all participants over the stretch of three weeks. We note that all recommendation services fall into the range from 0.5% to 1.0%. Further, we observe that some recommendation services obtained considerably larger numbers of requests. These systems have had a higher availability than their competitors. They produce less errors by providing valid suggestions in a timely manner. Figure 5 illustrates how the error rate relates to the number of requests received. Participants with high error rates received fewer requests than those who managed to keep their error rates low. We note that additional factors affect the number of requests. Some participants had low error rates but still received few requests. Their systems had not been active for as long as their counterparts with higher number of requests.

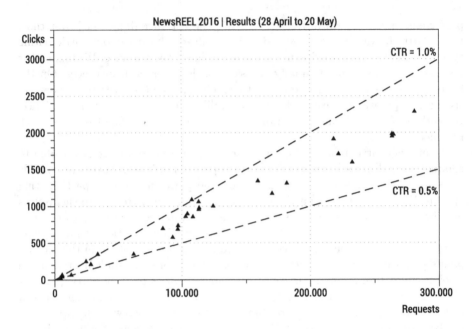

Fig. 4. Participating recommendation services delivered suggestions upon requests for period of three weeks. The figure shows how recipients responded in terms of clicks. Each triangle refers to a specific algorithm.

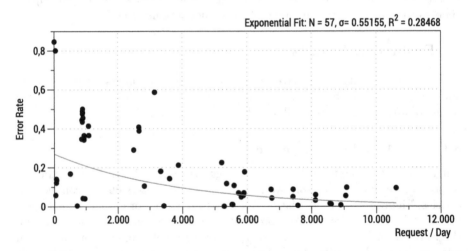

Fig. 5. Errors occur when recommendation services fail to timely return valid suggestions. ORP controls request delegation accordingly. The figure shows that the more errors systems produce, the fewer requests they receive.

6.2   Task 2: Offline Evaluation

Responding quickly to requests is essential for successful recommendations. We deployed two identical recommendation services to determine how network latency affects response times. Recommender service A replied from within the local subnet. Recommender service B replied from another net. Figure 6 illustrates the effect on response time. The orange line refers to recommender service A while the green line represents recommender service B. Both systems exhibit a bi-modular shape. System A has a higher peak at low response times. System B appears shifted toward higher response times. This illustrates the latency effect.

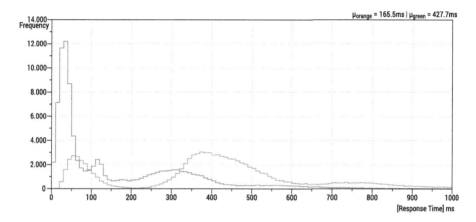

Fig. 6. Illustration of response times with identical implementation. The orange curve represents a system deployed in the local subnet whereas the green curve's underlying system operates from outside the local subnet. Network latency shifts the green distribution to the right. (Color figure online)

6.3   Comparing Online and Offline

Online and offline evaluations are frequently considered separately. Academia targets reproducible results on offline data sets. Businesses monitor user feedback continuously online. NewsREEL gives researchers the opportunity to compare performances in both regimes. Participants observe their performance in Task 1 and Task 2. Both settings support multi-dimensional evaluation. Task 1 reports click-through rates to assess how well systems cater to user preferences. Task 2 considers how accurately systems predict impressions. Impressions occur on various ways including browsing and search. Conversely, clicks are directly linked to recommendations. Thus, Task 2 is less affected by presentation biases of user interfaces than Task 1. Users might not perceive recommendations displayed online. Still, they can access articles that have been recommended. In contrast to Task 1, Task 2 would consider such user reading events as successful recommendations. As a result, we expect varying results as we compare online with offline accuracy. The question remains whether offline and online accuracy track each other. Task 1 determine reliability and scalability in terms of error rates. Recommendation services failing to return valid results obtain high error rates. Technical issues beyond the recommendation algorithm contribute to error rates. For instance, hardware defects, system maintenance, and network malfunctions induce errors not related to the recommendation algorithm. Task 2 simulates critical scenarios as it delegates requests at maximum capacity to the recommender system. This neglects the presence of periods with relatively low load in the online setting. Recommender systems only reply to a subset of requests in Task 1. Contrarily, Task 2 requires recommender systems to provide suggestions for all requests. As a consequence, systems can succeed online even though they exhibit inferior response times offline. Additionally, the offline evaluation lets participant detect flaws in their implementations.

6.4   Participation

In this year's edition, 48 participants registered for NewsREEL. Thereof, 46 signed up for Task 1 whereas 44 enlisted in Task 2. Multiple participants registered from the Netherlands (6), India (5), Turkey (4), Germany (3), United Kingdom (3), China (2), France (2), Norway (2), and Tunisia (2). Nine participants received virtual machines to deploy their recommendation service onto. This was meant to limit disadvantages due to network latency or the lack of hardware. We observed 21 teams competing with 73 different algorithms during the evaluation period of Task 1. In contrast, seven teams conducted offline experiments and shared their insights in form of working notes.

6.5   Discussion

The NewsREEL lab gives participants the opportunity to evaluate news recommendation algorithms. Analyzing the implemented strategies and discussing with the researchers, we find a wide variety of approaches, ideas, and frameworks. The performance as well as the response time of the algorithms varies with the algorithms and contexts. Thus, the performance ranking may change during the course of a single day. In order to compute a ranking, the challenge uses a comprehensive evaluation period (4 weeks in Task 1) and a huge dataset (consisting of ≈ 100 million messages in Task 2) respectively. The baseline recommender performs quite successfully, being always among the best 8 recommender algorithms. We observe that high error rates and low availability lead to few requests. This hampers comparing participants' systems. We cannot be sure that we can reproduce the ranking in a different context. For instance, the same set of recommenders performs differently 6 months later when an important event shapes users' interests in a different way. The CTR ranges from 0.5 % to 1.0 %.

7   Conclusion and Outlook

Suggesting news articles challenges recommender systems. Similarly to other domains, news recommender systems face streams of recommendation requests as visitors continue to interact with digital news websites. Streams make it challenging to update recommendation models and they also require scalable infrastructures. Additionally, systems have limited information about their users. Frequently, they lack any form of user profiles and rely on tracking them by session cookies. Furthermore, stories are continuously added to the collection of existing news items. For these reasons, establishing reproducible evaluation protocols is an ongoing struggle. Innovative strategies are needed to deal with this cumbersome problem.

CLEF NewsREEL provides participants with a unique opportunity to contribute ideas. Participants gain access to an operating news recommender system thus obtaining live feedback by actual users. In addition, they receive a large-scale data set covering news and interactions with news over a stretch of two months. Both tasks address not only preference modeling, but additionally they challenge participants to consider technical aspects such as scalability, reliability, and complexity. Other contests hardly address such factors even though businesses cannot ignore them. Task 1 measures the CTR as well as error rates. Task 2 measures how well algorithms predict future interactions as well as response times. By taking part in both tasks, participants can determine how well offline results transfer to online setting and what we can learn from them. This year's edition of NewsREEL allowed participants to evaluate their systems for several weeks online. Receiving several thousands request a day suffices to draw meaningful conclusions. However, we have to keep in mind that user preferences as well as news articles are continuously evolving. For this reason, algorithms providing the best suggestions today might fall behind in the future. Participants needed time to accustom themselves to ORP, which, in a yearly benchmarking cycle, means there is less time left for a long evaluation period.

Participants had the opportunity to provide feedback about the experiences with NewsREEL in an open conference call. We summarize what they suggested as improvements for future editions of NewsREEL. ORP ought to become more transparent and functional. As discussed above, currently, it is hard to track systems' success in terms of recommendations which are presented to users and then clicked. ORP does not explicitly provide references to recommendation requests when informing about click events. Instead, participants have to keep track of their recommendations and compare them with events from the continuous stream of messages. In addition, ORP currently disables recommenders producing errors without notifying participants. Thereby, participants' system availability decreases leading to fewer recommendation requests. Having been notified, participants could repair their system more quickly. In the future, we would like to allow for more time evaluating in order to have a more insightful comparison between offline and online performance. Additionally, we will clarify procedures and provide additional support for participants interested in offline evaluation. We plan to provide a ready-to-use installation of Idomaar on Amazon's S3 platform facilitating system setup.

Acknowledgments. The research leading to these results was performed in the Crow-dRec project, which has received funding from the European Union Seventh Framework Program FP7/2007–2013 under grant agreement No. 610594.

References

1. Balog, K., Kelly, L., Schuth, A.: Head first: living labs for ad-hoc search evaluation. In: Proceedings of the 23rd ACM International Conference on Conference on Information and Knowledge Management, CIKM 2014, pp. 1815–1818. ACM, New York, NY, USA (2014)
2. Blomo, J., Ester, M., Field, M.: RecSys challenge 2013. In: Proceedings of the 7th ACM Conference on Recommender Systems, RecSys 2013, pp. 489–490 (2013)
3. Brodt, T., Hopfgartner, F.: Shedding light on a living lab: the CLEF NEWSREEL open recommendation platform. In: IIiX 2014, pp. 223–226 (2014)
4. Chen, J., Nairn, R., Nelson, L., Bernstein, M.S., Chi, E.H.: Short and tweet: experiments on recommending content from information streams. In: Proceedings of the 28th International Conference on Human Factors in Computing Systems, CHI 2010, Atlanta, Georgia, USA, April 10–15, 2010, pp. 1185–1194 (2010)
5. Chen, Y., Berkhin, P., Anderson, B., Devanur, N.R.: Real-time bidding algorithms for performance-based display ad allocation. In: Proceedings of the 17th ACM SIGKDD International Conference on Knowledge Discovery and Data Mining, KDD 2011, pp. 1307–1315 (2011)
6. Diaz-Aviles, E., Drumond, L., Schmidt-Thieme, L., Nejdl, W.: Real-time top-n recommendation in social streams. In: Proceedings of the Sixth ACM Conference on Recommender Systems, RecSys 2012, pp. 59–66 (2012)
7. Ekstrand, M.D., Ludwig, M., Konstan, J.A., Riedl, J.T.: Rethinking the recommender research ecosystem: reproducibility, openness, and LensKit. In: RecSys 2011, pp. 133–140. ACM (2011)
8. Gantner, Z., Rendle, S., Freudenthaler, C., Schmidt-Thieme, L.: MyMediaLite: a free recommender system library. In: RecSys 2011, pp. 305–308. ACM (2011)
9. Garcin, F., Faltings, B., Donatsch, O., Alazzawi, A., Bruttin, C., Huber, A.: Offline and online evaluation of news recommender systems at swissinfo.ch. In: Eighth ACM Conference on Recommender Systems, RecSys 2014, Foster City, Silicon Valley, CA, USA - October 6–10, 2014, pp. 169–176 (2014)
10. Gebremeskel, G., de Vries, A.: Random performance differences between online recommender systems algorithms. (Manuscript submitted for publication) (2016)
11. Harper, F.M., Konstan, J.A.: The Movielens datasets: history and context. ACM Trans. Interact. Intell. Syst. **5**(4), 19: 1–19: 19 (2015)
12. Hopfgartner, F., Brodt, T., Seiler, J., Kille, B., Lommatzsch, A., Larson, M., Turrin, R., Serény, A.: Benchmarking news recommendations: The CLEF NewsREEL use case. SIGIR Forum **49**(2), 129–136 (2015)
13. Hopfgartner, F., Kille, B., Lommatzsch, A., Plumbaum, T., Brodt, T., Heintz, T.: Benchmarking news recommendations in a living lab. In: Kanoulas, E., Lupu, M., Clough, P., Sanderson, M., Hall, M., Hanbury, A., Toms, E. (eds.) CLEF 2014. LNCS, vol. 8685, pp. 250–267. Springer, Heidelberg (2014)
14. Kille, B., Hopfgartner, F., Brodt, T., Heintz, T.: The plista dataset. In: Proceedings of the 2013 International News Recommender Systems Workshop and Challenge, NRS 2013, pp. 16–23. ACM, New York, (2013)

15. Kille, B., Lommatzsch, A., Turrin, R., Serény, A., Larson, M., Brodt, T., Seiler, J., Hopfgartner, F.: Stream-based recommendations: online and offline evaluation as a service. In: Mothe, J., et al. (eds.) CLEF 2015. LNCS, vol. 9283, pp. 497–517. Springer, Heidelberg (2015)

16. Lommatzsch, A., Albayrak, S.: Real-time recommendations for user-item streams. In: Proceedings of the 30th Symposium On Applied Computing, SAC 2015, SAC 2015, pp. 1039–1046. ACM, New York, (2015)

17. Maksai, A., Garcin, F., Faltings, B.: Predicting online performance of news recommender systems through richer evaluation metrics. In: Proceedings of the 9th ACM Conference on Recommender Systems, RecSys 2015, pp. 179–186. ACM, New York, (2015)

18. McFee, B., Bertin-Mahieux, T., Ellis, D.P., Lanckriet, G.R.: The million song dataset challenge. In: Proceedings of the 21st International Conference Companion on World Wide Web, WWW 2012 Companion, pp. 909–916 (2012)

19. Di Noia, T., Cantador, I., Ostuni, V.C.: Linked open data-enabled recommender systems: ESWC 2014 challenge on book recommendation. In: Presutti, V., et al. (eds.) SemWebEval 2014. CCIS, vol. 475, pp. 129–143. Springer, Heidelberg (2014)

20. Said, A., Bellogín, A.: Rival: a toolkit to foster reproducibility in recommender system evaluation. In: RecSys 2014, pp. 371–372. ACM, New York, (2014)

21. Tavakolifard, M., Gulla, J.A., Almeroth, K.C., Hopfgartner, F., Kille, B., Plumbaum, T., Lommatzsch, A., Brodt, T., Bucko, A., Heintz, T.: Workshop and challenge on news recommender systems. In: Seventh ACM Conference on Recommender Systems, RecSys 2013, Hong Kong, China, October 12–16, 2013, pp. 481–482 (2013)

Overview of PAN'16

New Challenges for Authorship Analysis: Cross-Genre Profiling, Clustering, Diarization, and Obfuscation

Paolo Rosso[1], Francisco Rangel[2], Martin Potthast[3]([⊠]), Efstathios Stamatatos[4], Michael Tschuggnall[5], and Benno Stein[3]

[1] PRHLT Research Center, Universitat Politècnica de València, Valencia, Spain
[2] Autoritas Consulting, S.A., Valencia, Spain
[3] Web Technology and Information Systems, Bauhaus-Universität Weimar, Weimar, Germany
`martin.potthast@uni-weimar.de`
[4] Department of Information and Communication Systems Engineering, University of the Aegean, Mitilini, Greece
[5] Department of Computer Science, University of Innsbruck, Innsbruck, Austria
`pan@webis.de`
`http://pan.webis.de`

Abstract. This paper presents an overview of the PAN/CLEF evaluation lab. During the last decade, PAN has been established as the main forum of digital text forensic research. PAN 2016 comprises three shared tasks: *(i)* author identification, addressing author clustering and diarization (or intrinsic plagiarism detection); *(ii)* author profiling, addressing age and gender prediction from a cross-genre perspective; and *(iii)* author obfuscation, addressing author masking and obfuscation evaluation. In total, 35 teams participated in all three shared tasks of PAN 2016 and, following the practice of previous editions, software submissions were required and evaluated within the TIRA experimentation framework.

1 Introduction

Uncovering Plagiarism, Authorship, and Social Software Misuse (PAN) is a forum for the digital text forensics, where researchers and practitioners study technologies that analyze texts with regard to originality, authorship, and trustworthiness. The practical importance of such technologies is obvious for law enforcement and marketing, yet the general public needs to be aware of their capabilities as well to make informed decisions about them. This is particularly true since almost all of these technologies are still in their infancy, and active research is required to push them forward. Therefore, PAN focuses on the evaluation of selected tasks from digital text forensics in order to develop large-scale, standardized benchmarks, and to assess the state-of-the-art techniques. The targeted audiences in terms of research areas range from linguistics and computational linguistics to data mining and machine learning; targeted audiences in terms of users of envisioned tools are professionals, such as forensic

N. Fuhr et al. (Eds.): CLEF 2016, LNCS 9822, pp. 332–350, 2016.
DOI: 10.1007/978-3-319-44564-9_28

Table 1. Key figures of the PAN workshop series since 2009.

Statistics	SEPLN	CLEF						
	2009	2010	2011	2012	2013	2014	2015	2016
Follower	78	151	181	232	286	302	333	
Registrations	21	53	52	68	110	103	148	147
Runs/Software	14	27	27	48	58	57	54	35
Notebooks	11	22	22	34	47	36	52	26
Attendees	18	25	36	61	58	44	74	-

Table 2. Key figures of the FIRE workshop series since 2011.

Statistics	FIRE				
	2011	2012	2013	2014	2015
Follower					
Registrations	6	12	16	20	31
Runs/Software	6	8	8	17	20
Notebooks	6	2	6	4	6
Attendees	6	2	6	3	9

linguists, copyright protectors, lawyers, criminal investigators, and educators, but also laymen web users.

Previous editions of PAN have been organized in the form of workshops (2007–2009) as well as evaluation labs (2009–2015), and they were held in conjunction with the conferences SIGIR, ECAI, SEPLN, and in the recent years CLEF and FIRE. Tables 1 and 2 overview key figures of PAN/CLEF and PAN/FIRE labs. At PAN'16 we focused on authorship tasks from the fields of *(i)* author identification, *(ii)* author profiling, and *(iii)* author obfuscation evaluation. More specifically, the tasks will include two variants per field, namely author clustering and diarization, age and gender prediction, and author masking and obfuscation. A brief introduction to each of them follows, more details are given in the corresponding sections.

– Author Clustering/Diarization. Author clustering is the task where given a document collection the participant is asked to group documents written by the same author so that each cluster corresponds to a different author. This task can also be viewed as establishing authorship linking between documents. The training corpus comprised a set of author clustering problems in 3 languages (English, Dutch, and Greek) and 2 genres (newspaper articles and reviews). In PAN'16 we focused on document-level author clustering, while a variation of author clustering was included in the PAN'12 edition [23]. However, it was focused on the paragraph-level and therefore it is more related to the author diarization task. The task of author diarization is to identify different authors within a single document. Such documents may be the result of a collaborative work (e.g., a combined master thesis written by two students, a scientific paper written by four authors, ...), or the result of plagiarism. The latter is thereby a special case, where it can be assumed that the main text is written by one author and only some fragments are by other writers (the plagiarized or intrusive sections).

- Age/Gender Prediction. Since PAN'13 we have been organizing the shared task of author profiling [60,61], focussing mainly on age and gender identification (at PAN'15 also personality recognition [59]). While the goal in previous editions was to study different genres, at PAN'16 we aimed at evaluating age and gender identification in a cross-genre setting. The training was carried out on tweets, and the test on blogs, social media and hotel reviews, in the following languages: English, Spanish, and Dutch.
- Author Masking/Obfuscation Evaluation. While the goal of author identification and author profiling is to model author style so as to deanomyize authors, the goal of author obfuscation technology is to prevent that by disguising the authors. Corresponding approaches have never been systematically evaluated for quality, nor whether they are capable of confusing existing author identification and profiling software. The author obfuscation shared task at PAN aims at closing this gap. Concretely, author masking and author obfuscation evaluation aim respectively at perturbing an author's style in a given text to render it dissimilar to other texts from the same author, and at adjusting a given text's style so as to render it similar to that of a given author. The success of corresponding approaches has been evaluated considering readability and paraphrase quality. Our final aim is to check whether the state-of-the-art techniques of author identification and author profiling research fields (the software submissions to author identification and author profiling of previous years is available on our TIRA experimentation platform) is robust against author obfuscation technology.

2 Author Identification

Previous editions of PAN focused on author identification tasks that could be handled as supervised classification problems. In particular, the task was to assign documents of unknown authorship to one of the candidate authors. This was based on the fact that for each candidate author samples of their texts were available. Variations of this task considered cases where the set of candidate authors is either closed or open [4,23] as well as a singleton (*author verification*) [26,71,72]. At PAN'16, we focus on unsupervised author identification tasks where there is lack of candidate authors and samples of known authorship. In more detail, we focus on two main tasks: *(i)* given a set of documents, identify groups of documents by the same author (*author clustering*) and *(ii)* given a single multi-author document, identify parts of document written by the same author (*author diarization*).

2.1   Author Clustering

Author clustering is the task of grouping documents by their author in a given document collection [31,63]. This task is useful in multiple domains where there is lack of reliable authorship information in document collections [1,21]. For example, in a collection of novels published anonymously we might be able to decide that they are written by a single person. Given some proclamations published by terrorist groups we can identify proclamations, either of the same or different groups, by the same authors. Provided a collection of online product reviews by users with different aliases we can extract the conclusion that some of the aliases actually correspond to the same person.

In this edition of PAN we study two application scenarios:

(a) **Complete author clustering**: This scenario requires a detailed analysis where, first, the number of different authors (k) found in the collection should be identified and, second, each document should be assigned to exactly one of the k authors.
(b) **Authorship-link ranking**: This scenario views the exploration of the given document collection as a retrieval task. It aims at establishing authorship links between documents and provides a list of document pairs ranked according to a confidence score (the score shows how likely it is the document pair to be by the same author).

In more detail, given a collection of (up to 100) documents, the task is to *(i)* identify groups of documents by the same author and *(ii)* provide a ranked list of authorship links (pairs of document by the same author). All documents within the collection are single-authored, in the same language, and belong to the same genre. However, the topic or text-length of documents may vary. The number of distinct authors whose documents are included in the collection is not given.

To evaluate the complete author clustering task, we use *extrinsic* clustering evaluation (i.e., true labels of data are available) and, in particular, *B-cubed Precision*, *B-cubed Recall*, and *B-cubed F-score*. These measures have been found to satisfy several formal constraints including cluster homogeneity, cluster completeness, and the *rag bag* criterion (where multiple unrelated items are merged into a single cluster) [3]. As concerns authorship-link ranking, we use *mean average precision* (MAP), a standard scalar evaluation measure for ranked retrieval results.

Corpora. A new corpus was developed for this shared task comprising several instances of clustering problems in three languages (Dutch, English, and Greek) and two genres (articles and reviews) per language. A more detailed description of this corpus is following:

- English part: All documents have been published in the UK daily newspaper *The Guardian*[1]. Opinion articles about politics and UK were used in the training corpus while the evaluation corpus was based on opinion articles about society. Moreover, book reviews on the thematic area of culture were considered.
- Dutch part: It includes opinion articles from the Flemish daily newspaper *De Standaard* and weekly news magazine *Knack*. In addition, it comprises reviews taken from the CLiPS Stylometry Investigation (CSI) corpus [76]. These are both positive and negative reviews about both real and fictional products from the following categories: smartphones, fastfood restaurants, books, artists, and movies.
- Greek part: The opinion articles included in this part published in the online forum *Protagon*[2]. The training corpus was based on articles about politics and the evaluation part utilized articles about economy. In addition, this corpus comprises a collection of restaurant reviews downloaded from a relevant website[3].

For each combination of language-genre, we produced several instances of clustering problems corresponding to different ratios $r = k/N$, where N is the number of documents in a given collection. This ratio indicates the percentage of single-document clusters as well as the number of available authorship links. For instance, if r is high then most documents in the collection belong to single-document clusters and the number of authorship links is low. In this evaluation campaign, we selected to examine the following three cases:

- $r \approx 0.9$: only a few documents belong to multi-document clusters and it is unlikely to find authorship links.
- $r \approx 0.7$: the majority of documents belong to single-document clusters but it is likely to find authorship links.
- $r \approx 0.5$: less than half of the documents belong to single-document clusters and there are plenty of authorship links.

Table 3 shows statistics of the corpus used in this evaluation campaign. As concerns the length of documents, reviews in Dutch and Greek are shorter than the corresponding articles while English book reviews are longer than English articles. The number of documents per clustering instance ranges between 50 and 100.

Results. We received 8 submissions in the author clustering subtask. Following the practice of previous editions of PAN, the participants submitted their software in TIRA experimentation framework where they were able to apply their approach in both training and final evaluation corpora. The task of PAN

---

[1] http://www.theguardian.com.
[2] http://www.protagon.gr.
[3] https://www.ask4food.gr.

Table 3. Statistics of the author clustering evaluation corpus. Corresponding statistics of the training corpus are inside parentheses.

Language	Genre	Instances	Avg. Docs	Avg. words
English	articles	3 (3)	70 (50)	583.2 (751.1)
English	reviews	3 (3)	80 (80)	1,015.1 (1,032.3)
Dutch	articles	3 (3)	57 (57)	1,098.6 (1,137.1)
Dutch	reviews	3 (3)	100 (100)	152.6 (129.5)
Greek	articles	3 (3)	70 (55)	736.1 (739.1)
Greek	reviews	3 (3)	70 (55)	466.7 (573.4)

organizers was reduced to review the output of submitted systems and publish evaluation results. A summary of the evaluation results is presented in Table 4 (average values for all instances of the evaluation corpus). The baseline corresponds to a naive approach where the provided documents are randomly grouped in clusters. Average performance of 50 repetitions of this baseline approach is shown.

In both complete author clustering and authorship-link ranking, the submissions of Bagnall and Kocher achieved the best results. A high B-cubed recall indicates that an approach tends to produce large clusters while a high B-cubed precision usually corresponds to many single-item clusters. For the authorship-link ranking task, the approaches by Bagnall and Gobeill are significantly better than the rest of participants. A more detailed presentation of evaluation results is provided in [70].

2.2   Author Diarization

The author diarization task of the PAN'16 lab continues and extends the previous tasks from 2009–2011 on intrinsic plagiarism detection [46]. The original problem is related to the question, whether an author has misused text from others without proper references, and if yes, which text fragments are affected. Thereby the key word *intrinsic* indicates that potential plagiarized sections have to be found by inspecting solely the respective document, i.e., any comparisons with external sources are disallowed [74]. Consequently, authors have to be identified by analyzing the writing style in some way. This is not an artificial restriction, but has practical relevance in plagiarism detection systems, e.g., to limit or pre-order the search space, or to investigate older documents where potential sources are not digitally available.

Tasks and Corpora. Based on that, the shared task at PAN'16 focuses on identifying authorships within a single document. Thereby it is not only searched for plagiarism, but also for the contributions of different writers in a multi-author document. Among examples for the latter are collaboratively written student theses or scientific papers composed by a known number of cooperating

Table 4. Evaluation results for the author clustering task (submissions are ranked according to BCubed F-score).

Participant	B3 F-score	B3 Recall	B3 Precision	MAP
Bagnall	0.8223	0.7263	0.9765	0.1689
Kocher	0.8218	0.7215	0.9816	0.0540
Sari & Stevenson	0.7952	0.7330	0.8927	0.0399
Zmiycharov et al.	0.7684	0.7161	0.8521	0.0033
Gobeill	0.7058	0.7669	0.7373	0.1146
Baseline	0.6666	0.7140	0.6412	0.0015
Kuttichira	0.5881	0.7202	0.5122	0.0014
Mansoorizadeh et al.	0.4008	0.8218	0.2804	0.0085
Vartapetiance & Gillam	0.2336	0.9352	0.1947	0.0120

researchers. As an overall keyword for the task, the title *author diarization* has been chosen[4], consisting of three related subtasks:

(a) **Traditional intrinsic plagiarism detection**: Assuming a major author who wrote at least 70 % of a document, the task is to find the remaining text portions written by one or several others.

(b) **Diarization with a given number of authors**: The basis for this subtask is a document which has been composed by a known number of authors. Participants should then attempt to group the individual text fragments by authors.

(c) **Unrestricted diarization**: As a tightening variant of the previous scenario, the number of collaborating authors is not given as an input variable for the last subtask. Thus, before/during analyzing and attributing the text, also the correct number of clusters, i.e., writers, has to be found.

For all subtasks, distinct training and test datasets have been provided, which are based on the Webis-TRC-12 dataset [54]. The original corpus contains documents on 150 topics used at the TREC Web Tracks from 2009–2011 (e.g., [12]), whereby professional writers were hired and asked to search for a given topic and to compose a single document from the search results. From these documents, the respective datasets for all subtasks have been generated by varying several configurations like the number and proportions of authors in a document, the decision, if they are uniformly distributed or if switches in authorships are allowed to occur within a single sentence, at the end of a sentence or only between paragraphs. As the original corpus has already been partly used and published, the test documents are created from previously unpublished documents only. Overall, the number of training/test documents for the respective subtasks are: (a) 71/29, (b) 55/31 and (c) 54/29.

---

[4] The term "diarization" originates from the research field *speaker diarization*, where approaches try to automatically identify, cluster or extract different (parallel) speakers of an audio speech signal like a telephone conversation or a political debate [39].

Table 5. Intrinsic plagiarism detection results (Problem a).

		Micro			Macro		
Rank	Team	Recall	Precision	F	Recall	Precision	F
1	Kuznetsov *et al.*	**0.19**	**0.29**	**0.22**	**0.15**	**0.28**	**0.17**
2	Sittar *et al.*	0.07	0.14	0.08	0.10	0.14	0.10

Table 6. Diarization results (Problems b and c).

			BCubed		
#authors	Rank	Team	Recall	Precision	F
known (Problem b)	1	Kuznetsov *et al.*	0.46	**0.64**	**0.52**
	2	Sittar *et al.*	**0.47**	0.28	0.32
unknown (Problem c)	1	Kuznetsov *et al.*	0.42	**0.64**	**0.48**
	2	Sittar *et al.*	**0.47**	0.31	0.35

Results. The performance of the submitted algorithms have been measured with two different metrics. For the intrinsic plagiarism detection subtask, the micro-/macro-metrics proposed in [55] have been used, whereby the ranking is based on the macro calculation[5]. On the other hand, the diarization subtasks have been measured with the BCubed clustering metrics [3], as they reflect the inside-document clustering nature of those tasks very well. The final results of the 2 participating teams are presented in Tables 5 and 6. Fine-grained sub results depending on the dataset configuration, e.g., the number of authors in a document and their contribution rate, are presented in the respective overview paper of this task [70].

3   Author Profiling

Author profiling distinguishes between classes of authors studying their sociolect aspect, that is, how language is shared by people. This helps in identifying profiling aspects such as gender, age, native language, or personality type. Author profiling is a problem of growing importance in applications in forensics, security, and marketing. E.g., from a forensic linguistics perspective one would like being able to know the linguistic profile of the author of a harassing text message (language used by a certain type of people) and identify certain characteristics (language as evidence). Similarly, from a marketing viewpoint, companies may be interested in knowing, on the basis of the analysis of blogs and online product reviews, the demographics of people that like or dislike their products. Pennebaker's [43] investigated how the style of writing is associated with personal attributes such as age, gender and personality traits, among others.

---

[5] Conforming to previous PAN events.

In [5] the authors approached the task of gender identification on the British National Corpus and achieved approximately 80 % accuracy. Similarly in [20] and [8] the authors investigated age and gender identification on formal texts. Recently most investigations focus on social media. For example, in [28] and [66] the authors investigated the style of writing in blogs. On the other hand, Zhang and Zhang [79] experimented with short segments of blog post and obtained 72.1 % accuracy for gender prediction. Similarly, Nguyen et al. [41] studied the use of language and age among Dutch Twitter users. Since 2013 a shared task on author profiling has been organised at PAN [59–61]. It is worth mentioning the second order representation based on relationships between documents and profiles used by the best performing team of all editions [2,32,33]. Recently, the EmoGraph graph-based approach [57] tried to capture how users convey verbal emotions in the morphosyntactic structure of the discourse, obtaining competitive results with the best performing systems at PAN 2013 and demonstrating its robustness against genres and languages at PAN 2014 [58]. Moreover, the authors in [78] investigated on PAN-AP-2013 dataset a high variety of different features and showed the contribution of information retrieval based features in age and gender identification and in [35] the authors approached the task with 3 million features in a MapReduce configuration, obtaining high accuracies with fractions of processing time.

Tasks and Corpora. In the Author Profiling task at PAN'16 participants approached the task of identifying age and gender from a cross-genre perspective in three different languages: English, Spanish and Dutch. English and Spanish partitions were labelled with age and gender. For labelling age, the following classes were considered: 18–24; 25–34; 35–49; 50+. Dutch partition was labelled only with gender. The dataset was split into training, early birds and test, as in previous editions. Training partition was collected from Twitter for the three languages. For English and Spanish, early birds partition was collected from social media and test partition from blogs. Both were compiled from PAN'14's dataset. In case of Dutch, both early birds and test partitions were collected from reviews. The number of authors per language and age class can be seen in Table 7. The corpus is balanced per gender but imbalanced per age.

For evaluation, the accuracy for age, gender and joint identification per language is calculated. Then, we average the results obtained per language (Eq. 1).

$$\overline{gender} = \frac{gender\_en + gender\_es + gender\_nl}{3}$$

$$\overline{age} = \frac{age\_en + age\_es}{2} \tag{1}$$

$$\overline{joint} = \frac{joint\_en + joint\_es}{2}$$

Table 7. Distribution of authors with respect to age classes per language. Dutch partition is labelled only with gender information. The corpus is balanced per gender.

	Training			Early birds			Test		
	EN	ES	NL	EN	ES	NL	EN	ES	NL
18–24	13	16		35	8		5	2	
25–34	68	64		46	10		12	6	
35–49	91	126		51	8		16	13	
50+	39	38		40	4		5	5	
Σ	211	244	192	172	30	25	38	26	250

The final ranking is calculated as the average of the previous values (Eq. 2):

$$ranking = \frac{\overline{gender} + \overline{age} + \overline{joint}}{3} \qquad (2)$$

In summary, the Author Profiling shared task at PAN'16 focuses on the following aspects:

- **Age and gender identification:** As in previous editions, the task is to predict age and gender, and also the joint identification of age and gender for the same author.
- **Cross-genre evaluation:** The aim is at evaluating the performance of author profiling systems in a cross-genre setting. The training is provided in one genre (Twitter) and the evaluation is carried on another genre (social media, blogs or reviews).
- **Multilingual:** Participants are provided with data in English, Spanish and Dutch.

Results. This year 22[6] have been the teams who participated in the shared task. In this section we show a summary of the obtained results. In Table 8 the overall performance per language and users' ranking are shown[7]. We can observe that in general accuracies in both English and Spanish datasets are similar, although the highest results were achieved in Spanish (42.86 %). With respect to Dutch, were only the gender accuracy is shown, results are not much better than the random baseline (the highest value is equal to 61.80 %). It should be highlighted that this occurs even when the Dutch test set is the largest one. In Table 9 the best results per language and task are shown. A more in-depth analysis of the results and the different approaches can be found in [62].

---

[6] In the four editions of the author profiling shared task we have had respectively 21 (2013: age and gender identification), 10 (2014: age and gender identification in different genre social media), 22 (2015: age and gender identification and personality recognition in Twitter) and 22 (2016: cross-genre age and gender identification) participating teams.

[7] The authors of waser16 team found an error in their implementation when performing cross validation.

Table 8. Global ranking as average of each language joint accuracy. (*) Authors withdrew their participation due to a software error.

Ranking	Team	Global	English	Spanish	Dutch
1	Busger *et al.*	**0.5258**	0.3846	**0.4286**	0.4960
2	Modaresi *et al.*	0.5247	0.3846	**0.4286**	0.5040
3	Bilan *et al.*	0.4834	0.3333	0.3750	0.5500
4	Modaresi(a)	0.4602	0.3205	0.3036	0.5000
5	Markov *et al.*	0.4593	0.2949	0.3750	0.5100
6	Bougiatiotis &Krithara	0.4519	**0.3974**	0.2500	0.4160
7	Dichiu &Rancea	0.4425	0.2692	0.3214	0.5260
8	Devalkeneer	0.4369	0.3205	0.2857	0.5060
9	Waser *et al.**	0.4293	0.3205	0.2679	0.5320
10	Bayot &Gonçalves	0.4255	0.2179	0.3036	0.5680
11	Gencheva *et al.*	0.4015	0.2564	0.2500	0.5100
12	Deneva	0.4014	0.2051	0.2679	**0.6180**
13	Agrawal &Gonçalves	0.3971	0.1923	0.2857	0.5080
14	Kocher &Savoy	0.3800	0.2564	0.1964	0.5040
15	Roman-Gomez	0.3664	0.2821	0.1250	0.5620
16	Garciarena *et al.*	0.3660	0.1538	0.2500	0.5260
17	Zahid	0.3154	0.1923	0.2143	-
18	Aceituno	0.2949	0.1667	0.0893	0.5040
19	Ashraf *et al.*	0.1688	0.2564	-	-
20	Bakkar *et al.*	0.1560	0.2051	-	-
21	Pimas *et al.*	0.1410	0.1410	-	-
22	Poonguran	0.0571	-	-	0.5140

Table 9. Best results per language and task.

	Age and Gender		
Language	*Joint*	Gender	Age
English	0.3974	0.7564	0.5897
Spanish	0.4286	0.7321	0.5179
Dutch	-	0.6180	-

4   Author Obfuscation

The development of author identification technology has reached a point at which it can be carefully applied in practice to resolve cases of unknown or disputed authorship. For a recent example, a state-of-the-art forensic software played a role in breaking the anonymity of J.K. Rowling who published her book "The Cuckoo's Calling" under the pseudonym Robert Gailbraith in order to "liberate" herself from the pressure of stardom, caused by her success with the Harry Potter series. Moreover, forensic author identification software is part of the toolbox of forensic linguists, who employ it on a regular basis to support their testimony in court as expert witnesses in cases where the authenticity of a piece of writing is important. Despite their successful application, none of the existing approaches has been shown to work flawless, yet. All of them have a likelihood of returning false decisions under certain circumstances—but the circumstances under which they do are barely understood. It is particularly interesting if and how these circumstances can be controlled, since any form of control over the outcome of an author identification software bears the risk of misuse.

In fiction, a number of examples can be found where authors tried to remain anonymous, and where they, overtly or covertly, tried to imitate the writing style of others. In fact, style imitation is even a well-known learning technique in writing courses. But the question of whether humans are ultimately capable of controlling their own writing style so as to fool experts into believing they have not written a given piece of text, or even that someone else has, is difficult to answer based on observation alone: are the known cases more or less all there is, or are they just the tip of the iceberg (i.e., examples of unskilled attempts)? However, when the "expert" to be fooled is not a human but an author identification software, the rules are changed entirely. The fact that software is used to assist with author identification increases the attack surface of investigations to include any flaw in the decision-making process of the software. This is troublesome since the human operator of such a software may be ignorant of its flaws, and biased toward taking the software's output at face value instead of treating it with caution. After all, being convinced of the quality of a software is a necessary precondition to employing it to solve a problem.

At PAN 2016, we organize for the first time a pilot task on author obfuscation to begin exploring the potential vulnerabilities of author identification technology. A number of interesting sub-tasks related to author obfuscation can be identified, from which we have selected that of author masking. This task complements, and is built on top of the task of authorship verification, a sub-task of author identification, which was organized at PAN 2013 through PAN 2015 [26,71,72]:

Authorship verification:

Given two documents, decide whether they have been written by the same author.

vs.

Author masking:

Given two documents by the same author, paraphrase the designated one so that the author cannot be verified anymore.

Table 10. Average performance drops in terms of "final scores" of the authorship verifiers submitted at PAN 2013 to PAN 2015 when run on obfuscated versions of the corresponding test datasets as per the submitted obfuscators.

Participant	PAN 2013	PAN 2014 EE	PAN 2014 EN	PAN 2015
Mihaylova *et al.*	−0.10	−0.13	−0.16	−0.11
Keswani *et al.*	−0.09	−0.11	−0.12	−0.06
Mansoorizadeh *et al.*	−0.05	−0.04	−0.03	−0.04

The two tasks are diametrically opposed to each other: the success of a certain approach for one of these tasks depends on its "immunity" against the most effective approach for the other. The two tasks are also entangled, since the development of a new approach for one of them should build upon the capabilities of existing approaches for the other. However, compared to authorship verification, author obfuscation in general, and author masking in particular received little attention to date. A reason for this may be rooted in the fact that author masking requires (automatic) paraphrasing as a subtask, which poses a high barrier of entry to newcomers.

Notwithstanding the task's inherent challenges, 3 teams successfully submitted an approach. Keswani *et al.* [27] employ circular translation as a means of obfuscation, where the to-be-obfuscated text is translated to another language, and the resulting translation again, and so on, until, as a final step, the last translation goes back to the initial language. The presumption is that the original text will be sufficiently changed to obfuscate its author. Mansoorizadeh *et al.* [36] attack the feature of (stop) word frequencies on which many verification approaches are based and exchange the most frequent words in the to-be-obfuscated text with synonyms, carefully chosen not to distort the originals meaning. Mihaylova *et al.* [38] take a more "writing engineering"-based approach: it targets a number of style-indicating features that are frequently used within author identification approaches and tries to attack them by transforming the to-be-obfuscated text with certain rule-based and random text operations.

The performance of an author identification approach rests with its capability to achieve its goal of fooling a given expert, be it a software or a human. In this regard, we call an obfuscation software

- **safe**, if a forensic analysis does not reveal the original author of its obfuscated texts,
- **sound**, if its obfuscated texts are textually entailed by their originals, and
- **sensible**, if its obfuscated texts are well-formed and inconspicuous.

These dimensions are orthogonal; an obfuscation software may meet all of them to various degrees of perfection. However, achieving perfection in all three dimensions may not be necessary for practical applicability: for instance, if the fact that a text has been obfuscated is obvious, there may not be a problem as long as the changes made cannot be easily undone. To operationalize the three dimensions, we employ state-of-the-art automatic authorship verifiers to measure safety, and manual peer-review to assess soundness and sensibleness. Regarding safety, we measure the impact of author obfuscation on classification accuracy, whereas soundness and sensibleness are manually assessed on a Likert scale by multiple reviewers. In this connection, we also invite participants to conduct their own evaluation with regard to the aforementioned dimensions, giving them access to each other's obfuscations, thus crowdsourcing further ideas at evaluating author obfuscation approaches. As an evaluation dataset we employ the joint training datasets and the joint test datasets that were used for the authorship verification tasks of PAN 2013 to PAN 2015. This ensures compatibility between tasks and allows us to study the impact of the 3 author obfuscation approaches on the authorship verifiers submitted to the authorship verification tasks.

Regarding safety, Table 10 shows averaged performance drops when running the authorship verifiers submitted to PAN 2013 to PAN 2015 on obfuscated versions of the corresponding test datasets when compared to their performance on the original test datasets: the average performances drop significantly for each pair of obfuscator and year. The top average performance drop of -0.16 "final score" (i.e., the combination of AUC and C1) on the PAN 2014 test dataset comprising English novels has been achieved by the obfuscator of Mihaylova *et al.* [38]. The order of obfuscators by average performance drop remain stable across years, whereas the achieved drops differ based on the different test datasets. This result shows that the authorship verifiers are to some extent vulnerable to obfuscation. Regarding soundness and sensibleness of the texts, however, the texts produced by the safest obfuscator are less than ideal (i.e., while the original text's message can be partly inferred from the obfuscated text, many grammar mistakes are introduced). It is encouraging, though, that the obfuscated texts of Mihaylova *et al.*'s obfuscator achieve better soundness and sensibleness compared to the cyclic translations produced by Keswani *et al.*'s obfuscator. An in-depth analysis of the performances can be found in the full-length task overview paper [51]. This also includes a review of the results of peer-evaluation, where participants evaluated the runs of all obfuscators in anonymized form (knowing of course which of the runs was produced by their own obfuscator), and whether they are in line with our own evaluation results. Two of the submitted peer-evaluations were submitted by external reviewers who did not submit an obfuscator of their own.

5   Conclusions

PAN 2016 evaluation lab at CLEF attracted a high number of teams from all around the world. This demonstrates that the shared tasks on author identification, profile and obfuscation are of particular interest for researchers. New corpora have been developed covering multiple languages (English, Spanish, Greek, Dutch). These new resources will help fostering research in digital text forensics and future techniques will be able to be compared with the evaluation results obtained by the participating teams in the three shared tasks. The author obfuscation shared task will allow to shed light on the robusteness of state-of-the-art author identification and author profiling techniques against author obfuscation technology.

For the first time since 2009 a shared task on external plagiarism detection has not been organized at PAN/CLEF. A shared tasks on plagiarism detection will be organized at PAN/FIRE instead: after addressing previously text reuse in source code, at monolingual [13] and cross-language [14] levels, and plagiarirms in Arabic texts [7], this year the focus of the plagiarism detection task will be on texts written in Farsi[8]. Moreover, with respect to author profiling, a PAN/FIRE task on personality recognition in source code will be organized[9].

Acknowledgements. We thank the organizing committees of PAN's shared tasks Ben Verhoeven, Walter Daelemans, Patrick Juola. Our special thanks go to all of PAN's participants, to Adobe(http://www.adobe.com) and to MeaningCloud(http://www.meaningcloud.com/) for sponsoring the author profiling shared task award. The work of the first author was partially supported by the SomEMBED TIN2015-71147-C2-1-P MINECO research project and by the Generalitat Valenciana under the grant ALMAMATER (PrometeoII/2014/030). The work of the second author was partially supported by Autoritas Consulting and by Ministerio de Economía y Competitividad de España under grant ECOPORTUNITY IPT-2012-1220-430000.

References

1. Almishari, M., Tsudik, G.: Exploring linkability of user reviews. In: Foresti, S., Yung, M., Martinelli, F. (eds.) ESORICS 2012. LNCS, vol. 7459, pp. 307–324. Springer, Heidelberg (2012)
2. Álvarez-Carmona, M.A., López-Monroy, A.P., Montes-Y-Gómez, M., Villaseñor-Pineda, L., Jair-Escalante, H.: INAOE's Participation at PAN'15: author profiling task–notebook for PAN at CLEF 2015. In: Working Notes Papers of the CLEF 2015 Evaluation Labs. CEUR-WS.org, vol. 1391 (2015)
3. Amigó, E., Gonzalo, J., Artiles, J., Verdejo, F.: A comparison of extrinsic clustering evaluation metrics based on formal constraints. Inf. Retrieval **12**(4), 461–486 (2009)
4. Argamon, S., Juola, P.: Overview of the international authorship identification competition at PAN-2011. In: Working Notes Papers of the CLEF 2011 Evaluation Labs (2011)
5. Argamon, S., Koppel, M., Fine, J., Shimoni, A.R.: Gender, genre, and writing style in formal written texts. TEXT **23**, 321–346 (2003)
6. Bagnall, D.: Author identification using multi-headed recurrent neural networks. In: Working Notes Papers of the CLEF 2015 Evaluation Labs. CEUR-WS.org, vol. 1391 (2015)
7. Bensalem, I., Boukhalfa, I., Rosso, P., Abouenour, L., Darwish, K., Chikhi, S.: Overview of the AraPlagDet PAN@ FIRE2015 shared task on arabic plagiarism detection. In: Notebook Papers of FIRE 2015. CEUR-WS.org, vol. 1587 (2015)
8. Burger, J.D., Henderson, J., Kim, G., Zarrella, G.: Discriminating gender on twitter. In: Proceedings of EMNLP 2011 (2011)

---

[8] http://ictrc.ac.ir/plagdet/.
[9] http://www.autoritas.es/prsoco.

9. Burrows, S., Potthast, M., Stein, B.: Paraphrase acquisition via crowdsourcing and machine learning. ACM TIST **4**(3), 43:1–43:21 (2013)

10. Castillo, E., Cervantes, O., Vilariño, D., Pinto, D., León, S.: Unsupervised method for the authorship identification task. In: CLEF 2014 Labs and Workshops, Notebook Papers. CEUR-WS.org, vol. 1180 (2014)

11. Chaski, C.E.: Who's at the keyboard: authorship attribution in digital evidence invesigations. Int. J. Digit. Evid. **4**, 1–13 (2005)

12. Clarke, C.L., Craswell, N., Soboroff, I., Voorhees, E.M.: Overview of the TREC 2009 web track. In: DTIC Document (2009)

13. Flores, E., Rosso, P., Moreno, L., Villatoro, E.: On the detection of source code reuse. In: ACM FIRE 2014 Post Proceedings of the Forum for Information Retrieval Evaluation, pp. 21–30 (2015)

14. Flores, E., Rosso, P., Villatoro, E., Moreno, L., Alcover, R., Chirivella, V.: PAN@FIRE: overview of CL-SOCO track on the detection of cross-language source code re-use. In: Notebook Papers of FIRE 2015. CEUR-WS.org, vol. 1587 (2015)

15. Fréry, J., Largeron, C., Juganaru-Mathieu, M.: UJM at clef in author identification. In: CLEF 2014 Labs and Workshops, Notebook Papers. CEUR-WS.org, vol. 1180 (2014)

16. Gollub, T., Potthast, M., Beyer, A., Busse, M., Rangel, F., Rosso, P., Stamatatos, E., Stein, B.: Recent trends in digital text forensics and its evaluation. In: Forner, P., Müller, H., Paredes, R., Rosso, P., Stein, B. (eds.) CLEF 2013. LNCS, vol. 8138, pp. 282–302. Springer, Heidelberg (2013)

17. Gollub, T., Stein, B., Burrows, S.: Ousting Ivory tower research: towards a web framework for providing experiments as a service. In: Proceedings of SIGIR 12. ACM (2012)

18. Hagen, M., Potthast, M., Stein, B.: Source retrieval for plagiarism detection from large web corpora: recent approaches. In: Working Notes Papers of the CLEF 2015 Evaluation Labs. CEUR-WS.org, vol. 1391 (2015)

19. van Halteren, H.: Linguistic profiling for author recognition and verification. In: Proceedings of ACL 2004 (2004)

20. Holmes, J., Meyerhoff, M.: The Handbook of Language and Gender. Blackwell Handbooks in Linguistics, Wiley (2003)

21. Iqbal, F., Binsalleeh, H., Fung, B.C.M., Debbabi, M.: Mining writeprints from anonymous e-mails for forensic investigation. Digit. Investig. **7**(1–2), 56–64 (2010)

22. Jankowska, M., Keselj, V., Milios, E.: CNG text classification for authorship profiling task-notebook for PAN at CLEF 2013. In: Working Notes Papers of the CLEF 2013 Evaluation Labs. CEUR-WS.org, vol. 1179 (2013)

23. Juola, P.: An overview of the traditional authorship attribution subtask. In: Working Notes Papers of the CLEF 2012 Evaluation Labs (2012)

24. Juola, P.: Authorship attribution. Found. Trends Inf. Retrieval **1**, 234–334 (2008)

25. Juola, P.: How a computer program helped reveal J.K. rowling as author of a Cuckoo's calling. In: Scientific American (2013)

26. Juola, P., Stamatatos, E.: Overview of the author identification task at PAN-2013. In:Working Notes Papers of the CLEF 2013 Evaluation Labs. CEUR-WS.org vol. 1179 (2013)

27. Keswani, Y., Trivedi, H., Mehta, P., Majumder, P.: Author masking through translation-notebook for PAN at CLEF 2016. In: Conference and Labs of the Evaluation Forum, CLEF (2016)

28. Koppel, M., Argamon, S., Shimoni, A.R.: Automatically categorizing written texts by author gender. Literary Linguist. Comput. **17**(4), 401–412 (2002)

29. Koppel, M., Schler, J., Bonchek-Dokow, E.: Measuring differentiability: unmasking pseudonymous authors. J. Mach. Learn. Res. **8**, 1261–1276 (2007)
30. Koppel, M., Winter, Y.: Determining if two documents are written by the same author. J. Am. Soc. Inf. Sci. Technol. **65**(1), 178–187 (2014)
31. Layton, R., Watters, P., Dazeley, R.: Automated unsupervised authorship analysis using evidence accumulation clustering. Nat. Lang. Eng. **19**(1), 95–120 (2013)
32. López-Monroy, A.P., Montes-y Gómez, M., Jair-Escalante, H., Villasenor-Pineda, L.V.: Using intra-profile information for author profiling-notebook for PAN at CLEF 2014. In: Working Notes Papers of the CLEF 2014 Evaluation Labs. CEUR-WS.org, vol. 1180 (2014)
33. López-Monroy, A.P., Montes-y Gómez, M., Jair-Escalante, H., Villasenor-Pineda, L., Villatoro-Tello, E.: INAOE's participation at PAN'13: author profiling task-notebook for PAN at CLEF 2013. In: Working Notes Papers of the CLEF 2013 Evaluation Labs. CEUR-WS.org, vol. 1179 (2013)
34. Luyckx, K., Daelemans, W.: Authorship attribution and verification with many authors and limited data. In: Proceedings of COLING (2008)
35. Maharjan, S., Shrestha, P., Solorio, T., Hasan, R.: A straightforward author profiling approach in MapReduce. In: Bazzan, A.L.C., Pichara, K. (eds.) IBERAMIA 2014. LNCS, vol. 8864, pp. 95–107. Springer, Heidelberg (2014)
36. Mansoorizadeh, M.: Submission to the author obfuscation task at PAN 2016. In: Conference and Labs of the Evaluation Forum, CLEF (2016)
37. Eissen, S.M., Stein, B.: Intrinsic plagiarism detection. In: Lalmas, M., MacFarlane, A., Rüger, S.M., Tombros, A., Tsikrika, T., Yavlinsky, A. (eds.) ECIR 2006. LNCS, vol. 3936, pp. 565–569. Springer, Heidelberg (2006)
38. Mihaylova, T., Karadjov, G., Nakov, P., Kiprov, Y., Georgiev, G., Koychev, I.: SU@PAN'2016: author obfuscation-notebook for PAN at CLEF 2016. In: Conference and Labs of the Evaluation Forum, CLEF (2016)
39. Miro, X.A., Bozonnet, S., Evans, N., Fredouille, C., Friedland, G., Vinyals, O.: Speaker diarization: a review of recent research. Audio Speech Language Process. IEEE Trans. **20**(2), 356–370 (2012)
40. Moreau, E., Jayapal, A., Lynch, G., Vogel, C.: Author verification: basic stacked generalization applied to predictions from a set of heterogeneous learners. In: Working Notes Papers of the CLEF 2015 Evaluation Labs. CEUR-WS.org, vol. 1391 (2015)
41. Nguyen, D., Gravel, R., Trieschnigg, D., Meder, T.: How old do you think I am? a study of language and age in twitter. In: Proceedings of ICWSM 13. AAAI (2013)
42. Peñas, A., Rodrigo, A.: A Simple measure to assess non-response. In: Proceedings of HLT 2011 (2011)
43. Pennebaker, J.W., Mehl, M.R., Niederhoffer, K.G.: Psychological aspects of natural language use: our words, our selves. Ann. Rev. Psychol. **54**(1), 547–577 (2003)
44. Potthast, M., Barrón-Cedeño, A., Eiselt, A., Stein, B., Rosso, P.: Overview of the 2nd international competition on plagiarism detection. In: Working Notes Papers of the CLEF 2010 Evaluation Labs (2010)
45. Potthast, M., Barrón-Cedeño, A., Stein, B., Rosso, P.: Cross-language plagiarism detection. Lang. Resour. Eval. (LREC) **45**, 45–62 (2011)
46. Potthast, M., Eiselt, A., Barrón-Cedeño, A., Stein, B., Rosso, P.: Overview of the 3rd international competition on plagiarism detection. In: Working Notes Papers of the CLEF 2011 Evaluation Labs (2011)

47. Potthast, M., Gollub, T., Hagen, M., Graßegger, J., Kiesel, J., Michel, M., Oberländer, A., Tippmann, M., Barrón-Cedeño, A., Gupta, P., Rosso, P., Stein, B.: Overview of the 4th international competition on plagiarism detection. In: Working Notes Papers of the CLEF 2012 Evaluation Labs (2012)
48. Potthast, M., Gollub, T., Hagen, M., Tippmann, M., Kiesel, J., Rosso, P., Stamatatos, E., Stein, B.: Overview of the 5th international competition on plagiarism detection. In: Working Notes Papers of the CLEF 2013 Evaluation Labs. CEUR-WS.org, vol. 1179 (2013)
49. Potthast, M., Gollub, T., Rangel, F., Rosso, P., Stamatatos, E., Stein, B.: Improving the reproducibility of PAN's shared tasks: plagiarism detection, author identification, and author profiling. In: Kanoulas, E., Lupu, M., Clough, P., Sanderson, M., Hall, M., Hanbury, A., Toms, E. (eds.) CLEF 2014. LNCS, vol. 8685, pp. 268–299. Springer, Heidelberg (2014)
50. Potthast, M., Hagen, M., Beyer, A., Busse, M., Tippmann, M., Rosso, P., Stein, B.: Overview of the 6th international competition on plagiarism detection. In: Working Notes Papers of the CLEF 2014 Evaluation Labs. CEUR-WS.org, vol. 1180 (2014)
51. Potthast, M., Hagen, M., Stein, B.: Author obfuscation: attacking the state of the art in authorship verification. In: CLEF 2016 Working Notes. CEUR-WS.org (2016)
52. Potthast, M., Göring, S., Rosso, P., Stein, B.: Towards data submissions for shared tasks: first experiences for the task of text alignment. In: Working Notes Papers of the CLEF 2015 Evaluation Labs. CEUR-WS.org, vol. 1391 (2015)
53. Potthast, M., Hagen, M., Stein, B., Graßegger, J., Michel, M., Tippmann, M., Welsch, C.: ChatNoir: a search engine for the ClueWeb09 corpus. In: Proceedings of SIGIR 12. ACM (2012)
54. Potthast, M., Hagen, M., Völske, M., Stein, B.: Crowdsourcing interaction logs to understand text reuse from the web. In: Proceedings of ACL 13. ACL (2013)
55. Potthast, M., Stein, B., Barrón-Cedeño, A., Rosso, P.: An evaluation framework for plagiarism detection. In: Proceedings of COLING 10. ACL (2010)
56. Potthast, M., Stein, B., Eiselt, A., Barrón-Cedeño, A., Rosso, P.: Overview of the 1st international competition on plagiarism detection. In: Proceedings of PAN at SEPLN 09. CEUR-WS.org 502 (2009)
57. Rangel, F., Rosso, P.: On the impact of emotions on author profiling. Inf. Process. Manage. Spec. Issue Emot. Sentiment Soc. Expressive Media 52(1), 73–92 (2016)
58. Rangel, F., Rosso, P.: On the multilingual and genre robustness of emographs for author profiling in social media. In: Mothe, J., et al. (eds.) CLEF 2015. LNCS, vol. 9283, pp. 274–280. Springer, Heidelberg (2015). doi:10.1007/978-3-319-24027-5_28
59. Rangel, F., Rosso, P., Celli, F., Potthast, M., Stein, B., Daelemans, W.: Overview of the 3rd author profiling task at PAN 2015. In: Working Notes Papers of the CLEF 2015 Evaluation Labs. CEUR-WS.org, vol. 1391 (2015)
60. Rangel, F., Rosso, P., Chugur, I., Potthast, M., Trenkmann, M., Stein, B., Verhoeven, B., Daelemans, W.: Overview of the 2nd author profiling task at PAN 2014. In: Working Notes Papers of the CLEF 2014 Evaluation Labs. CEUR-WS.org, vol. 1180 (2014)
61. Rangel, F., Rosso, P., Koppel, M., Stamatatos, E., Inches, G.: Overview of the author profiling task at PAN 2013–notebook for PAN at CLEF 2013. In: Working Notes Papers of the CLEF 2013 Evaluation Labs. CEUR-WS.org, vol. 1179 (2013)
62. Rangel, F., Rosso, P., Verhoeven, B., Daelemans, W., Potthast, M., Stein, B.: Overview of the 4th author profiling task at PAN 2016: cross-genre evaluations. In: CLEF 2016 Working Notes. CEUR-WS.org (2016)

63. Samdani, R., Chang, K., Roth, D.: A discriminative latent variable model for online clustering. In: Proceedings of The 31st International Conference on Machine Learning, pp. 1–9 (2014)

64. Sapkota, U., Bethard, S., Montes-y-Gómez, M., Solorio, T.: Not all character N-grams are created equal: a study in authorship attribution. In: Proceedings of NAACL 15. ACL (2015)

65. Sapkota, U., Solorio, T., Montes-y-Gómez, M., Bethard, S., Rosso, P.: Cross-topic authorship attribution: will out-of-topic data help? In: Proceedings of COLING 14 (2014)

66. Schler, J., Koppel, M., Argamon, S., Pennebaker, J.W.: Effects of age and gender on blogging. In: AAAI Spring Symposium: Computational Approaches to Analyzing Weblogs. AAAI (2006)

67. Schwartz, H.A., Eichstaedt, J.C., Kern, M.L., Dziurzynski, L., Ramones, S.M., Agrawal, M., Shah, A., Kosinski, M., Stillwell, D., Seligman, M.E., et al.: Personality, gender, and age in the language of social media: the open-vocabulary approach. PloS One 8(9), 773–791 (2013)

68. Stamatatos, E.: A survey of modern authorship attribution methods. J. Am. Soc. Inf. Sci. Technol. 60, 538–556 (2009)

69. Stamatatos, E.: On the robustness of authorship attribution based on character n-gram features. J. Law Policy 21, 421–439 (2013)

70. Stamatatos, E., Tschuggnall, M., Verhoeven, B., Daelemans, W., Specht, G., Stein, B., Potthast, M.: Clustering by authorship within and across documents. In: CLEF 2016 Working Notes. CEUR-WS.org (2016)

71. Stamatatos, E., Daelemans, W., Verhoeven, B., Juola, P., López-López, A., Potthast, M., Stein, B.: Overview of the author identification task at PAN-2015. In: Working Notes Papers of the CLEF 2015 Evaluation Labs. CEUR-WS.org, vol. 1391 (2015)

72. Stamatatos, E., Daelemans, W., Verhoeven, B., Stein, B., Potthast, M., Juola, P., Sánchez-Pérez, M.A., Barrón-Cedeño, A.: Overview of the author identification task at PAN 2014. In: Working Notes Papers of the CLEF 2014 Evaluation Labs. CEUR-WS.org, vol. 1180 (2014)

73. Stamatatos, E., Fakotakis, N., Kokkinakis, G.: Automatic text categorization in terms of genre and author. Comput. Linguist. 26(4), 471–495 (2000)

74. Stein, B., Lipka, N., Prettenhofer, P.: Intrinsic plagiarism analysis. Lang. Resour. Eval. (LRE) 45, 63–82 (2011)

75. Stein, B., Meyer zu Eißen, S.: Near Similarity Search and Plagiarism Analysis. In: Proceedings of GFKL 05. Springer, Heidelberg, pp. 430–437 (2006)

76. Verhoeven, B., Daelemans, W.: Clips stylometry investigation (csi) corpus: a dutch corpus for the detection of age, gender, personality, sentiment and deception in text. In: Proceedings of LREC 2014 (2014)

77. Verhoeven, B., Daelemans, W.: CLiPS stylometry investigation (CSI) corpus: a dutch corpus for the detection of age, gender, personality, sentiment and deception in text. In: Proceedings of the 9th International Conference on Language Resources and Evaluation, LREC (2014)

78. Weren, E., Kauer, A., Mizusaki, L., Moreira, V., de Oliveira, P., Wives, L.: Examining multiple features for author profiling. J. Inf. Data Manage. 5(3), 266–280 (2014)

79. Zhang, C., Zhang, P.: Predicting Gender from Blog Posts. Technical Report. University of Massachusetts Amherst, USA (2010)

Overview of the CLEF 2016 Social Book Search Lab

Marijn Koolen[1,2]([✉]), Toine Bogers[3], Maria Gäde[4], Mark Hall[5],
Iris Hendrickx[6], Hugo Huurdeman[1], Jaap Kamps[1], Mette Skov[7],
Suzan Verberne[6], and David Walsh[5]

[1] University of Amsterdam, Amsterdam, The Netherlands
{marijn.koolen,huurdeman,kamps}@uva.nl
[2] Netherlands Institute for Sound and Vision, Hilversum, The Netherlands
mkoolen@beeldengeluid.nl
[3] Aalborg University Copenhagen, Copenhagen, Denmark
toine@hum.aau.dk
[4] Humboldt University Berlin, Berlin, Germany
maria.gaede@ibi.hu-berlin.de
[5] CLS/CLST, Radboud University, Nijmegen, The Netherlands
{mark.hall,david.walsh}@edgehill.ac.uk
[6] Edge Hill University, Ormskirk, UK
{i.hendrickx,s.verberne}@let.ru.nl
[7] Aalborg University, Aalborg, Denmark
skov@hum.aau.dk

Abstract. The Social Book Search (SBS) Lab investigates book search in scenarios where users search with more than just a query, and look for more than objective metadata. Real-world information needs are generally complex, yet almost all research focuses instead on either relatively simple search based on queries, or on profile-based recommendation. The goal is to research and develop techniques to support users in complex book search tasks. The SBS Lab has three tracks. The aim of the Suggestion Track is to develop test collections for evaluating ranking effectiveness of book retrieval and recommender systems. The aim of the Interactive Track is to develop user interfaces that support users through each stage during complex search tasks and to investigate how users exploit professional metadata and user-generated content. The Mining Track focuses on detecting and linking book titles in online book discussion forums, as well as detecting book search research in forum posts for automatic book recommendation.

1 Introduction

The goal of the Social Book Search (SBS) Lab[1] is to evaluate approaches for supporting users in searching collections of books. The SBS Lab investigates the complex nature of relevance in book search and the role of traditional and user-generated book metadata in retrieval. The aims are (1) to develop test collections

---

[1] See: http://social-book-search.humanities.uva.nl/.

© Springer International Publishing Switzerland 2016
N. Fuhr et al. (Eds.): CLEF 2016, LNCS 9822, pp. 351–370, 2016.
DOI: 10.1007/978-3-319-44564-9_29

for evaluating information retrieval systems in terms of ranking search results;
(2) to develop user interfaces and conduct user studies to investigate book search
in scenarios with complex information needs and book descriptions that combine
heterogeneous information from multiple sources; and (3) to develop algorithms
that can automatically detect book search requests and suggestions from online
discussions.

The SBS Lab runs three tracks:

- *Suggestion:* this is a system-centred track focused on the comparative evaluation of systems in terms of how well they rank search results for complex book
  search requests that consist of both extensive natural language expressions
  of information needs as well as example books that reflect important aspects
  of those information needs, using a large collection of book descriptions with
  both professional metadata and user-generated content.
- *Interactive:* this is a user-centred track investigating how searchers use different types of metadata at various stages in the search process and how a search
  interface can support each stage in that process.
- *Mining:* this is a new track focused on detecting book search requests in forum
  posts for automatic book recommendation, as well as detecting and linking
  book titles in online book discussion forums.

In this paper, we report on the setup and results of the 2016 Suggestion and
Interactive Tracks as part of the SBS Lab at CLEF 2016. The three tracks run
in close collaboration, all focusing on the complex nature of book search.

2   Participating Organisations

A total of 40 organisations registered for the 2016 SBS Lab, of which 29 registered
for the Suggestion Track, 19 for the Interactive Track and 28 for the Mining
Track. In the Suggestion Track, 10 organisations submitted runs, compared to
11 in 2015 and 8 in 2014. In the Interactive Track, 7 organisations recruited users,
compared to 7 in 2015 and 4 in 2014. In the Mining Track, which ran for the first
time this year, 4 organisations submitted runs. The active organisations are listed
in Table 1. Participation in the SBS Lab seems to have stabilised.

3   The Amazon/LibraryThing Corpus

For all three tracks we use and extend the Amazon/LibraryThing (A/LT) corpus
crawled by the University of Duisburg-Essen for the INEX Interactive Track [1].
The corpus contains a large collection of book records with controlled subject
headings and classification codes as well as social descriptions, such as tags and
reviews.[2]

---

[2] See http://social-book-search.humanities.uva.nl/#/collection for information on
how to gain access to the corpus.

Table 1. Active participants of the CLEF 2015 Social Book Search Lab, tracks they were active in (I = Interactive, M = Mining, S = Suggestion) and number of contributed runs or users.

Institute	Acronym	Tracks	Runs/Users
Aalborg University	AAU	I	14
Aix-Marseille Université CNRS	LSIS	M, S	8, 4
Chaoyang University of Technology	CYUT	S	6
Edge Hill University	Computing@EHU	I	12
Indian School of Mines Dhanbad	ISMD	S	6
Tunis EL Manar University	LIPAH	M	6
Humboldt University, Berlin	Humboldt	I	7
Know-Center	Know	M, S	8, 2
Laboratoire d'Informatique de Grenoble	MRIM	S	6
Manchester Metropolitan University	MMU	I	13
Oslo &Akershus University College of Applied Sciences	OAUC	I, S	15, 3
Peking University, China and Stockholm University, Sweden	ChiSwe	I	29
Radboud University Nijmegen	RUN	M	12
Research Center on Scientific and Technical Information	CERIST	S	6
University of Amsterdam	UvA	S	1
University of Duisburg-Essen	WGIS	I	21
University of Neuchtel Zurich University of Applied Sciences	UniNe-ZHAW	S	6
University of Science and Technology Beijing	USTB_PRIR	S	6
Total		I, M, S	111, 32, 46

The collection consists of 2.8 million book records from Amazon including user reviews, extended with social metadata from LibraryThing (LT). This set represents the books available through Amazon. Each book is identified by an ISBN. Popular works have multiple ISBNs, so often have multiple records in the collection. Based on an ISBNs to work mapping provided by LibraryThing,[3] the 2.8 million records represent 2.4 million distinct works. Each book record is an XML file with fields like *isbn, title, author, publisher, dimensions, numberofpages* and *publicationdate*. Curated metadata comes in the form of a Dewey Decimal Classification in the *dewey* field, Amazon subject headings in the *subject* field, and Amazon category labels in the *browseNode* fields. The social metadata from Amazon and LT is stored in the *tag, rating,* and *review* fields.

---

[3] See http://www.librarything.com/feeds/thingISBN.xml.gz.

To ensure that there is enough high-quality metadata from traditional library catalogues, we extended the A/LT data set with library catalogue records from the Library of Congress (LoC) and the British Library (BL). We only use library records of ISBNs that are already in the A/LT collection. There are 1,248,816 records from the LoC and 1,158,070 records in MARC format from the BL. Combined, these 2,406,886 records cover 1,823,998 of the ISBNs in the A/LT collection (66 %).

4   Suggestion Track

4.1   Track Goals and Background

The goal of the Suggestion Track is to evaluate the value of professional metadata and user-generated content for book search on the Web and to develop and evaluate systems that can deal with both retrieval and recommendation aspects, where the user has a specific information need against a background of personal tastes, interests and previously seen books.

Through social media, book descriptions have extended far beyond what is traditionally stored in professional catalogues. This additional information is subjective and personal, and opens up opportunities to aid users in searching for books in different ways that go beyond the traditional editorial metadata based search scenarios, such as known-item and subject search. For example, readers use many more aspects of books to help them decide which book to read next [13], such as how engaging, fun, educational or well-written a book is. In addition, readers leave a trail of rich information about themselves in the form of online profiles, which contain personal catalogues of the books they have read or want to read, personally assigned tags and ratings for those books and social network connections to other readers. This results in a search task that may require a different model than traditional ad hoc search [7] or recommendation.

The Suggestion track investigates book requests and suggestions from the LibraryThing (LT) discussion forums as a way to model book search in a social environment. The discussions in these forums show that readers frequently turn to others to get recommendations and tap into the collective knowledge of a group of readers interested in the same topic. The track builds on the INEX Amazon/LibraryThing (A/LT) collection [1], which contains 2.8 million book descriptions from Amazon, enriched with content from LT. This collection contains both professional metadata and user-generated content. In addition, we distributed a set of 94,656 user profiles containing over 33 million book cataloguing transactions. These contain an anonymised user name, book ID, book title, author, user rating and tags and cataloguing date.

The SBS Suggestion Track aims to address the following research questions:

- Can we build reliable and reusable test collections for social book search based on book requests and suggestions from the LT discussion forums?
- Can user profiles provide a good source of information to capture personal, affective aspects of book search information needs?

- How can systems incorporate both specific information needs and general user profiles to combine the retrieval and recommendation aspects of social book search?
- What is the relative value of social and controlled book metadata for book search?

Task Description. The task is to reply to a user request posted on a LT forum (see Sect. 4.2) by returning a list of recommended books matching the user's information need. More specifically, the task assumes a user who issues a query to a retrieval system, which then returns a (ranked) list of relevant book records. The user is assumed to inspect the results list starting from the top, working down the list until the information need has been satisfied or until the user gives up. The retrieval system is expected to order the search results by relevance to the user's information need. Participants of the Suggestion track are provided with a set of book search requests and user profiles and are asked to submit the results returned by their systems as ranked lists. The track thus combines aspects from retrieval and recommendation.

4.2   Information Needs

LT users discuss their books on the discussion forums. Many of the topic threads are started with a request from a member for interesting, fun new books to read. Users typically describe what they are looking for, give examples of what they like and do not like, indicate which books they already know and ask other members for recommendations. Members often reply with links to works catalogued on LT, which, in turn, have direct links to the corresponding records on Amazon. These requests for recommendations are natural expressions of information needs for a large collection of online book records. We use a sample of these forum topics to evaluate systems participating in the Suggestion Track.

Each topic has a title and is associated with a group on the discussion forums. For instance, topic 99309 in Fig. 1 has the title *Politics of Multiculturalism Recommendations?* and was posted in the group *Political Philosophy*. The books suggested by members in the thread are collected in a list on the side of the topic thread (see Fig. 1). A feature called *touchstone* can be used by members to easily identify books they mention in the topic thread, giving other readers of the thread direct access to a book record in LT, with associated ISBNs and links to Amazon. We use these suggested books as initial relevance judgements for evaluation. In the rest of this paper, we use the term *suggestion* to refer to a book that has been identified in a touchstone list for a given forum topic. Since all suggestions are made by forum members, we assume they are valuable judgements on the relevance of books. We note that LT users may discuss their search requests and suggestions outside of the LT forums as well, e.g. share links of their forum request posts on Twitter. To what extent the suggestions made outside of LT differ or complement those on the forums requires investigation.

Fig. 1. A topic thread in LibraryThing, with suggested books listed on the right hand side.

Topic Selection. The topic set of 2016 is a newly selected set of topics from the LibraryThing discussion forums. A total of 2000 topic threads were assessed on whether they contain a book search request by four judges, with 272 threads labelled as book search requests. To establish inter-annotator agreement, 453 threads were double-assessed, resulting a Cohen's Kappa of 0.83. Judges strongly agree on which posts are book search requests and which are not. Of these 272 book search requests, 124 (46 %) are known-item searches from the *Name that Book* discussion group. Here, LT members start a thread to describe a book they know but cannot remember the title and author of and ask others for help. In earlier work we found that known-item topics behave very differently from the other topic types [10]. We remove these topics from the topic set so that they do not dominate the performance comparison. Furthermore, we removed topics that have no book suggestions by other LT members and topics for which we have no user profile of the topic starter, resulting in a topic set of 120 topics for evaluation of the 2016 Suggestion Track. Below is one topics in the format as it was distributed to participants.

```
<topic>
  <topicid>107277</topicid>
  <request>Greetings! I'm looking for suggestions of fantasy
  novels whose heroines are creative in some way and have some
  sort of talent in art, music, or literature. I've seen my
  share of "tough gals" who know how to swing a sword or throw a
  punch but have next to nothing in the way of imagination. I'd
  like to see a few fantasy-genre Anne Shirleys or Jo Marches.

  Juliet Marillier is one of my favorite authors because she
```

makes a point of giving most of her heroines creative talents.
Even her most "ordinary" heroines have imagination and use it
to create. Clodagh from "Heir to Sevenwaters," for example,
may see herself as being purely domestic, but she plays the
harp and can even compose songs and stories. Creidhe of
"Foxmask" can't read, but she can weave stories and make
colors. The less ordinary heroines, like Sorcha from "Daughter
of the Forest" and Liadan from "Son of the Shadows," are good
storytellers. I'm looking for more heroines like these.

```
Any suggestions?</request>
<group>FantasyFans</group>
<title>Fantasy books with creative heroines?</title>
<examples>
  <work>
    <booktitle>Daughter of the Forest</booktitle>
    <author>Juliet Marillier</author>
    <workid>6442</workid>
  </work>
  <work>
    <booktitle>Foxmask</booktitle>
    <author>Juliet Marillier</author>
    <workid>349475</workid>
  </work>
  <work>
    <booktitle>Son of the Shadows</booktitle>
    <author>Juliet Marillier</author>
    <workid>6471</workid>
  </work>
</examples>
<catalogue>
  <work>
    <tags/>
    <rating>0.0</rating>
    <publication-year>2002</publication-year>
    <booktitle>Blue Moon (Anita Blake, Vampire Hunter, Book 8)</booktitle>
    <cataloging-date>2011-08</cataloging-date>
    <author>Laurell K. Hamilton</author>
    <workid>10868</workid>
  </work>
  ...
</catalogue>
</topic>
```

Operationalisation of Forum Judgement Labels. In previous years, the
Suggestion Track used a complicated decision tree to derive a relevance value
from a suggestion. To reduce the number of assumptions, we simplified the mapping of book suggestions to relevance values. By default a suggested book has
a relevance value of 1. Books that the requester already has in her personal
catalogue before starting the thread (pre-catalogued suggestions) have little
additional value and are assumed to have a relevance value of 0. On the other

Table 2. Evaluation results for the official submissions. Best scores are in bold. Runs marked with * are manual runs.

Group	Run	nDCG@10	P@10	MRR	MAP
USTB-PRIR	run1.keyQuery_active_combineRerank	0.2157	0.5247	0.1253	0.3474
CERIST	all_features	0.1567	0.3513	0.0838	0.4330
CYUT-CSIE	0.95Averageword2vecType2TGR	0.1158	0.2563	0.0563	0.1603
UvA-ILLC	base_es	0.0944	0.2272	0.0548	0.3122
MRIM	RUN2	0.0889	0.1889	0.0518	0.3491
ISMD	ISMD16allfieds	0.0765	0.1722	0.0342	0.2157
UniNe-ZHAW	Pages_INEXSBS2016_SUM_SCORE	0.0674	0.1512	0.0472	0.2556
LSIS	Run1_ExeOrNarrativeNSW_Collection	0.0450	0.1166	0.0251	0.2050
OAU	oauc_reranked_ownQueryModel	0.0228	0.0766	0.0127	0.1265
know	sbs16suggestiontopicsresult2	0.0058	0.0227	0.0010	0.0013

hand, suggestions that the requester subsequently adds to her catalogue (post-catalogued suggestions) are assumed to be the most relevant suggestions and receive a relevance value of 8, to keep the relevance level the same as in 2014 and 2015. Note that some of the books mentioned in the forums are not part of the 2.8 million books in our collection. We therefore removed any books from the suggestions that are not in the INEX A/LT collection. The numbers reported in the previous section were calculated after this filtering step.

4.3   Evaluation

This year, 10 teams submitted a total of 46 runs (see Table 1). The evaluation results are shown in Table 2 for the best run per team. The official evaluation measure for this task is nDCG@10. It takes graded relevance values into account and is designed for evaluation based on the top retrieved results. In addition, P@10, MAP and MRR scores are also reported.

The best runs of the top 5 groups are described below:

1. *USTB-PRIR - run1.keyQuery_active_combineRerank* (rank 1): This run was made by a searching-re-ranking process where the initial retrieval result was based on the selection of query keywords and a small index of active books, the re-ranking results based on a combination of several strategies (number of people who read the book from profile, similar-product from amazon.com, popularity from LT forum, etc.).
2. *CERIST - all_features* (rank 7): The topic statement in the *request* field is treated as a verbose query and is reduced using several features based on term statistics, Part-Of-Speech tagging, and whether terms from the *request* field occur in the user profile and example books.
3. *CYUT-CSIE - 0.95Averageword2vecType2TGR* (rank 11): This run uses query expansion based on word embeddings using word2vec, on top of a standard Lucene index and retrieval model. For this run, queries are represented by a combination of the *title*, *group* and *request* fields. Results are

re-ranked using a linear combination of the original retrieval score and the average Amazon user ratings of the retrieved books.

4. *UvA-ILLC - base_es* (rank 17): This run is based on a full-text ElasticSearch [3] index of the A/LT collection, where the Dewey Decimal Codes are replaced by their textual representation. Default retrieval parameters are used, the query is a combination of the topic *title*, *group* and *request* fields. This is the same index that is used for the experimental system of the Interactive Track (see Sect. 5.3) and serves as a baseline for the Suggestion Track.

5. *MRIM - RUN2* (rank 18): This run is a weighted linear fusion of a BM25F run on all fields, an Language Model (LM) run on all fields, and two query expansion runs, based on the BM25 and LM run respectively, using as expansion terms an intersection of terms in the user profiles and word embeddings from the query terms.

Most of the top performing systems, including the top performing run pre-process the rich topic statement with the aim of reducing the *request* to a set of most relevant terms. Two of the top five teams use the user profiles to modify the topic statement. This is the first year that word embeddings are used for the Suggestion Track. Both CYUT-CSIE and MRIM found that word embeddings improved performance over configurations without them. From these results it seems clear that topic representation is an important aspect in social book search. The longer narrative of the *request* field as well as the metadata in the user profiles and example books contain important information regarding the information need, but many terms are noisy, so a filtering step is essential to focus on the user's specific needs.

5   Interactive Track

The goal of the Interactive Track is to investigate how searchers make use of and combine professional metadata and user-generated content for book search on the Web and to develop interfaces that support searchers through the various stages of their search task. Through user-generated content, book descriptions are extended far beyond what is traditionally stored in professional catalogues. Not only are books described in the users' own vocabulary, but they are also reviewed and discussed online. As described in Sect. 4, this subjective user-generated content can help users during search tasks where their personal preferences, interests and background knowledge play a role.

The Interactive track investigates book requests and suggestions from the LibraryThing (LT) discussion forums as a way to model book search in a social environment. The discussions in these forums show that readers frequently turn to others to get recommendations and tap into the collective knowledge of a group of readers interested in the same topic. The track uses a subset of 1.5 million out of 2.8 million records of the A/LT collection (described in Sect. 3) for which a thumbnail cover image is available.

5.1   User Tasks

Participants started with a training task to ensure that they were familiar with system's functionality. Next, participants were asked to complete one mandatory task which was either a *goal-oriented* task (56 participants) or a *non-goal* task (55 participants). After completing the mandatory task participants were asked whether they had time to complete an *optional* task. 89 participants completed one of the eight optional tasks.

The *goal-oriented* task contains five sub-tasks ensuring that participants spend enough time to generate a rich data-set. While the first sub-task defines a clear goal, the other sub-tasks are more open to give participants the flexibility to interact with the available content and functionality. The same instruction text was used as in the 2015 track [8].

The *non-goal* task was developed based on the open-ended task used in the iCHiC task at CLEF 2013 [14] and the ISBS task at CLEF 2014 [6]. The aim of this task is to investigate how users interact with the system when they have no pre-defined goal in a more exploratory search context. It also allows the participants to bring their own goals or sub-tasks to the experiment in line with the "simulated work task" idea [2]. The same instruction text was used as in the 2015 track [8].

The *optional* task represent real Library Thing forum requests. 89 participants indicated that they had time for an optional task and were randomly given one of eight optional tasks, that were selected from the tasks used in the suggestion track. An example of an optional task:

> You're interested in non-fiction history books on the background to and the actual time of the Boer War in South Africa. Search the collection using any of the interface features to find at least one book that meets these criteria.

5.2   Experiment Structure

The experiment was conducted using the SPIRE system[4] [4], using the flow shown in Fig. 2. When a new participant started the experiment, the SPIRE system automatically allocated them either the *non-goal* or *goal-oriented*task. If they chose to undertake the *optional* task, they were also allocated one of the eight *optional* tasks. The SPIRE system automatically balances task allocation for both the main and optional tasks. Additionally each participating team was allocated their own experiment instance to ensure optimal balance both within and across the teams. Participants were not explicitly instructed to use only the interface and collection provided, so it is possible some users used other websites as well. However, given the lack of incentive to use external websites, we expect this issue to be negligible.

Participant responses were collected in the following five steps using a selection of standard questionnaires:

---

[4] Based on the Experiment Support System – https://bitbucket.org/mhall/experiment-support-system.

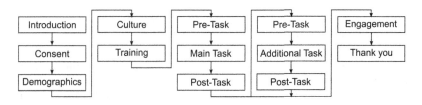

Fig. 2. The path participants took through the experiment. The SPIRE system automatically balanced task allocation in both the *Main Task* and *Additional Task*. After the first *Post-Task* stage, participants were asked whether they had time to do another task and if not, were taken directly to the *Engagement* stage.

- *Consent* – participants had to confirm that they understood the tasks and the types of data collected in the experiment.
- *Demographics* – gender, age, achieved education level, current education level, and employment status;
- *Culture* – country of birth, country of residence, mother tongue, primary language spoken at home, languages used to search the web;
- *Post-Task* – after each task, participants judged the usefulness of interface components and meta-data parts, using 5-point Likert-like scales;
- *Engagement* – after completing both tasks, they were asked to complete O'Brien et al.'s [12] engagement scale.

5.3   System and Interfaces

The user interface was both built using the PyIRE[5] workbench, which provides the required functionality for creating interactive IR interfaces and logging all interactions between the participants and the system. This includes any queries they enter, the books shown for the queries, pagination, facets selected, books viewed in detail, metadata facets viewed, books added to the book-bag, and books removed from the book-bag. All log-data is automatically timestamped and linked to the participant and task.

The backend IR system was implemented using ElasticSearch[6], which provided free-text search, faceted search, and access to the individual books' complete metadata. This is index was also used as a baseline system in the 2016 Suggestion Track (see Sect. 4.3). The 1.5 million book descriptions are indexed with all professional metadata and user-generated content. For indexing and retrieval the default parameters are used, which means stopwords are removed, but no stemming is performed. The Dewey Decimal Classification numbers are replaced by their natural language description. That is, the DDC number 573 is replaced by the descriptor *Physical anthropology*. User tags from LibraryThing are indexed both as text strings, such that complex terms are broken down into

---

[5] Python interactive Information Retrieval Evaluation workbench – https://bitbucket.org/mhall/pyire.

[6] ElasticSearch – http://www.elasticsearch.org/.

individual terms (e.g. *physical anthropology* is indexed as *physical* and *anthropology*) and as non-analyzed terms, which leaves complex terms intact and is used for faceted search.

The interface was designed to support users by taking the different stages of the search process into account. The idea behind the *multi-stage* interface design was inspired by Kuhlthau [11] and Vakkari [15] and it includes three distinct panels, potentially supporting different stages: *browse*, in which users can explore categories of books, *search*, supporting in-depth searching, and *book-bag*, in which users can review and refine their book-bag selections. An earlier model of decision stages in book selection [13] supports the need for a user interface that takes the different search and decision stages into account.

When the *multi-stage* interface first loads, participants are shown the *browse* stage, which is aimed at supporting the initial exploration of the data-set. The main feature to support the free exploration is the hierarchy browsing component on the left, which shows a hierarchical tree of Amazon subject classifications. This was generated using the algorithm described in [5], which uses the relative frequencies of the subjects to arrange them into the tree-structure with the most-frequent subjects at the top of the tree. The search result list is designed to be more compact to allow the user to browse books quickly and shows only the book's title, thumbnail image, and aggregate ratings (if available). Clicking on the book title showed a popup window with the book's full meta-data.

Participants switched to the *search* stage by clicking on the "Search" section in the gray bar at the top. The *search* stage presents a standard faceted search interface. Additionally if the participant had selected a topic in the *explore* stage, then the search was initially filtered by this as well. Participants could then select to search the whole collection.

The final stage is the *book-bag*, where participants review the books they have collected and can provide notes for each book. For each book participants could search for similar books by title, author, topic, and user tags, using the same compact layout as in the *browse* stage.

5.4 Participants

A total of 111 participants were recruited (see Table 1), 51 female and 60 male. 65 were between 18 and 25, 29 between 26 and 35, 16 between 36 and 45, and 1 between 46 and 55. 31 were in employment, 2 unemployed, 77 were students and 1 selected *other*. Participants came from 15 different countries (country of birth) including China (27 participants), UK (25), Norway (14), Germany (13), India (11), Denmark (10), resident in 8 different countries, again mainly in China, UK, Germany, Norway and Denmark. Participants' mother tongues included Chinese, English, German, Norwegian and 9 others. The majority of participants executed the tasks in a lab (74) and only 37 users participated remotely.

5.5   Procedure

The participants were invited by the individual teams, as described in Sect. 5.2, either using e-mail or by recruiting students from a lecture or lab. The following browsers and operating systems had been tested: Windows, OS X, Linux using Internet Explorer, Chrome, Mozilla Firefox, and Safari. The only difference between browsers was that some of the graphical refinements such as shadows are not supported on Internet Explorer and fall back to a simpler line-based display.

After participants had completed the experiment as outlined above (Sect. 5.2), they were provided with additional information on the tasks they had completed and with contact information, should they wish to learn more about the experiment. Where participants that completed the experiment in a lab, teams were able to conduct their own post-experiment process.

5.6   Results

Based on the participant responses and log data we have aggregated summary statistics for a number of basic performance metrics.

Table 3. Session lengths for the tasks. Times are in minutes:seconds and are reported median (inter-quartile range); Queries and Books Collected are reported median (inter-quartile range).

Task	Time	# Queries	# Books
Non-goal	7:38 min (9:38 min)	1 (5)	3 (3)
Goal-oriented	12:20 min (14:28 min)	5 (9)	5 (0)
South Africa	4:51 min (3:51 min)	1 (1.5)	2.5 (2)
Elizabethan	5:48 min (3 min)	3.5 (3.25)	2.25 (2.25)
Communication	4:58 min (2:47 min)	4 (4)	2 (2)
Painters	4:42 min (4:07 min)	4 (4)	1 (2)
Complex Mystery	3:36 min (4:22 min)	0 (0)	1 (0)
Astronomy	5:12 min (5:54 min)	3 (3.25)	2 (1)
Romance Mystery	2:21 min (3:15 min)	1 (2)	2 (1)
French Revolution	6:36 min (7:16 min)	4 (4.5)	1 (0)

Session length was measured using JavaScript. Table 3 shows median and inter-quartile ranges for all tasks. The data show clear distinctions between *non-goal*, *goal-oriented*, and optional tasks.

Number of queries was extracted from the log-data. Queries could be issued by typing keywords into the search box or by clicking on a meta-data field to search for other books with that meta-data field value. Both types of query have been aggregated and Table 3 shows the number of queries for each task. There is a clear difference between the *non-goal* and the *goal-oriented* task. On the *additional* tasks, more analysis is needed to investigate why the *south africa*, *complex mystery*, and *romance mystery* tasks have such low values for the number of queries. However, for the other *additional* tasks, it is clear that as far as complexity of the task and number of queries required, they lie between the *non-goal* and *goal-oriented* tasks.

Number of books collected was extracted from the log-data. The numbers reported in Table 3 are based on the number of books participants had in their book-bag when they completed the session, as participants could remove books they had previously collected.

The number of books collected is determined by the task, although the *elizabethan* and *south africa*, and *communication* tasks have different potential interpretations on how many books are needed to satisfy the task. As is to be expected, the *non-goal* task shows the highest variation in the number of books collected, as participants were completely free to define what "success" meant for them in that task.

6   Mining Track

6.1   Track Goals and Background

The Mining track is a new addition to the Social Book Search Lab in 2016. The goal of the Mining Track is twofold: (1) to detect book search requests in forum posts for automatic book recommendation, and (2) to detect and link book titles in online book discussion forums. The mining track represents the first stage in supporting complex book-related information needs. Later stages, such as the retrieval stage and user interaction with book search engines, have already been investigated in the Suggestion and Interactive tracks.

Up to now, these tracks have relied on the manual identification, analysis, and classification of complex search tasks as expressed in the LT discussion fora to serve as input in these tracks, as described in Sect. 4. Book search requests were manually separated from other book-related discussion threads by human annotators, and the suggestions provided by other LT users were used as relevance judgments in the automatic evaluation of retrieval algorithms that were applied to the book search requests.

However, to be able to fully support complex book search behavior, we should not just support the (interactive) retrieval and recommendation stage of the process, but also the automatic detection of complex search needs and the analysis of these needs and the books and authors contained therein. This is the goal of the Mining Track. The first edition of the Mining Track focuses on automating two text mining tasks in particular:

1. **Book search request classification**, in which the goal is to identify which threads on online forums are book search requests. That is, given a forum thread, the system should determine whether the opening post contains a request for book suggestions (i.e., binary classification of opening posts)
2. **Book linking**, in which the goal is to recognize book titles in forum posts and link them to the corresponding metadata record through their unique book ID. The task is not to mark each entity mention in the post text, but to label the post as a whole with the IDs of the mentioned books. That is, the system does not have to identify the exact phrase that refers to book, but only has to identify which book is mentioned on a per-post basis.

6.2 Track Setup

Task 1: Classifying Forum Threads

Data collection. For the task of classifying forum threads we created two data sets for training: one based on the LT forums and one based on Reddit. For the LT forums, we randomly sampled 4,000 threads and extracted their opening posts. We split them into a training and a test set, each containing 2,000 threads. These threads contained both positive and negative examples of book requests.

The Reddit training data was sampled from three months of Reddit opening posts published in September, October, and November 2014. The set of positive book request examples comprises all threads from the suggestmeabook subReddit, whereas the negative examples comprises all threads from the books subReddit. The training set contained 248 threads in total with 43 positive and 205 negative examples. The Reddit test data was sampled from December 2014 and comprises 89 threads with 76 negative and 13 positive examples of book requests.

Annotation. The labels of the Reddit *training* data were not annotated manually, as they were already categorized as positive and negative by virtue of the subReddit (books or suggestmeabook) they originated from. The Reddit *test* set originally consisted of 89 threads with the subReddit names as labels. In order to create a reliable ground truth for the test set, two track organizers manually classified the 89 test threads. All disagreements were discussed and we reached consensus on all 89 threads. 81 of the labels were the same as the original Reddit label; the other 8 were different. We use the manual labels as ground truth.

In the annotation process for the LT threads, positive examples of book requests consisted of all posts where the user described an explicit foreground or background information need and was searching for books to read. Examples include *known-item* requests, where a user is looking for a specific book by describing plot elements, but cannot remember the title; users asking for books covering a specific topic; and users asking for books that are similar to another book they mention. Posts where users ask for new authors to explore or where they list their favorite books and ask others to do the same are *not* classified as explicit book requests.

Task 2: Book Linking

Data collection. Book linking through the use of so-called 'touchstones' is an striking characteristic of the LT forum, and an important feature for the forum community. A touchstone is a link created by a forum member between a book mention in a forum post and a unique LT work ID in the LT database. A single post can have zero or more different touchstones linked to it. Touchstones allow readers of a forum thread to quickly see which books are mentioned in the thread.

For the book linking task we created a data set based on the touchstones in the LT forum. The training data consisted of 200 threads with 3619 posts in total. The test data for the linking task comprised 200 LT threads with 3809 posts in total. The task is to identify the LT work ID of all unique books mentioned in the post and link them to their specific post IDs.

In addition to the training data set, participants were encouraged to use the Amazon/LT collection used in the Suggestion Track to aid in the book linking task. This collection contains 2.8 million book metadata records along with their LT work IDs.

Annotation. In the annotation process, we annotated the posts in the LT threads (up to a maximum of 50 posts per thread) with all touchstones that were not added by LT users yet. Preliminary analysis has shown that around 16 % of all books are not linked [9]. We manually linked book titles in the posts to their unique LT work ID. Many books are published in different editions throughout the years with different unique ISBNs, but all of these versions are connected to the same unique LT work ID. If a book occurred multiple times in the same post, only the first occurrence was linked, so participants only need to specify each of the work IDs found in a post once. If a post mentioned a series of books, we linked this series to the first book in the series, e.g., the Harry Potter series was linked to "Harry Potter and the Philosopher's Stone". We did not link book authors. In some cases, a book title was mentioned, but no suitable work ID was found in the Amazon/LT collection. In this cases, we labeled that book title as UNKNOWN.

The annotation of book titles was found to be a difficult task for several reasons, in particular: (a) the definition of 'book reference' is not trivial: all sorts of abbreviations and author references are made; and (b) finding the book that is referred to, is sometimes difficult due to ambiguities and errors in titles. The latter was even more challenging in the case of book series.

In total, the dataset of 200 threads comprises 5097 book titles in 2117 posts.

6.3   Evaluation

For the book request classification task, we computed and report only accuracy, because this is a single-label, binary classification task. For the linking task, we computed accuracy, precision, recall, and F-score.

Both tasks are performed and evaluated at the level of forum posts. We detect whether a forum post was a book request in the classification task, and whether a certain book title occurred in a post. In case the same book title was mentioned multiple times in the same post, we only count and evaluate one occurrence of this particular book title. Each book title was mapped to a LT work ID that links together different editions of the same book (with different ISBNs).

During manual annotation, we came across several book titles for which we were unable to find the correct LT work ID. These cases were problematic in the evaluation: just because the annotator could not find the correct work ID, that does not mean it does not exist. For that reason, we decided to discard these examples in the evaluation of the test set results. In total, 180 out of the 5097 book titles in the test set were discarded for this reason.

Similarly, during the book request classification task, we also found some cases where we were unsure about categorizing them as book search requests or not and we discarded 26 such cases from the test set in the evaluation.

6.4   Results

Task 1: Classifying Forum Threads. For evaluation, 1,974 out of the 2,000 threads in the LT test set were used. For the 26 remaining threads, judges were unsure whether the first post was a request or not.

For the baseline system of the classification task, we trained separate classifiers for the two data sets (LT and Reddit) using scikit-learn[7]. We extracted bag-of-words-features (either words or character 4-grams) from the title and the

Table 4. Results for the classification task for the two datasets in terms of accuracy on the 1974 LT and 89 Reddit posts.

Team	Run	LT		Reddit	
		Rank	Accuracy	Rank	Accuracy
baseline	character_4-grams.LinearSVC	1	94.17	6	78.65
baseline	Words.LinearSVC	2	93.92	5	78.65
Know	Classification-Naive-Resutls	3	91.59	2	82.02
baseline	character_4-grams.KNeighborsClassifier	4	91.54	7	78.65
baseline	Words.KNeighborsClassifier	5	91.39	4	78.65
LIPAH	submission2-librarything	6	90.98	-	-
LIPAH	submission3-librarything	7	90.93	-	-
LIPAH	submission4-librarything	8	90.83	-	-
Know	Classification-Veto-Resutls	9	90.63	9	76.40
LIPAH	submission1-librarything	10	90.53	-	-
baseline	character_4-grams.MultinomialNB	11	87.59	11	76.40
baseline	Words.MultinomialNB	12	87.59	10	76.40
Know	Classification-Tree-Resutls	13	83.38	8	76.40
Know	Classification-Forest-Resutls	14	74.82	12	74.16
LIPAH	submission6-Reddit	-	-	1	82.02
LIPAH	submission5-Reddit	-	-	3	80.90

---

[7] http://scikit-learn.org/.

Table 5. Results for the linking task for the LT data set in terms of accuracy

Rank	Team	Run	# posts	Accuracy	Recall	Precision	F-score
1	Know	sbs16classificationlinking	4917	41.14	41.14	28.26	33.50
2	LSIS	BA_V2bis	4917	26.99	26.99	38.23	31.64
3	LSIS	BA_V1bis	4917	26.54	26.54	37.58	31.11
4	LSIS	B_V2bis	4917	26.01	26.01	35.39	29.98
5	LSIS	BUbis	4917	26.34	26.34	34.50	29.87
6	LSIS	Bbis	4917	25.54	25.54	34.80	29.46

body of the first post, and for LT also from the category (for Reddit, the category was the label). We used tf-idf weights for the words and the character 4-grams from these fields. We ran 3 classifiers on these data: Multinonial Naive Bayes (MNB), Linear Support Vector Classification (LinearSVC) and KNN, all with their default hyperparameter settings in scikit-learn.

Table 4 shows the results on the book search request classification task. We observe a clear difference in performance of the system on the LT and Reddit test sets.

Task 2: Book Linking. For evaluation, 217 out of the 220 threads in the test set were used, with 5097 book titles identified in 2117 posts. A further 180 book titles were found that could not be linked to works in the book metadata set of 1,925,024 books. These 180 unlinked book titles are ignored in the evaluation. Table 5 shows the results on the book linking task.

7 Conclusions and Plans

This was the second year of the Social Book Search (SBS) Lab. The SBS Lab investigates book search in social media from three different perspectives: (1) the evaluation of retrieval and ranking algorithms for complex book search tasks in the Suggestion Track, (2) studying how systems can support users in different phases of these complex search tasks in the Interactive Track, and (3) evaluating how well systems can identify book search tasks and book mentions in online book discussions in the Mining Track.

The Suggestion Track was changed little from the previous edition in 2015. In selecting topics, known-item information needs were removed to focus on recommendation requests. The user profiles and topic representations were enriched with more book metadata compared to previous years to give more information about the users and their information needs. Several of the best performing systems incorporated techniques for summarizing and reducing the rich natural language topic statement to remove irrelevant terms and focus on the need. Word embeddings were successfully used by several participants both for expanding queries and for summarizing the topic statements.

For the Interactive Track we simplified the experimental setup compared to 2015, such that users did only one mandatory task with at most one optional task. The optional tasks were based on book search requests from the LT forums, which result in notably different behaviour from the artificially created goal-oriented task.

The Mining Track ran for the first time in 2016, with the aim of evaluating systems that automatically identify book search requests and book mentions in online book discussions. Typical for the first year of a task, several issues with the task and its evaluation were identified. The classification task appeared to be straightforward, both in annotation as in implementation. The results show that the task is feasible and can be performed automatically with a high accuracy. The book linking task however posed a number of challenges, especially in annotating the data. The small number of participants in the track does not allow us to make informative comparisons between multiple different approaches to the tasks.

The 2016 SBS Lab saw the introduction of one new track and created further ways in which the tracks can collaborate and mutually inform each other. For the 2017 Interactive, we plan to introduce new features in the multistage system, such as building shortlists for searching with multiple example books and comparing the metadata of shortlisted books to build richer query representations. We expect these features will allow us to further investigate search stages and search strategies. The optional tasks in the 2016 Interactive Track have given us rich user interactions for a number of real-world complex book search information needs which we plan to use in the Suggestion Track as more structured representations of the information need. For the Mining Track the next step would be to expand and improve the two mining tasks in order to embed them in the social book search pipeline: starting with a complex book search request, find book titles that are relevant book suggestions and link them to their unique identifier. Alternatively, the classification task could be expanded to include the classification of different types of book search requests.

References

1. Beckers, T., Fuhr, N., Pharo, N., Nordlie, R., Fachry, K.N.: Overview and results of the INEX 2009 interactive track. In: Lalmas, M., Jose, J., Rauber, A., Sebastiani, F., Frommholz, I. (eds.) ECDL 2010. LNCS, vol. 6273, pp. 409–412. Springer, Heidelberg (2010). ISBN 978-3-642-15463-8

2. Borlund, P., Ingwersen, P.: The development of a method for the evaluation of interactive information retrieval systems. J. Documentation **53**(3), 225–250 (1997)

3. Elastic. Elasticsearch (2016). https://www.elastic.co/products/elasticsearch

4. Hall, M.M., Toms, E.: Building a common framework for IIR evaluation. In: Forner, P., Müller, H., Paredes, R., Rosso, P., Stein, B. (eds.) CLEF 2013. LNCS, vol. 8138, pp. 17–28. Springer, Heidelberg (2013). doi:10.1007/978-3-642-40802-1_3

5. Hall, M.M., Fernando, S., Clough, P., Soroa, A., Agirre, E., Stevenson, M.: Evaluating hierarchical organisation structures for exploring digital libraries. Inf. Retrieval **17**(4), 351–379 (2014). doi:10.1007/s10791-014-9242-y

6. Hall, M.M., Huurdeman, H.C., Koolen, M., Skov, M., Walsh, D.: Overview of the INEX 2014 interactive social book search track. In: Cappellato, L., Ferro, N., Halvey, M., Kraaij, W. (eds.) Working Notes for CLEF 2014 Conference. CEUR Workshop Proceedings, Sheffield, UK, 15–18 September, 2014, vol. 1180, pp. 480–493. CEUR-WS.org (2014). http://ceur-ws.org/Vol-1180/CLEF2014wn-Inex-HallEt2014.pdf

7. Koolen, M., Kamps, J., Kazai, G.: Social book search: the impact of professional and user-generated content on book suggestions. In: Proceedings of the International Conference on Information and Knowledge Management (CIKM 2012). ACM (2012)

8. Koolen, M., et al.: Overview of the CLEF 2015 social book search lab. In: Mothe, J., et al. (eds.) CLEF 2015. LNCS, vol. 9283, pp. 545–564. Springer, Heidelberg (2015). doi:10.1007/978-3-319-24027-5_51

9. Koolen, M., Bogers, T., Gäde, M., Hall, M., Huurdeman, H., Kamps, J., Skov, M., Toms, E., Walsh, D.: Overview of the CLEF 2015 social book search lab. In: Mothe, J., et al. (eds.) CLEF 2015. LNCS, vol. 9283, pp. 545–564. Springer, Heidelberg (2015)

10. Koolen, M., Bogers, T., van den Bosch, A., Kamps, J.: Looking for books in social media: an analysis of complex search requests. In: Hanbury, A., Kazai, G., Rauber, A., Fuhr, N. (eds.) ECIR 2015. LNCS, vol. 9022, pp. 184–196. Springer, Heidelberg (2015)

11. Kuhlthau, C.C.: Inside the search process: information seeking from the user's perspective. J. Am. Soc. Inf. Sci. 42(5), 361–371 (1991). ISSN 1097-4571, doi:10.1002/(SICI)1097-4571(199106)42:5⟨361::AID-ASI6⟩3.0.CO;2-#

12. O'Brien, H.L., Toms, E.G.: The development and evaluation of a survey to measure user engagement. J. Am. Soc. Inf. Sci. Technol. 61(1), 50–69 (2009)

13. Reuter, K.: Assessing aesthetic relevance: children's book selection in a digital library. JASIST 58(12), 1745–1763 (2007)

14. Toms, E., Hall, M.M.: The chic interactive task (chici) at clef2013 (2013). http://www.clef-initiative.eu/documents/71612/1713e643-27c3-4d76-9a6f-926cdb1db0f4

15. Vakkari, P.: A theory of the task-based information retrieval process: a summary and generalisation of a longitudinal study. J. Documentation 57(1), 44–60 (2001)

Overview of the CLEF 2016 Cultural Micro-blog Contextualization Workshop

Lorraine Goeuriot[1], Josiane Mothe[2], Philippe Mulhem[1], Fionn Murtagh[3,4], and Eric SanJuan[5(✉)]

[1] LIG, Université de Grenoble, Grenoble, France
[2] IRIT, UMR5505 CNRS, ESPE, Université de Toulouse, Toulouse, France
josiane.mothe@irit.fr
[3] University of Derby, Derby, UK
[4] Goldsmiths University of London, London, UK
[5] LIA, Université d'Avignon, Avignon, France
eric.sanjuan@univ-avignon.fr

Abstract. CLEF Cultural micro-blog Contextualization Workshop is aiming at providing the research community with data sets to gather, organize and deliver relevant social data related to events generating a large number of micro-blog posts and web documents. It is also devoted to discussing tasks to be run from this data set and that could serve applications.

1 Introduction

1.1 Context

Many statistical studies have shown the importance of social media; they seem to be now the main Internet activity for Americans, even when compared to email[1], and most of the social media. Chinese users spend an average of almost 90 min per day on social networks[2]. Social media is thus a key media for any company or organization, specifically in Business Intelligence related activities. Companies use social data to gather insights on customer satisfaction, but can also relate this data to key performance indicators [1], forecast product or services revenues [2] or measure and optimize their marketing. On the other hand, there are several levers that make social media popular in such ways. In the context of Twitter, Liu *et al.* mention content gratification ("content of the information carried through Twitter") and technology gratification ("easy to use") as the main gratifications influencing user intentions to continue to use Twitter; other gratifications being process ("searching for something or to pass time") and social ("interactivity with other parties through media") gratifications [3].

---

[1] http://www.socialmediatoday.com/content/17-statistics-show-social-media-future-customer-service, http://www.businessinsider.com/social-media-engagement-statistics-2013-12?IR=T.

[2] http://www.setupablogtoday.com/chinese-social-media-statistics/.

© Springer International Publishing Switzerland 2016
N. Fuhr et al. (Eds.): CLEF 2016, LNCS 9822, pp. 371–378, 2016.
DOI: 10.1007/978-3-319-44564-9_30

With regard to events such as festivals, social media is now widely used, and gathers various communities at cultural events: organizers, media, attendees, general public not attending the event. These communities are generally interested in different aspects of the generated information:

- the organizers: social media is a nice way to promote an event because it is community-driven. Social media is also useful during the event to get feedback from attendees and because it allows short and timely updates. After the event, data analytics on the discussion is also a useful feedback;
- the media: other media make use of the content put by organizers and attendees to report the event, as well as to inform the public;
- the public attending a festival: social media is a means to get information on the event, and communicate with other attendees on the event itself or related topics;
- the public not attending a festival: to get attendees and media feedback about the event using social media.

Social media is becoming a core component of communication for any event either professional or cultural.

Mining and organizing the information surrounding a cultural event can help broadening the perception and visualization of its social impact. In particular, micro-blogging is increasingly used in cultural events like festivals. For instance, more than 10 million twitts containing the keyword festival were sent and shared this summer 2015. On one hand this massive social activity can transform a local cultural event into an international event buzz. On the other hand, major festivals that do not follow the social mainstream could fail in attracting and renewing the public. Several national public scientific programs, such as "Tourism Australia's Social Media Program" or "The Travel Michigan Social Media Workshop Series", at the crossroads of computer science and humanities aim at studying this phenomenon, and its impact on the tourism industry as well as its impact on major national public institutions and society.

1.2   Aims of the Workshop

The aims of the Workshop are (1) to build a collection of twitts on targeted topics; we choose the case of festivals and collected millions of twitts. (2) to analyze the automatically built data set in order to extract the data set characteristics and to know better what is in the data collection. (3) to run the pre-defined tasks during several months and to define new tasks (during the Workshop day itself in September 2016).

In this paper, we present the corpus compiled for the CLEF Cultural micro-blog Contextualization and experimental tasks that make use of this corpus. This corpus has been built to study the social media sphere surrounding a cultural event, and contains micro-blog posts, a knowledge source, as well as all the web pages linked from the micro-blog posts.

More precisely, we first introduce use cases in Sect. 2, then we describe the data sets in Sect. 3. Section 4 gives some insights of the corpus while Sect. 5

depicts the experimented tasks which correspond to the pre-defined tasks. Section 6 concludes this paper.

2   Use Case Scenario

The goal of the CLEF Cultural micro-blog Lab is to develop processing methods and resources to mine the social media sphere surrounding cultural events such as festivals. twitts linked to an event makes a dense, rich but very noisy corpus: informal language, out of the language phrases and symbols, hashtags, hyperlinks... The information is also often imprecise, duplicate, or non-informative. The interest of mining such data is to extract relevant, and informative content, as well as to potentially discover new information.

The 2016 CMC Workshop is centred on festival participants, and focusing on, but is not limited to, the following use cases:

- An insider participant gets a micro-blog post about the cultural event in which he or she is taking part but needs context to understand it (micro-blog posts often contain implicit information). He or she needs also this background information before clicking on the link if any because the network activity is low or to avoid leaving the micro-blog application. The contextualization systems to be experimented with in this lab have to provide a short highly informative summary extracted from the Wikipedia that explains the background of the micro-blog post text.
- A participant in a specific location wants to know what is going on in surrounding events relative to artists, music or shows that he or she would like to see. Starting from a list of bookmarks in the Wikipedia app, the participant seeks a short list of micro-blog posts summarizing the current trends about related cultural events. She/he is more interested in micro-blogs from insiders than outsiders.

While our goal is to build data sets that will help research centred on the use cases above, we can foresee new research challenges that could be investigated with this data set: cultural events are often facing a big data challenge: direct stakeholders (organizers, artists, attendees), as well as indirect ones (media, public) can express themselves about the event, in different ways, media, and even languages. This data can be seen as a virtual sphere surrounding the event itself. Mining and organizing such data could bring very useful information on the events and their content. Besides the use cases given above, we believe such a corpus could lead to solve many other challenges in the domain.

For example, in the official web site for the Festival de Cannes 2015, in the part dedicated to the opening ceremony the May 13th, gives some excerpts of the speech of L. Wilson, but the tweet id = 598999849091084288, sent the May 15th, is about a TV talkshow commenting the opening ceremony with the actor S. Baker. This tweet does not depicts the ceremony and should not be relevant to describe the opening ceremony. On the contrary, the tweet id = 598636861280489473 lists some actress names (C. Deneuve, Noémie Lenoir,

Natalie Portman) which are not in the official site but that give interesting information about the actual ceremony and is then relevant to the opening ceremony.

The biggest foreseen problem encountered in this scenario is the "mapping" between events and posts. It is not one-to-many, but many-to-many: one microblog may be relevant to several events, and most of the time, a single event is mentioned in many posts. Moreover, one post may not be related to the events at all. Messages may be indirectly related to one event (a reply in a conversation for instance).

3 Datasets

3.1 Micro-blog Posts Collection

We collect all public micro-blog posts from Twitter containing the keyword festival since June 2015 using a private archive service with Twitter agreement based on streaming API[3]. The average of unique micro-blog posts (i.e. without re-twitts) between June and September is $2,616,008$ per month. The total number of collected micro-blog posts after one year (from May 2015 to May 2016) is $50,490,815$ ($24,684,975$ without re-posts).

Table 1. Fields of the micro-blog posts collection.

Name	Description	Comments
text	text of the twitt	99% of the twitts contain a non empty text
		66% contain an external compressed URL
from_user	author of twitt (string)	$62,105$ organizations among $11,928,952$ users.
id	Unique id of micro-blog	Total so far: $50,490,815$ posts.
iso_language_code	Encoding of the twitt	The most frequent tags: en (57%), es (15%), fr (6%) and pt (5%).
source	Interface used for posting the twitt	Frequent tags: Twitter Web Client (16%) iPhone and Twitterfeed clients (11% each).
<geo_type, geo_coordinates_0, geo_coordinates_1>	geolocalization	Triplet valued in 2.3% of the twitts

These micro-blog posts are available online on a relational database with associated fields, among them 12 are listed in Table 1. The "Comments" row in Table 1 gives some figures about the existing corpus.

---

[3] https://dev.twitter.com/streaming/public.

Because of privacy issues, they cannot be publicly released but can be analyzed inside the organization that purchases these archives and among collaborators under privacy agreement. CLEF 2016 CMC Workshop will provide this opportunity to share this data among academic participants. These archives can be indexed, analyzed and general results acquired from them can be published without restriction. The Workshop will organize a scientific peer reviewed process among participants to discuss and to check the validity and reproducibility of results.

3.2   Linked Web Pages

66% of the collected micro-blog posts contain Twitter t.co compressed URLs. Sometimes these URLs refer to other online services like adf.ly, cur.lv, dlvr.it, ow.ly, thenews.uni.me and twrr.co.vu that hide the real URL. We used the spider mode to get the real URL, this process can require several DNS requests. The number of unique uncompressed urls collected in one year is $11,580,788$ from $641,042$ distinct domains. Most frequent domains are: twitter.com (23%), www.facebook.com (5.7%), www.instagram.com (5.0%), www.youtube.com (4.5%), item.ticketcamp.net (1.1%) and g1.globo.com (1%)

3.3   Wikipedia Crawl

Unlike twitts and web pages, Wikipedia is under Creative Common license, and its contents can be used to contextualize twitts or to build complex queries referring to Wikipedia entities. Using the tools from INEX twitt conceptualization track[4] we extract from Wikipedia an average of 10 million XML documents per year since 2012 in the four main Twitter languages: English (en), Spanish (es), French (fr), and Portuguese (pt). These documents reproduce in an easy to use XML structure the contents of the main Wikipedia pages: title, abstract, section and subsections as well as Wikipedia internal links. Other contents as images, footnotes and external links are stripped out in order to obtain a corpus easy to process by standard NLP tools. By comparing contents over the years, it is possible to detect long term trends.

4   Micro-blog Corpus Insights

An extended version of the analysis in this section is in [7]. Previous work on determining and analyzing narrative flows are available in [9], using Twitter data from a designed experiment; and in [8], using film script.

A perspective on an analysis carried out, is as follows. twitts between 11 May and 31 December 2015 were used.

The following festivals are selected: Cannes Film Festival (13–24 May 2015); Fèis Île, Islay (Scotland) Festival (23–31 May 2015); Berlin Film Festival (19–21 May 2015); CMA, Country Music Association (Nov. 2015); Yulin Dog (June 2015); and Avignon Theatre Festival (4–25 July 2015).

---

[4] http://tc.talne.eu.

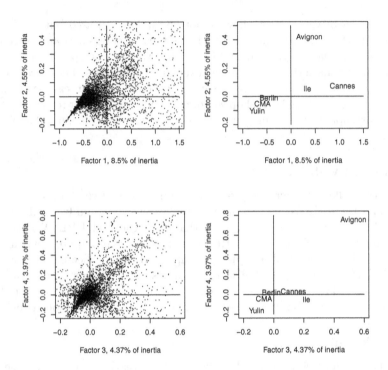

Fig. 1. The principal factor plane, in the top two panels, and the plane of factors 3,4 in the bottom two panels. The left panels display all words, with a dot at each word location. The right panels display the selected festivals.

Figure 1 displays the planes of principal axes, i.e. factors, 1, 2 and of axes 3, 4. This is Correspondence Analysis providing analysis of semantics. We do see here how the principal factor plane is especially a contrasting engagement with the Cannes Film Festival for axis 1, and the Avignon Theatre Festival for axis 2. Meanwhile, both axes 3 and 4 can be said to be especially relevant for the Avignon Theatre Festival.

Such festivals are the central focus of interest in this micro-blog corpus. Dealing with the complete dataset would require:

1. semantic characteristics of words in the twitts (or abbreviations, named individuals like performers, political or other happenings, web addresses, language used, etc.).
2. pattern recognition in the data, and discovery of, and characterizing, trends.
3. predictive modeling and other approaches (e.g. quantitative measures of impact or performance).

Overall, we may have the foundations here for Bourdieu-based social research [10, 11].

5   Experimented Tasks

Along with these three data sources (micro-blog posts, related Web and Wikipedia Encyclopedia), three types of search queries with related textual references will be provided to evaluate micro-blog systems:

- Contextualization based on Wikipedia where given a twitt as query the system has to provide a short summary extracted from the Wikipedia that provides all necessary background knowledge to fully understand the twitt.
- Summarization based on twitts where given a topic represented by a set of Wikipedia entities, extract a reduced number of twitts that summarizes main trends about that topic in festivals.
- Event link of a given festival program. Such information is useful for attendees of festivals, for people who are interested in knowing what happens in a festival, and for organizers to get feedback.

System outputs will be evaluated based on informativeness as in [4,5]. Manual runs and Questionnaire data will be provided by the French ANR GAFES project[5].

6   Conclusion

We presented in this paper the Cultural micro-blog Contextualization (CMC) corpus, a temporal comprehensive representation of the virtual sphere surrounding cultural events. This corpus is composed of twitts, URLs linked to by these twitts, and of one knowledge source.

The built corpus has the big interest to provide a snapshot of: (a) twitts, and, (b) web pages pointed to by the twitts. From a scientific point of view, it will be possible to rerun experiments on the exact same sets of web documents, even years after the event took place. The topics covered by the corpus have several benefits:

- The amount of data in the corpus is manageable by academic research teams (around 50 millions of twitts and URLs, possibly split into smaller subsets depending on the task expected). This point is important as we expect numerous participants to experiment their ideas on the CMC corpus;
- Forcing the corpus perimeter to festival cultural events still covers a variety of festivals (cinema, music, theater, ...) that may have different features regarding their related social spheres;
- The cultural domain is usually well documented in resources like Wikipedia, so the CMC corpus will not suffer from the lack of knowledge that may be used during retrieval.

---

[5] http://www.agence-nationale-recherche.fr/?Project=ANR-14-CE24-0022.

Without limiting the possible uses of this corpus, we foresee that the concurrent gathering of web pages and twitts may also pave the way to other studies inspired from [6,12], like co-evolutions of twitts and referred web pages over several occurrences of the same festival, or co-dynamics of topics in web pages and twitts.

We also presented some tasks associated with this data set. During the Workshop day at CLEF in September 2016, the collection will be discussed. We will discuss the quality of the data set based on analysis some participants have conducted, as well as the distribution of the corpus in accordance with the agreement we have with Twitter. During the Workshop day we will also discuss other possible tasks to be run over the data set.

References

1. Heijnen, J., de Reuver, M., Bouwman, H., Warnier, M., Horlings, H.: Social media data relevant for measuring key performance indicators? a content analysis approach. In: Järveläinen, J., Li, H., Tuikka, A.-M., Kuusela, T. (eds.) ICEC 2013. LNBIP, vol. 155, pp. 74–84. Springer, Heidelberg (2013)
2. Rui, H., Whinston, A.: Designing a social-broadcasting-based business intelligence system. ACM Trans. Manage. Inf. Syst. 2(4), 1–19 (2011). ACM, New York, NY, USA
3. Liu, I., Cheung, C., Lee, M.: Understanding twitter usage: what drive people continue to twitt. In: PACIS, 92 (2010)
4. SanJuan, E., Bellot, P., Moriceau, V., Tannier, X.: Overview of the INEX 2010 question answering track (QA@INEX). In: Geva, S., Kamps, J., Schenkel, R., Trotman, A. (eds.) INEX 2010. LNCS, vol. 6932, pp. 269–281. Springer, Heidelberg (2011)
5. Bellot, P., Moriceau, V., Mothe, J., Tannier, X., SanJuan, E.: Mesures d'informativité et de lisibilité pour un cadre d'évaluation de la contextualisation de twitts in Document Numérique, vol. 18(1), pp. 55–73 (2015)
6. Benz, D., Hotho, A., Jäschke, R., Krause, B., Mitzlaff, F., Schmitz, C., Stumme, G.: The social bookmark and publication management system bibsonomy. VLBD J. 19, 849–875 (2010)
7. Murtagh, F.: Semantic mapping: towards contextual and trend analysis of behaviours and practices (2016, Online proceedings)
8. Murtagh, F., Ganz, A., McKie, S.: The structure of narrative: the case of film scripts. Pattern Recogn. 42, 302–312 (2009)
9. Murtagh, F., Pianosi, M., Bull, R.: Semantic mapping of discourse and activity, using Habermas's Theory of Communicative Action to analyze process. Qual. Quant. 50(4), 1675–1694 (2016)
10. Le Roux, B., Rouanet, H.: Geometric Data Analysis: From Correspondence Analysis to Structured Data Analysis. Kluwer (Springer), Dordrecht (2004)
11. Le Roux, B., Lebaron, F.: Idées-clefs de l'analyse géométriques des données. In: Lebaron, F., Le Roux, B. (eds.) La Méthodologie de Pierre Bourdieu en Action: Espace Culturel. Espace Social et Analyse des Données, pp. 3–20. Dunod, Paris (2015)
12. Leskovec, J., Backstrom, L., Kleinberg, J.: Meme-tracking and the dynamics of the news cycle. In: Proceedings of the 15th ACM SIGKDD International Conference on Knowledge Discovery and Data Mining (KDD 2009), pp. 497–506. ACM, New York (2009)

Author Index

Printed in the United States
By Bookmasters